The New History of England

General Editors
A.G. Dickens and Norman Gash

The New History of England

*Probable publication 1987;
all other titles available

Authority and Conflict

England 1603–1658

Derek Hirst

Edward Arnold

© Derek Hirst 1986

First published in Great Britain 1986 by
Edward Arnold (Publishers) Ltd, 41 Bedford Square, London WC1B 3DQ

Edward Arnold (Australia) Pty Ltd, 80 Waverley Road, Caulfield East,
Victoria 3145, Australia

British Library Cataloguing in Publication Data

Hirst, Derek
    Authority and conflict: England 1603-1658.——
(The new history of England; 4)
    1. Great Britain——History——Early Stuarts,
1603-1649   2. Great Britain——History——
Puritan Revolution, 1642-1660
    I. Title   II. Series
    942.06   DA390

    ISBN 0-7131-6155-8
    ISBN 0-7131-6156-6 Pbk

Text set in 11/12pt Baskerville Compugraphic
by Colset Private Limited, Singapore.
Printed and bound by Richard Clay (The Chaucer Press) Ltd, Bungay, Suffolk.

Contents

For Lori, Sam and Nick

Preface

The series of which this volume is a part is intended to provide a narrative history of modern England. A narrative is particularly suited to relating political history – all the more so, perhaps, in a period of civil war and revolution, when so many actions and initiatives turn out to have been largely reactions to other events in a continuing crisis. Other developments too can appropriately be discussed in a narrative framework. Economic depression, or works of political thought, for example, have claims to inclusion in a narrative history of the period which produced them as legitimate as those they have to inclusion in the thematic surveys in which they more frequently figure. The supremely important developments in Scotland and Ireland in this period can also be integrated. Certain enduring features of English life – social and economic, religious and intellectual, even political – do, however, seem unsuited to such treatment. The narrative in this book is therefore prefaced by three detailed introductory chapters which are intended to set the course of events in a broader context. And it is succeeded by a concluding chapter which attempts to assess some of the consequences of the decades 1640–60.

That this book is among the longest in the series stems from both historical and historiographical factors. At the opening of *Behemoth*, his history of the civil wars, Thomas Hobbes remarked, 'If in time, as in place, there were degrees of high and low, I verily believe that the highest of time would be that which passed between 1640 and 1660.' Such high times require something more than a cursory account if they are to be understood. Furthermore, other scholars have engaged with the complex history of this period, and recent years have seen an outpouring of works unmatched in perhaps any other field of history. A text-book of the usual dimensions cannot easily introduce readers to the wealth of novel insights that have recently been made available. Nor could such a work readily explain very much, when the historiography is now so diverse.

The author of a general work such as this, which incorporates both original research and the fruits of the labours of others, necessarily incurs debts. Such debts are the greater in that the publishers' injunction that the footnotes be kept to the barest minimum precluded any acknowledgement in the text. Footnotes have been used to indicate original research, and not even then where the sources are obvious enough for scholars in the field to need no direction. For its part, the bibliography can make few amends to the scholars whose work has been plundered: I can only assure them they have my gratitude. Some obligations must, however, be recognized. I have benefited from reading numerous unpublished PhD theses, especially those by Richard Cust, Anne Hughes, B.W. Quintrell, Nick Tyacke and Keith Wrightson, and most of all those by Tom Cogswell on the politics of diplomacy in the 1620s and by Henry Reece on the military presence in the 1650s. Tom Cogswell, Jack Hexter, J.R. Jones, John Morrill, James Robertson, Conrad Russell, Margo Todd, Richard Tuck and Keith Wrightson have all read and commented on sections of the text in manuscript; Gerald Aylmer kindly undertook the heroic task, amidst many other duties, of reading through the whole, as did A.G. Dickens, one of the general editors of this series. They have all saved me from innumerable errors and solecisms; those that remain are of course my own. I also owe debts of a different sort to the members of various research seminars in Cambridge in the early 1970s, for without their widening of my horizons I doubt whether I could have undertaken such a project as this. Additionally I must thank Conrad Russell, for much of whatever sophistication the first half of the narrative manifests must be attributed to discussion and argument with him over a period of years.

Practical help in the research for this book was given by the faculty research fund of Washington University, by the American Philosophical Society, the National Endowment for the Humanities, the Guggenheim Foundation, the Folger Shakespeare Library, the Henry E. Huntington Library, and my old colleagues the Master and Fellows of Trinity Hall, Cambridge. But my greatest debt, for reasons which need no listing, is to my wife, Lori.

Derek Hirst
St Louis, Missouri

1 Economy and Society

The State of the Nation

Change and continuity accompany each other in most times and places, and England in the early seventeenth century was perhaps no more and no less Janus-faced than any other society. Nevertheless, the ambiguities have invited historians to come to very different conclusions. In politics intervals of purely royal rule were sandwiched between increasingly excitable parliaments; then came civil war, revolution and republic. Yet by the end of our period the republic looked surprisingly monarchical, and within two years the Stuart dynasty was to be restored, to rule as well as reign over a body politic which, many historians now assert, had resolved few of the issues which troubled it. The social record is no more clear cut. If there was a 'crisis of the aristocracy' in the generation around the turn of the sixteenth century, then the 1660s dawned on a society which was fast entering the 'age of oligarchy'. And so in economics: by the end of our period agriculture was still by far the largest employer and textiles still England's major industry and export; yet the so-called 'commercial revolution' had begun, with colonial imports and re-exports diversifying England's pattern of consumption as well as its trading account. But perhaps the cruellest ambiguities could be found in the world of the mind, where we can with equal justice see England in the 1650s as experiencing the birth of yet another, scientific, revolution, or struggling still in the destructive toils of the wars of religion. Against the humane activities of Robert Boyle and his friends must be set the eminently unenlightened parliament of 1656 which reacted to the misguided Quaker James Nayler by voting a punitive mutilation whose brutality paled beside the savagery many MPs demanded. In every area authorities were being called in question, but the longing for authority remained an inescapable fact of life.

The England of the 1650s was therefore far from the complacent 'pudding time' which the accession by courtesy of parliament of a new dynasty a half century later was to usher in. But already some of the preconditions for stability existed. Not least, the worst of the

1

demographic storm had been weathered, and with it the crest of the
inflationary tide.

   In the century before the 1640s the population of England and
Wales had almost doubled, from around three million to over five
million; the most spectacular growth occurred in London, which had
some 40,000 inhabitants in 1500, and around 250,000 in 1600. Its
population then soared to more than 400,000 by 1640, making it a
genuine metropolis, the largest city in Europe let alone in England.
The consequence of such increasing pressure on the market in a
period when farming techniques changed only slowly and in the
adverse climate of the 'little ice age' from *c.*1550 to *c.*1700, was a
rapid rise in prices, and particularly in the price of food. The price of
bread-corn had by the end of the 1640s risen between eight- and
ten-fold from its level in 1500, rents had marked a parallel path, and
though wages had also risen in the general inflationary surge they had
not kept pace. Real wages in the early seventeenth century seem to
have been about half their level of a hundred years before. The net
outcome was living conditions in the decades 1620–50 which have
been called amongst the worst that England has experienced. But by
the 1650s prolonged hardship seems to have taken its toll of the
emotional reserves of English men and women, and thereafter in
parishes across the country couples began to marry later and to have
fewer children. The ensuing reduction of the remorseless pressure of
demand on resources allowed real wages to recover, permitting some
of the poor to divert income away from the crude necessities of food
and rent. The ground was thus laid for the expansion of domestic
demand which proved central to the economic take-off of the eighteenth century.

   That happy outcome was in 1600 unimaginable. Widespread
deaths from famine in the later 1590s, and the recurrence of mortality
crisis in the relatively isolated north-west in the catastrophic year
1623, reveal how far England yet was from a sufficiency in the
necessaries of life. Preoccupation with the weather was therefore not
the polite conversational gambit that it is for most westerners today,
but rather a natural concern with what could be quite literally a
matter of life and death. On average a bad harvest occurred every
four years, and low crop yields meant that one failure bred deficiency the following year since the small farmer was soon driven to eat
his seed corn. The consequences for the labouring poor who in normal years may have spent 70 per cent of their income on rent, food
and drink could be disastrous: meat dwindled in their diet, and the
switch to coarser foods left them vulnerable to other ailments. But
rainy summers did not only bring hunger. Soaring food prices left
ordinary consumers with a smaller margin of income to spend on

other commodities, so harvest failure only too often caused industrial depression as demand dried up. The misery of high prices was then intensified by lowered incomes. This conjunction accounts for the abnormal suffering in 1623 and the later 1640s, when the hungry took to the roads in alarming numbers, in a desperate search for jobs or charity.

Bad weather also sapped the nation's productive resources. When agriculture was the largest employer, prolonged rain, or heavy frosts, halted the work of many. Non-manual sources of power were equally vulnerable to interruption, since the variability of water and wind prevented mills grinding, contrary winds left cold Londoners without their 'sea coal' from Newcastle, and water-intensive industries like tanning and soap-boiling perforce slackened off in dry summer months. Much of the labour force accordingly had no prospect of year-round employment.

Low productivity was built into the structure of the economy. Appalling hygiene and still more dismal medical skills left average life expectancy at birth wavering in the mid-30s; even if a child survived the most dangerous years of infancy, a fourteen-year-old could only count on an average of another forty years or so of life. That ensured that at most 50 per cent of the population fell within the age-range of efficient work, between about 15 and 60, compared with over 60 per cent even in the ageing population of today. The various ailments – from 'griping in the guts' to toothache – consequent on the chronic dietary deficiencies common to all classes diminished efficiency still further. The lack of incentives other than hunger also lowered productivity, and explains the widespread belief in the rationality of starvation wages. The relative scarcity of consumer goods, and of avenues for social mobility, appear to have generated amongst the work-force a high preference for leisure once basic needs had been met. The incessant fulminations from the pulpit against idleness and drink, especially in years of low food prices, are hardly surprising: in one week in 1632 more than 30 per cent more malt, for beer, was brought into London for sale than bread-corn.* The predictable failure of moral reformers left it to the increasing variety and cheapness of consumer goods in the later seventeenth and more particularly the eighteenth century to generate new habits.

Other factors of production were scarcely better prepared than labour to raise the economy above the provision of a modest sufficiency. There were surprisingly few bottlenecks in the supply of either raw materials or fuel for industry: contrary to legend, reserves of wood were not burned out, and except in London coal was still very

---

* *Privy Council Registers 1632–1633*, p. 249.

much a supplement rather than a replacement. Yet demand
remained too weak to put much pressure on production, for most
people had little left after the purchase of necessities. Consequently,
although the water-powered blast furnace was introduced in iron
manufacture in the sixteenth century, output remained low – under
25,000 tons a year in the 1650s – and England continued to import
high-grade products from Sweden. The one significant labour-saving
invention, the stocking-frame, developed late in Elizabeth's reign for
weaving hosiery, spread only slowly, not helped by governmental
suspicion of a device which threatened to increase unemployment.
And if technology did little to transform the economy, the formation
of capital was scarcely intensive enough to meet the demands posited
by modern development economists, since industrial prices rose even
slower than wages, and permitted little accumulation of profits.
Thus, the returns on the production of woollen cloth in the early
seventeenth century have been estimated at a mere 13 per cent. Given
the prevailing insecurity, and the relatively high cost and short duration of loans, such levels were unlikely to generate take-off. Matters
were not helped by the tendency of early-modern governments to
treat the economy as a source of plunder. Customs tariffs drew few
distinctions between exports and imports, manufactures and raw
materials, and penniless monarchs readily granted out monopoly
patents – which usually increased costs and diminished supplies – to
courtiers whom they had few other means of rewarding.

A consideration of foreign trade, the sector so beloved by traditional economic historians, seems to highlight the undynamic nature
of the English economy. London's exports were in 1640 still dominated by textiles as they had been a century before: almost 87 per cent
of the value of total exports came from cloth, with other manufactures
providing a mere 2.3 per cent. The one significant sign of change
was that by 1640 re-exports, largely colonial products, amounted to
6.4 per cent in value of the capital's exports: by the mid-1660s
re-exports probably contributed almost one quarter to the value
of England's total exports. Our period therefore saw England
advancing some way towards the role of Europe's entrepôt which it
was to capture by the end of the century. Nevertheless, exports give a
gloomy picture of the economy, and recurrent crisis would probably
be a fair assessment of the state of foreign trade after the short-lived
boom that came with peace in 1604. The mainstay, broadcloth, the
product of the old-established textile industry in areas like Wiltshire,
faced growing competition in Europe. The industry was handicapped
by restrictive practices, by shifting patterns of sheep-rearing which
affected the quality of the fleece grown, and most important from
1620 by currency manipulations in the major market of the Baltic and

north Germany which dramatically diminished English competitiveness. The trade with Spain and the Mediterranean, which provided an increasingly important market for the lighter 'new draperies', and a valuable source of luxuries and spices, brought less consolation than it might have done, for it was repeatly disrupted in the decades after 1620 by political instability in war-torn Europe and ultimately in England too.

The newer branches of trade offered as yet little recompense. The East India Company, which was by the end of the century to prove so lucrative, was faltering badly in the second quarter. The dazzling promise of the early years after its foundation in 1600 had faded by the 1620s, as Dutch competition – at its most brutal in the Amboyna massacre of 1623 – drove the company out of the Spice Islands (now Indonesia), and left its activities largely confined to India, which had not yet shown itself a rewarding market. The company was further handicapped by political problems at home. It was unpopular because it exported bullion – critically important for an adequate domestic currency before the development of a credit market – to bring back its spices, silks and calicoes; and insolvent monarchs and courtiers regarded it as a rich cow to be milked.

The westward trade was equally dispiriting. England's American colonies were not the Eldorado for which the Elizabethan explorers had hoped. Although there were by the Civil War some 50,000 English colonists in the western hemisphere, they offered, such were their distance and their difficulties, neither a regular nor a wealthy market for English products. Nor were their own products sufficient to revitalize the English economy. Only the wholesale importation of African slaves from around mid-century transformed the faltering tobacco economies of the Caribbean settlements into the labour-intensive sugar producers on which much of England's re-export prosperity was to be based in subsequent decades. The other tobacco-growing colony, Virginia, fared even worse for much of our period. The hopes of its backers, the gentry and merchants who flocked to invest in the Virginia Company in the early years of James's reign, that it would yield bullion soon dwindled along with their investments. Competition from the superior tobacco of the Spanish colonies, and ill-prepared settlers, left the colony's prospects bleak, and after nearly collapsing in the 1610s and 1620s it was only saved by the introduction of a better strain of tobacco. By 1640 Virginia and Maryland (founded in 1633) were exporting about two million pounds of tobacco yearly.

The other cluster of colonies, the New England settlements established in the 1620s, were still more disappointing economically. Although it is often thought that these were quite different in character

from the southern colonies, since the first colonists fled religious persecution rather than economic hardship, recent research has shown
that in fact most of the early migrants were driven by pressures of
over-population and economic depression in England just as were the
Virginia or Caribbean settlers. And judged economically, the hard
soil and harsh climate made New England a poor substitute for the
riches of Mexico and Peru, or even for the Spice Islands lost to the
Dutch. It was only by the end of the century that its potential role as a
supplier of vital naval stores such as ships' masts became clear; and
already by then its ship-building and fishing industries, and its trade
with the Spanish colonies to the south, made New England more of a
competitor with than a contributor to the English economy.

The gloomy tone of so much economic writing before 1660 is therefore hardly surprising. England seemed to have picked the wrong
sites to build its empire; its main export product, broadcloth, was
losing ground; and in every area the Dutch, with their more advanced
credit organization and their far more effective ship-building techniques, were edging out English competition. The only exception was
the Mediterranean, where the bulky Dutch *fluits* were ill-suited to
withstand Barbary corsairs. The English response was characteristically defensive. Commerce ought as much as possible to be organized
in great trading companies, like the East India or the Levant companies, where it could be regulated and protected. As much as possible
Dutch ways should be emulated. And where they could not be
emulated the Dutch should be excluded: that of course was the
rationale of the Navigation Act of 1651 and the subsequent measures
of the Restoration period, and of the three great wars against the
Dutch, beginning in 1652, which were eventually to break their trading power.

Economic Change

Concern with the balance of foreign trade did not represent the irrational protectionism that Victorian free-traders used to envisage. A
deficit occasioned an outflow of payments, and in a society without
effective credit mechanisms a shortage of coin could bring economic
activity to a stop. The crisis of the early 1620s resulted at least partly
from such a shortage. But on the whole historians' fixation with
foreign trade has resulted more from the fact that the records are
there, in the customs figures, than from its intrinsic importance.
For although exports allowed the import, in return, of goods which
were eventually, as they cheapened, to prove crucial in helping to
change ordinary tastes, the export trade was dwarfed by an unquanti-
fiable and often highly localized internal economy. Furthermore, in

contrast to the doubtful health of the export trade, the internal economy was diversifying and growing considerably in our period.

While it might not be wholly accurate to call London the 'engine of growth', its growing impact on the nation was the most obvious aspect of internal development. The concentration of the sale of England's major export, broadcloth, at the single mart of Antwerp for much of the sixteenth century had elevated nearby London's role as the other axis of the trade. Provincial 'outports' like Southampton and Boston had been overwhelmed by the competition, and increasingly the nation's commercial and financial activities centred in the capital, although at the price of provincial resentment. London's predominance continued to grow: while it shipped 77 per cent of the country's new drapery exports in 1610, the figure had risen to 85 per cent by the 1640s. Despite the outports' losses, the very concentration helped generate further economic advance. The growth of Newcastle, and of the coastwise shipping industry, is inconceivable without the demand of the coal- and grain-hungry Londoners. The establishment of the Virginia colony by London merchants stands in contrast to the failure of southwestern merchants who lacked their resources. And as the booming capital drove its supply lines far up the east coast as well as deep into the midlands it did much to stimulate agricultural advance, most particularly in the development of intensive market gardening in its immediate hinterland.

London's role as the social and political capital of the nation was as important as its commercial dominance. The location in London of all the main law courts attracted an ever-growing procession of litigants as the economy expanded. Similarly, the final abandonment by the early Tudors of medieval traditions of peripatetic kingship and their expansion of the royal administration in London brought almost as great a flood of suitors to the City and to its twin, Westminster. As the nation's leaders beat a path to London, a service sector developed to cater to their expensive tastes. Gentry sent their sons to the inns of court, London's equivalent of a law school, for a year or so to acquire polite ways as well as a smattering of legal knowledge; amusement centres like the Spring Gardens were established; and by the end of our period the beginnings of the London 'season' for polite society were apparent. By that date too the wealthier and more cosmopolitan aristocratic and gentry families had begun to purchase town houses, indicating that they now looked on London visits as regular occurrences, rather than as being dictated by their litigation or their political needs. The less smoky west end was already beginning to be laid out in fashionable squares and a 1632 government census found almost 25 per cent of the peerage (though less than 1 per cent of the gentry) resident in London without good reason. The upshot was that

the city increased not just in numbers but also in riches: by mid-
century, while it contained one-twelfth of the nation's population it
also contained one-eighth of the assessed wealth. But London was not
yet megalopolis. Paupers certainly huddled in squalid tenements,
behind the fashionable quarter in the west, in alleys and yards hidden
by merchants' palaces in the City, and in some sections of the poorer
east: one building in the relatively prosperous City parish of St
Michael, Cornhill, had over ten inhabitants to a room in 1637.
Nevertheless, most housing was occupied by single families. Open
tracts like Moorfields still dotted the landscape, and to the south and
east Southwark and Stepney were genuinely separate communities.
By mid-century the population of the eastern suburbs was probably
only around 50,000. It was still possible to walk from end to end of the
metropolis in a morning, though the smoke pollution was such that on
a clear day in January 1652 a Dutch visitor to St Paul's Cathedral was
unable to see the Tower from the roof.

Urbanization elsewhere was more tenuous. The 'poet' John
Taylor, visiting the cathedral city of Winchester in 1623, thought
there were 'almost as many parishes as people within its walls'.
Although about 800 market towns have been identified, the claims of
many to urban status are suspect. The scale of urban life can be
appreciated from the fact that apart from London only Norwich had
over 20,000 inhabitants, with the other provincial centres of Bristol,
Newcastle and York exceeding 10,000. In third-ranking towns with
a population of 5,000 or more, such as Worcester or Northampton,
streets were likely to end in open country, orchards dotted the
'townscape', and dungheaps and wandering pigs were common traffic hazards. London and the provincial centres were clearly genuinely
urban, with a wide range of specialized occupations. Outside that
select group Northampton had its concentration of leather-workers
and Wigan its pewterers. But most towns should on the whole be
thought of as rural service centres, and contrasted with their hinter-
lands not so much occupationally or socially as in density and
administrative structure.

Domestic commercial organization was no more specialized than
were many towns. Regional specialization in agriculture was already
far advanced, with Cheshire famous for its cheese and Worcestershire
for its orchards. Yet the hazards of inland transport still ensured that
some grain for bread and beer was grown in predominantly pastoral
regions – sensibly enough, for the average price of wheat in Devon
late in the dearth year of 1631 was 50 per cent higher than in neighbouring Dorset.* The degree of isolation and the badness of the roads

*Calendar of State Papers, Domestic, 1631–1633, p. 186.

can certainly be exaggerated. Although the council's letters might amble at 2 m.p.h. towards the king in 1607, news and rumour could travel fast – over fifty miles in a night in the Irish scare of 1641. And transport was sufficiently regular for John Taylor to publish the *Carrier's Cosmography* in 1637, giving details of carriers linking London with all regions. But areas distant from navigable waterways did suffer. Outlying upland counties periodically had difficulty in sending taxes to London, especially in winter, since so little traffic went that way. Cross-country contacts were even more difficult, and money collected in Dorchester in the south-west for relief of the starving in distant Lancashire in 1648 could not be sent because none knew how to convey it. *

Nevertheless, England had made further progress towards commercialization than had any other part of Europe save northern Italy and the Netherlands. The great medieval general fairs like Stourbridge outside Cambridge were losing their functions, and brokers and middlemen increasingly traded in bulk in roadside inns. A further novelty was the slow spread outwards from London of the permanent retail shop. Indeed, there are signs of a critically important shift towards consumer values. Most sixteenth-century Warwickshire probate inventories listed livestock first, while a century later all began with household goods, which were growing in both number and variety. Even quite humble families increasingly cooked in brass instead of iron pots, ate off pewter instead of wooden bowls, and wore knitted stockings. A further major change of attitudes was associated with the very rise of the lighter textiles of the 'new draperies'. Clothing for ordinary people up to the late sixteenth century was a household good: thick broadcloth garments endured, to be left to children in parents' wills. But from around the start of our period a new concern for fashion appeared, for which the lighter, more highly coloured fabrics like bays and perpetuanas were well suited, and which the availability of the new cloths must have done much to create. The age of the consumer society, and of civility, was dawning: by the 1650s a major landmark was visible with the appearance of coffee shops in London and Oxford.

It is therefore imperative to recognize both the existence of change and its slow pace. The growth of London and the forging of a national economy were indissolubly linked to developments in production in both agriculture and industry, but it would be unwise to speak of a 'revolution' in either sector. In agriculture the slow spread of new techniques was reinforced by a new vogue in handbooks, like Walter Blyth's *The English Improver* of 1649. Their very existence is significant, although equally revealing is Sir Richard Weston's

*C.H. Mayo, *Municipal Records of Dorchester* (1908), p. 546.

acknowledgement of the Low Countries' pre-eminence in his *Discourse of Husbandry used in Brabant and Flanders* (1645). Additionally, as market pressures gradually affected the whole country more attention was given to the type of crops and farming practices best suited to local soils. More striking still, in the course of our period some farmers – not all of them large – were sufficiently attuned to the market to convert to new cash crops like madder for dye and, especially in the Severn valley, tobacco, as well as to market gardening around towns. Although the full impact of the new crops was only to be felt later, when slackening demand after mid-century encouraged farmers to concentrate on raising productivity, the steady commercialization of agriculture meant that England slowly outstripped much of the rest of Europe in its ability to feed a growing population. Starvation in the crisis of 1623 was limited to the north-west; and thereafter, although hardship in the later 1640s was appalling, famine seems to have been more or less eliminated. Nevertheless, growth remained slow and it has been strongly argued that increases in food production in the period owed as much to the cultivation of previously waste land as to new techniques. And even here the gains were small-scale. The grandiose and glamorous projects for disafforesting woodland and draining the fens in which royal, aristocratic and merchant speculators engaged in the 1630s achieved far less at first than did piecemeal encroachments, for the very scale of their activities provoked fierce local resistance.

Industrial change was similarly piecemeal. Assertions based on the expanding production in the north-eastern coalfields that there was an 'industrial revolution' in this period have not stood up to questioning. Certainly, output did rise fast, but it rose from a very low base, and coal was put to relatively few industrial uses – as in glass-making after 1612, or in the production of salt and the manufacture of nails and other low-grade metal wares. Smaller-scale innovations were probably more important in the industrial sector. Thus, in textiles new techniques were brought by immigrants from the more technologically advanced Low Countries during Elizabeth's reign. The government too played a role in such advances, since the Tudor state could see social advantages in increasing employment, economic advantages in reducing imports, and hoped for political or military advantages from autarky, or self-sufficiency. Not surprisingly, metallurgy and mining were the main fields to benefit, but the crown also backed some consumer industries like dyeing through the issue of monopoly patents. The readiness of entrepreneurs as well as farmers to respond, once they were assured of a market, points to a healthy flexibility in the economy. Notable steps towards diversification were the establishment of the new draperies, especially in East Anglia, and of glove- and lace-making, the introduction of crops like woad and madder for commercial dyeing, and the localized development of a domestic metalware industry in the west midlands, producing such items as nails, needles and pins. By 1640 the value of new drapery exports was beginning to vie with the product of the – admittedly depressed – traditional broadcloth industry.

With a few famous exceptions, such as the larger coal mines of the north-east, industrial production occurred in cottages. The entrepreneur, who might deal with few outside his own family in the textile areas of west Yorkshire or up to perhaps 500 in the new draperies belt of southern Suffolk, provided workers in their homes with their raw materials and sometimes even with their tools; he then collected their product, usually paying them piece rates. The prevalence of domestic production in most of the major industries, textiles, leather-working and most branches of the metal industry, means that it is impossible to measure the suffering inflicted by the deteriorating economic conditions of the first half of the century. Cost-of-living figures measure prices in the market. An unknown but very large proportion of the population was engaged in both agriculture and industry, whether the small farmer whose wife and servant did some subsidiary spinning or leather work, or the artisan miner with a small plot of land attached to his cottage. The numbers of entirely landless grew, but we have no ideal of totals. Again, although real wages fell markedly, the availability of *some* work for the whole family in many areas meant that while people had to work much harder to keep alive than their ancestors in 1500 had done, the dismal wage rates did not cause total privation. It was in this connection that the new industries proved critical, providing some support for an expanding and otherwise probably unemployed labour force. The diary of the Essex clergyman Ralph Josselin shows that in the dismal years of the later 1640s it was the diversity of the local economy that preserved the poor. Over a longer period it helped England escape the horrors of starvation which hit France in the later seventeenth and eighteenth centuries. And over a longer period too, in a context of falling food prices the new industries provided sufficient extra income for the poor to enable demand to come together with supply and thus to create a potent new market for consumer goods.

Social Structure

Early-seventeenth-century England was not therefore bound to the unchanging values of the soil. Economic change was accompanied, and indeed facilitated, by a surprising flexibility in what was still a fundamentally hierarchical social order. The dangers of rigid analytical models, whether built around class or status, are apparent. A major ingredient in class formation must be class consciousness, and while the rhetoric of the Levellers of the 1640s – the first genuine popular political movement in history – did display a strain of class hostility, the 1640s were extraordinary times. When both agricultural and industrial production were firmly rooted in the family workers were more likely to identify with a family in whose household they might live, rather than with workers elsewhere. Poor communications and localized horizons made the latter identification still less likely. Probably most thought of themselves primarily as residents of a particular village or town, or as weavers, blacksmiths, or whatever, than as members of the 'commons'. Status-analysis equally runs into difficulties, since while contemporary commentators did talk of birth and style of life they also listed as characteristics of the various social groups wealth, possessions and power, the concerns of modern class analysts. Their ambivalence testifies to the relative fluidity and openness of English society on which foreigners remarked.

The most obvious feature of society is the presence of a titular nobility. On the whole English peers had rent rolls of over £3,000 p.a., and influence to match; they were also *de facto* members of the House of Lords, and figured disproportionately on the king's privy council. But despite their scarcity when compared to the proliferating nobilities of France and Spain – there were fewer than sixty peers in 1603, and rather more than twice that number a generation later – the peers did not form a caste. They were not exempt from taxation, nor barred from marrying commoners, or engaging in trade. The demands of blood, lineage and land were further confused when the early Stuarts ennobled great merchants and financiers such as Lionel Cranfield, earl of Middlesex, and Baptist Hickes, Viscount Camden. But the nobility did not need new blood to teach them that status was empty without money. The fourth earl of Bedford was perhaps the greatest property speculator of his day, and most noblemen eagerly exploited any mineral resources found on their estates. They provide a warning against any simplistic dichotomy between 'feudal' and 'capitalist'. Too many peers were amongst the kingdom's greatest industrialists, or indeed amongst the most aggressive landowners: thus, successive earls of Pembroke outpaced the inflationary curve by their estate policies.

There may have been a financial 'crisis of the aristocracy' in the late sixteenth century as the peers adjusted slowly to the pressures of inflation. Traditionally, lettings had been for periods of lives rather than for terms of years, and were often not flexible enough to finance the lavish new buildings – the 'prodigy' houses such as Hatfield and Hardwick – and styles of clothing which Elizabethan and Jacobean high fashion demanded. But as tenancies fell in, the nobility more than compensated by raising entry fines for new tenants as well as by raising rents. The recovery was made easy for them by the extent of their landholdings in a period of fierce land hunger, and by 1641 the peers were richer than their predecessors had been in 1558. There was, however, a price to pay. As landlords, and particularly as absentee landlords – which owners of great estates almost necessarily were in parts of their holdings – they risked the resentment of their tenants and a consequent loss of political influence. The costs of landlord aggression were made distressingly clear in the sacking of the earl of Salisbury's house at Cranborne in Dorset in 1643.

That the relative position of the aristocracy had changed is evident in the different forms that civil war took in the fifteenth and seventeenth centuries. Nevertheless, the stress should fall on the word *relative*. The peers had grown richer; but so too had other groups. The combined income of the five richest peers may have been less than £75,000 p.a., when the total income of the untitled gentry in pre-war Kent alone probably ran close to three times that figure; at the same time non-landed, urban wealth increased dramatically, and both literacy and religious division grew apace. Society was becoming pluralist, and the position of the peerage was bound to be affected. Morale may also have suffered from the crown's sale of titles in the 1610s and 1620s, which increased the number of earls, for example, by 141 per cent. Yet the adulation shown in print and in public demonstrations during the 1620s for godly protestant noblemen like the earls of Pembroke, Essex and Southampton suggests little fall in the prestige of the aristocratic order as such. There is very little to show that noblemen were on the eve of the Civil War in anything so dramatic as a crisis, and the demise of the House of Lords in 1649 seems to owe almost everything to political rather than to social change.

The contours of the next tier down the pyramid, occupied by the gentry, are notoriously indistinct. Commentators agreed that gentle birth and way of life – which meant a sufficiency of money for a leisured existence – were necessary for all. But what was that way of life when in 1642 one-third of those deemed gentlemen in Yorkshire had less than £100 p.a., while two had over £4,000 p.a.? A plausible solution is to divide the status-group of gentlemen along economic lines, distinguishing parochial gentry, whose estates were limited to a single parish or settlement, from county gentry, whose lands spread more widely, and from the greater gentry, such as the Yorkshireman Sir Thomas Wentworth, whose estates might fall in several shires. Since this was still a basically landed society, the degree of landholding had the appropriate political consequences: the more land a gentlemen held, the higher he might rise in local government and politics. Ultimately, however, to be a gentleman was to be thought a gentleman by one's neighbours, and to discuss gentility in hierarchical terms can be misleading. The newly-rich, buying an estate and aping gentry ways, might very soon be thought gentlemen. As Sir Thomas Smith, an Elizabethan commentator, concluded, 'Gentlemen be made good cheap in England.' The contrast with France or Spain, where the connection between land and commerce was far more tenuous and where status was much more a matter of descent, was important both for England's socio-political and its economic development.

The relative ease of access to gentility meant that the numbers of gentry increased fast in a period when both the profits from land and the population as a whole were multiplying. There were for example seventy-eight more gentry families in Lincolnshire in 1634 than there had been in 1562, and over England as a whole gentry numbers probably tripled between 1540 and 1640, from 5,000 to 15,000. In this sense at least it is possible to talk of the 'rise of the gentry', one of the old subjects of historians' controversy. Its product is visible in the manor houses dating from the sixteenth and seventeenth centuries which dot the English countryside, in the increasingly ornate tombs with which gentry families flaunted their status, and in the growing preoccupation with genealogy, through which gentlemen manufactured evidence to bolster the status they claimed. By the early seventeenth century the gentry made up between 2 and 3 per cent of the populace, and owned perhaps 40 per cent of the land.

Shading away gradually from the bottom ranks of the gentry were the yeomen, who can best be characterized as large farmers of up to perhaps 100 acres, depending on soil type. Like the gentry, the yeomen were on the whole getting richer, as the profits of large farms producing for the market grew. The evidence is again visible in the buildings, and also in probate inventories, which show increasing domestic comfort, with pewter and sometimes even silver utensils replacing wood, and with glass in the windows and cloth 'hangings' to keep out the draughts. Below the yeomen on the lower rungs of the landed hierarchy clustered the hard-pressed husbandmen, small or marginal farmers with perhaps twelve to fifty acres. Beneath these proliferated the cottagers and labourers, whose lives grew more miserable as prices rose.

Changes were occurring at this level as well as at the top. The degree to which English farming has ever been 'peasant', or largely egalitarian and subsistence in character, can be exaggerated, but detailed local studies have found that at the beginning of our period many communities were closer to the stereotyped peasant cluster of near-subsistence farms than they were at the end. While 'fielden', or arable, areas already contained many large capital-intensive farms employing landless labourers, in most regions significant numbers of husbandmen still worked the land, with no large pool of the landless beneath them. Half a century later conditions were changing. Continued population growth drove the burgeoning poor to areas where they could find living-room and livelihoods, particularly to the towns and to woodland regions with sufficient waste land where they could erect squatters' hovels. While the core of yeomen and husbandmen in the swelling villages of the forest of Arden in Warwickshire, or in Myddle in Shropshire, remained relatively stable, a new class of landless paupers, comprising about one-third of the population, had appeared below them by the end of our period. In many fielden villages too an agricultural proletariat was forming. Although the lords of the manors could often restrain immigration, and the proliferation of the poor that accompanied it, they could not check all economic forces. Thus, in Orwell in Cambridgeshire the disastrous harvests of the late 1590s and the continuing difficult conditions in the new century combined to wipe out many marginal farmers, polarizing the inhabitants into rich and poor even more effectively than did the expansion downwards of the populations of the woodland and urban zones. Throughout the arable belt, the spread of commercial farming, coupled with inflation, encouraged landlords to put pressure on marginal smallholders unable to pay rents per acre which might seem economic to the larger farmer producing for the market. The provocative transformation of Cotesbach in Leicestershire, which made it one of the centres of agrarian protest in the abortive 1607 Midland Rising, stemmed almost entirely from its landlord's aggressive estate policy. The overall consequence was clear. In 1600 between a quarter and a third of England's rural populace were labourers, but by 1700 that fraction had risen to around a half.

In the long run, social polarization helped to pacify agrarian England. The growing wealth of the yeomen, often the purchasers of the lands of failed husbandmen, left them rather closer to their gentry superiors than to their inferior neighbours; they were therefore less likely to share the interests and concerns of the numerous poor, or to give them a political lead as once they had. Even in the most troubled areas, the more slowly polarizing fenlands of eastern England and some forest regions in the south-west, the countryside after 1650 was far less troubled by popular disturbance than it had been in the previous century. But the present reality – and a frightening one to many observers – was the relative and absolute growth in the numbers of the poor.

If the countryside was divided into 'haves' and 'have-nots', the inequalities in the towns were as great. A fortunate few, the merchant oligarchs who dominated all towns, might enjoy a half or more of the property and wealth. But the scale of urban wealth can be exaggerated. Despite immense fortunes like those of Cranfield and Hickes, most merchants, even in the City, were no richer than parochial gentry; in the smaller provincial towns the comparison would be with yeomen.   Nevertheless, the contrast with the lot of most of their neighbours remained glaring. The larger early-modern towns had some of the same powers of attraction as their modern third-world successors, and the life of the poor newcomers huddled 'at the town's ends', dependent on occasional labouring jobs and on charity, was marginal. In depressed Sheffield in 1616 one-third of the populace was described as 'begging poor'. Perhaps another 20 per cent, poorer artisans, might need occasional relief in any town during industrial depressions. The growing evidence of distress helps account for the deep unease voiced by many parliament-men in the 1620s.

The increasing numbers of townsmen caution against any attempt to categorize English society in terms of the landed hierarchy. So too does the rise of the professions, which can in practice be limited to three – the law, medicine and the church. Professionals grew in number even faster that did the gentry, a sure sign of national prosperity. At least twenty-two physicians practised in the prosperous cathedral city of Canterbury between 1603 and 1643; and the number of attornies active in the counties of Devon, Hertfordshire and Warwickshire quadrupled between 1580 and 1640. More business and greater numbers ensured that the proportion of urban wealth held by professionals in the town of Northampton rose to one-tenth by 1640, from nil around 1600. But such signs of social diversification by no means represented a challenge to the values or ways of landed society. While 'professional' qualifications became increasingly necessary, inherited connection was often almost as important to success in a profession as it was to landowning families. The legal dynasties, the Bacons, the Whitelockes, the Finches, are notorious. They are matched amongst the clergy, and the tomb of the wife of the Jacobean archbishop Mathew of York could proclaim her close relation to two archbishops and five bishops. More generally, one-quarter of the Jacobean incumbents in the diocese of Exeter had succeeded to their fathers' church livings, giving another meaning to the legal fact that such livings were accounted freeholds. Landed society and professional society interpenetrated at every level. Younger sons of gentry looked for advancement – thus, their numbers amongst the clergy doubled between 1600 and 1640. Conversely, successful lawyers bought landed estates; the greatest of them, Sir Edward Coke, held enough acres to gain election to parliament for two separate counties in the 1620s. The leading clerical dignitaries were also landed magnates, and, lower down, the ordinary country minister was often a working farmer too, on the glebe lands attached to his living.

The social claims of the professions were, however, by no means wholly accepted. Many were the complaints – perhaps justified, since it has been estimated that only a half of those called to the bar were sons of gentry – against upstart and grasping lawyers. The protests swelled to a crescendo in the revolutionary years, with calls for the abolition of the whole profession. And despite their rising educational standards, the clergy's aspirations to status did not match their material rewards. Although bishops still sat in the House of Lords, they married their children into gentry families – and some said they were lucky to do that when Archbishop Laud was the son of a Reading clothworker and Archbishop Neile of York the son of a London tallowchandler. Similarly, although the parish minister might be addressed as a gentleman he was usually no richer than a yeoman, despite the efforts of benefactors from Laud to Cromwell to improve his lot. It is not unlikely that the hostility to clerical pretensions which ran so strong in the 1640s and 50s drew some of its fire from such discrepancies.

One further group, comprising half the population, was of and yet not of the hierarchy. The military origin of land law and of the chivalric orders meant that in their own right women could hold neither land nor – unless by special grant – title. This period did remove some of the legal disabilities of women as the equity court of chancery began to offer them some relief in the only matter that was held to concern them, their rights to inheritances and to property settled on them at marriage. Furthermore, the growing prosperity of merchants and yeomen meant that more people made wills, and in due course many of these appointed their wives executrix. Women thus gained a legal standing in certain courts which contributed to the relative freedom, by European standards, of propertied English women by the eighteenth century: indeed, earlier visitors from abroad too were sometimes struck by the social latitude allowed to women. But only in widowhood did women achieve a significant measure of independence, with control over property or, in many towns, the right to practise their husbands' trades. Amongst the middling and meaner sorts women always played a central role in the domestic economy, helping on the farm or in the shop as well as managing the household. Yet the subordination of women was intensive, and did not only stem from the landed concerns of the gentry. 'Skimmington rides', popular charivaris or shaming rituals directed at households where the wife ruled the roost, occurred over a wide area of England. Still more harsh was the lot of poor and ugly women: eccentric behaviour could earn for these an accusation of witchcraft.

Male dominance did not necessarily mean callousness. While preachers and moralists instructed wives to obey they urged husbands to cherish, and the evidence in diaries of emotional reciprocity and the sharing of decisions is buttressed by the wills which made the widow the executrix. Nevertheless, though there were clearly influential women, like Lady Joan Barrington, the matriarch of the powerful East Anglian gentry family, it is equally clear that such figures only achieved political independence in exceptional circumstances – the roles of the redoubtable Lady Brilliana Harley and the countess of Derby during the Civil War sieges of their absent husbands' houses are examples. Most telling is the case of the Levellers, who advocated a remarkable degree of democracy in the 1640s. But while women figured prominently in their demonstrations, and while Elizabeth, the wife of John Lilburne, one of the Leveller leaders, was a leader of the movement in her own right, they stopped short of demanding political rights or legal reforms for women. The renowned role of women as religious patrons and religious enthusiasts of all kinds, both in England and elsewhere, therefore probably owes much to their inability to act on other stages. In particular, the readiness of the protestant sects at mid-century to accept that God spoke directly to the individual, of either sex, and that those to whom God spoke might participate fully in the church's affairs, probably underlay the prominence of women in groups like the Quakers. That fact also helps explain the fierce male reaction the sects provoked.

Economic change, urbanization, commercialization, at a time when the pyramid of status and wealth rested firmly on the land seems a recipe for social stress. The disproportionate number of younger sons staffing the parliamentary bureaucracy in the 1640s and 1650s, and the probability that a victorious royalist regime would have been little different, suggest that at least some expectations had been frustrated. Yet as we have seen, the social structure was flexible enough to avert the worst tensions.

Education was, after apprenticeship, probably the most common route to advancement for the common people. Many were the local notables, whether gentry, clergy or merchant, who piously paid the school or university fees of clever sons of the village poor – in Dorset there were both county and town collections for this purpose in the early seventeenth century.* Yet education was not simply provided to

*C.H. Mayo, *Muncipal Records of Dorchester*, p. 541.

those whom the better sort co-opted. The growth of the professions stemmed from the pressure of those who would be upwardly mobile as well as from the demand of the wealthy for their services. The university sector best reveals the extent of the surge, for student numbers at the two universities of Oxford and Cambridge roughly tripled between the mid-sixteenth century and the 1620s, to upwards of 1,000 entrants a year. The demand for an educated, preaching clergy and for a laity that could comprehend their teaching combined effectively with the humanists' insistence that the gentry be educated for their station. It has been argued that in consequence a larger proportion of English male adolescents received tertiary education in this period than was to be the case again until the twentieth century. The eyes of many were set on a clerical career, for between a half and three-quarters of the much smaller number of graduates seem to have become clergy. The bulk probably came from the sons of clergy, merchants, yeomen and artisans who made up well over a half of the entrants – many of them supported on the 500 or so scholarships established in the philanthropic wave between 1560 and 1640, while others worked their way as servants. But by no means all students had professional ends in view. At least one-third of the intake by the 1620s was of gentle birth, adolescents sent to acquire civility, learning and godliness. Doubtless all they gained for their fees, often enough, were some social graces and a smattering of Latin tags.

The combination of philanthropy and private interest which brought the physical growth of the universities also contrived to multiply the number of grammar schools. There were around 700 endowed grammar schools by mid-century, and perhaps double that number of private schools, whose teachers depended wholly upon fees. The object of the pious benefactors of the endowed schools had usually been to impart godliness and sufficient learning to enable students to enter university and, by extension, to become clergy. The effects on the curriculum were predictable. The private schools, which usually shared the same objectives, differed little in the subjects taught, although over the century both sectors balanced the prevailing stress on Latinity with a growing concern for mathematics and for English composition. Despite the conservative curriculum, the schools' services were evidently in demand. By mid-century most small towns possessed a grammar school of some kind, some of the larger ones several. Thus, twelve Leicestershire market towns had endowed schools, and most of the populace of Kent – admittedly a well-provided county – lived within ten miles of a grammar school. Schooling was therefore accessible to most people who could afford fees, which were often as low as £1 a year. Not surprisingly, thoughtful conservatives like Francis Bacon worried about the social consequences of over-provision.

The popularity of the grammar schools, which only adjusted slowly to the demands of an expanding commercial sector, perhaps testifies to the force of educational inertia. It was at the lowest level, in the petty schools, that education was most socially rational. The growing complexity of the economy generated a wide demand for schooling, sufficiently strong to enable one London teacher of writing to adults to afford a summer house down the river in fashionable Greenwich. Over half the parishes in the poor midland diocese of Lichfield had schoolmasters for some time between 1584 and 1642, and nationally probably the large bulk of the population lived within walking distance of an elementary school. The expansion of a market economy meant that farmers needed to be able to read contracts; similarly, more and more artisans and traders had to confront bills and written instructions and, if they were wise, to cast accounts. The demand for a literate laity capable of reading its Bibles reinforced this economic pressure, but the latter clearly predominated. Literacy was both socially and occupationally highly specific. While literacy rates soared from the later sixteenth century, until by 1642 almost one-third of the adult male populace was literate, the figures were patchy. Townsmen were around two-thirds literate, and the higher the status and the greater the complexity of the trade the more complete the literacy. And so in the countryside, while gentry were completely literate, cottagers and labourers were largely illiterate. The poor had less economic need for literacy, although the urge to read the Bible or pressure from a conscientious clergyman might move a minority.

Similar factors applied to the education of women. Barred from the universities and grammar schools, their role as mothers of potentially godly children might still have justified schooling them to the level of Bible-reading, and certainly many were the preachers and moralists who urged this. Many did go to elementary schools. But education for women as much as for men was for a station in life, and most parents seem to have been reluctant to pay fees for little tangible benefit. Increasing numbers of schools for daughters of the better sort were established in the course of the seventeenth century, especially around London; although these certainly taught reading and the Bible, they seem to have concentrated most on polite accomplishments appropriate for gaining a husband. Overall, however, the female literacy rate was only around 10 per cent by mid-century, though there are of course abundant instances of literate country-women arguing scripture in the civil war period. Women in the provinces on the whole received as little schooling as did the labouring poor.

The socially specific character of literacy therefore cautions against any exaggeration of the impact of education in undermining social barriers. The avenues for social mobility remained narrow, and other safety-valves were more important in easing the demographic and economic strains. The most obvious was poor relief, whether private charity or official provision.

The compulsory poor rate, established by statute in the later six-teenth century, came to be levied on householders almost as a matter of course in the gloomy years of the 1620s and 1630s. That develop-ment is a measure of the failure of the gifts of gentry and merchants to keep pace with the growing numbers of poor or even with inflation. Thus, it has been estimated that known charitable gifts in the county of Kent over the period 1480–1660 were the *per capita* equivalent of a half-day's wages for a local plough-boy. In the new draperies town-ship of Coggeshall in Essex in the 1630s private charities yielded about one-third as much as the official poor rate. But official relief was no universal safety-net. Poor parishes were often unable to bear their own burdens, and had to hope – usually vainly – for aid from wealth-ier neighbours when crises occurred. A more serious deficiency lay in the contemporary concept of poverty, which focused primarily on the aged and women with dependent children – that is, the truly help-less. These received niggardly pensions, and their begging from door to door was usually tolerated. Much less notice was taken of pauper householders, whose numbers increased as depression worsened, and whose begging was frowned upon but, perforce, allowed. Rural and urban parishes were driven to resort to the occasional dole, which imposed increasingly strict requirements about proper conduct as the scale of the problem became evident. In the industrial areas town authorities and county magistrates were often compelled to go fur-ther. They found themselves regularly subsidizing sales of grain to the poor or even, in the disastrous 1620s, setting up more ambitious pro-grammes such as Salisbury's famous municipal brewery.

These were, however, hardly long-term solutions, and the almost inevitable consequence of an intractable problem was the hardening of hearts: the churchwardens' accounts for West Ham, Essex, refer-red laconically in 1652 to the burial of 'a poor woman that died in the cage'. 'Sturdy' migrants and pregnant girls likely to add further burdens to the parish poor rates were whipped back to their last places of residence, communities acting for themselves or with the aid of the county quarter sessions blocked the construction of pauper cottages, and often pressure was applied to prevent the poor from marrying and bringing more poor into the world. The summary powers vested in local officials by statute could be put to a variety of uses and abuses. Emigration was the natural human response. In the first instance the poor might look for work and subsistence in nearby or even distant towns, but eventually many were driven as squatters to woodland areas, and beyond. Almost 2 per cent of the English population emigrated in the 1630s, and a similar proportion in the 1640s. By mid-century there were probably 50,000 English colonists in the Americas, and many more had perished there. Ireland was probably still more important as a safety-valve for a booming population in a sluggish economy. It has been estimated that as many as 100,000 English and Scots may have left for Ireland in the century of confiscation and settlement after 1589.

Family Life

England's expansion outwards underlines the remarkable rate of geographical mobility, at all social levels. Demographers have suggested that almost 2 per cent of the provincial population must have moved to London each decade to allow it to grow as it did despite its appalling mortality rate. And while many migrants would have been the wandering poor, desperate for jobs or for relief, those slightly above them seem to have been not much more rooted. Even amongst the freeholding, and therefore more secure, families at Laxton in Nottinghamshire in 1612, over a half seem to have been on their holdings for less than two generations; in the Northamptonshire village of Cogenhoe over half the population disappeared and was replaced between 1618 and 1628, and mortality alone cannot explain such flux. Most people moved at least once in their lives, although for the most part movement occurred within a fifteen-mile radius. Then as now, the young were the most mobile. Young people left home to enter service, whether domestic or in husbandry – almost two-thirds of the 15–24 age group were servants. Others became apprentices; there were probably 20,000 apprentices in London at any time, while apprentices came to Bristol from some thirty counties. Service allowed parents to get surplus mouths away from the family table, and allowed the children in their turn to accumulate wages, or skills, with which to set up on their own. The result was of course that marriage partners were as often as not found outside the village as in, and that horizons expanded and news travelled.

   For probably the majority of the population certain fundamental aspects of life seem therefore to have been little different from what we know today. Personal mobility aided personal independence. Status and the preservation of the family inheritance were vital considerations to those who had something to preserve, and strong parental pressure was often applied to determine the marriage choice of offspring. The daughter of the fierce old lawyer Sir Edward Coke was probably not alone in being whipped at the bedpost into obedience, but many wealthy parents clearly allowed their children at least a veto over selections made for them. Where there was less to gain or lose there was less point in parental exertions, and often young adults made their own choices. That is not to say that for the poor selection of a mate could be a matter of unsullied romance or lust. Prospective partners needed to be sure of their mutual abilities to establish and maintain a home, and ages at marriage were therefore relatively late for the bulk of the populace. Numerous local studies show ages of males at marriage falling in the 27–9 years range in the first half of the seventeenth century; as communities gradually responded to the years of hardship the average age of women at marriage sometimes went even higher than that around mid-century.

Family formation was no more subject to physiological determinism than it was to parental control. It is easy to imagine that before modern forms of contraception birth rates ran close to the biological maximum. But what has been called the peculiarly European pattern of late marriages allowed England and her neighbours to escape the 'poverty trap' consequent on near-maximum family size which has beset other regions. The planned spacing of children was clearly impossible. Yet whether through sexual abstinence or other techniques, the population was capable around mid-century of reducing its fertility, as well as raising its age at marriage still further, in order to cope with deteriorating conditions. Smaller family sizes, coupled with the growing agricultural flexibility generated by the increasingly market-oriented economy, then permitted some improvement in English living standards in the later seventeenth century.

A further factor in preserving living standards was the relative rarity of the extended families which elsewhere ate into any surpluses that family farms might produce for the market. The nuclear family was very much the rule. Surviving listings suggest that household size averaged around 4.5, though nobles and gentry might have dozens of servants under their roofs. The scale of family life was partly fortuitous: mortality rates ensured that relatively few grandparents lived to need supporting in old age. Amongst the poor, children were likely to depart early for that great safety-valve, service, while more substantial households were restricted by convention. The English pattern of inheritance for land, like that of most of western Europe, was broadly primogenitive. There were regional variations, and partible inheritance was fairly common in non-fielden regions, and especially amongst poorer farmers; but on the whole eldest sons were likely to remain on the family holdings, while younger sons and daughters received a portion of the family's possessions and an entry into service or apprenticeship. The pressures of primogeniture were particularly strong amongst the gentry, since considerations of status demanded that estates remain intact. Not for nothing did the Digger Gerrard Winstanley take the hapless younger brother as his metaphor for the poor of the earth. Most were left to make their own way in the world with an annuity grudgingly given by their elders, an opening into the professions, an apprenticeship or – increasingly important when too few new occupations were opening – a sea passage as an emigrant. Mortality rates did ensure, however, that advancement often came earlier than it does today, and the youth of some civil war commanders is striking: John Lambert was only 40 when his political career came to an end at the Restoration.

The intimate landscape is familiar in other respects. Too much has been made by historians of one alleged consequence of low life-expectancy, and that is the coolness of relations within the family. Conscious of the likelihood of any child's early death, parents, it is argued, feared to invest emotional capital in it. They allowed this distancing to reinforce a distaste for the uncivilized 'natural' being that was the child, a distaste which had its roots in fears for a fragile social order as well as in protestant teachings on original sin. The result was, allegedly, parent conduct towards children that might range from callous to brutal. Particularly amongst the propertied élite family relations could certainly be cold, and the gossip John Aubrey noted that prior to the 1650s, 'the child perfectly loathed the sight of his parents, as the slave his torturer.' Yet the picture can be over-drawn. A careful reading of diaries and letters suggests that, just as many marriages seem to have been built around affection and respect, so those qualities were not absent from relations between parents and children even amongst the gentry. Writing of her young son to her absent husband, that parliamentarian stalwart Lady Brilliana Harley reported that he was 'as merry as his little soul can be, till he is asked where you are, and then he makes some moanfull tune.' However much more frequently it happened than today, the death of children could still prove devastating. And even in the dismal years of the early 1630s a major cause of the thwarting of the government's plans for the compulsory apprenticeship of poor children as a relief measure was the reluctance of 'foolish poor parents' to part with their offspring. Charity then as now began at home. The point is reinforced by the recent suggestion that in the seventeenth century as well as the twentieth much mental distress originated in family tensions that sit ill with assumptions of distant personal relations.

Little emerges from such a survey of the economic and social characteristics of seventeenth-century England to lead one to conclude that political upheaval stemmed from socio-economic change. Indeed, paradoxically, continuities may have been at least an important as change. The failure of the economy to grow as fast as did the population meant that there were dangerously large numbers in 1642 ready to seek their fortunes in arms. Similarly, the prominence of primogeniture, with its attendant problem of the younger brother, undoubtedly helped both king and parliament find their enthusiastic supporters. Had economy and society been better matched there might have been fewer extremists seeking to rise by means of total victory. But in no way does the social structure appear fundamentally unstable. Many were hungry in 1642, but it was not the hungry who took the political lead. Indeed, social animosities seem to have been rather greater in, for example, 1549 than a century later. The signs of social stress visible in the early seventeenth century were scarcely unconnected to the passions of civil war, for as we shall see they led some to suspect the hand of Antichrist and others to clutch more violently at hierarchical controls. Nevertheless, on the whole the causes of the war have to be sought in the realm of politics and religion, and in the domain of folly and misunderstanding.

The diversification of the economy and the growing complexity of the social structure did help shape if not cause the political upheaval. The economic dominance of the great landowners, whether crown or magnates, was diminishing as the commercial sector grew in strength. Their power was certainly undercut by a variety of economic and social developments – population mobility, literacy, the increasing numbers and self-confidence of the gentry, and so on. If the Civil War and its outcome did not resemble the baronial wars of the thirteenth or fifteenth centuries, then the divergence must in large part be traced to the emergence of a less hierarchical society and to new political forces.

2 The Body Politic

Central Government

In England government was the king's government, and the monarch ruled as well as reigned. That age-old convention was certainly subject to both modification and challenge in our period, as that steady revival of classical learning and of classical political theory helped stimulate thought of an impersonal state. Thus, a sermon preached at the university church in Cambridge in 1632 argued that treason against the state was a greater crime than treason against the king, and, not surprisingly, traces of novel analyses of political responsibility can be seen in the parliamentary attacks on Charles I's ministers. Such changing attitudes help explain the ability of parliament in 1642 to claim it was preserving king, government and law even while fighting against him. But the flowering of the impersonal state came only slowly during the republic. Prior to that, officials served the king.

Not only did the king control the distribution of office and favour, but he also determined policy. To some extent the latter stemmed from the former. When James carefully balanced a pro-Spanish with an anti-Spanish secretary of state for most of his reign, he ensured that policy would not lean heavily in either direction, and thus reinforced his hopes of acting as Europe's peacemaker. Similarly, Charles's revealing appointments to bishoprics after 1628 changed the character of the church of England. But the king's control over the formulation of policy was also more direct. Despite historians' jibes at James's devotion to hunting and young men, his servants could never take his royal *fiat* for granted. Not even the alliance of Prince Charles, the duke of Buckingham and parliament could hurry the king into war against Spain in his last, allegedly declining year. And Charles in his turn steadfastly refused to consult either his Scottish or his English councils over his catastrophic Scottish policy until too late.

To enable him to govern the country the king had certain prerogatives, recognized at law. The royal prerogative was a blend of powers and rights which included sole control over foreign policy, regulation

of overseas trade and of the coinage, pardoning of criminals, and –
although there was dispute over this – regulation of the church.
Looming over all these was the king's duty to take, as he alone saw fit,
emergency action to preserve the state; it was this 'absolute prerogative' which was to be the focus of so much tension in the early
seventeenth century. The king's power of government was indicated
most clearly of all by his ability to issue proclamations, reinforcing, or
filling gaps left by, the less flexible instrument of statute. His possession of quasi-legislative as well as executive – and, as we shall see,
judicial – functions thus counsels against thinking in modern cate-
gories of separated powers. Proclamations were particularly useful in,
for example, the promulgation of measures against epidemics, all the
more so when parliaments met only infrequently; but unless statutes
specifically provided, proclamations were not enforceable in the
common law courts.

The precise relations between the prerogative and the common law
were something of a grey area. That the king possessed prerogatives
was undoubted; the assumption ran that he would observe ancient
conventions and the public weal in his use of them. Indeed, when
early in James's reign the Commons expressed doubts about the
constitutional implications of the recent use of proclamations the
crown rapidly returned to more traditional paths. But as we shall see,
greater difficulties arose when financial exigency drove kings to use
undoubted prerogative powers to raise revenue, and to transform
extraordinary into ordinary use. At this point collision occurred
between two absolutes, the right of the subject to his property and the
right of the king to act as he saw fit in what he deemed to be an
emergency. There was no obvious arbiter. As Chief Justice Hobart
said in 1623, 'The prerogative laws are . . . the law of the realm for
the king, as the common law is the law of the realm for the subject.'
More generally, insoluble problems confronted a monarchical state
when a king set himself to follow policies which a sizeable body of his
subjects condemned, for the undoubted royal right to determine
policy left them little redress. Parliament's attempt to distinguish in
1642 between the errant person of the king and the inerrant office of
the king revealed the confusion generated by the clash of constitutional truths with political realities. Such contortions nevertheless pay
signal testimony to the general acceptance of the rights and powers of
the crown.

Since the king could not deal personally with all the business of
government he needed advice and assistance. This he could take from
whomever he chose. Indeed, a feature of Charles's rule that caused
considerable resentment was his tendency to ignore the normal
sources of advice and to turn instead to the duke of Buckingham alone

in his early years and to a motley crew, which included the papal agent and Scottish and Irish Catholic courtiers, in the later 1630s. Some historians have argued plausibly that central to the politics of Charles's reign is the problem of counsel, the problem of ensuring that the king listened to the right sort of advice. And though, short of civil war, it proved impossible to define or impose such advice, most commentators agreed that the king ought to rely on his privy council. This was an executive body in its own right, although it acted only in the king's name and with his allowance. Among its members were the great officers of state, the heads of what we should think of as departments, like the lord treasurer and the two secretaries of state; it also included leading officers of the royal household like the lord steward and lord chamberlain, as befitted a government centred on the person of the king. The council's broad executive powers might be used to the full when James was away hunting, but were less indulged when Charles was in the 1630s deciding matters with a few intimates. The council ranged in size from fifteen at the end of Elizabeth's reign to over forty in Charles's. At the latter point it was unmanageable as either an executive or an advisory instrument. Although Charles appointed a series of overlapping sub-committees, his council reflects his unfortunate hankering for secrecy, and his readiness to make policy in an informal fashion.

Not even an effective council could cope with the tasks it confronted, for there were very real constraints on the government's freedom of action. In an important sense government was 'private', in that many offices at what might be called the administrative if not at the policy-making level were granted for life and viewed effectively as freeholds. Office-holders recruited their own servants and expected to make money from the public in fees and other perquisites, rather than from an appropriate salary. The distance of this system from nineteenth-century bureaucratic ideals can be appreciated from what is now the generally accepted estimate that the annual income of officials from fees – which could of course easily cross the impossibly blurred line separating them from bribes – equalled at least 40 per cent of royal revenues. Even senior 'political' figures like the two secretaries of state received only £100 p.a. each in salary, and were expected to live at a level appropriate to their station with the aid of fees. A further 'unbureaucratic' feature of government is that administrative offices and 'reversions', or future appointments, were often sold, although the practice was never systematized as it was in France for the king's benefit – all too often courtiers pocketed the proceeds. The king therefore possessed less control over his administration than might be imagined.

A consideration of royal finances underlines the 'private' nature of government. Government was in more ways than one the king's, since he paid for it and the subject ordinarily did not. Kings were expected to 'live of their own,' to which end they enjoyed certain 'ordinary', or recurring, revenues, from fines and from residual feudal dues, from the customs, as well as from the ancient crown lands. Taxation, which was viewed as an extraordinary and usually wartime affair, had to be granted by parliament, on the maxim that the subject's property was his own. Even the customs, which were of critical importance, can be seen as 'private', since the king's ministers had at the very beginning of James's reign confessed their inability to manage any large-scale undertaking by replacing direct administration with a 'farm', or lease, of the collection to merchant contractors. Farming was variously attractive. It guaranteed fixed sums of revenue instead of an unpredictable flow; it gave courtiers an opportunity for manipulation and bribery when arranging the lease – thus, the earl of Salisbury received £6,000 from the successful syndicate in 1604; and most important of all, the customs farmers could be coerced into providing credit, the most urgent need of all governments.

As the history of the customs suggests, government was minimal in scale. The central administration was exiguous even by contemporary European standards, and was probably smaller under Charles I than the royal government of the single French province of Normandy. What we might term the central executive consisted of up to ten clerks of the council, and the two secretaries of state, with perhaps fifteen clerks under the latter. Not surprisingly, individual ministers, the council collectively, and even the king himself, handled often the most trifling complaints from petitioners, about family squabbles and the like. Although these may have made an impressive reality of patriarchal monarchy they ought to have ended up in an outer office, had there been enough outer offices. Instead, they intensified the irrepressible tendency of this kind of government to delay.

The lack of a bureaucracy limited the sources of information open to the central government. 'Policy' tended to be merely *ad hoc* responses to whatever landed on ministers' desks – normally, petitions from interested parties – and consistency was lost in a fog of ignorance and amid the often conflicting cries of vested interests. The government's perpetual shortage of funds increased its difficulties. Not until the so-called 'financial revolution' of the 1690s could governments afford the luxury of formulating policies; earlier, they simply reacted to circumstances. And even when policy was declared, the same factors of scale and lack of information limited enforcement.

Court and Patronage

The corollary of personal monarchy was that the royal court was the nation's political centre. Since all channels of government emanated ultimately from the king, and since parliament met only occasionally, anybody wanting to obtain anything significant needed royal or conciliar approval. Quite literally, he had to find 'a friend at court' to help him. The court was, essentially, composed of the king's friends and servants, some of them high-ranking nobles like the earl of Pembroke or the Scottish duke of Lenox, others personable intimates like Endymion Porter. Amongst the servants can be included the political (as opposed to the middle-ranking legal and financial) office-holders, and around these clustered assorted hangers-on, those hopeful of office or favours, and servants of the king's servants. Foreign agents and representatives were also part of the court, a politically unfortunate fact when most European diplomats and exiles were Catholics. Although the court's floating membership might run into the hundreds, it was a world of intensely personal rivalries. There were insufficient jobs for the aspirants who were all competing for the king's ear. Furthermore, in days before bureaucratic standards of official morality rewards for the few top jobs could be enormous, as indicated by the immense piles built by those Jacobean lord treasurers, the earls of Salisbury and Suffolk; the competition was therefore all the hotter. Those with access – and here lay the influence of the king's intimates in the privy and bed chambers – acted as brokers and charged for their favours; and patronage and reciprocated benefits were the rules of the game. Not surprisingly, a large literature on the corruption and expense of court life developed, which contains gems like the defeated Sir Walter Raleigh's verdict that the court 'glows and shines like rotten wood', and that the purposes of its statesmen were only 'ambition, their practice only hate.'

The suspicions of the moralists and advocates of economy in country and parliament were not unjustified: after all, the 2,000 or so employees of the royal household in the 1630s made up, with their families, one of the half-dozen largest communities in the country, with a huge impact on London's economy. There was bound to be room for reform. But the court was more than just a place where pigs plunged their snouts into the trough. Those with policies to forward had to go to the same sty. Identifiable groups of courtiers in the 1620s, especially those surrounding the third earl of Pembroke, backed war with Spain and the preservation of England's protestant identity, while others, most notably the earl of Middlesex, urged peace and financial retrenchment. The existence of such political, as well as personal, divisions prevented distaste for the court, or dislike of royal policy, building to dangerous proportions. The anxious puritan appalled by James's pacific ways in his last years and outraged by signs of religious decay could hardly reject outright an establishment which contained allies like Pembroke. Division at court then, far from being a sign of weak rule, helped avert alienation by offering contacts to dissidents. Far more dangerous was the court Charles created, which, if it did not become ideologically monolithic, only allowed the airing of a single viewpoint. Incomprehension in the country, and a fatal alienation, were the predictable outcome.

The court offered practical as well as ideological contacts to the country. Local magistrates needing extraordinary relief – for example, permission for the export of grain in breach of the grain regulations – or gentlemen seeking local office had to seek out friendly courtiers or councillors, normally men with local roots, to smoothe their way. And since membership in virtually all local commissions was determined at the centre, it behoved the aspiring gentleman to make friends there. The attempt of several recent historians to discuss the politics of the early seventeenth century in terms of innate hostility between court and country is therefore ill-advised. Members of the one might scorn rural bumpkins, and of the other, corrupt parasites, but ultimately neither could survive alone.

Detailed studies of probably the two best-documented county figures, Sir Thomas Wentworth in Yorkshire and Sir Robert Phelips in Somerset, have shown how symbiotic were the connections of court and country, and how intently the man who would domineer in his county must look to the court. Favour at court enabled the gentleman to deploy influence locally, but conversely the scale of a man's following helped guide courtiers when they chose whom to patronize. The local gentleman had to propitiate both his neighbours and the distant 'great ones' at Whitehall if he were to establish his local standing and gain the due rewards in prestige and power. As the fiscal demands and changing character of the court in the later 1620s alienated the less sophisticated lesser gentlemen and freeholders who composed the electorate, parliaments and parliamentary elections caused Phelips some unease as he tried to tread his tortuous path. The most telling comment on the relationship of court and country came in 1642, when both split down the middle.

Patronage was the essential lubricant in this world. It worked at all levels. If young men wanted university fellowships or if towns wanted changes to their charters, they had in a pre-professionalized age to find those who could help them to what they wanted. Still more in high politics did patronage oil the wheels and prime the pumps. Candidates for jobs were found amongst the cousins, friends or dependents of those with influence. The existence of a 'spoils system', and the absence of any principles of entry through merit, do not mean that early-modern morality was inferior to our own. The personal nature of government meant that just as the king was expected to enjoy the rewards of his position, so were his servants. That they turned to their friends when appointing subordinates was hardly surprising: there were no political parties yet, nor party loyalties. Politics was furthermore a dangerous game, which still cost men their lives – the headsman's axe claimed Sir Walter Raleigh's and the earl of Strafford's even before the passions of civil war broke loose. Who better for a magnate to trust than those who were personally loyal? Such considerations were of course reinforced by the natural human emotion of pride: politicians like to have followings. The rules of the game were enduring, and were not abrogated by the fall of the monarchy. The town worthies of Leeds urged the election to parliament of one army officer in 1654 because General Lambert was his patron, 'and he strikes with great hammer!' All must look upwards for advancement and aid; and in so doing they acknowledged the demands of hierarchy.

The ties of patronage rested on reciprocity, however, not unthinking submission. A client's performance reflected on his patron, and therefore the latter had to concern himself with qualifications: thus, that Jacobean earl of Northampton took pride in having introduced the astute merchant Lionel Cranfield to the king's service. And clientage did not necessarily entail utter sycophancy. While Charles's favourite the duke of Buckingham expected his clients to protect him against impeachment, beyond that they could and did give him conflicting advice. Furthermore, since gratitude was the quality commended in clients, superiors must show generosity if their inferiors were to show deference. A patron had to deliver the goods. When James's lord treasurer, the earl of Suffolk, was disgraced for corruption in 1618 he soon found himself isolated not just at court but also locally as his neighbours realized he could do nothing for them. The dictates of hierarchy were therefore not quite as straightforward as they may seem, and superiors sometimes found themselves bowing to their inferiors' wishes. The notorious Catholicism of the earls of Worcester may have stemmed as much from their need to retain the respect of the highly Catholic south Wales gentry as from personal preference. Equally, the readiness of the very unpuritanical Buckingham to employ and protect puritans, including, ironically, a staunchly puritan patronage secretary in John Packer, surely owed more to his estimate of the concerns of the political nation with which he had to work than to his own tastes.

Nevertheless, religious passions could weaken the patronage tie. The dominance of the earls of Derby in Lancashire was undercut by the crystallization of mutually hostile puritan and Catholic loyalties amongst their neighbours: unlike the earls of Worcester they could not even lead from behind in these circumstances. Equally, the well-deserved historiographical reputation of the earl of Pembroke as the Hamlet of English politics in the 1620s indicates that the task of squaring his position as the champion of the godly with the demands of court politics was neither comfortable nor very productive.

More damaging was the accession of a king who was as incapable of seeing the need for distributing favours to those who mattered as he was effective at provoking ideological confrontation. Charles's austere temperament led him throughout his career to expect unquestioning submission, not talk of a *quid pro quo*. When the earl of Suffolk tried to bargain over a post the king exploded, demanding 'Where is your obedience?' The scant support noblemen and even courtiers and councillors gave Charles in 1640–2 reflects his frigidity. As the disappointed earl of Arundel – who was to leave the country to avoid the fighting – remarked, 'It is an ill dog that is not worth whistling.'

The Courts and Parliament

To stress the personal nature of monarchy and the court as the very personal centre of politics is not to imply that government was primitive. There were bureaucratic elements, most particularly in the ancient revenue administration, the exchequer, with its elephantine official memory for debts due the king and its equally elephantine procedures. Equally bureaucratic, in the worst sense of the word, were the law courts.

Instead of the modern division into departments of state, early-modern government featured an overlapping series of courts. Even the central administrative organ, the privy council, was also a law court of a kind, as were its offshoots in the peripheries, the councils in the north, at York, and in Wales and the Welsh marches, at Ludlow. The commonest justification of the existence of kings was the administration of justice and the safeguarding of property rights, and James in particular took seriously his role as the fountain of justice. Not for nothing did his funeral sermon talk of him as Britain's Solomon, for at least until the crisis in the courts of 1616 his council intervened frequently as a sort of supreme arbitrator, at all stages of litigation. Under Charles too a steady trickle of petitioners sought quasi-judicial aid from the council, especially to mitigate the common law's draconian remedies for bankruptcy. Reinforcing the conciliar arm was the more formal tribunal of star chamber where councillors, reinforced by judges, sat to hear and punish with fines and corporal – although not capital – sanctions offences against a wide range of government concerns and dangerous breaches of the peace. But, as they did with the council proper, litigants and petitioners diverted star chamber's energies to their own use by alleging riot in the course of property disputes: accordingly, star chamber business increased probably ten-fold between 1550 and 1625. The provincial councils, less hampered by affairs of state, were still more eagerly used by litigants, and the councils at York and Ludlow probably handled nearly 2,000 cases a year under James.

Those 'prerogative courts' – so-called because they were the judicial manifestation of the royal prerogative – were not the only tribunals serving the king. If there was a single major centralizing force in English history it was the central courts, the great common law courts of king's bench and common pleas and the equity court of chancery. As the outcome of successive constitutional test cases in the period demonstrates, the judges inclined strongly towards the interests of the crown. Thus, all the opinions in the 1637 ship money case recognized that in emergencies the rights of the individual must give way to the needs of the state, and that those needs could only be defined by the king. The judges quite properly saw themselves as protectors of the *king's* peace in the *king's* courts. The crown was more than merely the symbol of national unity, and medieval baronial pretensions had been struck down in the courts as much as on the battlefield. Chief Justice Hobart was not therefore adopting a threatening new position when he opined in 1623 that in the courts 'everything for the benefit of the king shall be taken largely, as everything against the king shall be taken strictly.' The judges were merely unfortunate in that as politics became more polarized they found themselves more frequently attempting to hold the ring. Their activities were all the more provocative in that however much Sir Edward Coke, the greatest of them, cast the judges as servants of a sovereign common law, and however much they strove honestly – as most did – to live up to that ideal, the judges were also the paid servants of the king. A standard career pattern was for the attorney general, the king's chief legal officer, to succeed to a judgeship, frequently as chief justice or lord chancellor. Parliament's impeachment for treason in 1641 of all but one of the surviving common law judges of the 1630s was their unlooked-for reward for such a close association with the king's government.

The courts were agencies of centralization in a wider sense, for they drew ever more litigants from all over the kingdom. The momentum grew in the early modern period as the expanding population and economy, and the accelerating land market, bred disputes. Litigiousness, and the complexity of title to land, could expose a landowner to years of expensive defence against hungry relatives. But the courts did not simply wait for business to come in. Not surprisingly, since the income of officials as well as lawyers came from fees, each court strove to create work for itself. Venues for suits did exist outside Westminster, in the provincial councils, or the chancery court of the ancient palatine – or semi-autonomous – jurisdictions of Lancaster and Durham; the duchy of Lancaster court dealt with around 2,000 bread-and-butter cases a year before 1641. But the losing party with a deep enough purse could begin proceedings anew in the central courts.

As competition heated in the early seventeenth century the hungry central common law courts launched volleys of 'prohibitions', or orders banning further proceedings, against other courts; since they were formally superior they usually won unless the privy council intervened. The rivalry for business brought bitter confrontation between king's bench and chancery, which came to a head in 1616, and Charles too was compelled to intervene in a series of jurisdictional disputes in the early 1630s, to little lasting effect. Only the sweeping away of the conciliar jurisdictions in the deluge of civil war and revolution seemed to bring a final solution. Nevertheless, the petitions from the north in the 1650s for the restoration of the regional tribunals, and Cromwell's re-establishment in 1654 of the Lancaster palatine jurisdiction, suggest that they had met a real need for local and – relatively – speedy justice in a period when communication with London was both slow and expensive.

Centralization was not therefore an unmitigated blessing, for the Westminster courts found themselves swamped by business. The business of king's bench quadrupled between 1560 and 1580, and doubled again by 1640; the other courts were not far behind. Delays mounted alarmingly, encouraged by the common law's preoccupation with procedural technicalities. The lawyer-MP Edward Alford, admittedly a hostile witness, reported in the parliament of 1621 that the average duration of cases in chancery was twenty-three years; but his comment, that three years should be enough, damned the common law courts too. The calculation of fees by the number of pages in documents invited prolixity and abuse. The twice-yearly exodus from Westminster of the judges on their assize circuits through the counties to hear both criminal and civil business did divert some pressure from the central common law courts, but it is unclear how much of a safety-valve two days in each county provided. When the assize judges seem to have averaged about one civil case every twenty minutes in the mid-seventeenth century, and when an overworked trial jury might hear a dozen criminal cases in succession, then the system was clearly creaking under the strain of business. Equally disturbing was the vulnerability of proceedings to incompetence and abuse, since all those involved, apart from the judges and counsel, were effectively amateurs and all were paid by fees. Reports of partisan sheriffs impanelling partisan juries, and of jailers brutalizing and exploiting prisoners, or alternatively allowing them to escape, were legion. In many respects the law was unpredictable. The property laws in particular were draconian, yet perhaps only 10 per cent of convicted felons were executed, thanks largely to the practice of allowing 'benefit of clergy' – branding for first offenders – to males who could read. Such latitude contrasted with the treatment of debtors, who were consigned to gaol remediless, and of prisoners: a visitor to London in 1652 was told that some twenty poor prisoners died of privation in Newgate every month. Radicals were not alone in fulminating against both lawyers and courts in the years of upheaval at mid-century.

Although parliament retained a broader popularity in the political nation than did the law courts, it was perhaps as ineffective at bringing practical relief. A fundamental characteristic of parliament (or rather, strictly, of *parliaments*, since each was legally distinct) before the 1690s is its dependence on the will of the king, who called it into being and dissolved it as he saw fit. Kings summoned parliaments for money, or, less often, for some other business, and not because they were constitutionally bound to submit themselves to criticism. The prime constitutional role of parliament was therefore as a meeting-ground, a place for the doing of business, both royal and private, and not as a point of conflict. Conflict accorded ill with prevailing notions of harmony in the body politic, a harmony symbolized most potently by the inescapable fact that the king was a part of parliament, was king-in-parliament when that body met; similarly, most of his councillors sat in one house or other. Had conflict been what parliaments were about kings would have seen little value in them – and indeed, when in our period conflict for various reasons came to outweigh the doing of business kings did come to see little point in them. We need not go so far as to argue that parliaments were *events*, rather than an institution, for they possessed some continuity in personnel, in business, in their records, and most of all in their sense of corporate identity. But parliaments only sat for about four and a quarter years between 1603 and 1629.

The famous break in the history of parliaments, between 1629 and 1640, did not therefore mark a total discontinuity with the immediate past. Nor was it altogether a surprise, for the 1620s had been full of gloomy predictions that England would shortly see 'the last of parliaments'. Those predictions reflected less royal aspirations towards absolutism than the fact that parliament's practical value was open to question. Its legislative record was spotty in the extreme, and –

contrary to Tudor norms – no statute emerged from the meetings of 1614, 1621, 1626 and the first parliament of 1640. While procedure did grow more sophisticated, the most notable developments, in the Commons' committee system, were as much to free loquacious figures like Sir Edward Coke from the rules of debate as to improve the house's legislative capacity. Furthermore, and most important, both the value and the frequency of the taxes parliaments granted were as we shall see declining.

Its relative failure as a legislature did not mean that parliament was instead living up to the Victorian ideal of restraining the government. True, the outcry in the Commons in 1610 dissuaded James from further swingeing impositions of duties on foreign trade; and the storm over monopolists in 1621 did act as something of a deterrent. But despite repeated efforts, the Commons failed to persuade the crown wholly to abandon impositions; and, in another business that really mattered, the efforts in parliament in 1628–9 to alter the king's religious policy failed miserably.

Parliament's problems were intensified by the absence of any clear sense of the institution's role. The great wave of legislative activity in the sixteenth century, which reformed the church and provided a broad framework of socio-economic regulation, left the crown with little need for further statutes. After James's first parliament dashed his hopes of a legislated union of England and Scotland, neither he nor his son looked to parliament for much other than money. The emptiness of so many opening speeches by kings and their servants points to some uncertainty as to the positive contribution parliament might make to government, and may account for the lack of concern the crown showed for the techniques of management. Others were similarly unsure. Apart from isolated sessions like 1624, when the agenda was largely set by Prince Charles and the duke of Buckingham, or the Long Parliament of 1640, when the parliamentary genius John Pym gradually took the lead, members of the Commons in particular tended to spend much time pursuing local priorities, such as the deepening of the river Ouse or the setting of a new light on Dungeness. While these mattered greatly to those concerned, and while they bolstered the Commons' sense of representing the nation, they did not always facilitate the establishment of a common agenda.

Such local priorities were at least partly forced on members by an increasingly active electorate. County constituencies, both more prestigious and more populous, were often contested, Yorkshire and Somerset repeatedly so between 1604 and 1640: and although many small borough constituencies were subservient to neighbouring landowners or to powerful officials such as the chancellor of the duchy of Lancaster, the electorate was too large to be entirely subject to

magnate interest. The forty-shilling freeholder franchise in the counties and the hotch-potch of urban franchises potentially included
around one-third of the country's adult male inhabitants. Not surprisingly, MPs frequently testified to their concern to satisfy their
localities, and on occasion – notably after the large grant of taxation
in 1624 – a few experienced their neighbours' wrath for not doing so.
Furthermore, MPs fixed their gaze firmly on their localities because
they too were primarily local men. As MPs they were part-timers,
and most spent most of their lives looking to their harvest or their
case-load as JPs. As often as not they sought their seats in a local
competition for status rather than with any clear sense of national
purpose. They then hurried home as fast as they could, or as fast as
London's delights would let them. The costs of life in the capital gave
them all the more reason to do so – as Sir Simonds D'Ewes observed
gloomily in 1642, 'we all know that by our attendance here we are few
of us savers'. Symptomatic of the level of consistency and statesmanship to be expected of such amateurs was the failure in the 1620s of
bills to reform the antiquated militia; indeed, England's humiliating
military performance in the 1620s was not altogether unconnected
with the largely local horizons of its parliament-men. The many congenital back-benchers amongst them were unlikely to seek eagerly to
involve themselves in government, or to push for control over the
executive.

  The peers in the suggestively named upper house were as much a
part of parliament as were the Commons, and their approval, as well
as the king's, was needed for the passage of any statute. The Lords'
institutional superiority to the Commons was underlined in the 1620s
when the upper house acquired a judicial capacity as a sort of appeals
court, though that role was virtually to overwhelm it in business by
the 1640s. But institutional superiority is no guarantee of political
initiative: Despite the presence in the Lords of a solid block of royal
supporters in the twenty-six bishops – over one-sixth of the total
members in the 1620s – and of privy councillors and prominent
courtiers, much of the political running was made by the Commons.
Since the crown's financial plight meant that the main business
confronting parliaments throughout the pre-war years was taxes,
constitutionally very much the Commons' preserve, the relegation of
the Lords to a back seat was predictable. The upper house did not on
the whole adjust well. The role of individual peers as royal servants,
great patrons or even political managers cannot be denied. Thus, the
earl of Pembroke was the greatest patron of the 1620s, and his men
were crucial in the foreign policy debates of 1624 and in the attack on
Buckingham in 1626. But in the corporate capacity of the Lords
claims for a 'crisis of the aristocracy' find some justification, for the

peers collectively show signs of having lost their sense of purpose. In 1614 the Commons revealingly agreed to proceed quickly with some bills 'to find the Lords something to do', and in 1624 one jaundiced gentleman noted accurately how few public bills came from the Lords any more. Most remarkable of all, at one point in the troubled session of 1628 peer after peer rose to move for an adjournment on the grounds that their thin house had not 'any business to do until the Commons shall send [some] up to them'.

Various explanations can be advanced, in addition to the priority of fiscal business. The house of Lords often saw itself as something of a broker between king and Commons; yet Charles's attempt in his Answer to the Nineteen Propositions of 1642 to appeal to the peers by stressing their role as a 'screen or bank' between crown and people suggests how uncomfortable that posture could become as political tensions grew. The Commons were always eager to maintain a united front with the Lords, yet when in 1628 the peers tried to placate the king by softening the Petition of Right the lower house brushed aside their reservations. More generally, as Lord Chancellor Ellesmere testified after James's first parliament, the peers were at a disadvantage in conference encounters as the learning of the lower house grew. As controversy came to centre on legal questions they grew uneasy in face of lawyers in the Commons of the stature of Sir Edward Coke and John Selden, and only as political crisis in the early months of the Long Parliament drove the ship of state out into uncharted waters did the Lords regain some of their old prominence as the Commons' leaders sought advice, reassurance and, if possible, unity. But while in most of the radical initiatives of 1641-2 the Commons were encouraged by a minority of opposition peers, the fact remains that the lower house usually put pressure on the upper rather than vice versa. Historians' concentration on the Commons in earlier parliaments, if not their frequent assumption that parliament *was* the Commons, is therefore to some extent justified.

If the two houses were so unproductive of legislation, why did parliament bulk so large in governmental as well as popular estimations? Part of the answer for the government is easy. When kings lived so much from hand to mouth, no addition to their revenues could be ignored, and the taxes granted in the session of 1606 in particular, and in 1624 and 1628, were substantial. Although it might seem with hindsight that the sums were hardly worth the labour and the concessions expended – most importantly in the crown's restraint over impositions after 1610 – the council in its intensive debates in 1615 and in the winter of 1627-8 on raising revenue could think of few alternatives. There was always the hope that the Commons might at last appreciate the crown's problems and show the generosity

expected of them. For a central function of parliaments was, supposedly, to cement unity between king and people: each, acquainted
with the concerns of the other, would then come together in common
purpose. All agreed that a king's strength lay in the love of his people,
and conciliar assertions to this effect were not necessarily empty piety.
One councillor, Sir Thomas Edmondes, could confide in 1621 that
'Abuses were grown to such a height of ill as the kingdom had been
undone, if we had been much longer without a parliament.' While, as
we shall see, scepticism could sometimes be heard within the council,
councillors had had much the same upbringing as had other MPs in
Elizabethan assumptions about the virtues of unity in an organic
body politic. MPs could give the king the benefit of their local experience; they could help him with extraordinary taxation; and an affirmation of unity could give practical strength as well as comfort in a
crisis. Despite its financial flimsiness, James did not treat as con-
temptible the Commons' declaration of support in 1621 for his efforts
in Europe. The courtiers and councillors who in the crisis of 1639–40
hoped for a rapprochement with the nation in parliament should not
therefore be seen as turncoats.

An emphasis on conflict has been the main historiographic legacy
of the study of early-seventeenth-century parliaments. Yet procedure
within parliament aimed less at divisions than at obtaining 'the sense
of the house', at unity and consensus. Until 1641 divisions were fairly
rare. Similarly between Commons and king: William Hakewill, an
outspoken critic in 1610 of the royal fiscal policy of impositions, said
at about the same time that MPs were 'all of counsel with the king and
commonwealth indifferently'. It was a common refrain. If the king
unquestionably possessed the powers of government and there was no
gainsaying his will, then whether England was well or ill governed
must hinge on the counsel he received. And few parliament-men even
in 1640–1 foresaw parliaments acting as constant counsellor. They
left that role to the privy council. Rather, drawing on members' local
knowledge, parliaments must present abuses to the king for rectifica-
tion and, if necessary, remonstrate against corrupt councillors and
royal servants. Parliaments, even meeting occasionally, were essential for the well-being of the kingdom, and the most common metaphors for parliament were phrases like 'the physician of the
commonwealth', 'the eye of the kingdom', 'the grand jury of the
realm'.

Until the eve of civil war, few parliament-men had any thought of
corporate involvement in government. Indeed, there was little reason
why men in the Commons should. If government was the business of
the privy council then it might be thought more a concern of noblemen
than of commoners, since kings took their servants disproportionately

from the nobility, and tended to ennoble those who rose from below. Accordingly, the troubles of the parliaments of the later 1620s, with their attacks on Buckingham, by no means stemmed from bids to enforce ministerial responsibility to parliament, as historians anachronistically preoccupied with parliament used to argue. Instead they centred on attempts to end a situation where 'all the king's council rode upon one horse'. In other words, the proper involvement in government of the council, not of parliament, was the goal. Pressure was finally exerted in late 1641 to establish parliamentary control over the council and over the sword. Yet that came only at the end of long and ultimately abortive negotiations between Charles and the parliamentary leaders aimed at replenishing the council with 'good lords'. Furthermore, the rate of absenteeism suggests that the growth of a parliamentary administration owed more to political crisis than to the aspirations of most members.

The Commons were therefore by no means self-confidently aggressive. Procedural uncertainty or unease at the course proposed could throw the Commons – and the Lords too – into long periods of uneasy silence. Only a few dozen members 'speechified', to use a later expression, and the reticence of many country gentlemen and merchants may have made the house easier to influence than we think. The Commons often showed a remarkable readiness to pass over slights and get on with business, and even to vote taxes in unpromising circumstances. Interest, both local and personal, was a powerful factor, and no matter how worthy a bill it was unlikely to proceed without committed advocates.

But parliaments, and parliamentary behaviour, cannot be reduced to a single strain. It is as misleading to focus exclusively on the deference and petty-mindedness of the Commons as it is to portray members as incessantly hungering after power. The preference for local business may indeed have undermined the Commons' effectiveness, yet the inadequate grants for war in the 1620s, which had such fatal consequences, stemmed also from a fully conscious conviction that the war was not the right war and that it was being mismanaged. However aware parliament-men were of their duty to aid and counsel the king, they also knew that they had to 'speak for their country'; and that country might be both neighbourhood and nation. That last imperative was becoming all the more powerful in view of the elimination by nascent absolutisms throughout Europe of the medieval heritage of representative assemblies. Sir Robert Phelips's declamation in 1625, 'We are the last monarchy in Christendom that yet retain our original rights and constitutions', is justly famous.

Parliament-men therefore knew how to use arguments of principle against an issue which seemed fundamentally threatening. When they were confronted with what they took to be a frontal assault on their privileges, as in James's attempt at the end of the 1621 parliament to control debate, they could dig in their heels in full awareness of the constitutional significance of the episode. Most MPs were realists and recognized that extraordinary measures might be forced on even benevolent rulers. But when those measures were claimed as a right inherent in the crown they could no longer be passed quietly by in the interest of doing business. Reactions to impositions – which many MPs realized had been levied by Elizabeth – to the royal power of arrest in 1627, and later to ship money, indicate that gentlemen and lawyers correctly saw as crucial the distinction between tacitly acknowledged and publicly asserted powers.

There were other explanations for the ambivalent behaviour of so many parliament-men. They were spokesmen at the centre for their localities and yet they often had, on their return, to explain and implement royal policy as JPs or deputy-lieutenants. A more fundamental ambiguity lay in England's problematic inheritance of what has been called a 'double majesty'. On the one hand stood a fairly coherent theory of kingship and authority, guaranteed in the last resort by the king's 'absolute prerogative'; and on the other an equally powerful theory of law, rights and custom, articulated and defined not just in the law courts but also in parliament. Both demanded respect and allegiance, yet political circumstances – especially the crown's repeated requests for money – seemed to be drawing them apart.

For all their exaggerations, older accounts of the crown and Commons as adversaries were thus not *wholly* wide of the mark. By the end of the 1620s some members were not averse to making their case to the country, most obviously with the Three Resolutions of 1629, when they found the king rejecting their advice. Hakewill's balanced responsibilities were coming into conflict under pressure of events. And significantly, it seems to have been conflict rather than consensus that attracted popular attention as the ways of court and crown became more unpopular. The failure of legislation in the 1620s ought to have undermined the legitimacy of parliament in any consensus model of politics. Yet the rapid and turbulent sequence of parliaments seems instead to have established parliament more firmly in the political nation's estimate of what was the proper political structure. The widespread declarations of devotion to parliament which greeted the fiscal devices of 1626–7 are revealing.

Local Government

Much recent scholarship has been directed towards exploring the implications of the minimal scale of central government. Since the privy council did little other than respond to petitions placed before it by private parties and local bodies, most government was local self-government by local dignitaries. The rediscovery of the local perspective alerts us to another source of political tension. Noblemen and gentlemen might react just as angrily to challenges to local institutions which maintained and reflected their own local standing as they did to affronts to the dignity or competence of parliament.

The medieval plenipotentiary in the counties, the sheriff, had by this time been reduced to humdrum tasks, impanelling juries, collecting certain ancient royal revenues, and the like. Not surprisingly, every autumn gentry laboured their court contacts frantically to ensure that they were not 'pricked' as sheriff. But the office of justice of the peace, or JP, was a different matter. Although unpaid and involving duties which, if conscientiously performed, could be extremely onerous, the post attracted no shortage of candidates, for it was the prime demonstration of a gentleman's membership of the county's élite. Furthermore, it also brought local power, the ability to protect friends and strike at enemies in innumerable petty ways. The most obvious of the JP's functions was his role as lay judge, attending at the county's quarter sessions court to try a wide range of cases – though capital felonies were increasingly dealt with by the assize judges on circuit. Beyond that, acting alone, the JP took depositions and evidence, and bound over suspects in preparation for the sessions.

Quarter sessions were the main administrative institution in the counties, as well as a criminal court. Sixteenth-century legislators had thrust onto the backs of the JPs 'stacks of statutes', and JPs therefore combined their judicial role with setting local rates for bridge and highway repair, appointing constables, providing for the upkeep of bastards, and so on. Some hurled themselves enthusiastically into their tasks. The Calvinist vision of a godly commonwealth seems to have inspired many JPs, and recent local studies have painted vivid pictures of godly magistrates, such as the Bacon family in Norfolk and the Lewkenors in Suffolk, who combined fierce moral correction with a disciplined charity. But as poverty, vagrancy and all the allied social ills multiplied late in Elizabeth's reign the privy council came to doubt the ability of the JPs in sessions to cope. It knew well how gentry competition for honour was driving up the numbers of county JPs past the limits of effectiveness: when the Northamptonshire commission, an extreme case, rose from 43 in 1562 to 113 in 1616, it was easy for an individual JP to assume others would do the work. The council's concern was even sometimes shared in that stronghold of the gentry, the House of Commons, which is normally thought to have adulated the JP, the MP's *alter ego*. One lawyer MP in 1614 claimed there were 300 statutes requiring enforcement by JPs, 'and few of them knew fifty of them'.

The council had other grounds for concern about the local governors. Localism was sometimes as great a handicap as laxity to the smooth maintenance of social order. In a crisis local magistrates often responded with remarkable energy. The economic disaster of 1629–31 drove the JPs in Essex to investigate both supply and demand, checking the amount of grain stored in barns and the acres still to sow, and seeking from the constables information on the sizes of households in their jurisdiction; after balancing the equation they decreed the amount of grain to be sold weekly in the markets. Too often, however, local administrators refused to depart from their accustomed ways. Thus, county benches everywhere rejected the council's laudable proposal, made in the good harvests at the end of the 1610s, that local grain stores be established to alleviate future dearth. Equally sacrosanct were local boundaries, and the unwillingness of the Huntingdonshire authorities to aid nearby Essex in the invasion scare of 1625 is notorious. Local administration was therefore constantly disrupted by rating disputes, squabbles between one jurisdiction and the next over who should bear the burden for what.

Mounting regulatory problems drove central governments from the Elizabethan onwards to strive to press this unpromising material into responsiveness to central concerns. Dearth or economic crisis was the normal trigger for these drives for enforcement, but they came so frequently that they can almost be spoken of as that early-modern rarity, a policy. In their frustration, and in their quest for revenue, successive monarchs frequently sought to co-opt private interest in the implementation of much of the regulatory framework. For example, since JPs in the clothing areas, who depended on local deference for their local standing, rarely enforced the statutes regulating textile workmanship, Charles appointed by letters patent, for a monetary consideration, a patentee who was to search for abuses and receive part of the penalties. As MPs ought to have recognized when they themselves drafted regulatory statutes providing for prosecution by mercenary informers, the patentee was a realistic device for coping with the deficiencies of local government by unpaid amateurs. But the deployment of private interest in enforcement invited corruption; moreover, JPs often reacted angrily to outsiders interfering in their preserves. Accordingly, although Elizabeth occasionally threatened to systematize the use of patentees to compensate for the ineffectiveness and factiousness of JPs, and although James in his financial difficulties appointed so many patentees that alarmed MPs suspected a system, patentees never became an officially acknowledged element in local government. They were at least partly eliminated by statute in 1624.

The key to attempts to tighten up local government was therefore the use of the assize judges. From the late 1580s the judges were regularly 'charged' before their departure on circuit with the needs of government. They were to keep a tight rein on jurors, suspected not merely in government circles of using their position to profit themselves; they were to galvanize the JPs; and to report on their performance. Increasingly, the judges submitted to the JPs sets of articles requiring action, chiefly in the field of regulation of and provision for the poor. However few the sanctions at its disposal, the Jacobean council attempted to formalize these directions in the years after 1605, and economic crisis in the early 1620s caused council and judges to return to the fray. Attention was diverted by the military activity of the later 1620s, but peace and renewed economic crisis in 1630 brought a new and fierce flurry of regulatory activity when the celebrated books of orders of 1630–1 were dispatched into the counties for (the council hoped) general enforcement.

The council's 1605 orders had also instructed the JPs to ease the pressure on quarter sessions by holding regular 'six-week sessions' in which two or more JPs acting informally in their neighbourhoods were to bind over, take sureties, and oversee the petty regulation of the parishes. Such 'petty sessions' had already emerged on an *ad hoc* basis in many counties as conscientious JPs tried to cope with the range of tasks confronting them in the Tudor years; the strident insistence on petty sessions in the 1631 book of orders was therefore not altogether needed. It is indeed a measure of the gradual responsiveness of English local government that by 1640 petty sessions, now monthly, and collections for the poor rate had everywhere become firmly established. Economic adversity clearly underlay much of this activity; but equally worthy of note is the activity of the Jacobean council. That activity cautions against assuming that early-modern governments in general, and James's in particular, were wholly unable to follow a consistent policy.

Governmental lassitude was much more evident in the oversight of the militia, the military arm of local government. In the mid sixteenth century statutes had decreed some modernization in the arms and training of a reconstituted militia; further, a permanent hierarchy of command emerged in the wartime crisis at the end of Elizabeth's reign, with the senior resident peer in a county usually serving as lord lieutenant, assisted by three or four of the leading resident gentry or minor peers as deputy-lieutenants. The main element in the militia was the trained bands, usually consisting of the 'discreeter' householders, or their sons. The reluctance of gentlemen to put arms in the hands of the 'meaner sort' was given substance by the non-performance of the Northamptonshire trained bands against agrarian rioters in the county in 1607. The militia's officers, drawn from the local gentry, provided further social reassurance, since contemporaries were almost as concerned about domestic unrest as about external threats.

There was, however, a price to pay. The Elizabethan Spanish wars had imposed deeply resented burdens on the localities in a time of soaring food prices, and the 1604 parliament seized eagerly on the opportunity presented by peace with Spain, and the desire of government strategists to reform the now technologically outmoded provisions, to repeal the Tudor legislation. But, probably as a result of competing legislative priorities as well as of lack of urgency in the council, parliament enacted no new code. The militia was thus left dependent on the royal prerogative. While the prevailing deference to authority allowed the council at the end of the 1610s to cajole the trained bands into equipping themselves with expensive new muskets, the questionable legal footing of the militia was to prove debilitating in the war-torn 1620s when the crown sought to raise money as well as arms by the prerogative alone. Deputy-lieutenants in county after county regretted their lack of unquestionable 'compulsive' powers. Many gentlemen did seek to impart some reality to their traditional chivalric vocation by short periods as volunteers in the warring armies of the continent, and others, especially younger sons and those without a patrimony, became mercenaries – the future parliamentarian captains-general, Essex and Fairfax, are examples of the one, and those supreme professionals George Monck and Philip Skippon of the other. Nevertheless, England became more than ever a military backwater. It was fortunate that Europe's great powers, Spain and France, were too distracted in the 1620s to seek to chastise Charles for his belligerence.

Urban corporations were no less introverted than the neighbouring gentry. Having narrower interests to protect than did county JPs, town corporations often clung to them fiercely; thus, Bristol corporation was in the 1610s even fining its citizens who took suits to the central courts. The correspondence of many deputy-lieutenants therefore resounds with squabbles with unco-operative town fathers, while in their accounts of the civil war from opposite ends of the political spectrum both the earl of Clarendon and Lucy Hutchinson condemned the insubordination of towns. For his part, the town clerk of Warwick urged all towns to beware the gentry, who used towns only 'as they do their stirrups to mount to their horse'.

Towns were usually enclaves of intense government as well as of self-government. Certainly, some industrial settlements, such as the Essex new draperies towns of Coggeshall and Braintree, were unincorporated and had to rely on an often unfriendly neighbouring JP. But most towns had their own officers, from mayor and aldermen down to the humble ale-conner, regulating all areas of life, from prices in the market to the precedence of wives. Sixteenth- and seventeenth-century monarchs sought to buttress the forces of order against the disruptive potential of expanding urban populations by strengthening the powers of urban magistrates; nevertheless, despite the steady entrenchment of self-selecting oligarchies, urban populations as a whole were not depressed into an under-class. The poor immigrants who clustered as lodgers in alehouses and tenements may indeed merely have experienced authority as victims. But the urban freemen, those free to practise a trade, who often comprised a half of a town's adult male inhabitants, had a wide range of minor offices in ward, parish and trade guild open to them. It has been estimated that one in ten of London's adult males was serving at any one time in some post. Such a prolonged education in civic responsibility undoubtedly played a part in fostering that urban 'independence' which conservative commentators like Clarendon deplored. Nevertheless, the authorities need not have worried that in the towns they faced a 'many-headed monster'. London, which had the most poor, also had the most developed poor-relief system in England, with doles, almshouses, charitable apprenticeships and subsidized education. To maintain the effectiveness of London's system, parish officers kept regular and detailed lists of their neighbours, whether householders or lodgers. In Ipswich constables went the rounds of alehouses hunting absentees from Sunday services, and in town after town godly magistrates and ministers joined to exert a fierce moral discipline, exemplified by the bloody whipping-post at Bury St Edmunds.

While the JPs left the bulk of the working papers, and therefore determined the judgment of subsequent ages, their importance has perhaps been exaggerated. Order had in the last resort to be preserved in the villages, not in the counties, since JPs were often very thin on the ground: in the extreme case of Amounderness in Lancashire one JP governed more than 7,000 people. Standing between the JPs and the people were lesser figures, the high constable, the petty constable, the churchwarden and the overseer of the poor, each playing a vital role. Not merely did they transmit commands in one direction and information in another, but they also initiated processes.

The high constable, acting over a division of a county – a hundred, lathe or wapentake – was selected by the JPs from the minor gentlemen, or occasionally from the yeomen. He played a crucial role in helping apportion county-wide rates, and he reported at assizes or sessions on local abuses and grievances, as well as on the doings of the petty constables. The latter, often called parish constables or headboroughs, did frequently give grounds for concern to their superiors, since in many townships they were selected by annual rotation amongst the householders. The unpopularity of a job which involved considerable work and carried with it the risk of financial liability for escaped suspects encouraged those who could afford it to find paid substitutes to perform the duties; this practice ensured a degree of disreputability, incompetence or crippling illiteracy in those appointed.

The extension into the parishes of a sterner vision of order throws a revealing light on the position of the petty constable and on some of the tensions involved in local government. Charged with implementing the orders of the JPs, the constable was the last link in the chain stretching from privy council to people. He was also the one with whom the better sort in town and country had to deal in their efforts to reform such traditional expressions of good neighbourliness as alehouses and village dancings. Too officious in his pursuit of order, a constable might be beaten up or ostracized after his year in office; too indulgent towards his neighbours, he risked prosecution. Indeed, prosecutions of constables at quarter sessions for refusals to serve or for slackness abound in periods of crisis. The neighbourly constable might not wish to harry the unemployed weaver for trying to feed his children from the profits of an illicit alehouse; similarly, refusals to take on the office increased in the later 1630s, when the collection of ship money caught the constable between the wrath of council and sheriff on the one hand and the sometimes violent resentments of villagers on the other. The dilemma became most painful with the soaring levies of the civil war, during which not a few constables fled or were murdered. It can best be felt in the lament of one Wiltshire constable, scrawled on an order from a local garrison commander, 'Woe is me, poor bastard.'

Fortunately for all concerned, the public officials did not stand alone between order and chaos. In villages which contained a resident gentleman, and particularly in areas – largely in the central belt of the country – where the boundaries of manor and parish more or less coincided, social discipline might be well maintained by an alliance of squire and parson. Many manorial courts still possessed considerable vitality. Thus, the large Staffordshire manors of Cannock and Rugely sent only a handful of cases to the JPs around the turn of the century, while the manor courts exercised effective jurisdiction over both misdemeanours and petty debts. The potential for informal control from above is evident too in the Gloucestershire manors of Farmcotte and Postlippe where a 1608 census recorded five-sixths and more of the men as employed by a single gentleman. But while such settlements were by no means the norm, lesser mortals could fill the gap elsewhere. The process has been most closely studied at Terling in Essex. There, by the 1620s householders alarmed by the extent of social change were insistently using petty political power to buttress the order from which they benefited, as churchwardens and overseers of the poor withholding charity from the disorderly poor and as jurymen presenting the stubbornly wayward to the appropriate secular or ecclesiastical court. The pattern appears to hold elsewhere. Significantly, the available evidence, particularly from the home assize circuit around London, suggests a steady growth of prosecutions – which were initiated privately – through the later sixteenth century to a peak in the 1620s, as the better sort strove to protect themselves. Thereafter, prosecutions declined to a lower plateau in the later seventeenth century as improved living standards and the smoother operation of formal and informal controls made the world safer. The scanty evidence indicates a decline in both murder and bastardy rates after mid-century.

Informal Controls

Since policing was so scanty, informal controls were the key to the maintenance of order. The incessant noseyness and back-biting so characteristic of much early-modern village life made such controls stronger than might be thought today. Thus, it has been estimated that perhaps one in seven of the population of turn-of-the-century England was denounced by his or her neighbours for sexual deviance. But neighbourly interests might also avert conflict. For while the frequency of litigation testifies to the intensity of parochial feuds, probably the majority of prosecutions were averted locally. The costs of prosecution when there was no public prosecutor, the resentments inspired, and the reluctance of village worthies to jeopardize the life of a neighbour, if not of a vagrant, unless he or she were a persistent trouble-maker, all combined to make mediation and persuasion the main guarantors of the local peace. And at a deeper level, a complex of attitudes about the proper order of personal relationships underpinned the stability of the larger society.

Men, women and children were expected to recognize their place in a hierarchy. In the last resort, the courts could be used against those who failed to pay deference, but normally an insistent social conditioning seems to have done its work. Villagers doffed their hats to the squire, addressing him as 'sir', 'your worship', or 'your honour'; he in turn might address a yeoman as 'goodman Green', while the rest simply heard their names called. The authoritarianism implicit in such conduct was, however, both softened and reinforced by a constant appeal to paternalist values. As with all generalizations, qualifications are needed. The alternative values of the market place and of contract were gaining ground; furthermore, the unnumbered assertive women who suffered the humiliation of the ducking stool or of a 'Skimmington ride' might have questioned how far the hierarchy of male domination was ever softened. But magistrates repeatedly had held before them the patriarchal ideal, combining as it did love with justice. The influential puritan Richard Sibbes surely had society as well as theology in mind when he wrote, 'The word "Father" is an epitome of the whole gospel.' The fifth Commandment, 'Honour thy father and thy mother', was, despite its reference to both parents, the most frequently cited justification of obedience to political authority in the seventeenth century. Christian teachings about God the Father thus buttressed contemporary reality, since mortality rates ensured that around half the population was under the age of twenty. The insistence that children submit and show respect to their elders made good social sense.

The father was in effect co-opted as a petty magistrate and peace-keeper. James and Charles repeatedly enjoined the nobility and gentry to forego the delights of the metropolis and instead pacify their neighbourhoods by maintaining hospitality in their households. And in times of stress authorities reminded fathers as householders of their responsibility for the actions of their servants and apprentices. Similarly, householders were assumed to be the vital core of the parish, since they would instruct their families. The churchwardens of All-hallows the Great, London, were in 1615 instructed to check off householders, rather than all the inhabitants, attending church and fine absentees. Indeed, everybody was expected to become part of a family, and subject themselves to family discipline; only widows and widowers, and the gentry, could live alone without attracting disapproval. The 'masterless man', the single independent male, threatened society's image of itself as an organic whole, an interdependent family, and was denounced as the source of all disorder, whether criminal or political. Social ideology as much as social reality underlay the harsh treatment of the vagrant.

It seems safe to assume that the concept of hierarchy did have political consequences. Although conditions worsened markedly for the poor in our period social tensions did not become explosive. Prior to the civil war such friction as did develop was limited in every sense. The central records yield evidence of only about forty food riots in the whole period 1585–1640; and the only significant agrarian disturbances were in the midlands in 1607 and in the eastern fenlands and south-western forests in the 1630s. The behaviour of the poor in the few times of trouble is equally instructive. Whether in agrarian or food riot, the pattern of popular unrest manifests general acceptance of a patriarchal scheme of authority. Protesters invariably first approached the neighbouring magistrate to complain about what they saw as anti-social activity, whether by landlords or food traders. Only if rebuffed did the poor act for themselves, and even then they neither challenged the social order, nor attacked the rich as rich. Food riots occurred not in the areas of greatest suffering, but where the existence of a grain trade gave provocation; moreover, rioters often handed over to local authorities the grain they seized.

The attitude of the authorities also helps explain why popular disturbances were more akin to demonstrations than violent outbursts. The government balanced denunciation of disorder with a surprising understanding. Many Tudor proclamations and statutes, especially in the 1590s crisis, had condemned economic exploitation by the rich, and rioters not surprisingly claimed that they had the law on their side: they merely demanded enforcement. The council evidently sympathized with their view. Thus, after the Midland Rising of 1607 against aggressive landlordism in the arable plain, the council issued wholesale pardons to the rioters while fining several landowners in star chamber. Such a response was certainly economically irrational, for much of the midlands was and still is best suited to pasture, not the arable farming for which the rioters clamoured. But as social policy it made sense, and perhaps helps explain the remarkable social stability in the years of economic and politic upheaval of the 1620s and still more the 1640s. Greater alienation from the social order can be discerned, notably in the violent rioting in the Stour valley in Essex and Suffolk in the turbulent summer of 1642; but that incident underlines both the potential dangers of the unprecedented concentrations of industrial workers that were developing, and the very different behaviour of the rest of the country.

The prevailing deference cannot always be attributed to mere fear of the landlord, since so many villages lacked resident gentry. More important was the near-universal acceptance of a common set of values. Even that apparently most alienated of all figures, Gerrard Winstanley, the theorist of the proto-communist Diggers in the years around 1650, gave fathers a large part to play in the new republic he outlined in *The Law of Freedom*.

Stability and Instability

The machinery of the state in England was, it should now be apparent, limited. Although it possessed a single legal system, England
notoriously lacked an organized police force and, for most of this
period, a standing army. The privy council therefore depended on the
voluntary co-operation of the gentry in their localities, and they in
their turn had to count on often lethargic constables. The question
remains, did the structural characteristics of the English body politic
weaken royal government and help usher in civil war?

We need to remember that bureaucracies and police guarantee
neither efficient government nor political stability. There is little sign
that early-modern England was abnormally badly run – indeed, until
the catastrophe of civil war, quite the contrary. Although in certain
respects English administration was deficient, so was that of any European state in the period, and in some areas the English record was striking. Thus, the most challengeable, and challenged, of the government's fiscal measures, the forced loan of 1626–7 and ship money, at
least until 1637, achieved remarkable yields by European standards.

England had certain administrative advantages, one of which was
actually a consequence of the scale of government. Minimal standing
forces meant minimal taxation, which until 1635 came rarely, fell
lightly, and fell on few individuals. There were compensations for
the obvious drawbacks of the ineffectual military displays of the
1620s and 1639–40. In the long term England's economy benefited
markedly from the smallness of the slice carved out by the state. If in
1600 a new consumer society was developing in Europe it was in the
Low Countries, which set the pace in urban, in mercantile and in
agricultural development. Yet by 1700, impoverished by their long
years of war against Spain, and then against England and against
France, the Netherlands were lapsing into their eighteenth-century
backwater, while the English, their resources relatively untapped by
their rulers, were left free to spend on the new goods on the market.
The short-term political consequences of the light tax load were
almost as important as the longer-term economic. The political
troubles of the 1620s, and the violent attacks on excise collectors in
1647, underlined the risks of heavy taxation in years of economic
crisis. The fact that agrarian protest in England was so much less
violent than the outbreaks of the *Nu-Pieds* or *Croquants* in France may
be partly explained by the fact that the crown was not joining landlords in raiding pockets already emptied by bad harvests and industrial depression. Correspondingly, the high yields of the forced loan
of 1626–7 and ship money in the 1630s surely owe much to the rarity
of taxation.

The early Stuarts were also fortunate in England's long tradition of relatively centralized government. This helped drill subjects into the habit of obedience to the crown, and, later, to parliament. A single legal system, centred in the capital, and a single representative institution, parliament, in sharp contrast to the patchwork-quilt of jurisdictions and institutions in the slowly-evolving nation-states of France and Spain, still more of the Netherlands, intensified national consciousness and national loyalties. Such an assertion jars with perhaps the most prevalent argument of recent scholarship on the early seventeenth century. Historians have noted the petty bickering of local magistrates and taxpayers and claimed that the fundamental governmental reality was the 'county community', even that the counties represented a 'federation of semi-autonomous republics', often vociferously unhappy in their union. It was allegedly a 'revolt of the provinces' that brought down the royal government, and which hamstrung successive field armies on both sides during the civil war.

There is considerable justice in the characterization. Probably a majority of gentry married within their counties – over 70 per cent in relatively isolated areas like Kent and Lancashire, only 43 per cent in Warwickshire – with sometimes boggling 'ideological' consequences: thus, the daughter of the prominent Kent royalist Sir Thomas Peyton married the son of one of the Kent regicides. Many gentry families had lived in their counties since pre-Tudor days, and amassed both a dauntingly extensive cousinage and a powerful sense of roots and local identity. Quarter sessions did much to develop a county consciousness amongst the gentry, compelling them to look beyond their parishes; and certainly the sessions, and the grand juries at assizes, were likened to county parliaments.

Yet the case probably owes as much to the fact that archives have been organized in county record offices as to historical reality. Only 18 per cent of the gentry families in pre-war Warwickshire dated back to before 1500; and everywhere the greater gentry – the county leaders – were far more likely to marry outside the county than were mere parish gentlemen. The sprawling East Anglian cousinage which linked the Rich family in Essex with the Hampdens in Buckinghamshire and the Cromwells in Huntingdonshire could be matched in other regions. And although the county was the historical administrative unit, it was not necessarily a natural one. Apart from the assize court and parliamentary elections – which were themselves an injection of the centre into the county – there were no county-wide meeting-grounds in large counties like Yorkshire, Lincolnshire and Sussex, which had separate quarter sessions for the different regions of the county; while in Norfolk and Warwickshire the sessions rotated regularly from town to town, and different groups of gentry attended each. Local rivalries, particularly those between county and town, regularly gave the privy council the chance to mediate and thus to exert itself. The barrier presented by localism can be exaggerated.

Local ties anyway competed with other loyalties. Catholic gentry (admittedly largely excluded from local government) regularly sought suitable brides outside the county; devout puritans were not far behind – the East Anglian connection is a reminder once again. Such contacts extended far beyond the altar into political and religious life. Distant but like-minded gentlemen might lodge together when attending parliament, or recommend suitable ministers to each other. Always there were litigants returning from the law courts and carters bearing news as well as goods to alert even the home-bound to the wider world. At the close of parliamentary sessions in the 1620s the Suffolk minister John Rous made a point of bustling across to hear the news from a returning MP. Although national issues may have been refracted for local eyes, illumination still occurred. Oxford and Cambridge colleges often had regional affiliations, and informal county dining associations met fairly regularly at London inns. Yet a polite education could not help but reduce introversion – with immeasurable consequences, when one-third of all heads of gentry families in Warwickshire in 1640, and a far higher proportion of the county leaders, had attended either a university or an inn of court, or both. It may be that introversion increased in proportion to distance from London, though the rousing election address delivered in Cheshire by Sir Richard Grosvenor in 1624 suggests that this was no invariable rule. Nevertheless, it seems likely that a Frenchman, or a Scot, was infinitely more a foreigner than was someone from beyond the county line. Maps of England were as popular as were county maps, and every localist ultimately acknowledged the supremacy of the nation state. Centre and locality were not opposite poles, and each could usually recognize the practical advantages in co-operating with the other.

Early-modern governments did not, however, entirely succeed in containing regional passions. Then as now it proved too easy to forget that England was and is part of Britain, and while Wales had been effectively subordinated to English law and English institutions in the early sixteenth century, the outlying kingdoms of Ireland and Scotland proved more troublesome. The leader of the last great Gaelic revolt against English rule in Ireland submitted in Elizabeth's dying weeks, but little was done to bring the country by peaceful means into England's orbit. Instead, the gap between the two kingdoms widened as the Counter Reformation at last made its mark on Irish parishes in the 1620s and added dangerous religious hostilities to the old ethnic and economic tensions. That English rule should have changed at just that point from malign neglect, concerned only to exploit and to maintain a shadowy supremacy by force of arms, to the energetic administration of Wentworth was to bring tragedy.

Scotland's was to prove an equally uncomfortable throne for an English king. An independent kingdom until James VI succeeded Elizabeth to become James I of England, Scotland was subsequently largely ignored. The hopes of profit Scottish nobles had entertained were soon dashed, for relatively few Scottish courtiers grew fat in the English sun. Instead, James became an absentee, confident in his choice of able servants in Edinburgh, and Scottish visitors to the English court were increasingly ridiculed for their uncouth ways. Matters grew worse under Charles, who lacked even the advantage of personal familiarity with the Scottish magnates. Resentments at relegation to the status of distant provincials were intensified by new and unwelcome attention the Scots received in the second quarter of the century.

Scotland and Ireland provide manifestations of a phenomenon common to much of Europe in this period. Everywhere outlying provinces and kingdoms, often acquired by dynastic accident, protested against increasing subjugation and exploitation by the core state of the dynastic empire. The gathering revolt in Scotland in 1637–40 and the Irish revolt of 1641 mirror contemporaneous events in the Spanish Habsburg dominions of Portugal, Catalonia, Naples, and also in some of the French crown's less unified provinces. The troubles stemmed largely from Charles's more activist foreign policy in the later 1620s and beyond; this led him to impose new burdens on jealous kingdoms drawing few benefits from his rule, and often to ignore local customs and immunities in so doing. Moreover, in his intense commitment to Renaissance principles of uniformity and symmetry he strove foolhardily to reduce all to a single, English, pattern. Disaster ensued from the blithe assumptions of James and still more of Charles that though they cast few glances north and west they would be able to shape religious practices by mere command. Whatever English hostility to ship money, and whatever John Pym's skill in manipulating domestic political forces in 1640–1, the Stuart monarchy fell first at Scottish and Irish, not English fences.

The English state was, nevertheless, better placed than its neighbours to extract submission from its native subjects. The process of subordinating the English nobility to the crown had been effectively completed during the Tudor period. This left the gentry looking only to the crown when the humanists indoctrinated them into the duty of service to the commonwealth. Their loyalties were reinforced by their new-found belief, from which many Englishmen drew a sense of common purpose rivalling that of Spaniards of the *Reconquista*, that

England was God's elect nation. Eager to rally behind the godly prince, the new Constantine, their equal eagerness to identify and confront Antichrist only proved dangerous when Charles refused to follow Elizabethan and Jacobean traditions.

A further aid to political stability was the scarcity of the blood royal. Unemployed princes could lend respectability to any protest, as the saga of the prince of Condé showed in mid-seventeenth-century France. England too had a faint taste of these dangers in the strange 1624 parliament, when prince Charles seemed to lead a 'reversionary' interest against his father. Nevertheless, the isolation of kings could be two-edged, rendering upheaval, if and when it came, catastrophic. Had the Tudors, or James I, been more fertile the effusion of blood and words in the 1640s might have been avoided, for opponents of Charles I could have turned to an ambitious member of the royal family to rescue them through a regency just as opponents of James II looked to Mary and William in 1688.

If one major difference between the seventeenth-century and the fifteenth, that time of dynastic civil wars, was the scarcity of royal blood, another was the absence of figures like Thomas Neville, better known as Warwick the Kingmaker. While we tend to think of this as a political advantage for rulers who no longer had to face 'over-mighty subjects' in the provinces, like most changes it was not an unmixed blessing. A central government with – that pre-modern rarity – a policy to enforce needed powerful agents in the localities on whom it could depend. At last brought to appreciate this fact, Cromwell in 1655 dispatched the major-generals into the countryside. The record of ship money in Essex in the 1630s suggests a similar conclusion. From being one of the most recalcitrant counties at the beginning, Essex towards the end became something of a model of conformity, in large part because Charles put enormous pressure on another earl of Warwick, Robert Rich. But few magnates had the kind of influence Warwick possessed in Essex. Although it may be problematic to talk of a crisis of the aristocracy, social change had gradually diminished the relative prominence of the nobility; meanwhile religious passions might, as we have seen, ignore the dictates of hierarchy. And as Charles strove to shape his court in his own image, and turned it into a kind of social centre for conformist and quiescent peers, he contrived to erode the local influence of those who were drawn in, and who became identified with its unpopular ways. Although pre-civil war parliaments, and the alignments of 1642, showed that the crown consistently enjoyed the support of the house of Lords and of a majority of the active peers, the nobility was no longer such a valuable prop as once it had been. The imposition of reform from above was therefore that much harder.

The absence of powerful local magnates who might have given a lead left the crown helpless before the greatest impediment to dynamic government, the force of inertia. The forced loan and ship money were novel, and therein lay both their political weakness and their practical strength. For the council geared itself up unprecedentedly to make them work, and to overawe those who damned them as unconstitutional. But in more familiar fields, such as in the collection of the subsidy – the tax granted by parliament which fell mostly on lands – the council was content to follow, and to let others follow, ancient ways. Yields lagged miserably, as assessors and collectors made no attempt to adjust for the impact of inflation on land values, or to tax new owners as land changed hands. Thus, the average assessment of seventy Sussex gentry families dropped from £61 to £14 in the period of inflation which spanned the 1540s and the 1620s, while by the early seventeenth century probably only 10 per cent of households in the nation were assessed. In consequence, the yield of a subsidy fell steadily, from £137,000 in 1559 to £55,000 in 1628 – in real terms, allowing for inflation, to about one-fifth of the 1559 level. This was a pre-professional age, and as the council itself acknowledged in 1638, most officials were more diligent when commanded by 'express letters . . . than in such things as are of ordinary course incident and belonging to their office'.

The remorseless decline of the parliamentary subsidy provides considerable justification for the approach of older historians who searched for long-term causes of the civil war and talked of a 'crisis of the constitution'. It does, however, shift the terms of the analysis away from ideological and social factors. The decline drove the English government perilously close to what has been called 'functional breakdown', the inability to do what it and others expected in the crucial field of war. Parliamentary taxation, whose major purpose had been to pay for war, was proving more incapable than ever of supporting a war. But the crown was squeezed from both sides, for changing technology and tactics, the inexorable consequences of the application of gunpowder, were making wars more expensive: one official calculated that the 1625 Cadiz raid cost four times as much as Drake's Elizabethan attack on the same port. Such changes were also eroding the critical distinction between peace and war. The traditional assumption was that the customary royal revenues should pay for peace-time costs. Yet the medieval expedient of conscripting merchant ships for naval purposes proved ineffective at Cadiz in 1625, and indicated that an expansion of the royal navy was needed as a peace-time preparation for any war which might occur. A further cause of weakness lay in the unsophisticated nature of both central and local government, which could ill cope with the growing logistical difficulties of organizing a war-effort. The administrative and financial, as well as the political, crises of the 1590s and still more of the late 1620s and 1639–40 exposed the ramshackle nature of the early-modern English state.

The urgency of the structural problems can be exaggerated. Although war and diplomacy lay at the core of the mystique of kingship kings did not have to fight, as James wisely recognized. Again, a different sort of war in the 1620s would almost certainly have attracted more parliamentary support, which might have modified hasty modern assertions about the debility of the English body politic. Furthermore, James's notorious profligacy must bear some responsibility for the crown's problems. Nevertheless, as Cecil realized after his experience in organizing a war against Spain and in Ireland in the 1590s, some restructuring was essential: the crown must have some capacity for action. Cecil's solution, articulated in the abortive Great Contract of 1610, was to abandon the medieval practice of seeking taxation only for extraordinary purposes, and to obtain more regular parliamentary funding of the ordinary needs of government. Charles I, after experiencing another war, took the opposite, if equally logical, course, and tried to raise money from his subjects outside parliament. The eventual solution to the deficiencies of Tudor practices might therefore have gone either way: closer parliamentary involvement with – if not necessarily in – government, or a crown financially independent of parliament.

Yet it seems unwise to reduce the equation to such simple fiscal terms, and we should remember constraints all too familiar to earlier historians. The growth of a constitutionalist creed, centred on the common law, statute and consent, and hardened by a widespread awareness of the rise of what has come to be called absolutism in Europe, shaped the way in which events and actions were viewed, and therefore helped determine responses. Reform, which necessarily meant innovation, became a sensitive subject – all the more so when reforms were attempted by monarchs with a provocative affection for theories of divine-right monarchy. The suspicious response to the Great Contract, the failure of the 'benevolence' of 1626, and the increasing problems besetting ship money in its later years, were to point to the ideological limits under which governments operated.

This is not to argue that the eventual outcome, a monarchy firmly based on parliament, was inevitable. The achievements of Richelieu and Mazarin in France showed what could be achieved when a nation faced a credible external threat. The Stuarts' misfortune may then have been that for all the fear of Antichrist, Armageddon remained for most a distant prospect. Again, the early Tudors, and the later Stuarts, exploited strong memories of civil war to establish the dominance of the crown, but such means were hardly open to James I and Charles I. What a consideration of the nature of English government does indicate is the folly of Charles in attempting to innovate doubly. He might have succeeded in restructuring the financial base of the monarchy. But, however responsive he made the local governors, he simply did not possess the resources to undertake that task while at the same time trying to alter the face of the English church.

3   Hearts and Minds

The Church

The church was an integral part of the fabric of early-modern life. As its greatest defender, Richard Hooker, had argued in the 1590s, the church was but another facet of the body politic. All Englishmen were by law members of the church of England, and compelled by statute to attend its services every Sunday. The king governed the church as well as the state, and was not alone in mingling secular and ecclesiastical roles. The bishops of the church sat (as they still do) in the House of Lords, and were in many respects temporal magnates. The bishop of Durham was at least nominally the fount of temporal authority in the county palatine of Durham, and every bishop and every dean – the head of the cathedral clergy – wielded local authority not only as a major landlord but also, usually, as JP: thus, the dean and chapter of Salisbury governed a quarter of that city. The hierarchy of church courts had jurisdiction over laity as well as clergy, not merely in spiritual matters but also over probate and marital litigation. Furthermore, the church courts catered to a wide market by handling defamation cases, a vital business, since in days before impersonal credit ratings a person's credit amounted to his or her estimation in the local community.

Most important of all, the church was a social and political cement. At a fundamental level the church was supposed to bind together the community. The statutory compulsion on all parishioners to worship together was reinforced by the widespread practice of almost corporate communions by the whole parish four times a year – protestant England had not yet severed itself from the ways of medieval Europe, where the corporate Easter communion was an important device for healing local feuds. And at a more 'political' level the church insistently enjoined obedience. The general stress on the fifth Commandment was made more particular by regular prayers in parish churches for all magistrates and for the royal family, and by prayers and sermons on special occasions.

It was no wonder that contemporaries abhorred those who

separated themselves from the church, whether Roman Catholic recusants or the handful of protestant separatists. Not only did such dissidents breach the cardinal principle of unity, and implicitly deny the existence of a corporate body politic; they also called their political loyalty into question. The century before 1650 was, after all, an era of assassination plots and of religious war, in England as well as in Europe, and contemporaries with the horrors besetting Germany and France clear before them, as well as petty village brawls, thought twice before they opened divisions of conscience. Charles I was therefore no cynic when in the political negotiations in the aftermath of defeat in 1646 he saw the king's power over the church as no less fundamental than his power over the sword. In his most famous saying, James I in 1604 had stressed the symmetry and interdependence of church and state, 'No bishop, no king'.

The English Reformation and the Elizabethan settlement had hinged on royal and parliamentary action. It was therefore easy for the estranged to denounce the church as a mere creature of the state. Yet the church's spiritual functions remained of vital significance to many, and these functions were changing fast. The pre-Reformation priesthood can be characterized as primarily sacramental. The personal attributes of the priest mattered little, for it was the power inherent in the sacraments he administered and the ritual he performed that reconciled his essentially receptive congregation to God. The protestant reformers in reaction fiercely attacked ritual for inculcating passivity and even idolatry, and for encouraging the people to look for mediators between themselves and God. Protestants instead demanded a 'lively faith' of the individual, who faced God alone, and for whom the only mediator was Christ. To mainstream protestant opinion in England the clergy's central function was to expound that gospel, not to administer the sacraments; they became ministers of the Word, not a priesthood. Generations of protestants therefore heralded preaching as 'the ordinary means to salvation', the instrument for awakening the requisite faith in the people.

The character of the clergy changed accordingly. Although only between one-quarter and one-half of clergy had degrees in 1600, the proportion had risen to over three-quarters by 1640. The gradual dispersal throughout England of ministers capable of preaching the Word had at last, by the eve of the civil war, seemed to make a practical possibility of the early Reformers' dream of rendering England a fully protestant nation. Indeed, one of the most important features of the early-modern period was the attempt to persuade the whole population to internalize and apply to itself the teachings of the Reformation. The pre-civil war church was thus a missionary church, as well as a political arm. It aimed not merely to preach

Christianity to an unschooled peasantry, but also to extract an intense
protestant response from the individual.

The intermingling of church and state at all levels might seem to
conflict with that missionary drive, but surprisingly few critics
expressed serious doubts. In his hugely popular *Acts and Monuments*,
better known as the *Book of Martyrs*, the Elizabethan John Foxe had
proclaimed the church militant led into battle with the Roman
Antichrist by the godly prince, the new Constantine. His audience
only applauded a king who advanced the cause of the church. There
was certainly by 1640–1 abundant hostility to the other side of the
coin, the political role of the bishops, but that was because of what the
church had become in the 1630s rather than a development of tensions already evident in 1603. And that other likely grievance, the
church courts, was at the start of the century a singularly
uncontentious issue. The bills periodically advanced in parliament to
define or limit the courts' practices seem to have owed most to common lawyers' dislike of other jurisdictions, and not to wider pressure
to limit the activities of the church. Significantly, in the localities the
godly used the courts eagerly enough to discipline their neighbours.

If the social and political role of the church was not in principle a
source of disillusion, how well equipped was it to handle its spiritual
tasks? The laws compelling attendance ought to have helped the
church enormously, but in fact prosecutions seem to have been
extremely sporadic. Anyway, the physical obstacles to attendance
were sometimes overwhelming. The huge parish of Whalley in
Lancashire, covering 180 square miles and including almost forty
separate townships with some 10,000 inhabitants, was exceptional, ·
but many parishes in the north were too big for practical purposes,
and it is clear that many northerners could not go to church at all. The
situation was little different in wooded areas elsewhere, for the scattered settlements left too many inhabitants unable to walk easily to
church. The liability of the sprawling parishes in the Sussex and Kent
Weald to religious dissent – the puritanism of Cranbrook in Kent
was notorious – or to paganism and witchcraft, is unsurprising, since
the established church catered inadequately to its congregations.
Towns too suffered, for parochial structures had been established in
demographic conditions often very different from those of the seventeenth century. The single parish church of burgeoning Sheffield
could scarcely hold the town's several thousand inhabitants. The
proportion of England's population that did not go to church must
remain unknown, but it was probably substantial: it is likely to have
included the majority of children and perhaps of young servants too,
especially the women. Too many people were outside the reach of the
church in their most impressionable years, a fact which helps to

explain the appeal of wandering missionaries, whether Baptist or Quaker, in the revolutionary years.

The physical problems of provision were intensified by the poverty, or rather the inequitably distributed wealth, of the church. Archbishop Whitgift calculated in 1584 that only 600 parish livings, out of over 9,000, were adequate to support learned clergy, especially clergy with families. He was unduly pessimistic, for probate evidence of parsonage furnishings and libraries suggests that from perhaps the mid-Elizabethan period clerical living standards on the whole improved markedly. Where a minister possessed the glebe land attached to the parish church he might farm comfortably as a yeoman, as that voluminous diarist Ralph Josselin did at Earl's Colne in Essex; still more where he also possessed the 'great' tithes, those on his parishioners' arable produce, he might be a rich man in an era of rising agricultural productivity and prices. The senior cathedral clergy were of course even wealthier. But there is no denying the existence of parochial poverty, especially in the four-ninths of all livings whose revenues were left 'impropriate' to laymen by the accidents of the Reformation. Although many patrons could be outstandingly generous – Lady Joan Barrington in Essex regularly succoured several local incumbents – others were content to leave stipends fixed at the exiguous levels of a century before. The elaborate church surveys carried out under the republic show too many livings, usually those which were impropriate, valued at scarcely more than a day labourer might earn – fifty-one Lancashire curates earned less than £15 a year. That so many ministers spent much of their time as schoolmasters, physicians or veterinarians was a matter of necessity. A still more damaging consequence was that some livings were left empty. To cite an extreme case, the eight parishes of Colchester were for part of our period served by two ministers largely dependent on voluntary contributions.

A further obstacle in the church's path was anticlericalism. The growing professional competence, the pride in university qualifications and theological learning of a reformed clergy, as well as their tendency to intermarry among themselves, distanced them from their parishioners. More generally, anticlericalism can be called the inseparable obverse of the clergy's missionary role. As ministers castigated sinners and strove to establish a godly moral order they incurred the resentment of the unregenerate. The vindictive sermon preached by the Cheshire minister John Murcot on the plague death of a parishioner who had defied him over some local festivities, and the angry response of the 'rabble rout', illuminate the tensions an active ministry could arouse.

Nevertheless, the church's prospects under James did not look unduly gloomy. Not only were the clergy more educated, but there were widespread efforts to better their preaching. Although Archbishop Whitgift had in the late 1580s crushed the non-episcopal, quasi-presbyterian attempts, known as 'prophesyings', to provide regular occasions for clerical performance before a lay audience, 'lectures by combination' quietly fulfilled many of the purposes of moderate Elizabethan puritanism in improving clerical standards by self-help. In these episcopally sanctioned exercises, panels of neighbouring parish ministers agreed to preach, or lecture, usually in monthly sequence, in local market towns, and then to meet informally afterwards for criticism and for discussion of common problems. Scattered clergy thereby gained a sense of collegiality, and an opportunity to make more practical contacts; they also gained access to a wider audience, since the lectures were usually held on market day, when the surrounding countryside came in to trade. And the towns in their turn benefited, for in an age of sometimes heroic sermon-going preaching was a spectator-sport, and might therefore attract business. As the jaundiced Bishop Wren later complained, 'not a market, or a bowling-green, or an ordinary [inn]' could survive without a lecture. While by no means all the clergy were drawn in, combination lectures were found under James from Cornwall to Yorkshire, some of them having endured for decades; they were to be found again widely in the puritan Interregnum. Not altogether without reason, churchmen were by the 1620s extolling their colleagues as the 'wonder of the world' for their learning and proficiency.

More important, many clergy recognized the need to translate their university training into terms suitable to a popular audience. Leading polemicists from William Perkins at the start of our period to Richard Baxter at the end urged their colleagues to preach in a 'plain style' – to, not above, their congregations. While that advice often conflicted with the need of insecure ministers to establish their social position, genuine and far-reaching efforts were made to cope with the problems of a semi-literate culture.

The degree to which this was still primarily an oral culture is apparent even in ostensibly educated circles. The most widespread feature of pre-civil war piety was undoubtedly what has been generally termed 'household religion'. At home after a sermon countless godly households recapitulated the heads of the preacher's argument, sometimes in turn, sometimes with the parents catechizing children and servants; a Dutch Calvinist, Lodewijck Huygens, visiting London in 1651–2, was struck by the presence at sermons of innumerable adult note-takers, who were presumably preparing to venture forth into their households. Clergy unable to purvey a logically structured argument to parishioners still largely immersed in an oral culture themselves responded with the question-and-response format of catechism, although the early reformers had in their concern for personal illumination damned such cold learning-by-rote. The demand for catechisms, which seem to have been aimed primarily at a household rather than a parochial audience, is plain in the at least forty-four editions that the Jacobean Stephen Egerton's *Briefe Method of Catechizing* went through by 1644. Equally popular were the pious works in dialogue form, such as Arthur Dent's *Plain Man's Path-way to Heaven* of 1601, which were just as much pitched to the needs of oral discourse.

Churchmen of the early seventeenth century thus had some reason to feel moderately confident. Although the growth of protestantism and literacy further increased expectations of the ministry, the battle against gross ignorance in the clergy's own ranks had been largely won, and that against ignorance in the wider world at least begun. And most important, the church enjoyed an enviable degree of internal peace.

Puritanism

What then of the problem of puritanism, which has so vexed modern historians? Some have sought its essence in theological, some in organizational, some in liturgical differences within the English church. Others, more ambitious, have linked puritanism with the birth of the modern world, seeing in it a major factor in the rise of individualism, of science, of radical politics, or of recognizably modern social attitudes, a 'new world of discipline and work'. Most have agreed that the rise of puritanism was a prime cause of the English civil war. The scope of such claims has predictably invited a reaction, and several recent scholars have denied the existence of anything that can usefully be called puritanism. They maintain that since, until Laud's rise to power, there was such a broad consensus within the church, or alternatively that since differences were so random, we should entirely cease talking of puritanism, lest we breed confusion and false distinctions.

There are real difficulties in defining a puritan. To contemporaries it was usually a term of abuse, whose typical object resembled Zeal-of-the-land Busy in Ben Jonson's *Bartholomew Fair* – an extremist, probably hypocritical and disreputable. When we call a respectable minister or gentleman a puritan we are using the word in a way most contemporaries would not have recognized until the Laudian years. Furthermore, the grey areas to which critical historians have pointed cannot be ignored: how do we regard Bishop Morton, whose Calvinism drove Laud to set a spy on him, but who was certainly a loyal

son of the church? Nevertheless, the term 'puritan' is helpful if it is
used with care to indicate a person manifesting at least some of a
cluster of attitudes rather than as a hard party label. Not only did
Laud see an enemy to attack, but more sympathetic observers had a
sense of who were 'the godly', or 'the hotter sort of protestants', or
even (especially in the later part of our period) 'the saints'.

There are few means to distinguish with certainty between
Jacobean puritans and non-puritans. Formal theology will not do.
Prior to the reaction which became apparent in the 1620s and gathered speed in the Laudian years of the 1630s, the orthodox theology of
the English church was largely Calvinist, stressing an omnipotent
God's foreknowledge of all things, and the inefficacy of the will and
works of sinful man in attaining salvation. The Calvinist bishop John
Davenant was rightly perplexed at the success of Laud's challenge to
the theology of predestination: 'Why that should now be esteemed
puritan doctrine, which those held who have done our church the
greatest service . . . I cannot understand.' Indeed, the strength of the
pre-Laudian consensus is suggested by the fact that Elizabeth's Archbishop Whitgift, for all his harrying of dissidents over the church's
liturgy and organization, had also helped suppress academic ques-
tioners of Calvinism. Although his successor, Bancroft, primate from
1604 to 1611, was not in the same theological mould, George Abbot,
archbishop of Canterbury from 1611 to 1633, had learned his divinity
from Geneva; so too had King James. And since theology in this
strenuously learned age shaped the religious outlook of those who
took their religion seriously, the existence of a theological consensus
helped blunt other points of conflict. A case in point is the ceremonial
of the church. The 'dregs of popery' retained by Elizabeth in her
church – the minister's surplice, the sign of the cross in baptism, and
the like – remained controversial in James's early years, but after an
initial drive for conformity he put little pressure on his bishops; they
in turn on the whole tolerated the scruples of nonconformist ministers
who were often among the more conscientious evangelizers in their
dioceses. Nonconformists found sympathizers in, amongst others,
Archbishop Matthew of York and Bishop Montague of Winchester.

Such tolerance in turn helps explain why the episcopal structure of
the church was so little at issue in James's reign. Although separatists
like the Mayflower Pilgrims were ready to go into exile, the lack of
controversy over the church in most of James's parliaments surely
indicates its basic acceptability. There is abundant evidence, in correspondence, sermons and parliamentary speeches, that before the
accession of Charles the bishops were widely respected: 'fit to be
made examples for all ages', as Sir John Eliot declaimed nostalgically
in 1629. Most important of all, if preaching was the main instrument

of conversion and therefore vital to the godly, the bishops were on the right side. Most supported lectures by combination, and many were themselves herculean preachers. Even the non-Calvinist Samuel Harsnet, bishop of Norwich in the 1620s, had a sabbatarian dislike of distractions from Sunday services; and despite the cares of office, Archbishop Matthew's sermons averaged one a week for over forty years.

It makes as little sense to see puritans as necessarily subversive of authority in the state as in the church. Conscientious pre-Laudian ministers were often to be found working amicably with the local secular authority, whether godly JP or town corporation. This was hardly surprising, since the church was in an important sense dominated by lay property-owners, most of them gentry (although the largest single one was the crown). The same lay take-over of the church at the Reformation which had put much of its tithe wealth in lay hands had done the same for its patronage. Thus, almost three-quarters of the parish advowsons, or rights of presentation to parish livings, in Somerset were controlled by laymen; twenty-two livings, chiefly in Essex, were at the disposal of the earl of Warwick. Lay influence was further increased as pious merchants and town corporations ensured that virtually all sizeable towns possessed lectureships, or preaching posts, for regular sermons to large urban audiences. Laud, who prized clerical independence so highly, saw lecturers as particularly vulnerable to the pressure of paymasters, and with some reason: thus, one London bequest was to be withdrawn 'if there be any alteration in religion'.

Accordingly, although the clergy may have aimed to change the world, their close involvement with the lay élite ensured that they directed themselves only towards the elimination of sin and the erection of a godly discipline. They did not strive to subvert the established order by preaching an individualist creed. Many magistrates, in city and country, steadily supported godly ministers whose liturgical views branded them puritan, and in Exeter, in Salisbury, in Norwich, as intimate a parochial alliance of church and state existed as that between king and bishops. Though the ministers in their turn urged on the magistrates the duty to punish sin, they urged on the people reverence to their godly superiors. The classic instance of such a relationship is the lavish support of Ipswich corporation for the renowned Samuel Ward, who was content to remain town preacher there from 1605 to 1638. Although Ward was repeatedly in trouble with the higher powers for his views on foreign policy and on the liturgy, the reverence for order he preached in Ipswich makes him at best an ambiguous radical.

Still less can the character of a puritan be deduced from economic attitudes. Puritans certainly glorified the discipline of work, and urged their audiences to strive in their callings – the *Treatise of Vocations* by the great late-Elizabethan William Perkins is the classic exposition. Many puritan diaries also reveal a tendency to interpret material blessings providentially, as signs of God's favour: their authors must have found an incentive to work all the harder. Some historians have accordingly seen in puritanism a key to the genesis of capitalist attitudes. Yet capitalist methods were hardly new to sixteenth-century Europe, and religious exhortations to members of the various social orders to do their duty had long been heard. Exhaustive analysis of the sermons of a wide range of early-modern clergy on economic matters has discovered little more than a protestant – and indeed, earlier, a humanist – consensus on the duty of the individual to work in his calling and in so doing to glorify God, and on the wrongfulness of the getting of money for its own sake. Perhaps the most that can be said is that puritans did insist louder than most on work, and elevated the doctrine of divine providence, to which we shall turn shortly. This had its value for those who wanted to work hard in the world anyway in offsetting moralists' and puritans', attacks on worldliness. And there were of course more of this 'industrious sort of people' in the new context of economic opportunity. As (the puritan) Thomas Scott preached at the Norfolk assizes in 1620, it was easy for a merchant to echo the godly in stressing the first table of the Ten Commandments, which focuses on man's duty to God and which 'touch not the corruptions of his profession' as does the second table, whose emphasis falls on man's duty to his fellows. It seems no coincidence that words such as 'conscientious' and 'religiously' gained new meanings related to work and time-keeping in the period roughly from 1550 to 1650. In other words, protestantism, and puritanism, helped legitimate – and therefore did foster – certain economic practices. But it would be unwise to go further and seek a specifically puritan socio-economic doctrine.

To question the clarity of distinguishing marks does not, however, mean that no distinctions can be drawn before the rise of Laud and the Arminians in the 1620s made theological issues clearer and the Thirty Years War made them more urgent. On the one hand it does seem possible to identify a point of comparison. Many scholars have denied the appropriateness of the term 'Anglican', laden as it is with nineteenth-century connotations. Yet when 'puritans' came into their own in the 1640s it became clear that in addition to the mere conformists, 'the common sort of protestants', there were many – non-Laudians, lay and clerical alike – who were prepared to suffer persecution for the sake of certain ecclesiastical practices and traditions. The constant use of an Elizabethan prayer book which had

made no radical break with the pre-Reformation order of worship had
by the civil war generated a specifically 'Anglican' commitment,
protestant yet ceremonial. Such a commitment was evident earlier, in
the poet-clergyman John Donne, in that other – although rather
more ceremonialist – clerical poet George Herbert, or in James's
favourite bishop, Lancelot Andrewes. All combined a fully protestant
theology with devotion to the institution of the church and its practices; and being less sure than some that they could identify the godly,
they tended to see the church as an organic expression of Christian
society rather than as the preserve of the elect. We might even include
James himself with such figures. He was always more concerned with
securing conformity to his wishes as prince than with defining doctrine
– even his famous support for the rigid Calvinists at the Dutch synod
of Dort in 1618 was qualified, and probably owed as much to diplomatic as doctrinal qualifications – and the range of his episcopal
appointments suggests the typically 'Anglican' aim of accommodat-
ing differences. His policy was not unsuccessful, for Calvinist bishops
such as Archbishop Abbot, or Arthur Lake of Bath and Wells, tended
towards a ceremonialism in office which more rigorous divines might
have condemned.

If there is something to be said for the later phrase 'Anglican', the
contemporary phrase 'the godly' is of much greater use. Those who
took their religion seriously were likely to be called 'puritans', as was
Richard Baxter's father, derided by his Shropshire neighbours for his
pious life. The characteristic puritan stress was on a 'lively' faith,
one that was 'experienced'. 'Godliness' meant internalizing and living out a creed to which 'the common sort of protestants' paid only lip
service.

Not suprisingly, all centred on the matter of salvation. Since the
early Reformation protestant theologians everywhere had recognized
the twin dangers of fatalism and hedonism inherent in the doctrine of
justification by faith alone, and their attribution to God of sole
responsibility for infusing saving faith into the individual. Calvin's
more emphatic assertion of the omnipotence and inscrutability of
God called man's action yet further into question. Since salvation lay
in the hand of God alone, the fate of the soul became a matter of deep
and often agonized concern to the individual. In face of the pastoral
need to reassure anxious congregations, and the political need to
make Calvinism socially respectable by explaining why a certain way
of life as well as belief mattered, Calvinist ministers accordingly
modified in the pulpit their formal academic stress on divine predestination. While still maintaining the ultimate and the total responsibility of God, with William Perkins they counselled that would-be
believers could gain an internal 'assurance' that they were amongst

the elect. Although useless before God, works might testify to
election, since only the true faith granted by God could breed in
believers the proper hatred of sin and love of God and of their neighbours. Still, since God alone held the key the believer's status was
likely to remain always in doubt.

In that insecurity lay the vital barrier against hedonism. The godly
were repeatedly advised that their very lack of confidence could be a
sign that God was with them, and they accordingly strove all the more
for assurance through internal discipline and action in the world. The
Thirty-Nine Articles, the church's formulary of faith, insisted that the
doctrine of election could be 'full of sweet, pleasant and unspeakable
comfort', and the will of Sir Francis Hastings, a prominent gentleman in early Jacobean Somerset, suggests how this could be. Hastings's God, 'in his foreknowledge, and before I was to work either
good or evil, hath chosen me to be his child and predestinated me to
eternal salvation.' But it was not always so. As the popularity of
Richard Baxter and other clerical 'physicians of the soul' suggests,
the persistence of doubt often brought deep depression. John
Bunyan's spiritual autobiography, *Grace Abounding unto the Chief of
Sinners*, is the finest account of the painful quest for assurance.

In the 1590s William Perkins responded to some of the central
problems raised by predestinarian theology by systematizing the doctrine of the covenant. Seeking to account for the life of faith required
of the faithful he set out what was to become an enormously influential thesis, that God covenanted with man through the offer of the
Christ of the New Testament while the elect convenanted with God to
strive to obey the law of the Old. But despite the efforts of convenant
theologians, the requirement of godly living still seemed to conflict
with the formal theology of predestination. The perplexity of the
questioning countryman in Dent's best-selling *Plain Man's Path-way*
gains ready sympathy from modern readers, as does the ability of the
fallen angels in Milton's *Paradist Lost* to spend an eternity debating
God's eternal decrees.

Nevertheless, if the logic remained obscure the consequences for
daily life were apparent. The godly man was the active man, and
Milton's denunciation in *Areopagitica* of 'a fugitive and cloistered virtue' was typical. Each preacher provided a slightly different map of
the godly course, and emphases tended to vary with the changing
generations – still more when the clerical monopoly over public
expression broke after 1640. Yet all would have agreed with John
Preston, perhaps the most influential of godly divines in the 1620s,
when he enjoined his readers to 'labour to get humiliation': the pros-
tration of sinful man before a just God urged by all protestants
acquired an active quality. Thereafter, the road towards sanctification

from that abject state was above all by way of the Bible – and hence the widespread protestant concern for literacy and schooling. Preston urged, 'Study the scriptures, much meditate in them day and night . . . and thou shalt find this, that grace will follow.' The goal of puritan scripturalism was not, however, the contemplation of Christ so characteristic of non-puritans like Donne or of Catholic devotionalists. Although Christ's sacrifice had earned grace for men, they had to engage in the incessant struggle with sin demanded by the covenant in order to avail themselves of it. Perkins warned that though 'it is an hard thing for a man to search out his own heart', nevertheless 'it is the duty of every Christian to try and examine himself whether he be in the faith or not.' The diaries which were so much a puritan product recorded those self-examinations; and in 1656 John Beadle even produced a guide to the keeping of such records, *The Journal or Diary of a Thankful Christian*.

Amongst the heroic diarists of the early seventeenth century was Archbishop Laud, a fact which cautions us once more against over-hasty generalizations. But there were aspects of contemporary religious life where distinctions were clearer. St Paul, that all-important authority for protestants, had instructed the godly to seek 'edification' in the church. Conformist Calvinist clergy interpreted that injunction as counselling Christians to avail themselves of the aid of the institutional church: not, as Catholics would have it, through the sacraments but rather through 'practical' sermons on faith and morality, reinforced by the pious works – such as Perkins's *How to Live, and That Well*, or Bishop Bailey's *The Practice of Piety* – that poured from the presses. Others, with some warrant in the text, understood St Paul to have used 'edifying' in a more active sense, and saw extempore prayer and repetition of sermons in godly fellowship as essential to the cultivation of a lively faith. Accordingly, godly neighbours associated informally, often enough with the parish minister present – 'our society', as Ralph Josselin, minister of Earl's Colne, Essex, called them – to make good the deficiencies of the formal services in parish churches whose members included the ungodly as well as the saints. What were in effect extensions of household religion thus assumed enormous scriptural importance for puritans. Indeed, the significance of godly fellowship calls in question the assumption of those who locate in an appeal to the individual conscience the essence of puritanism: as Cromwell forcefully reminded dissident comrades in his approximation to a gathered church in the army in 1647, 'Thus far as we are agreed, I think it is of God.'

Such neighbourly gatherings provided the main spiritual outlet in pre-war days for thousands who yet remained loyal to the ideals of national church and national reformation. Occasionally, as in the case of those around the future New Englander John Cotton at Boston in Lincolnshire, such groups even convenanted together to 'walk in the ways of the Lord' – their sense of exclusiveness thus led them to become partial or semi-separatists while remaining within the church. One of the greatest strengths of the pre-Laudian church lay in its relative tolerance even of such practices, despite their implication of religious pluralism, for it thus permitted to the godly what was, by European standards, unprecedented latitude while retaining their adherence to the principle of unity.

The upheaval of the 1640s which saw some at least of this Christian fellowship burst out into open separation also exposed other tensions within radical protestantism. The excitement of the early European Reformation had occasioned several outbursts in which the zealous took to an extreme the twin protestant teachings that the dispensation of grace in the New Testament superseded that of the law in the Old, and that the overthrow of the tyranny of the mediating priesthood had brought 'Christian liberty' to believers. Radicals had an alarming tendency to claim that spiritual illumination freed them from the bonds of the moral law. It was partly to counter such antinomian excesses that mainstream protestant theologians became so insistently moralist, and also so insistently scripturalist. That the Bible remained a living religious force is indicated in Henry Newcome's feeling comment on his Cheshire parish of the 1640s, 'The people came with Bibles, and expected quotations of scripture.' Yet scripture manifestly also served as a restraint on the dangerous appeal to the Holy Spirit and to the individual conscience. While conformist clergy differentiated themselves from puritans by their respect for the institution of the church – even the Calvinist Jacobean bishops tended to talk of the church as 'mother' – mainstream puritans in their turn appealed to scripture against both episcopal and sectarian foes. For the temptation to antinomianism endured: the dramatic events of the early 1640s were to convince many that further revelation was in train. As English history seemed to some to follow the prophecies of the Book of Revelation radicals – not surprisingly, often unlearned laity – concluded that truth was no longer simply locked up in the pages of scripture. The Holy Spirit was acting again in the world, bringing fresh illumination and full Christian liberty. As Independents and those beyond on the radical fringes claimed 'more light', conservative puritans fortified themselves in an anguished biblical legalism which many modern readers find incomprehensible and distasteful.

There were other obstacles to reformation besides luke-warmness and excesses of zeal. But obstacles were only what the saints expected. If they knew that the faithful were but a small company they also knew that they faced a potent enemy. Indeed, another common puritan trait lay in the intensity of their belief in the existence of Antichrist.

The detection of Antichrist in all hindrances to true religion, and the tracing of Antichrist to Rome, were born jointly of a practical need and an intellectual tendency. On the one hand, the traumatic upheaval of the Reformation had to be justified, and the prophecies in the books of Daniel and Revelation seemed to provide the means; and on the other, protestant scriptural literalism impelled the believer to take seriously those disturbing texts. The apocalyptic interpretation was sanctioned and intensified in the pages of John Foxe's *Acts and Monuments*, which became undoubtedly the most influential defence of the English church: the parish church of Waltham Cross, Essex, possessed one Bible yet three copies of Foxe in the mid seventeenth century.* The identification of England with Israel, and of its enemies with God's enemies, was encouraged by the general fondness for the providential histories of the Old Testament, for those histories told of God's doings with his chosen people. The experience of the Elizabethan wars and the pope's attempt to preach a crusade against England then cemented the orthodoxy. Qualifications are indeed needed, as so often. Until the foreign and domestic disasters of the 1620s, and again briefly in 1641 when the domestic enemy seemed broken, English puritans insisted on their membership of the international protestant community. More important, the agreement of Archbishop Whitgift and King James that the pope was Antichrist indicates that an embattled anti-Catholicism was not peculiar to a minority. But as with so much else, the fervour of belief is in question. Although the Gunpowder Plot of 1605 gave Antichrist firmer shape in James's mind, the king tended to see Satan as the Jesuits, operating on the international stage. For the puritan, the enemy was within as well as without, for like God Antichrist was omnipresent. Although the intensity of the belief in an imminent apocalyptic struggle varied with the political climate, gaining strength with the Catholic successes in the Thirty Years War, a potential for millenarianism lay deep in the protestant mainstream. The orthodox Calvinist William Prynne was not alone in assuming after 1649 that the execution of Charles I – ostensibly by protestant radicals – had in fact been an Antichristian Jesuit plot to discredit protestantism. Such beliefs were not, it should be stressed, entirely flights of fancy. Many Catholics equally believed in an apocalyptic struggle, and 'dirty tricks' were played. Thus, a Catholic agent, the 'false Jew of Newcastle', attempted in the early 1650s to set the protestant congregations at odds by pretending to be one of the Jewish converts who were widely believed to herald the approaching millennium.

*Essex Record Office, D/P 75/5/1, f.173v.

The war with Antichrist necessitated more than ever the elimination of sin, for as the history of the Jews showed, God would turn his back on a sinful nation. The establishment of a godly commonwealth by whipping the people into church on the sabbath was not just a matter of public decency, or even of the glorification of god. It would also determine national survival. Accordingly, the Long Parliament's closing of the theatres was an integral part of its war effort. The moral discipline which seems so characteristic of puritanism was thus paradoxically linked to the central protestant doctrine of an immediately providentialist God.

There was of course no doubting the ultimate outcome, for God would prevail. More disturbing was the immediate prospect, for nation or individual. But some comfort lay in God's very omnipotence and responsibility for every occurrence. Since God was the interventionist God of the Old Testament, punishing sin in this world and the next, a continuous check on his purposes might be obtained from a scrutiny of events. The world was, in the title of the book by Oliver Cromwell's tutor Thomas Beard, *The Theatre of God's Judgements*. Although all knew well the story of Job, scourged by God for no apparent reason, many were the puritans who chronicled in their diaries God's 'providences', their escapes from danger, catastrophes afflicting themselves, their neighbours or the nation, in order to determine God's judgment of them. Of course, the broad protestant consensus meant that the sense of a providentialist God was as little the exclusive preserve of puritans as was anti-Catholicism. But it does seem to have been only a certain sort of protestant who internalized that message, to an extent that could be both disconcerting and superstitious. The north-western minister Henry Newcome was able to distinguish between 'bye', 'ordinary', 'particular', 'special' and 'extraordinary' providences in his affairs, while Simonds D'Ewes in 1622 saw 'the retrograde growth of beans' as a portent. The morally dangerous potential in this outlook for the exaltation of worldly success – which has encouraged some historians who seek to explain the 'commercial revolution' of the seventeenth century – needed a proper spiritual humility to restrain it. Cromwell was as capable of reading divine punishment of his and the nation's sins into the failure of his 'western design' against Spain as he was of seeing the hand of God in his victories. More emphatically, Charles Fleetwood, his son-in-law and successor as commander of the republic's forces, greeted the collapse of the republic with the cry, 'God hath spat in our faces.'

What made a person a puritan? The distribution of godliness across the social spectrum suggests that in the last resort everything hinged

on a random spiritual variable. Amongst the gentry, much clearly
depended on upbringing; neighbourhood too was not without effect,
and for several generations gentry families in east Sussex tended to be
more zealous than did their neighbours in west Sussex. Yet efforts to
go beyond that simple observation always run up against anomalies
like the puritanism of Robert Rich, earl of Warwick and the luke-
warmness of his brother Henry, earl of Holland. And if it is difficult to
establish a social background conducive to the development of puritanism, it is equally difficult to identify a puritan 'type'. Warwick's
joviality and high fashion hardly fit the conventional image of the
puritan. It must be remembered that members of the élite can rarely
be classed as *simply* puritan, for most had been to university, and had
there imbibed an education shaped by the humanists of the sixteenth
century. In John Milton, Lucy Hutchinson and many others, the
classical and the scriptural could co-exist with only occasional strains.
The kill-joy legend fits ill with Milton's pride in his writing or
Cromwell's not at all unusual delight in his music.

Lower down the social scale certain factors may have encouraged
the development of puritanism. At any time there are those who value
the comradeship and exclusiveness brought by shared membership of
a spiritual élite, and the disappearance after the Reformation of the
medieval religious guilds left a large gap. The gathering of neighbours
for 'edification' in godly households provided the protestant substitute. The characteristic puritan modes of address, 'brother', 'sister',
testify to the spiritual fellowship such associations of the godly could
bring. They perhaps help explain something of puritanism's notorious appeal to townspeople, so many of whom were newcomers to the
urban world, uprooted from the community of their villages. The
attractions of puritanism to townspeople may also have been related
to literacy, since both books and godliness were concentrated in
towns.

If puritanism did have a social appeal – and the argument has been
contested – it probably lay in the desire for discipline. Gentry, merchants and substantial householders, the beneficiaries of a social
order the fragility of whose underpinnings they might recognize in
times of crisis, had grounds for apprehension in the century or so
before 1650. The reassuring medieval vision of an ordered, earth-
centred, man-centred universe came under increasing challenge from
the new philosophers and the scientists; soaring food prices brought
in their wake recurrent ripples of popular discontent; and unprecedented levels of demographic mobility fuelled the dramatic expansion of London and pushed up to dangerous levels the numbers of
poor in many a village and country town. In such circumstances
the omnipotent, wilful Calvinist God might provide an attractive

explanatory system, and the puritan stress on moral discipline an attractive tool for stabilizing the world. The general reasoning is clear enough. Since ale ate up barley, the bread-corn of the poor, the popularity of tippling worried many of the propertied – that their fears were not groundless is shown by a 1644 survey which listed one alehouse for every twenty households in parts of supposedly godly Essex. For their part, puritan ministers tended to fulminate more insistently than most against drunkenness and all the other sins committed in the alehouses which competed with the church for attendance. Their repeated warnings of imminent judgment on the land thus coupled alehouses and dearth in a way the anxious magistrate must have found immediately comprehensible. Similarly, the fact that between 10 and 30 per cent of all brides were pregnant at the altar aroused fears that every new twist in the spiral of economic depression might leave prospective grooms unable to set up households, thus turning pregnant brides into destitute bastard-bearers and burdens on the parish poor rate. Fierce puritan denunciations of idleness and fornication, and of dancing and alehouses as the chief means to the latter, were thus guaranteed an approving, and often vindictively punitive, audience.

It therefore seems plausible to see the stress placed by protestantism in general, and puritanism in particular, on Bible-reading and sermon-going as a deliberate assault on the old patterns of communal culture. Those patterns had centred on the neighbourliness of village green and alehouse, and had their dangerous corollary in the corporate, ritualized worship of the medieval church. Only such a major confrontation can account for the impassioned denunication by one Gloucester puritan. 'So many paces in the dance, so many steps to hell', or the fierceness of the storm kindled by James's issue in 1618 of the Book of Sports authorizing various Sunday pastimes, and by its more determined reissue by Charles in 1633. The passions associated with sabbatarianism can be inferred from the acquittal in 1614 of a Sussex butcher accused of committing murder during a Sunday football match, the jury finding that the victim died by divine visitation. But however violent the moral fervour against dancing and drunkenness, it could not have strained the body politic as it did had there not also been social grounds for concern.

It would be foolish, nevertheless, to give too much prominence to a specific social appeal. There were puritans amongst the poor, and conversely probably a significant majority of gentry and yeomen, not all of them bucolic debauchees, saw maypoles, dancing and village games as harmless amusements, and puritan attempts to suppress them as socially divisive. King James's Book of Sports was after all extracted from him by sympathetic Lancashire gentlemen; equally, there could have been no civil war had not division existed within all classes. Nevertheless, some of the appeal of puritanism seems to have lain in the opportunities it presented for social discipline.

What, then, of puritanism's role in the causation of the Civil War? Puritans scarcely formed a mass movement, bearing down a reactionary king and state church – the repeatedly expressed conviction of the godly that they were few, a remnant, bears remembering. Rather, it was the rooting of puritanism amongst the local magistrates that made it so potent a factor. As we have seen, puritanism was not inherently subversive of order. The devotion accorded by the godly to great patrons like the Elizabethan earl of Leicester or the earl of Warwick in the Laudian years and beyond, despite their unpuritanical lives, suggests how compatible puritanism could be with the existing order. The contingent fact of Charles's and Laud's ecclesiastical policy brought out a potential which might otherwise have lain hidden. Nevertheless, that is not to deny that there was an inherent potential. For puritans the position of the magistrate was no longer simply a natural phenomenon in an organic world, as was supposed by the dominant inherited metaphors of the tree of the commonwealth and the body politic. The magistrate did not simply *exist* in the world as it was; he had to *act* to make the world as it should be. Calvinist authority had a dynamic purpose. Thus, the puritan minister Richard Sibbes demanded of magistrates 'a holy violence in the performance of all duties'. Thus too, when those godly and discontented lords, Saye and Brooke, contemplated emigration in the 1630s they found to their dismay that the godly colonists of New England were far from wedded to the doctrine of the hereditary nature of authority.

The ideal of the godly governor was Ignatius Jourdain, who remained at his post to organize relief in the great Exeter plague of 1625 when his aldermanic colleagues had fled, who zealously whipped fornicators and who in parliament demanded the death penalty for adulterers. But the activity demanded of the magistrate might sometimes go beyond suppressing sin, and Jourdain left no doubt locally of his hostility to Charles's Scottish policies. The conditional nature of godly authority became brutally apparent when in 1637 the magistrates of Ipswich stood by and watched a substantial local riot against the bishop of Norwich.

More importantly, if less definably, it may not have been entirely coincidental that those who felt driven to challenge ship money openly were the eminently godly John Hampden and Lord Saye, backed by the sprawling puritanical cousinage which was so closely involved in the New World. Saye, and Oliver St John, Hampden's counsel, certainly had links late in the 1630s to the rebellious Scottish covenanters, and clerical clients talked resistance theory in the earl of Warwick's garden. Calvin's guarded advocacy of the duty of the lesser magistrate to act to preserve the commonwealth could bear fruit in conditions of political dissatisfaction. It may be that the English preoccupation with unity was so great that only pressure from outside, from Scotland and Ireland, could push men to violence. Nevertheless, the dissonant notes sounded by Warwick's friends, or the willingness of Thomas Scot, MP for Canterbury, or of that future conservative parliamentarian Simonds D'Ewes to confide to their diaries in the 1620s their longings for a rebellion suggest that the strains may have been greater than we have appreciated.

Although before the Civil War puritanism may have been a conservative force for order, Laud's suspicions were not without foundation. Not least among the Calvinist seeds of civil war was the Bible. The Geneva Bible had been compiled in the 1550s in a time of defeat and exile, and the margins of its Old Testament were studded with observations on the duties of kings and the fate of royal sinners. Similarly, the Genevans undermined the classic New Testament justification of obedience, Romans xiii ('Let every soul be subject unto the higher powers'), by noting that it applied merely to the 'private man', leaving the problematic case of the lesser magistrate discreetly veiled. The Authorized Version of 1611 offered some competition, but the Geneva Bible retained its status as the most popular text for much of our period – Cromwell's scriptural citations show it was a formative influence on him. Generations of readers were thus educated in a very limited version of monarchy. Furthermore, covenant theology, with its stress on the individual's co-operation with God to fulfil God's plans, did make it easier to contemplate voluntarist associations for extraordinary purposes and to move outside the conventional limits of natural authority. The Scottish national covenant, John Pym's repeated demands in the early 1640s for oaths of association to bind the nation to itself and to God, and the Leveller Agreements of the People are at least in part applications of covenant theology to politics in an elect nation. Only fierce anti-Catholicism was needed to breed a strident political activism.

That such a creed had consequences is apparent. Since in puritan thought all men were alike responsible to God, negligent superiors did not excuse inferiors for inactivity. Thus, Sir Richard Grosvenor, presiding as sheriff over the 1624 Cheshire election, urged all the voters to note the religious threats at home and abroad, and to follow their consciences. Still more remarkably, by the end of the decade he was urging juries to present all Catholics, including landlords, for punishment. Such action was within the law, if outside the social norms. More alarmingly, in 1640 the godly London turner Nehemiah

Wallington noted that many of his friends went armed to church in fear of an assault by papists led by the crypto-Catholic Lord Cottington, a leading councillor, from his bastion in the Tower. The dangerous ambiguity of the puritan appeal, to the yearnings of the better sort for discipline and to all the undifferentiated godly as a religion of personal commitment and personal responsibility to God, was made horrifyingly clear when the political crisis finally broke. In the lynching and flaying of a Catholic officer by troops headed for Scotland in 1640, and in the unprecedented anti-Catholic violence which broke out in the Stour valley in East Anglia in the summer of 1642 we can see the impossibility of defining puritanism as merely a disciplinary creed. In those events lay the seeds of radical departures in the 1640s, and the seeds too of the developing reaction towards the king of appalled conservative gentlemen who seemed part of the parliamentary puritan opposition in 1640.

In sum, although puritanism did not drive men eagerly to preach resistance, it did contribute enormously to the climate of mistrust which helped deprive Charles's Scottish policy and ship money of willing support. Once again we encounter the consequences of Charles's attempt to do too much with limited resources in an inherently difficult situation. And when crisis did come, the inculcation of a sense of godly duty into a by no means insignificant segment of the population was found to have undermined the constraints against extraordinary action.

Furthermore, since it takes two to quarrel, the impact of puritans emerges in the hostility widely shown them. Puritans saw themselves as at war with the world, and the world reciprocated. When Thomas Hooker, whose lectureship at Chelmsford in Essex was suppressed by Laud in 1630, gloatingly told the unregenerate in his audience before his departure for New England that Christ and his saints would require 'an account for all thy abominations, nay for all thy speeches against the people of God, upon thy ale-bench when thou didst toss them to and fro', he invited the denizens of the ale-bench to show an equal aggressiveness. Puritans were a minority who sought to discipline the rest, and Richard Baxter's account of the rabbling of godly ministers in the Welsh borderlands on the eve of the war suggests that social tensions were the consequence. The war showed that – as they might have predicted – the puritans had earned the hostility of a surprising number of ordinary Englishmen who were devoted to the liturgical and corporate religion of the Prayer Book, and still more of the 'good fellows' of the ale-bench, whose culture and whose popular pastimes the godly had sought to extirpate.

Other Beliefs

Historians have often considered puritanism, and indeed English protestantism in general, in isolation. But since puritanism in part was anti-Catholicism, it is unwise to ignore Catholics when talking of protestants: all the more so since much of protestant doctrine was worked out in polemic with Catholics. Furthermore, protestant evangelism, which took its most energetic English form in puritanism, was part of an evangelical drive affecting all of Europe, since both protestant and Catholic reformers alike faced a largely uneducated people given to superstitious ritualism. Catholic bishops strove to improve the standards of their priests as did their protestant counterparts, and similarly encouraged catechising and devotional literature for the lay audience. Ironically, the lack of a protestant tradition of pietism forced many English readers to turn to sometimes adapted Catholic works until a suitable domestic supply appeared with the writings of Bailey and others. Thus, the youthful Richard Baxter profited from 'Bunny's' *Resolutions*, the work of the Jesuit Robert Parsons.

The common concerns, and common approach to the problem of the christian life, nevertheless failed to dampen the fires arising from theological and ecclesiastical differences. Catholic priests still climbed the scaffold in the seventeenth century as they had in Elizabeth's reign. To proselytize for Rome was not only an act of political disobedience, since the king was head of the supposedly all-inclusive state church; it also directly breached the cardinal principle of unity in a way that the implied religious pluralism and voluntarism of puritanism did not. And most important, it seemed to urge obedience to a foreign power whose hostility had culminated in papal attempts to depose Elizabeth. But although Catholic priests risked execution for treason, and laity who obstinately stayed away from church – recusants – risked potentially heavy fines, the penal laws were little different in their operation from any other early-modern statutes. They were for extraordinary, not continuous, use. Thus, although James wished no more than had Elizabeth to create martyrs, the Gunpowder Plot of 1605 pushed him into a flurry of executions. But after the twenty-five deaths up to 1618 there were no more until the excitement of civil war brought another twenty-four victims in 1641–6, and a last two in 1651–4. And so too with the laity: the normal sufferer was the prominent Catholic whom central or local authorities sought to press into conformity as an example. There is little evidence of families being ruined by fines, and, as with other penal laws, the pressure for enforcement came from hungry courtiers anxious to make money from fines. Thus, the main punitive years were the 1630s, despite the numbers of prominent Catholics at

Charles's court, while the puritan republic brought a marked relaxation.

Such laxity did little damage, for after the fatal escapade of 1605 lay Catholics were far more loyal to the crown than to the pope. Indeed, most leading Catholics in the countryside were unlikely rebels, since many probably remained Catholic from sheer cultural conservatism, seeing in their faith continuity with their ancestors and in its adhesion to hierarchy a welcome contrast to protestant individualism. In yet a further irony, lay Catholicism came curiously to parallel lay puritanism. Their need for refuge drove missionary priests to attach themselves to gentry households and to ignore the potentially rich harvests in the unevangelized upland areas of the north and west, 'dark corners of the land' to the established protestant church. In consequence Catholicism became very much a household religion. The remarkably well-documented Blundell household of Little Crosby in Lancashire experienced a constant round of catechising and exhortations to moral and social duty of which any godly puritan might have approved.

Why then was anti-Catholicism such a potent force? The answer lay not just in Catholics' breach of unity and in their adherence to Rome; more particularly, the numbers of English Catholics were growing. The Counter-Reformation was taking effect in England as elsewhere. There were probably between 30,000 and 40,000 recusants, or principled absentees from church, in England in 1603; by 1641 there were about 60,000. Although their relative numbers may have been small – in Yorkshire, a more Catholic county than many, recusants probably never numbered more than 2 per cent of the population – they compensated by their prominence. Around 10 per cent of the peerage in 1641 was Catholic, and, fatally for Charles, there were unknown numbers of Catholics at court. Worst of all, the number of priests soared from 250 in 1603 to over 700 in the 1630s, with the number of the Jesuits, the most feared, quadrupling. The rumours, and reports of gatherings in London and at court, took on an alarming tinge in light of the political advances of Catholicism in the Thirty Years War and of Charles's Catholic bride.

While the godly blamed all their troubles on Rome, the real obstacle to protestant advance lay not in popish wiles but in sheer indifference or primitive superstition. Because this was an age of religious war it is tempting, but wrong, to assume that everybody was a concerned Christian. To the unknown number who did not go to church must be added the still greater number who, though forced to go, only slept. Clerical complaints indicate that the temper of many seventeenth-century English men and women differed little from that of the majority of their twentieth-century descendants, and that the abolition in 1650 of compulsory attendance partly emptied the churches.

In all probability the lot of the early-modern protestant clergy was harder than that of either their predecessors or their successors. Social historians have pointed to the value of the corporate ritual of the pre-Reformation church to a peasant society whose dull routine was disrupted only by the vagaries of the weather and disease. The church's ritual year paralleled the agricultural year and thus exalted it – the feast of the Annunciation coincided with the spring sowing, Martinmas with the hay harvest, Michaelmas with the cereal, and so on. Perhaps most important, an essentially sacramental religion gave the church magical attributes on which parishioners eagerly called in emergency, using holy water, ritual prayers and blessings for sick animals and failing crops. The protestant Reformation was as much an attack on such practices – which came to be condemned too by the Catholic Counter-Reformation – as it was on the theology of the Catholic church. But in partially de-sacramentalizing worship, the Reformers deprived countrymen of an important crutch and earned a predictable animosity. Puritan campaigns against communal festivities as disorderly and superstitious desecrations of the sabbath only intensified the passions.

The sad tally of executions of witches in England as well as in Europe in the century or so after the Reformation points to the dislocation brought by the attempts of devout protestants and Catholics alike to eliminate superstitious practices. The importance of such aids to negotiating the hazards of life is evident in the presence in many post-Reformation villages of 'wise women' or 'cunning men', who dispensed charms and magical and sometimes herbal remedies for a variety of disasters, thus filling the gap left by the withdrawal of a church whose ritual had given it a quasi-magical quality. Popular witchcraft was not, it should be said, the 'black magic' with which it is now usually identified. Until the remarkable East Anglian career of the 'witchfinder-general' Matthew Hopkins during the disruption of civil war, accusations of witchcraft in England did not arise from the allegations of devil worship often encountered on the continent. The inquisitorial legal processes found in Europe and Scotland allowed the élite to dominate proceedings at all stages, and to give free rein to the fashionable neo-Platonism of the Renaissance. That system of beliefs, which conceived of the world as composed of opposites in dynamic tension and which was reinforced by a vision drawn from the Old Testament, was certainly common enough in England. Thus, the otherwise tolerant Sir Thomas Browne argued in his *Religio Medici* that to deny the existence of witches was to deny the existence of God. But the dependence of accusations on local juries of presentment ensured that English witch trials centred instead on charges of specific acts of malice (*'maleficium'*) arising from personal or local social tensions. It may have made little difference to the thousand or so women and men who between the Reformation and the Restoration went to their deaths in England for witchcraft. But the procedural barriers which limited any fusion of intellectuals' prejudices with the superstitions and suspicions rife in the villages may have helped England avoid the still bloodier records of Scotland and France.

As disturbing to the puritan as residual superstition was blind worldliness. The demands for a godly sober discipline, and for diligent attendance at services and sermons, often held little appeal for youths of both sexes and all social groups. The period of apprenticeship and service, whether in house or farm, freed as it was from family cares, was in some measure a time of licence when the pleasures of dancing and the alehouse were widely allowed. The associated commonplace that fornication was 'but a trick of youth', rather than a desperate sin, had its fruit in the high level of bridal pregnancy. That unconcern was widespread has been indicated by research into sexual offences, which were of course not entirely the preserve of youth. Over a half of those cited before the church courts for moral causes failed to respond and were excommunicated for contumacy, despite the social as well as spiritual difficulties involved in principle if not always in practice. The poor, and poor women in particular, having less need to worry about the social stigma and less money to pay the fees, often did not trouble to seek absolution. It has been estimated that 5 per cent of the population was excommunicate at any time, a figure which must be expanded to include their households, since they too suffered consequent disabilities.

Ultimately, puritans were no more able to overcome such recalcitrance – which gave some plausibility to the doctrine of the elect few – than were the bishops whom they castigated for luke-warmness. However much puritans cultivated a 'plain style' of preaching, the sermon, their main evangelical tool, was a weak weapon against the unconverted, and to extend it to two or three hours as so many did was scarcely an improvement. Worse, their emphasis on bible-reading demanded widespread literacy when literacy was extremely socially specific. Even that pastoral genius Richard Baxter confessed failure when after the Restoration he disowned 'the rabble that can not read'. It was no wonder therefore that puritans insisted that the lay magistrate had to impose a godly rule, and reacted so violently when Archbishop Laud seemed to take that hope from them.

Political Thought

The popular readiness to see in witches, readily visible malevolent agents, an explanation for a world of troubles resulted from an imperfect understanding of, and control over, that world. The outlook was characteristic of polite society as well as of unlettered peasants. Perhaps the most obvious feature of political analysis in the period is the prevalence of what another age has come to know as conspiracy theory. Charles in his proclamation dissolving the 1628-9 parliament blamed 'the malevolent dispositions of some ill affected persons', while his opponents habitually denounced 'evil counsellors'. Such flawed judgments arose from a deep complex of attitudes about the composition and working of the body politic.

Sharing a reverence for the past common to all predominantly agricultural, and hence traditional, societies, most English men and women shied away from the concept of change. Symptomatic is the clarion call issued by the opinionated lawyer and protestant hero William Prynne, 'THE OLD IS BETTER'.* Equally revealing is the general eagerness to deny that a Norman Conquest had ever altered English ways: thus John Pym claimed in 1628, 'The Conqueror himself, though he conquered the kingdom, conquered not the law.' Structural reform was thought dangerous because it would jolt the body politic from its known paths. Indeed, as the mixed metaphor might suggest, the very concept of structural reform is anachronistic. The body politic could only be treated by the physician, or at worst the surgeon.

Accordingly, since men feared the consequences of admitting that problems which beset them resulted from genuine difficulties, they tended to blame corrupt individuals rather than faulty institutions. To take an example: fundamental reform in the law was anathema, for it was the law which was thought to transmit the defining characteristics of England. When by 1640 many had come to the conclusion that the law had failed in its other prime function, the protection of liberty and property, the angry response of the house of Commons was to accuse the judges of treason rather than to set up a commission to revise the law. In other words, the hunt for conspirators could be an evasion of what we would see as the real issue. But the intensity with which protagonists of all sorts hunted malevolent agents also reflected the conviction that in an harmonious society upheavals could only originate in ill will. The anxiety to identify conspiracies rather than to contemplate reform might, however, be counter-productive as well as simply unproductive. On one level it inclined Jacobean MPs to point to corruption and extravagance at court and to overlook the genuine financial problems which Salisbury tried to bring to their notice. On

*The capitals are Prynne's, in his *Independency Examined* (1644), p. 2.

another it tended to sap that trust which is essential to the working of any body politic. In this context the inflammation of religious passions was to prove doubly damaging. The prevalence of conspiracy theories, the 'fears and jealousies' which were the common currency of politics, put insurmountable barriers in the way of co-operation in 1641.

The intellectual framework of early-seventeenth-century England impeded political change in another important respect. English thought remained curiously insular, and not simply in its well-known commitment to the common law which differentiated it from the Roman Law traditions of the rest of Europe. In Italy, France and the Netherlands philosophers were turning their attention to the problem of the state, an increasingly obtrusive feature of the turbulent political scene. Everywhere – except in England – thinkers commented on the analysis of the problems of power in a violent world advanced long ago by Tacitus in imperial Rome. 'Necessity', to which Charles I ominously appealed to justify his fiscal demands in the 1620s and 1630s, lay at the centre of European political debate. Contemporaneously, the great Dutch jurist Hugo Grotius formulated lasting rules for dealings between states. But the apologists for the embattled England of Elizabeth had cast its mission as a religious one, and the queen as a second Judith, and their stress on the dignity and religious aura of monarchy was eagerly seconded by that royal theologian, James I. Discussions of the English polity were in consequence overwhelmingly cast in the legal terms espoused by the great Sir Edward Coke,* or in the religious language of divine kingship beloved of the king. There was little latitude for innovation in either vocabulary. Most lawyers saw the law as sovereign, limiting both prince and people, while James and his clerical apologists talked as much of the duties as of the rights of Christian kings.

The assimilation of protestant theology into political culture intensified the English preoccupation with human agents and human actions. It became easy to see right conduct – whether godly obedience or godly rule – as the central concern of public life. There was, however, a further reason for the focus of so much comment on personal conduct. The execution of the earl of Essex in 1601 and the treason charges successfully pressed against Sir Walter Raleigh and Lord Cobham in 1604 reflect the grim urgency infused into courtly competition as royal finances deteriorated. Corruption, vice and decay seemed all around, all the more so after the massive scandals of James's reign. In response, those who had received a humanist education in the classics looked increasingly to classical thinkers who had faced analogous problems, and they found them in writers of the

*See below, pp. 120–1, 152.

Roman empire. Virgil, Tacitus, Seneca, all had concerned themselves with the moral perils of public life and with the importance
– both political and personal – of preserving virtue. The appropriateness of their Stoic philosophy led that critical courtier Ben
Jonson to write Virgilian country house poems and to choose those
dark figures of Rome, Sejanus and Catiline, as subjects for plays
which seemed dangerously close to commentaries on English politics.
It was no accident that *Catiline* became the most cited of all plays.
Further models from the same period were found in the hugely
popular *Lives* of Plutarch.

  The neo-stoic preoccupation with virtue in politics gave rise to
another striking feature of early-seventeenth-century thought. On the
basis of the intense legalism on Coke's generation, historians have
often talked of the 'common law mind' of insular, conservative Englishmen; but we might as well speak of the 'commonplace mind'.
Increasingly from the mid-sixteenth century students who had
learned from the humanists the classical vision of a history that was
cyclical, and therefore repetitive, and therefore to be learned from,
plundered the classical past as well as modern historians. They
sought, and noted down copiously, not simply the precedents so dear
to the common law mind but also exempla, aphorisms, maxims,
commonplaces, that would bring both successful *and* virtuous models
of conduct to vivid and easily remembered life. The quest for examples in the past cannot be dismissed as just a pedantic, academic, or
snobbish affectation, for established figures from Francis Bacon to the
earl of Bedford kept commonplace books. More strikingly, in their
disenchantment in the 1620s with the decline from glory and virtue,
two aged ex-Elizabethans – the great antiquarian William Camden,
a genuine historian in his own right, and Fulke Greville, Lord Brooke
– founded at Oxford and Cambridge respectively England's first history lectureships. They sought to bring before the nation's future
élite examples of classical virtue in action.

Implicit in the preoccupation with public conduct and virtue is an
aristocratic political order. Appropriately, Greville also wrote the *Life*
of his friend Sir Philip Sidney, whom a whole generation saw as the
supreme embodiment of protestant nobility in public life; nor is it
surprising that Milton's advocacy of a life of commitment was coupled with an intensely élitist vision. Yet there was a fundamental
restraint on such thinking. England's was a monarchical order, never
more so than in the perorations of that enthusiast of divine-right
thinking, James I. Whatever his more subtle practice, James's delight
in the tributes paid by the Book of Psalms to kings – 'Even by God
himself they are called gods' – left little room for noblemen, other

than to say 'Amen'. His son's assumptions were little different, and Charles promptly squashed the lectures on Tacitus delivered under Greville's auspices at Cambridge in 1627. The Stuarts' sense of the exaltation of their position was not peculiar to themselves. Every nobleman, when challenged, would have admitted that the elevation of their ancestors to nobility depended on the actions of kings, 'the fountains of honour'. Similarly, John Pym in 1640 was, perhaps with a touch of rhetorical flourish, to see in the king 'the fountain of justice, of peace, of protection; . . . the royal power and majesty shines upon us in every public blessing we enjoy.'

To a logical mind divine-right kingship seems to exclude every other claim to authority, or to a right to political action. But the merits of analytical logic seemed less clear in the early-seventeenth century than they do today, for most educated contemporaries were persuaded of the harmonious nature of their universe. The Platonic renaissance of the sixteenth century had popularized the belief that the world was created of opposites and dissimilarities in fruitful tension – '*concordia discors*', harmony in discord, or so the theory ran. It was therefore less difficult for the early-modern than for the modern mind to conceive of both a sovereign king and a sovereign common law, or absolute royal pre-rogatives and absolute rights to property. Just as in a more private world men and women were expected to keep their passions and their 'humours' – their temperaments – in balance, so too in the political world. Indeed, the power of the dominant organic metaphor for society, the 'body politic', can best be appreciated from the origin of the word 'constitution', which emerged in the early-modern period from the theory of the physical balance of the bodily humours.

The many parliamentary critics of the crown's fiscal demands in the early seventeenth century were not therefore indulging in unlikely flights of fancy when they contended that to respect the subject's rights to property would be to strengthen the king. Men confident of what was their own would – and this became an urgent consideration after the assassination of Henry IV of France in 1610 – 'love' their king and thus be more easily governed. They would fight more bravely – 'No property, no valour,' as Sir Nathaniel Rich put it in 1628. More generally, mutual respect for the constituent elements of the body politic would invigorate the whole. From their different posi-tions, Thomas Wentworth, lord president of the council in the north, and Pym concurred in 1628 in believing that each part received 'strength and protection' from the whole, and vice versa. Until 1642, and even beyond, probably a large majority of Englishmen clung to the conviction that conflict was not only improper but impossible. The deluge of petitions to king and parliament in the spring of 1642 testified vividly to the belief that harmony and balance ought to prevail.

Unfortunately, such thinking offered little guidance when conflict did occur, and most of the polemic of 1642–3 has an almost casuistical tone as writers sought loopholes in the ramparts of consensus through which to appeal for support. As Philip Hunton observed bleakly in 1643 in his impressive *Treatise of Monarchy*, if prerogative and liberty, prince and people, did come into conflict, then the individual would be left alone with only his conscience to guide him. It was an alarming conclusion, and the Kent gentleman Henry Oxiden prayed for some 'omnipotency' to help him avoid it. Thomas Hobbes sought to answer such prayers with his *Leviathan*.

The stridency of the assertions of balance and harmony did not always reflect a total confidence. As circumstances and the crown's fiscal demands imposed strains, an air of apprehension, even evasiveness, became apparent. The lawyer and MP Robert Mason had wisdom on his side when he commented on some additions touching the power of the king which the Lords tried to make to the Petition of Right in 1628: 'The next word is "trusted", which is very ambiguous, whether it mean trusted by God only as a conqueror, or by the people also, as kings which are to govern by laws *ex pacto* [made by agreement]. In this point I will not presume to venture.'

Fears of generating tensions which might prove impossible to resolve set limits to intellectual activity in this period. Telling instances of such restraints are to be found in the key field of historical scholarship. In history lay political arguments: lawyers sought precedents, and the humanist-influenced discovered models to be applied as the cycles of time repeated themselves. Advances certainly occurred, most particularly as the evidence of the past was made more available. An energetic keeper of the government's records in the Tower was appointed in 1606, and the first guide to them appeared in 1622; furthermore, next door to Westminster the magnificent private collection of Sir Robert Cotton furnished what was almost a reference library for parliament-men and courtiers alike. At the start of our period the antiquarian William Camden in his *Annals* and *Britannia* pioneered a return to the pragmatic historiography of the Italian humanists, in reaction to the providentialism beloved of John Foxe. Without doubt the finest achievement of the developing historical consciousness was the research by John Selden and Sir Henry Spelman into the nature of feudalism and feudal law; though perhaps more striking is the remarkable *Oceana* of 1656, in which James Harrington expounded a view of history in which economics was a dominant force, with the distribution of power within a 'commonwealth' reflecting the distribution of wealth.

Yet caution was essential. As the archival activity suggests, and as legal arguments emphasized time after time, precedents to support the crown abounded. The historically-minded attorney-general William Noy was accordingly able to guide Charles into an aggressive, fiscally-inspired legalism in the 1630s. Nevertheless, certain avenues of investigation were more or less closed. In 1604 James dissolved the society of antiquaries for fear that the precedents it discovered might prove embarrassing; and in 1627, as we have seen, Charles terminated the Cambridge history lectures. But censorship was not merely royal, and others thought it dangerous to challenge assumptions. John Selden was scarcely averse to polemic, and in his famous *History of Tithes* of 1617 willingly pricked clerical bubbles. Yet he was remarkably reticent in the next turbulent decade on the not dissimilar question of the status of parliaments, though his researches into the historical origins of law had given him ample ammunition to use against those, from Coke to Pym, who thought authority rooted in age. Many readers would have nodded their agreement when Sir Walter Raleigh in the preface to his *History of the World* warned historians not to follow truth too close by the heels lest they get their teeth kicked out.

Science

Intellectual progress was more evident in the realm of science, and much of this progress has been tied to the enduring religious ferment. Insular scholars have held that it required the triumph of puritanism in seventeenth-century England to displace the hidebound Aristotelianism of the medieval past. In their analysis, the critical spirit fostered by puritanism's appeal to the individual conscience, and the stress placed by godly divines on *experience* of the message of God's grace, jointly prepared the way for a new empiricism. Since the 'intellectual revolution' was one of the lasting legacies of the period it behoves us to examine such claims.

Puritan scientists can certainly be found, as for example in Henry Briggs, the first geometry professor in Jacobean Oxford, with his interest in logarithms and in a decimal currency, or in the youthful Robert Boyle of the 1640s, the greatest English scientist before Newton. Yet historians have often been beguiled by the fact that the rise of science occurred in the same century as the triumph (if also the collapse) of puritanism into merely assuming a causal relationship. They have sought scientists of one religious bent or another with as much diligence as other historians used to hunt rising or falling gentry, with a similarly inconclusive outcome; for there were far too many non-puritan scientists for us to assume any simple connection. Thus, the most vocal proponent of the new science, and opponent of sterile orthodoxies, was Francis Bacon, briefly James's lord chancellor. However out of touch he was with the mathematical field which was to yield the most fruitful discoveries, Bacon's strident calls for systematic observation of the natural world, for the inductive-experimental method, and for co-operative research were to provide the watch-words for most English scientists of the Restoration period. Yet Bacon's religious views, if any, were opaque; and his concern for the social utility of science, for which he is so often celebrated, seems closer to the 'commonweal' interests of Tudor humanists than it does to the godly divines of his day. Equally problematic for any linkage of puritanism and science is the fact that most anatomical research seems to have been carried out by men who were to sympathize with the royalists; indeed, William Harvey, the foremost anatomist and discoverer of the circulation of the blood, joined the king at Oxford. Moreover, of the two great 'political arithmeticians', or statisticians, of the 1650s and beyond, one, William Petty, was apparently a sceptic who had been educated at a Jesuit college and had done his early work in France, and the other, John Graunt, was a Catholic.

Modern proponents of the impact of puritanism have been able to make their case only by exaggerating the rigidity of the turn-of-the-century academic world. The two universities were by no means simply conservative bastions of theology. Although the curriculum remained largely classicist and Aristotelian, it was not exclusively so. The *raison d'être* of the universities was after all to teach the universe of learning, and the Aristotelian synthesis proved able to expand to take account of many of the new discoveries. Freshmen at St John's College, Cambridge, were even required by the statutes of 1547 to spend their first seven months in the study of mathematics and geometry, the vital building-blocks of the scientists. Recent research has shown that however out of sympathy they were with many of the new discoveries, some lecturers felt compelled to refer to them. The foundations were thus slowly laid for further, and more rapid, development.

That scientific activity did take place at the universities is only now coming to be appreciated. The distinctly non-puritan Jacobean bishop, Lancelot Andrewes, a powerful figure in Elizabethan Cambridge, had maintained a lively and critical interest in mathematics and astronomy, and many were the colleges with extensive collections of scientific instruments in their libraries, and lecturers on the use of such instruments among their fellows. It is therefore less surprising that so many university-educated gentlemen could become the practising scientific *virtuosi* of the later seventeenth century. Still more clear is the record at Oxford. There the non-puritan Sir Henry

Savile established university professorships in astronomy and geometry in 1619, with the intention that they should propagate the new science. The posts' occupants, both puritan and non-puritan, took him at his word, as did the university, which after 1620 made attendance at the lectures compulsory for advanced students. The Laudian triumph seems to have made little difference to the pace of scientific activity at Oxford, and indeed, one of Laud's considerations in establishing a lectureship in Arabic in 1636 was access to Arab mathematical knowledge. Against this background, the 'scientific revolution' of the later seventeenth century looks somewhat less revolutionary.

Those historians who have advanced a single cause for the rise of science have overlooked the sheer difficulty presented by the astronomical hypothesis of Copernicus, the cornerstone of the new science, which contradicted common sense with its insistence that the earth spun on its axis. Once supporting evidence became available in the early seventeenth century, through the observations of Galileo and through research into the variations of the magnetic needle, heliocentrism was rapidly accepted by many of the learned, throughout Europe. And the European dimensions of the pursuit of scientific knowledge in this period make it both parochial and unwise to see scientific research as the preserve of a single group in England. The rise of science owes more to the general cultural milieu than it does to any narrow set of causes.

The sixteenth century had been a time of intellectual upheaval. The geographical discoveries undermined the assumptions of centuries, while the new availability in the Renaissance of non-Aristotelian, non-organic, ways of looking at the world challenged prevailing beliefs about both cosmos and matter. On the one hand neo-Platonic theories of a universe dominated by spirit substances brought with them the cult of the *magus*, the adept. Through illumination the *magus* – such as the figure of Prospero in Shakespeare's *The Tempest* – gained access to the mysteries of the universe. Although this dream of illumination and control influenced variously both Bacon (especially in his *New Atlantis*) and Newton at opposite ends of the century, it also led many adepts deep into alchemy, astrology and, it was feared, heresy. On the other hand, mechanistic materialism, paying court to Archimedes and given stature above all by the discoveries of Galileo, was to lead ultimately to the grim and perhaps godless world of Thomas Hobbes's *Leviathan*. Some found the new avenues unnerving. John Donne's famous lament, 'all coherence gone', in his poem 'The Anatomie of the World' testifies to an unease similar to that which led Rome to condemn Galileo, the leading shaker of the contemporary world. But that intellectual upheaval also bred a genuine excitement so widespread that it crossed all narrow confessional boundaries and drew men into 'natural philosophy' for the sheer delight of it. The famous story of Hobbes, enraptured when first coming across Euclid's theorems, tells us as plainly as does the existence later of the numerous gentry *virtuosi* that science was exhilarating.

In one area, however, a case can be made for the partisan affiliations of science. The illumination claimed for the *magus* by the neo-Platonists had a certain likeness to the claims to divine inspiration advanced by many radical protestants. The most important of the sixteenth-century continental *magi* was the alchemist, and chemist, Paracelsus, who saw in his own observations and experiments the key to the age of the Holy Spirit in which all things would be revealed. The resemblance of that vision to the millenarian hopes of many protestants is apparent, and Paracelsus had considerable influence on thinkers in central Europe – such as Jan Amos Comenius, who was to come to England in 1641 – as the troubles of that region intensified. Comenius's dreams of the protestant millennium combined the spreading enlightenment of which Paracelsus and Bacon had written extensively with the provisions for social betterment, particularly through educational reform, characteristic of north European humanism.

It was no accident that the works of Paracelsus were published in English, and by radicals, in the 1640s. For at that point the prophecy in the Book of Daniel, that in the last times 'many shall run to and fro and knowledge shall be increased', took on a new urgency. Indeed, technological utopianism became a major characteristic of the ferment of the revolutionary years, as Comenius's leading disciple, the tireless visionary Samuel Hartlib, urged that in the last days man would be restored to that 'dominion over nature' which Adam had enjoyed. Much of the effort of Hartlib's circle was directed towards moral and social reform, often of a fairly unrealistic kind. Nevertheless, some of his associates did engage in the chemical researches – for example, seeking a substitute for charcoal in the smelting of iron – to which Paracelsians so often turned. The early chemical work of Robert Boyle can also be set at least partly in this context. But the significance of the Hartlib circle, one of the few concrete instances of a connection between religion and scientific thought – albeit Petty, a Hartlibian, was scarcely a millenarian protestant – can be justly questioned. Ceaseless demands for scientific and practical education do not make those who urge them scientists; rather, Hartlib, with his proposals for an Office of Addresses to act as a scientific labour exchange and patent office, should like many of his allies be seen as a popularizer rather than as a scientist.

Nevertheless, the mechanical approach had still to eliminate its competitors in the race to enlightenment. Robert Boyle in the late

1640s felt that astronomical observations could only be justified if they proved useful to mankind – presumably by way of astrology. Otherwise, he remarked slightingly, 'we know them only to know them.' Similarly, Isaac Newton was to spend far more time in alchemical pursuits than he did on the mathematics associated with his optical and gravitational discoveries. But while in the early seventeenth century neo-Platonism made astrology and alchemy viable subjects of enquiry, their status was to change. Where the Hartlibians did inspire contemporary criticism was in the social implications of their ideas. The neo-Platonists' argument that God, or rather divine spirits, inhabited the material world, and that true knowledge of God could be found in the study of – or even sympathy with – that world appealed to sectarians in the 1640s who had grown convinced that God had poured the Holy Spirit out into the world. Nature could therefore be apprehended through the spirit, and God approached through nature. What Paracelsus and Comenius stood for seemed to become clear in the revolutionary decades. Radical sects – Baptists, Ranters, Quakers alike – practised faith-healing; William Dell, master of Caius College, Cambridge, in the 1650s, demanded the replacement of the traditional university curriculum by the teaching of science and trades; the Ranter leader Laurence Clarkson turned to astrology; while the insistence of Gerrard Winstanley the Digger that God and the world were one gave his calls for scientific education alarming implications. It was no wonder that Hobbes in *The Leviathan* directed such ridicule at theories of a world populated by spirits – not that such theories seemed to most contemporaries inherently absurd; rather, they were dangerous. Nor was it any wonder that Boyle, son of the earl of Cork, reacted so completely against arguments for an animate universe that he grew reluctant even to admit the concept of laws of nature which matter might be said to obey.

Old-fashioned histories of science used to suggest that science was an autonomous pursuit, a noble and rarefied endeavour. Such a judgment is facile. The devotion of the energies of so many astronomers to solving the problem of longitude, and the interest of so many mathematicians in matters relating to the measuring of land area, show that science cannot be isolated from economic change, from commercial and navigational developments, or from the new estate-management practices associated with the growth of the surveyor's profession. The interest of members of the London merchant community in the practical application of scientific, and particularly mathematical, techniques is clear in the foundation of Gresham College in 1597, which placed a greater emphasis on lectures on science than did the old universities. The practical utility of the new mathematics is also indicated by the great survey of Ireland carried out by

William Petty for the conquering English authorities in the 1650s. Furthermore, industrial and technical advance facilitated scientific progress by making available more reliable instruments and consequently more accurate measurements. Without earlier improvements in glass-making and metallurgy it would have been difficult for Robert Hooke after the Restoration to conduct his fundamental researches into microscopy. Nevertheless, it would be equally absurd to argue that economic change triggered and shaped the research of a period whose most characteristic scientific concerns were the nature of motion and of matter.

Similar balance is essential in any assessment of what historians have seen as the other direct stimulus to scientific endeavour. The case of the Hartlibians suggests that religious change did indeed have some impact in the revolutionary years. But it was less than is sometimes argued; and the insistence of countless godly ministers before the civil war that faith and faith alone was what counted can have given little encouragement to scientific enquiry.

The connections with religious and political change are likely to have been of a different order. The very well-informed Restoration gossip John Aubrey felt that 'the searching into natural knowledge began but since or about the death of King Charles the first' in 1649, and indeed the groundwork for many later advances does seem to have been laid in the 1650s. But instead of turning to arguments about the anti-authoritarianism of revolutionaries we should note the way in which the political ferment caused thinkers of all hues to consider the nature and grounds of opinion, of knowledge, of authority. Also, and more important in the short term, the reaction against the violence and destruction stimulated scientific enquiry. Undoubtedly the most significant of all the antecedents to the Royal Society of the Restoration were the scientists who met in Oxford in the 1650s, particularly those associated with John Wilkins at Wadham College. With interests ranging from mathematics to optics and chemistry, and with similarly broad political sympathies, Wilkins, John Wallis, Seth Ward, Christopher Wren, Petty, Boyle and others were united by a distaste for enthusiasm and dogmatism as well as by their intellectual curiosity. If the passions of war finally exposed the dangers of spiritual illumination as a means of knowing, and brutally underlined the costs and risks of public life, then indeed the upheavals and the flowering of science were intimately related.

It would be misleading to close a survey, however partial, of the English outlook in the early seventeenth century with the high ground of science. Rusticated courtiers and godly divines often agreed in condemning the earthy concerns of the bulk of those with whom they had to deal. The popularity of bloody sports such as bear- and bull-baiting, and public hangings, might incline a modern observer to echo the verdict. The frequency with which educated ladies such as Lady Margaret Hoby and Lucy Hutchinson involved themselves in medical care in their neighbourhoods certainly indicates the sparsity, or perhaps the incompetence, of physicians in the countryside; it also speaks to the boredom and frustration attending the country life, especially that of women. Yet the mental world of this period was not narrow and coarse of necessity. By 1640 most major provincial towns had a bookseller, often more than one. The number of works printed annually in England between 1600 and 1640 rose from 259 to 577; thereafter it soared. Nor were even a majority of those books manuals of devotion: the presses in 1623 published 120 religious works as against some 189 on a variety of other topics, which included eighty-nine on current events. The appearance in the early-Stuart period of salaried newsletter-writers, such as John Pory and Captain Rossingham, and the proliferation in gentry family archives of letters full of news and gossip, testify to a widespread appetite for information of all kinds. The popularity of Plutarch's *Lives*, of maps and travel books – such as Richard Hakluyt's *Voyages* – even the beginning in fashionable circles of what was to become the 'grand tour' of Europe, show that horizons were broadening.

4 The Failure of Reform
1603–1620

In March 1603 an observer in London noted that 'many men, both noble and others, have made very great provision of armour, munitions and victuals'. Forty-five years had passed since the uncertainty on the last change of monarch, and when the dynasty too died with Elizabeth there were fears of worse. But to widespread wonderment, there was 'no tumult, no contradiction, no disorder . . . every man went about his business readily, as peaceably, as securely, as though there had been no . . . news ever heard of competitors.' The credit for the smooth succession of James VI of Scotland should be distributed variously, to the tireless backstage workings of Elizabeth's chief minister, Sir Robert Cecil, to James's own diplomatic efforts to ingratiate himself with all and sundry, and perhaps too to the distracted and exhausted state of both France and Spain, which had once toyed with alternative claimants. Characteristically, James preferred to see in the enthusiastic reception he was accorded a testimony to his own skill and, most of all, a sign of divine goodwill towards him, God's lieutenant on earth.

James was in many ways a welcome change from Elizabeth. An adult male with two sons and a daughter, he conformed more closely to the image of kingship and promised at last a secure succession. His renowned yearning for the peace of Christendom delighted taxpayers, groaning under the burden of Elizabeth's wars, if not the military contractors and the young men with their way to make. Furthermore, while a financial case can certainly be made for the old queen's niggardliness, the bitterness of the competing factions in the 1590s had been at least partly the result of her sheer unwillingness to offer rewards. James, recognizing the political importance of patronage, made no such mistakes. Many of the traits for which he has been so condemned by historians seem less culpable when set in context. He perpetrated an 'inflation of honours', but so did the kings of France and Spain, who equally faced the need to accommodate prospering landed and commercial sectors of society, and could see the money to be made in selling titles. He was munificent; but as a foreigner and first of a new dynasty he could count on no inherited loyalties, and had to create them. Moreover, he was under pressure, and when his extravagance was questioned in the Commons in 1610 he retorted aptly that most there had either had or asked for something. But he put up little enough resistance.

James's generosity and his famous taste for lively and handsome young men may alike be related to his troubled youth. His rigorous upbringing as an orphan had bred in him a prodigious and pedantic learning and love of philosophy, whose fruits were seen in the books he wrote on divine kingship, on witchcraft, on tobacco. But he had as a child been starved of the affection and approval he felt his due as a divinely ordained king, and perhaps not surprisingly, he later showered favours on those who smiled on him. His yearnings were not satisfied by marriage to Anne of Denmark, a woman who was at odds with him in temperament and soon in religion; he was, accordingly, nowhere happier than in the crude physical fellowship of a group of hunting companions, or joking with a young favourite. Most contemporary kings had their favourites, or *privadoes*; and we shall never know whether James was actively homosexual. But his declaration at the height of his later infatuation with George Villiers, that as Christ had his John he had his George, was unusual. His tastes had political consequences. Some contemporaries were disturbed when they saw the king fondling his favourite in public, or when in the later years they saw the careful decking out of a handsome 'myrmidon' which went with each new faction's attempt to gain the king's ear. His unquenchable passion for hunting perhaps casts doubt on the view of some contemporaries that his renowned aversion to war and to duelling stemmed from cowardice rather than conscience. But one item in the legend is unchallengeable: James's hunting could disrupt business. His anxiety to be free of politics for the chase bred weak royal control over the administration and a dangerous tendency – which brought disaster at the end of the 1621 parliament – for the king to be fifty miles of bad roads away from events.

Although he was reluctant to devote himself to business, and was fortunate in his early years in being served by the omnicompetent Cecil, James was no pleasure-loving cypher. His memories of the turbulent Edinburgh mob, and perhaps his consciousness of his own awkward appearance and speech, made him shun Elizabeth's dazzling example of courting popularity. Nevertheless, his ability to balance the factions in court and church was fully as developed as hers, and he avoided the dangerous alienation of those out of favour that was to disfigure his son's reign, and that had marred too the last years of Elizabeth in the strife between the earl of Essex and Cecil. His flexibility and his skill at letting sleeping dogs lie served him well in dealing with parliaments and with protestant zealots. The charge so often levelled, that he was 'the wisest fool in Christendom', is patently unjust, for he often belied doctrinaire words with extreme shrewdness, and when he put his mind to it his assessment of individuals and situations could be incisive. His verdict on William Laud, who was to be at the root or so many of Charles's problems, reveals both his acuity and his desire to pacify rather to provoke: 'He hath a restless spirit and cannot see when matters are well, but loves to toss and change and bring things to a pitch of reformation floating in his own brain.'

But James made less use than he might of his skills. His objectives in Scotland had been to survive. When so many of his later political difficulties were associated with English resentment of his extravagance, the suddenness of his journey from penury to riches may have been significant. The material discomforts of Scottish life had, however, been overshadowed by the political. James spent his years north of the border wary of a nobility allowed to become over-assertive in the upheavals of sixteenth-century Scottish history; in consequence he learned to divide and rule, and succeeded brilliantly in separating the intransigent Scottish presbyterian clergy from noblemen frustrated at new restraints. With some justice James prided himself on his 'kingcraft' when he reminded his English subjects that he was no mere novice. But his Scottish experience was formative in more ways than one. In his preoccupation with survival he failed to appreciate not just the need but also the opportunities for reform in England, where kings possessed far more authority than did their Scottish counterparts. His solitary initiative, laudable though it was, was to press for the unification of England and Scotland. Had he also backed either of his reforming ministers, Cecil or Cranfield, as thoroughly as his contemporary Henry IV of France did Sully the record might have been very different.

Despite a plague epidemic which devastated both London and the provinces that summer, the political auguries seemed good. James's motto, '*Rex pacificus*' [the royal peace-maker], points to his conviction that his mission lay in the bringing of unity and harmony. In particular, he saw in his own person the opportunity to heal the centuries-old enmity between the English and the Scots. Accordingly, he promptly had himself proclaimed king of Great Britain and took a lively if prurient interest in Anglo-Scottish marriages. But James's dreams of peace spread wider than the northern border along the river Tweed. A fundamentally tolerant ruler himself, he saw little reason for the religious fortifications which stretched across Europe, and hoped to breach them. With the glories of Drake's years long past, war-weariness created a favourable climate for him to set in train moves which were to bring peace with Spain in 1604. While Cecil, brought up an Elizabethan protestant, was less hopeful than James that the wider world could be pacified by building bridges to the Catholic foe, he recognized that England by now had little direct interest in fighting. Although radical protestants greeted the ensuing peace of London as a desertion of England's Dutch allies, who were still embroiled with Spain, others applauded the treaty of London's promise of an end to war taxation and its opening of the Spanish trade – which was to prove important to the burgeoning new draperies – to English merchants.

James's vision of himself as peace-maker extended alike to domestic affairs. Since the Reformation, each new reign in England had begun with a religious settlement, and while James let his respect for the Elizabethan establishment be known, he also intimated his belief that there was room for improvement. The king's genuine interest in reform cannot be doubted: in the middle years of his reign he attempted to limit the non-residence of clergy, and throughout he refrained from plundering the church's revenues as the more cynical Elizabeth had done. Nevertheless, his motives in summoning a group of bishops and puritan clergy to confer at Hampton Court in 1604 were probably less reformist than relish at the prospect of a theological disputation and at the chance to air his own views. The conference has become legendary as a confrontation with die-hard presbyterians, and James contributed to the legend. Either misunderstanding the debate and believing he had found his more resolute Scottish foes lurking behind craven Englishmen, or eager to make a political point, he at one point asserted the mutual dependency of episcopacy and monarchy, 'No bishop, no king,' and denounced the presbyterianism he claimed to detect as a threat to the state. But the reforms the puritans urged on him were studiously moderate, for there was little left of the presbyterian anti-episcopal agitation of Elizabeth's reign. Alarmed by the theological differences evident at both universities in the 1590s, some called for a more rigid definition of Calvinist orthodoxy. Otherwise, the complaints focused on essentially practical and disciplinary matters, and on certain 'popish' ceremonies, such as the ring in marriage and the cross in baptism, to which the godly had long objected. The discussion was generally as harmonious as the demands were low-key.

The outcome of the conference was correspondingly mixed. James refused to meet the doctrinal demands, lest he jeopardize that tolerant ecclesiastical comprehensiveness at which he aimed throughout his reign. He did, however, respond promptly to other concerns by ordering a new translation of the Bible, which appeared in 1611 and gained subsequent renown as the 'King James' or Authorized Version.

Its clear and everyday prose was to help shape the popular conscience, even if it did not immediately displace its main, Genevan, rival, whose sometimes radical marginal comments the king hoped to counter. The other consequences of Hampton Court were negative. Alarmed by what the petitioning occasioned by the conference revealed of lay and clerical organization, and disdainful of the apparently trivial nature of the puritan demands, James showed he could be jolted out of his conciliatory intentions by a challenge to his regal position. On Whitgift's death in 1604 he appointed as archbishop of Canterbury the equally disciplinarian Richard Bancroft. Pressed by the king, Bancroft then assiduously enforced the canons that emerged from the separate ecclesiastical convocation of 1604. While mainly concerned with house-cleaning the church, these slapped at dissidents by requiring clergy not merely to conform, but to conform *willingly*, to the doctrine and ceremonies prescribed. Hopes that Elizabeth's death would bring a public relaxation withered.

The road from Hampton Court was for some a direct one, first underground and then eventually to New England. But while the conference may have been a climacteric for a few godly consciences, it was not so for the church as a whole. Despite the disappointment, most clergy were too committed to the ideal of national church, to their pastoral charges, and to their livelihoods, to resist; only about ninety ministers, around 1 per cent of the total parish clergy, lost their livings. And the promotion of Bancroft proved an aberration, for unlike Elizabeth James was a 'godly prince' who accepted the need for a preaching clergy. The succession of good Calvinists whose episcopal appointments followed Bancroft's explains why puritanism in any ecclesiastical sense figures so small as a grievance in the Jacobean parliaments, with even the purge of 1604–5 dying as an issue by 1614.

For all their importance to James's sense of mission, the moves to peace in Europe and in the church were something of a side-show. The main preoccupation of all political actors was the helter-skelter of patronage in a new reign.

These were tense months. Their flavour is perhaps best caught in the ruthlessness with which Cecil deployed the hard skills he had learned in the factiousness of the 1590s to destroy other rivals, lord Cobham and Sir Walter Raleigh, for their alleged involvement in Catholic plotting. For his part, James's record was, as in so much else, neither as good nor as bad as it might have been. While Elizabeth had conferred frustratingly few knighthoods, the 906 James bestowed in his first four months were too many, and generated some resentments. His material generosity to Scottish cronies was hardly surprising; it became more objectionable when it continued into the reign, with, for example, £67,498 of the £90,688 he gave away in 1611 going to eleven Scotsmen. But the exhilarating ride south, when all rushed to greet the rising sun, had not overwhelmed his Scottish canniness. He balanced his favour to his friends by rewarding most of Elizabeth's councillors for their aid in his succession. Thus, the all-important Cecil, secretary of state, became Viscount Cranborne and then earl of Salisbury, and the lord treasurer, Thomas Sackville, Lord Buckhurst, became earl of Dorset. Reaping the fruits of office, the one soon built the huge pile of Hatfield House while the family name of the other was popularly inverted to 'Fill-Sack'. It may have been to check and balance the self-interest of these two that James elevated Lord Henry Howard, one of the great schemers of Elizabeth's last days, to high favour and the earldom of Northampton; for the risks of any factional monopoly of power had only too recently been made evident in Essex's violence against the overweening Cecils. If so, the move would have been more impressive but for Northampton's syco-phantic air and his crypto-Catholicism.

As important as the signs of continuity in creating a surge of good feeling was the hearing that James gave to the case for administrative reform. His own sense of it may only have been skin deep, but Salis-bury, for all his own ambition, had learned from his uncomfortable experience of trying to run the wars of Elizabeth's reign from hand-to-mouth that reform must come.

Elizabeth's financial legacy was ambiguous. Some military expenses continued, but with peace the war was over: thus, the cost of governing Ireland fell nearly ten-fold between 1603 and 1607. Elizabeth had furthermore left a small annual surplus on her 'ordi-nary', or regular, account, which in peace-time ought to have covered the higher costs of the court of a king with a family. The ruinous aspect of Elizabeth's reign was fiscal and administrative ossification. Neither she nor her chief minister Lord Burghley, Salisbury's father, had had any remedy for the strains imposed by inflation other than cost-watching. While other large landlords were capitalizing on demographic pressures by multiplying their rent-rolls, the royal estates were left virtually unsurveyed in Elizabeth's long reign, and their economic potential was thus unknown. One example will tell much of the story. In 1587 Elizabeth agreed to a long lease on some Bermondsey property for £68 p.a; when the lease finally fell in, in 1636, it was found to be worth £1,071 p.a. Similar paralysis was evident elsewhere. Revenues from the crown's feudal dues declined, though they were by contrast to rise markedly under the early Stuarts. Furthermore, in the period of rapid inflation between Mary's death and 1604 there was no revision of the book of rates, the artifical valuations at which customs were levied on imports and exports.

To a degree Elizabeth's plight must command sympathy. Religious division and an uncertain succession may have made her anxious to avoid the discontent which her successors were to provoke by raising their revenues. The crown more than most landlords had to see in lands a source of patronage as much as an economic resource. But a comparison with what other early-modern rulers managed to achieve in wartime suggests the importance of sheer inertia. The queen's motto, '*Semper eadem*' ['always the same'] was not inappropriate.

The short-term solutions sought by Elizabeth and Burghley had soured the political atmosphere. The queen had attempted to limit expenditure by failing to compensate her servants directly for the prevailing inflation. This forced officials to turn to indirect means, which might amount to blatant self-help in the form of higher fees or bribery and extortion. They also availed themselves of royal grants of economic privileges, for the novel degree of government intervention during the sixteenth century had made milking the economy all the easier. The chief device the crown used to foster the new industrial techniques which were to transform the English economy was the issue of patents conferring monopoly privileges; the potential for exploitation was obvious to courtiers or speculators willing to claim they had found a new method of producing an article, such as playing cards, in common use. A similar fate befell the regulatory, or 'penal', statutes which had proliferated in the Tudor period, most of which naturally left considerable scope for executive discretion. As it became clear that much of the system of enforcement was a seamy method of supporting the court and its hangers-on attacks on governmental corruption mounted, to culminate in the storms over monopolies in Elizabeth's last parliaments of 1597 and 1601. A potentially dangerous phenomenon had appeared in incipient disenchantment with the court.

Salisbury initially saw hope in the altered climate created by a new king and peace. Not only would peace ease the fiscal pressure on the subject; it ought also to permit financial recovery, since customs would grow with trade. While it is difficult to deduce a coherent programme from a series of initiatives spread over some years, Salisbury's long-term aim seems to have been broader – the creation of sufficient goodwill between crown and Commons to allow lasting reforms. But it proved impossible to restrain James's growing expenditure, and Salisbury's task was accordingly complicated by a mounting burden of debt. The need to cope with the short-term problem of a growing shortage of cash then led him to search for revenue by systematically exploiting the customs. Although he regarded the fortunes of crown and parliament as closely interrelated, he fatally underestimated the degree to which the Commons would see exploitation of the customs as a threat to their traditional control over taxation.

Salisbury's reformist credentials are clearest in his attempts to sell off the ramshackle edifice of ancient rights that has been called fiscal feudalism. The most important of these rights were purveyance and wardship. Purveyance was the system whereby officials bought up supplies for the crown in local markets at fixed prices far below cost. The incidence was obviously inequitable, and despite the growing practice of 'compounding', or paying money in lieu, the opportunities for abuse were legion. Although the crown's profits were appreciable – around £30,000 p.a. in 1604, rising to about £40,000 in the 1620s – Salisbury was attracted by the greater administrative simplicity of regular parliamentary supply. His readiness to abandon wardship is still more striking, since as master of the court of wards his own profits probably averaged about one-sixth of the almost £20,000 p.a. which the crown gained from wards in the years around 1600. Wardship stemmed from the ancient right of the feudal lord to provide a guardian for the lands and heir of a tenant who by reason of age or sex was unable to fight for him. However anachronistically, much land was still held by military tenure, and in the court of wards the hard-pressed Tudors and early Stuarts sold rights over the land and marriage of wards. Although the relatively low yield to the crown probably explains Salisbury's willingness to dispense with wardship, its importance was not merely financial. To the ward it could mean the devastation of the estate and, perhaps, an unwelcome marriage, although as a rule of thumb such disasters normally only afflicted a family one generation in three. And to the crown, 'Patronage and protection [is] the end of wardship', as Salisbury put it in 1610. Wardship had enormous symbolic significance for James, emphasizing as it did his benevolent overlordship of the nation; and it had great patronage value, for it allowed the crown or Salisbury as master of the court of wards, to reward courtiers with grants of wards on favourable terms. As the government's prolonged hesitation in 1610 was to show, the equation was difficult to balance. *If* parliament were generous, a larger and more regular revenue might be secured; but abandonment of wardship would severely limit the crown's patronage resources, and the Common's attitude to regular taxation was scarcely propitious.

The parliamentary prospects seemed bright enough. While Elizabeth's fiscal demands had caused unease in her last parliaments, in other respects she had faced far less turbulence than in her earlier years. Peace, and the euphoria at the new reign, might allow that quieter tone to continue. For his part, James emphasized his desire for harmony by choosing to meet parliament at all in 1604. He was unable to request new taxes while Elizabeth's last subsidies were being collected, and therefore all he could hope for was mutually beneficial legislation – not least, the enactment of his cherished union between England and Scotland.

A government with a legislative programme had other assets besides the political climate. The usually loyal bishops in the Lords were reinforced by the goodwill of the secular peers, who as a group had benefited handsomely from James's generosity. Although it is misleading to talk of a government 'interest' in the Commons, since the quasi-freehold nature of many posts imposed few obligations of political responsibility on their holders, a certain loyalty was presumed. The privy council practised no direct electoral management; yet courtiers and office-holders made up between a quarter and a third of the almost five hundred members, thanks to the efforts of friendly magnates and the eagerness of borough constituencies to gain friends at court. The taciturnity of most members meant that energetic courtiers might have a disproportionate impact. But unfortunately for Salisbury, most courtiers were no more active than their country neighbours, and Francis Bacon, striving hard for promotion, too often soldiered on with whatever help Salisbury's unofficial contacts in the house could provide.

Financial reform had competition on the agenda, from the union of the kingdoms, from a host of private bills, and from unexpected developments. Indeed, the chaotic opening of the parliament indicates how little of an actual agenda there was. Disorganization soon gave place to dissension when the Commons discovered that government lawyers had by sharp practice sought to reverse the result of the Buckinghamshire election, in which a privy councillor, Sir John Fortescue, had been defeated in a local squabble. Although not personally concerned, James reacted angrily when the Commons declared that they were the only judge over elections. Doubtless as a result of his experience with the theocratic claims of Scottish presbyterians he abhorred assertions of autonomous jurisdiction, and provocatively lectured the Commons on the origins of their privileges in the grace of earlier kings. Alarmed, the Commons concluded that that grace could be withdrawn, and their privileges lost. But neither side was anxious to dig itself into a rigid position, and James's eventual tactful compromise was eagerly accepted. The crown was to attempt no further challenge to the house's control over its own composition.

Once the storm passed the Commons resumed business, and with clear support and encouragement from Salisbury in the Lords they turned to the elimination of purveyance and wardship. But they soon faltered at the problem of compensating the king, for distant counties, which suffered little from purveyance, were naturally reluctant to contribute equally with the south-east, and wardship raised similar difficulties, since not all were held by military tenure. When members appreciated that they were being asked to establish a permanent tax their feet grew colder and progress slower.

Even peace, towards which the government was hastening, seemed unlikely to usher in an era of good feelings. The expected trade boom inflamed the jealousy of the provincial ports for London, since the outports feared that London would extend its growing commercial dominance into the newly reopening Spanish market. The threat posed by the greater resources of the London merchants was intensified by the tightness of their organization: about half of London's exports, the traditional partly-finished broadcloths sent to Germany and the Low Countries, were shipped by one company, the Merchant Adventurers; and half of this trade was in the hands of twenty-six men. The provincial members saw London itself as 'a head too big for the body', reducing the rest of the kingdom to poverty, and blamed the commercial companies for accelerating that process. The merchants' cries were echoed by gentry MPs responding to constituency grievances or realizing that their own fortunes were bound up with the price of wool and the fortunes of the cloth trade. The pressure to open the trading companies to provincial merchants – and not for 'free trade' in nineteenth-century terms – gained nothing in 1604, and some relaxation in the Spanish trade alone in the next parliamentary session of 1606; but it irritated a government which believed strongly in the virtues of organization and whose credit was closely tied to the London merchants.

James's patience, already sapped by repeated displays of particularism, broke when crude English chauvinism thwarted his dream of a union of his kingdoms. The Commons' fears that unification under the name of Great Britain would wreak havoc with all laws that referred specifically to England had some legal plausibility. Nevertheless, the debates made clear that much of the resistance was purely xenophobic – and MPs' prejudices were probably shared by peers jealous of Scottish rivals at court. The insults to his native land clearly angered the king, and he gave vent to his accumulated frustrations by castigating the Commons for finding fault with all his propositions and for meddling in his finances. Here he was on weak ground, and when a Commons' committee prepared a defence, the famous Apology, it aggrievedly pointed out that the financial discussions had been 'upon motion' of privy councillors.

The Apology was never presented, for as usual James thought better of his anger and rapidly closed the session with a conciliatory prorogation. But it is important for what it reveals of early-Stuart parliament-men. Earlier historians erred in believing that the Commons were embarked on a campaign of constitutionalist aggression. The house had shown itself localist and leaden-footed when reforms were suggested, and the initiatives came from elsewhere. The most renowned passage of the Apology is appropriately defensive: 'All experience shows that the prerogatives of princes may easily and do daily grow [while] the privileges of the subject are for the most part at an everlasting stand.' Yet however conservative the outlook, the Commons thought they knew where they stood. The Apology confidently asserted that the privileges of parliament, threatened in the Buckinghamshire dispute and by other slights, were essential for the liberties of the subject.

The aftermath of the 1604 session warned zealous protestants that peace with Spain could be at best only a truce with their old enemy in Rome.

While most English Catholics were at least as loyal to the crown as to the pope, the religious struggles of the sixteenth century had been fought out in an international context, and a small number of zealots and conspirators looked abroad for aid in returning England to the Catholic fold. In their frustration at James's peaceful succession some had engaged in the half-baked Main and Bye Plots; these had little effect other than in bringing Raleigh and Cobham to the steps of the scaffold and in shocking the tolerant James into agreeing to new sanctions against recusants – the spring of 1605 brought over 5,000 convictions and fines. But the peace with Spain came as a greater disappointment to those who had looked to Madrid and, alienated and alone, they turned their thoughts to a 'sudden blow'. The opening of the new session of parliament, scheduled for November 1605, seemed their chance to destroy the whole persecuting political élite as well as the protestant king. Ironically, they failed because they were not alienated enough, and in this they offer the clearest example of the advantages of ideological division at court. Some were fatally reluctant to see Catholic lords blown up with the rest, and so the secret leaked out.

The Plot predictably occasioned a new burst of persecution. Though prosecutions proved powerless to halt the growth of recusancy, new sanctions enacted in 1606 made life more uncomfortable for the propertied who could be blackmailed by informers or who attracted the attention of needy courtiers. And the Plot had one unlooked-for by-product. A statute of 1606 imposed on Catholics an oath of allegiance denying the pope's claim to depose kings. Catholic polemicists denounced this as an intrusion into matters of faith, while

James contended it was merely civil, and in the ensuing international controversy James developed more systematically the views on the divine origins and responsibilities of kingship which he had adumbrated in his long struggle with the Scottish presbyterians. The greater intensity after 1606 of his rhetoric of lieutenancy to God, which at least some MPs came to find distasteful, can be traced to the conspiracy.

The most immediate result of the Gunpower Plot was, however, a strengthening of national unity behind its protestant prince. Despite the peace with Spain, the monarch could still be cast as a new Constantine leading the godly against a satanic popish foe. The subsequent celebration of 5 November showed how much anti-Catholicism entered the fabric of national life. In the ensuing parliamentary session, in 1606, the outburst of patriotic fervour far outweighed the resentment at James's spending evident in the one-vote margin of the eventual vote on supply. Despite peace the royal debt had nearly doubled since Elizabeth's death; there was little to show for it, little sign of future improvement, and the Commons had accumulated a list of material grievances. Though they remained unwilling to heed Salisbury's promptings over fiscal feudalism, they displayed unprecedented generosity by voting the king £453,000 in peacetime supply. They were moved to do this, not by another reform programme aimed at cultivating goodwill, but simply by the realization of how vulnerable and how valuable was the person of their sovereign.

Though protestant Englishmen might unite behind their prince, their good feelings did not extend to their neighbours. Whatever delight the king took in the second, 1606, session of parliament rapidly dissipated in the course of the third session in 1606–7 when he was again rebuffed over the union. The Commons baulked at even minor proposals, and in a clever wrecking move one prominent MP, Sir Edwin Sandys, disingenuously advanced his alternative of a 'perfect union'. The scheme's 'perfection' lay in its suggestion that Scottish law be totally abrogated in favour of the – as Englishmen saw it – incomparably superior English law. The fears for the common law voiced in the 1604 debates would thus be laid to rest. James's initial reaction was to lash out, although once again he tactfully moderated his displeasure by closing the session by prorogation. His eventual good grace stemmed, ominously, in part from his realization that he did not need parliament to gain all his objectives. Soon after the prorogation the government brought a collusive action, the *Post-Nati* case, in which the judges resolved that birth in Scotland, or any other territory owing allegiance to the king of England, *ipso facto* conveyed naturalization. The decision had little immediate effect, for those affected – the *post-nati* – were of course born in or after 1603. But after so blatantly flouting the clear wishes of the Commons James recognized that there was little hope of further parliamentary cooperation on a union, and ceased to press the point. He may correspondingly have begun to lose interest in parliaments. But for the moment he turned his attention to the peaceful settlement of the 'middle shires' of his British kingdom, the old trouble-spot of the Borders, while reminding sneering Englishmen of the laudable obedience of the Scots, who could be governed by a stroke of the pen from distant Whitehall.

Another outlying area, across the Irish Sea, proved more recalcitrant than the Borders. The great Gaelic uprising of the 1590s, centred on the stronghold of Ulster and led by Hugh O'Neill, earl of Tyrone, had finally collapsed as Elizabeth lay dying. But though Tyrone was defeated his position was not destroyed, and he proceeded to improve it by appeals to the conciliatory James. Not for the last time an unfortunate gap opened between the policy of the government in London and its agents in Ireland. James and Salisbury were inclined to check the excesses of Elizabeth's last years and doubted the value of punitive anti-Catholic measures in the absence of a viable protestant alternative. But their local agents remembered only the recent upheaval, and hungered for land. English policy in Ireland therefore wavered, breeding uncertainty and insecurity in those it affected, and in 1607 the Ulster chieftains, Tyrone and his neighbour, the earl of Tyrconnel, fled to safety in Europe.

English officials were not inclined to look a gift horse in the mouth. The 'flight of the earls' offered a dramatic solution to the problem of Ulster, the most recalcitrant region of Ireland, since the local leaders, and major landowners, had gone. The government happily assumed that those who stayed were equally involved in conspiracy, and almost immediately plans were afoot for the systematic extension throughout Ulster of the device of colonization with loyal settlers from the mainland which had been used piecemeal elsewhere since Mary Tudor's reign. By the middle of the next decade the character of the new Ulster was emerging, divided into shires and subjected to English justice. But the new planters' resources proved inadequate to meet the crown's demand that the bulk of the native Irish be displaced. Accordingly, while there was some settlement by protestant small farmers – some 40,000 came from Scotland, and were made yet more zealous in their presbyterianism by proximity to Irish Catholics – colonization normally consisted of a veneer of protestant estate-owners, dependent on the labour and rack-rents of the Irish. The troubled Ulster of the protestant supremacy was taking shape.

Whether close attention from London would have made any difference is doubtful, but like all English governments James's was infinitely more concerned with domestic than with Irish problems. And those problems, which were more than ever Salisbury's to wrestle with when he succeeded on Dorset's death in 1608 to the lord treasurership, were overwhelmingly financial. Although there were genuine obstacles on the road to solvency, such as the need to secure Ireland, the major impediment was the king. Despite his periodic vows that no longer would every day be a Christmas he steadily amassed more debt as he succumbed to the requests that flooded in.

It must be stressed that the royal finances were not irretrievably doomed. A debt which was of the order of twice the ordinary, or regular, revenue was scarcely catastrophic had rational policies been followed. Of these Salisbury still had hopes, and with Dorset he had initiated a long, although generally abortive, series of commissions to examine 'projects', or means of raising money. But when James's support was too intermittent and the administrative resources too scarce to implement the reforms needed it was easy to conclude that the quickest road to the reduction of the debt was by way of the crown lands. Extra income could indeed be raised from this source: the belated surveys Salisbury ordered in 1608 almost quadrupled the crown's rents from its Yorkshire lands, and retrospectively damned Elizabeth's inertia. But since the interest on the debt was 10 per cent while the yield of land was commonly accounted at 5 per cent sales seemed more promising, whatever the loss in patronage and political influence. The campaign of planned sale which Dorset began shortly before his death had by 1610 raised almost £450,000. Had expenditure fallen too the liquidation of capital combined with the 1606 subsidy would have more than eliminated the debt. But although sales, subsidy and other windfalls brought in £1,185,000 between 1606 and 1610, the debt fell in the same period by a mere £455,000, to £280,000, as expenditures rose apace. Characteristically, James celebrated the 1606 subsidy by giving three of his Scottish friends £44,000 to pay off their debts, and by spending £800 on 'spangles' for the guard.* The knowledge that the king's will was no more subject to restriction than was the tide drove Dorset and Salisbury to the fateful decision to exploit the customs.

The prospect of a major breakthrough appeared with an internal dispute among Levant Company merchants. This occasioned a decision by the revenue court of the exchequer in 1606 that duties imposed for the regulation of commerce were an unchallengeable

* University of Kansas, KSRL Ms. E191.

element in the crown's foreign policy prerogative. The potential of the *Bate's Case* decision was obvious, for if the crown claimed it was regulating trade it could impose any duties it wished. In the summer of 1608 Salisbury accordingly imposed new tariffs on virtually every import except basic foodstuffs, munitions and ships' stores. As the chancellor of the exchequer, Sir Julius Caesar, gloated, the day would be 'the most gainfull to the king and his posterity as any one day's work'. The 1608 impositions brought in about £70,000 p.a., and by the 1630s further impositions yielded about £218,000 p.a. in all. At stake now was the late-medieval balance between crown and parliament in which revenue-raising required consent.

Salisbury had not been deterred by the defeat of his earlier parliamentary efforts to liquidate fiscal feudalism, and despite the very different promise held out by *Bate's Case* he still hoped for major fiscal reforms. Although by 1610 the king's ordinary revenues had risen to about £460,000 from their 1606 level of £315,000, the failure to reduce the debt warned Salisbury that any new war would destroy his gains. Technological change necessitated greater military preparedness, and to what must have been Salisbury's delight, one of the judges in *Bate's Case* had held that kings must have peace-time supply for the defence of their kingdom – in breach of the convention that kings lived off their own resources in time of peace. Salisbury clearly hoped for a parliamentary settlement to that end, but the atmosphere for his far-sighted 'Great Contract' of 1610 was poisoned by the recent impositions. As the lawyer James Whitelocke was to warn the Commons, if kings could impose at will, 'Considering the greatest use they make of assembling of parliaments, which is the supply of money,' there was little future for parliaments.

The Contract was the last attempt until the very different conditions of 1641 to restore the crown's finances through harmony with parliament. In tense negotiations in the summer of 1610 agreement seemed to have been reached. For £200,000 p.a. the king was to surrender wardship, purveyance and the much-resented use of informers to raise money on penal statutes; additionally, James separately indicated his willingness to forego any further impositions without parliamentary consent. Members of the Commons were told to consult their neighbours over the recess about what was a massive constitutional innovation, regular taxation for the upkeep of government. But when parliament reassembled in November both parties had thought better of the bargain. The Commons attacked the Scots as the likely beneficiaries, and James demanded immediate payment of all his debts. Despite Salisbury's efforts, parliament was soon dissolved.

The causes of failure must be sought partly in the arithmetic. Many MPs were reluctant to subsidize what they saw as sheer extravagance, and Sir Edwin Sandys alleged that James's court cost four times as much as its French or Spanish counterparts. Moreover, since only a section of the populace had been liable to feudal dues the proposal that a general tax should replace them was resoundingly denounced in the constituencies, while landowners were equally hostile to the alternative, a permanent tax on lands liable to feudal dues. On the other side, the basic operating principle by which the government staggered along was at risk, for the Contract made little provision for replacing the indirect pickings, from rich wards, by which courtiers supported themselves. Salisbury's determination to press on testifies to his sense of the gloomy future under an unthrifty king and to his awareness of the political tensions that would be provoked should the disputed revenues be raised further. But as Caesar in particular amongst the king's advisers realized, the Contract left too little margin for reducing the debt. Worst of all, it asked the king to sacrifice flexible revenues for a fixed income in an era of inflation.

Graver issues of reciprocated fears for the future underlay the practical problems. The king's occasional outbursts against the Commons did not arise from any inveterate hostility, for he took seriously his rhetoric about his divinely ordained duty to preserve the laws and constitutions of the kingdom. Indeed, despite the very different rhetoric each used, James was at first rather more of a 'parliamentary prince' than Elizabeth had been. In her last, wartime, years Elizabeth had been single-minded in her use of parliament, calling it for frequent but brief meetings to gain money. James on the other hand allowed three separate sessions of his long first parliament of 1604–10 to pass without a grant of taxes, and this was not wholly because he was rebuffed. Furthermore, the legislative record reveals that parliament was playing a more positive role in social and economic regulation under James than it had under Elizabeth. The frustrated interests which had gained an average of only thirty-three statutes from the queen's last three parliaments could triumph in the seventy-two acts of the 1604 session and the fifty-six of 1606. Indeed, until the Long Parliament of the civil war, the total legislative achievement of James's first parliament was second only to the monumental Reformation Parliament. The detailed work on the regulation of alehouses, draining of fenland and reformation of corporations tells an important story of collaboration between king and country. Nevertheless, James did hold certain views which were not those of most of his subjects. He repeatedly voiced the belief that all property was held of the king as the ultimate lord and that all laws and rights originated in royal grace. He was therefore a receptive audience for those, such as

Lord Chancellor Ellesmere and perhaps also the earl of Northampton, who urged the indignity of bargaining away the rights of the
crown, and who resented the growing prominence of the Commons –
at the expense of the Lords as much as of the crown – as money
matters became central.

Ellesmere's apprehensions were mirrored by the express doubts of
some MPs about parliament's prospects should the king receive the
adequate annual revenue he now seemed to claim as his due from his
subjects. Such doubts were reinforced by the realization that any
bargain made might prove insecure. For the judges in *Bate's Case* had
held, and James reiterated, that since prerogatives were for the good
of the kingdom they were inalienable. Any of the prerogatives compounded for in the Contract might therefore be resurrected if a future
king withdrew his grace from his subjects. And indeed, although
James's practical politics were essentially conciliatory, a thread of
suspicion of the crown's discretionary power runs through the sessions of this long parliament. The causes are hard to seek, but in all
probability men conscious of European trends towards enhanced
princely authority looked at James's Scottish background and saw in
the civil law practised there, and the institutional weakness of the
Scottish parliament, an elevated vision of kingly authority. Not
surprisingly in view of his hopes of union and his repeated remarks
about the royal dignity, many Englishmen suspected James of yearning for unEnglish ways. Their response was to assert that the common
law and the rights, especially to property, it protected were the
ancient 'inheritance' or 'birthright' of Englishmen, fully as inalienable as was the crown's prerogative. When impositions, which looked
suspiciously like the excise taxes on which so many European princes
had built, created the prospect of a potentially limitless non-
parliamentary revenue, lawyer-MPs like Whitelocke, William
Hakewill and Thomas Hedley proved capable of articulating long
and coherent constitutionalist objections.

The failure of the Great Contract marked a watershed in early-
Stuart politics. Those who came after Salisbury merely worked within
the limits of the prevailing system. Like Cranfield in the years around
1620 they might vainly try to give substance to the convention that the
king's ordinary revenue sufficed for ordinary expenses; but nobody
strove to build the new relationship with parliament that Salisbury
had sought. Remarkably, neither was there much sign before the
1630s – and precious little even then – of any willingness to pursue
his alternative, and contradictory, strategy, of purposefully
exploiting the customs, with all the risks of a breach with parliament
that that brought. Salisbury's failure and his lack of support from the
throne must have dampened the ardour of other would-be reformers.

The crown's task therefore increasingly became survival rather than advance.

The immediate outcome of the failure of the Contract was scarcely division between crown and Commons, for with parliament dissolved politics once again centred on the court. And there the major event was the decline of Salisbury, who had angered James by dragging his revenue and prerogative onto the stage to no good end, and by permitting the attacks on the Scots. Confident he could check and balance any ensuing factionalism as he had in Scotland, James determined to let none succeed again to Salisbury's commanding position. Conveniently enough, it was at this time that he became deeply attached to a favourite, the Scot Robert Carr, in 1611 created Viscount Rochester and later earl of Somerset. For whatever the personal details, a favourite could be an asset for a monarch wishing to assert himself, and although the charming Carr was no intellectual match for many of those he dealt with he provided a valuable screen for his master.

The experiment did not prove a happy one for James, in part at least because he would not apply himself to business as his new regime required. But he was also unlucky in the scandals of the period. Again, some of these were his own responsibility, since in his first years he had rewarded servants by direct bounty, but with his resources exhausted his servants were forced back onto self-help. Unfortunately too, some courtiers had a knack for attracting ill-fame of other kinds. Newsletters and correspondence were soon to reveal a resurgence of that antipathy to a corrupt court that had marred the last years of Elizabeth.

The failure of the 1610 bid for a parliamentary revenue settlement meant that it was once again business as usual, and the first priority was raising money. The hallmark of James's later years was the 'projects' which betray the hand-to-mouth finances of the crown. Salisbury had of course during his primacy himself examined various schemes, most of them abortive, but in the years after 1610 the attention devoted to projects intensified. Private individuals pestered courtiers, and courtiers the king, with splendid devices to benefit everybody – and not least the projector – and harm nobody. The seamy world on the fringes of court and City which fathered the projects was savagely satirized by Ben Jonson in *The Devil is an Asse*, and the discredit was unfortunately balanced by little gain for the king. The one significant exception was the invention and sale in 1611 of the hereditary title of baronet. Status-hungry gentlemen eagerly paid the asking-price of £1,095, and by 1614 baronetcies had brought in over £90,000. But the penurious James and his courtiers could not resist the temptation to sell as much as could be sold. With the promise of a fixed number ignored, the market was soon saturated and by 1622 the price had fallen to £220. The crown's role as the fountain of honour was cheapened, albeit briefly, and the vital concept of 'degree' called in question in jokes and gossip. Cynicism about the court grew.

Divisions at court compounded the cash crisis. Salisbury's decline saw Northampton and his nephew the earl of Suffolk challenge a looser group which comprised notably the earl of Pembroke, Ellesmere, Chief Justice Sir Edward Coke and the Calvinist George Abbot, appointed archbishop of Canterbury in 1611 after James's fears of militant puritanism had subsided. The growing factionalism steadily hemmed James in. Salisbury's unlamented death in 1612 left the key offices of lord treasurer, secretary of state and master of the wards vacant, but in his anxiety to avoid polarizing the court further James gave the wards to a political nonentity and left the other posts empty, putting the treasury under a body of commissioners and declaring he would be his own secretary with Somerset's help. These were unfortunate years, for the two-year vacancy in the two greatest political offices loosened control over the whole administration. Extravagance and corruption grew. Moreover, the reputed homosexual relation of king and favourite enhanced the court's reputation for immorality; the occasional air of drunken incapacitation which James acquired from his disease of porphyria, which affects the central nervous system, did not help.

Although the court rivalries centred on patronage and perquisites, contemporaries did detect other differences. While Pembroke and his friends urged a fresh approach to parliament, the Howards, not without justification after the experience of 1610, questioned whether any parliamentary grant would be worth the concessions and frustrations it would entail. The groups also disagreed on foreign policy at a time when Europe seemed once again about to descend into war. Pembroke, Abbot and their allies concluded that the safest course was to reforge Elizabeth's ties to the Dutch and to prepare for war with Spain. The Howard connections' preference for peace probably owed less to the notorious crypto-Catholicism of several of their number than to a proper sense of the cost of war.

James for his part inclined towards the views of the Howards, for he still clung to his hopes of acting as the peace-maker of Europe. He saw Spain as over-extended, involved on three continents, anxious for peace, and also impressively regal in its ways; conversely, he disliked the Dutch not only as distasteful republicans but also as dangerous trading rivals. But in the 1610s his dreams were threatened by events.

The assassination in 1610 of the moderate Henry IV of France exposed once again the dangers of intransigent Catholicism, whose international dimensions were revealed the following year in a marriage alliance between France and Spain; at the same time renewed religious war in Germany seemed likely over the succession dispute to the strategic duchy of Cleves-Julich. Reluctantly, James allowed himself to be edged off the fence into a marriage alliance between his daughter Elizabeth and Frederick, ruler of the Rhineland Palatinate and leader of the German Protestant Union. At such a delicate moment the ever-canny James shied away from appointing obviously partisan figures to key domestic offices.

Zealous protestants found little cause for rejoicing in the diplomatic implications of Elizabeth's 1613 wedding. Sunk in mourning already for the death the previous year of James's elder son, Prince Henry – an aggressive figure who, had he lived, might have led England down a very different road in the ensuing European struggle – they soon gained new occasion for despondency. In hope of detaching James from the protestant alliance, Madrid in 1613 dispatched a new ambassador, don Diego Sarmiento, better known by his later title of Count Gondomar. The close friendship he built up with the king, which came with an increasingly eager pursuit of a Spanish bride for James's second, and now only, son Charles, has often been taken as evidence of the ailing king's gullibility. Yet like so many verdicts on James this is unfair, for he had no firm alliance from which he had to be pried loose. He was eager to revert to his pacific policy if the Catholic world would allow him, and in 1614 gladly helped mediate the Cleves-Julich dispute. A Spanish marriage – of which he had long dreamed as an appropriately grand match for his eldest son – might balance the Palatine connection and allow him to mediate the larger European quarrel. Accordingly, he slowly allowed the Howards to fill some of the political void left by Salisbury's death. The growing public exaltation at this time of the memory of Queen Elizabeth, whose death had been little mourned, was no coincidence.

Much of the black legend about the Howards has been discredited by modern scholarship. Although Northampton in particular was a crypto-Catholic the clan was by no means the lackey of Spain – all politicians accepted gratuities, from Spain or anybody else, since salaries failed so badly to keep pace with the standards of display expected. Nor were the Howards altogether corrupt leeches on the public revenues. That Thomas Howard, earl of Suffolk and lord treasurer, could eventually be tried for corruption indicates that at least some thought he had overstepped a line; but it was a much more difficult line to draw than it is now when office is seen largely as a

matter of public service. Furthermore, self-interest did not rule
wholly supreme. All things being equal, an office would not be given
to an incompetent, whose performance would reflect on his patron.
Northampton accordingly employed some able and open-minded
advisers, and had for his own part to prove that he could benefit the
king. In an unsuccessful bid for the lord treasurership in 1613, Northampton stressed his reformist credentials by introducing to James and
to public life the former London merchant Lionel Cranfield, who was
to become the leading reform figure of the next decade.

Nevertheless, the Howard years saw the nadir of Jacobean scandal
and indebtedness, and did damage the court. Northampton's religion
and the high prerogative views for which he was notorious inspired
grave distrust; worse, the manner of the clan's accession to power
hardened the growing sense that the court was dangerously corrupt.
James's favourite, Somerset, fell in love with Suffolk's daughter, the
rather tarnished Frances Howard, who was at the time married, in
mutual unhappiness, to the young earl of Essex, son of Elizabeth's
tragic favourite. Hugely scandalous divorce proceedings on the
grounds of Essex's impotence were eagerly followed in 1613 in manuscript newsletters in country houses across England, as James pressed
and packed a tribunal of shame-faced ecclesiastics to bring in the right
verdict. And when Suffolk gained the treasurership in 1614 the palace
he built for himself at Audley End, largely financed from official
balances, drew from James the appropriate but fatally lax comment
that it was too big for a king but big enough for a lord treasurer. Not
surprisingly, the annual ordinary deficit under Suffolk ran at the
alarming level of £160,000; the debt therefore steadily mounted.

These years brought few compensating financial departures, for
like all their rivals at court the Howards were daunted by the scale of
the problems. Fear of the reaction of a parliament which most
assumed must eventually come deterred them from looking further to
the customs – an investigatory commission in 1613 listed raising customs duties 'to the highest value' under the heading 'Projects not
likely to prove well'. But the equal helplessness of those courtiers who
advocated a parliament was made clear by the proposals of the new
attorney-general, Sir Francis Bacon, and of Sir Henry Neville. Despite their own considerable experience in the lower house, and despite
Neville's role as a critic of the government in 1610 – a role which
vividly illustrated the fluidity of politics – neither had any solution to
the burning question of impositions, nor anything other than minor
sops to offer to the Commons in return for supply. Bankrupt of ideas
and nearly bankrupt of funds, James drifted reluctantly towards
another parliament in the spring of 1614.

Preparations for a parliament were handicapped by the king's continuing disinclination to fill vacant offices. His eventual choice as secretary of state of the diplomat Sir Henry Winwood, an aggressive protestant but hardly a front-rank figure, was probably part of his old policy of playing off the factions, since the other secretary, Sir Thomas Lake, was a Howard client. Winwood was only appointed a week before the parliament, and the delay was unfortunate, since it left the new secretary too little time to familiarize himself with his new office to act effectively as the crown's chief spokesman in the Commons. A more serious consequence of the divisions around the throne was that others did make preparations.

The confusion at court is almost, though not quite, a sufficient explanation of the disaster of 1614. As usual, there was no conciliar campaign to pack parliament, and the composition of the Commons was much like any other. But with Northampton sinking into his final illness Suffolk and Somerset determined on disruption, probably as part of their court struggle against Pembroke, the parliament's leading supporter. They encouraged reports that someone was 'undertaking' to manage the lower house, and the newly assembled Commons soon put together the rumours of undertaking with an isolated case of electoral intimidation by a councillor, Sir Thomas Parry, at Stockbridge in Hampshire. Fears of an attempt to subvert and destroy parliament took vivid shape, and the hapless Winwood and the few supporters of the king's requests for supply lost control. Although a contrite Neville eventually stilled the uproar over 'undertakers' by pointing to the innocence of his own proposals, the move to substantive business did not improve tempers. MPs deplored the relaxation in the laws against recusants which had come with friendship for Spain, and could not be deflected by Winwood's obvious sympathy for their protests. The cries that good laws without enforcement were pointless expose the limited role of parliament in government – and many feared that that role might become still smaller in view of the government's systematic use of impositions. The 1614 debates on these reveal some highly sophisticated political thought. One member took up the theme of inexorable aggrandizement glanced at in the 1604 Apology when he gloomily held that there were '3 sorts of kingdoms: elective, successive, and tyrannical, and accordingly did each extend his [sic] prerogative.' In the heat of debate Sir Edwin Sandys spoke the unspeakable when, pointing to the ominous French parallel, he warned, 'Nay, so do our impositions increase in England as it is come to be almost a tyrannical government in England.'

But the Commons were not parliament. Only the support of the Lords could allow protests against impositions to emerge from the lower house, let alone reach the statute book, and here the Commons stuck. When the Commons learned that Bishop Neile had branded

the Commons as seditious for disputing something adjudged a prerogative of the crown, a ruinous confrontation over privileges developed between the two Houses. Although some MPs strove vainly to
overcome their colleagues' exasperation at James's spendthrift ways
in the hope that he might once again be 'in love with parliaments', the
angry king saw no chance of supply and hastily dissolved this 'Addled
Parliament'. It had done nothing, other than to turn James yet further against parliaments.

The failure of parliament did not disappoint everybody. The
Howards were at last able to gain their reward in the lord treasurership and mastership of the wards; since they also controlled access to
the king through Somerset their position was assured. They were,
however, no nearer a solution to the unending problem of money.
    James's decision to sacrifice the parliament rather than impositions
can hardly be faulted financially after the experience of 1610, but the
immediate future was bleak. He found only the most temporary solution in a disingenuous appeal to popular sentiment: pointing to the
Catholic threat, James demanded of all the taxpayers as an extraordinary 'benevolence' the subsidy the Commons had allegedly
intended to give before the dissolution. The nation's compliance in
this underlined remarkably parliament's key function as the arena
for the expression of dissent. Whatever his views once elected, a
gentleman in his locality had to submit to commands from 'above'.
The alarmed constitutionalism of many in the 1614 parliament did
not therefore herald polarization in the country. But the council too
prized harmony, and the nation's respect for the will of the ruler was
not misplaced. In yet another intense quest for revenue in 1615 the
councillors agreed that restoration of the king's finances could only
come through parliament, and to that end, most urged concessions on
impositions. But Lord Chancellor Ellesmere and Lord Treasurer Suffolk were pessimistic: the matter of right and power was involved, and
Suffolk 'knew not how it could be salved'. Whatever the wishes of the
council, uncomfortable ideological positions were being dug under
pressure of events, as they had been in the Commons: the importance
of impositions was apparent to all. Nevertheless, hopes of conciliation
survived, and the council shied away from imposing provocative new
customs duties as it had in 1613. James plumped instead for the
greatest 'project' of all.
    Cockayne's Scheme is one of the classic cases of ill-conceived gov-
ernment intervention in the economy. William Cockayne, a London
alderman, was an Eastland Company merchant trading to the Baltic.
Like many others he wished to break into the lucrative Merchant
Adventurers' trade in unfinished broadcloth without staking the large

capital required by the company, and backed up his bribes to courtiers and king with plausible arguments. The labour-intensive finishing stages of cloth manufacture, a speciality of the Netherlands, added half or more of the final cost of the product. If the finishing were done in England then not only would employment be generated, but more money would be brought into the country; such reasoning had for some time led the crown to back the diffusion of dye crops in England. The treasury could also expect increased customs revenues if finished rather than unfinished cloth were sold abroad. Cockayne therefore proposed that the export of unfinished cloth should be phased out; to ensure this, the projectors should take over the Merchant Adventurers' privileges. But the scheme rested on false assumptions of English domination of wool and cloth production. Although cloth exports had surged by 25 per cent since the 1604 peace with Spain, English broadcloth was a traditional and therefore high-cost industry. Newer centres were starting up in the lower-wage areas of eastern Europe, often using Spanish wool. By the end of James's first decade merchants were warning that the north European markets were clogged and that cloths were harder to sell, especially as clothiers tried to cut their costs by reducing quality. Without reforms in production any tampering was likely to be dangerous.

It soon became clear that the Cockayne group was far more interested in itself selling unfinished cloth to the old markets than in establishing a finishing industry. The real disaster of the project then emerged. Cloth production, hingeing on the annual wool clip, was seasonal; the merchants bought large quantities from the clothiers in a short period, to be sold gradually. Considerable mercantile capital was thus tied up. But the new company was under-capitalized and could not afford to keep its limited funds inactive as the more creditworthy Merchant Adventurers had done. Inevitably, it was unable to purchase enough cloths, and unemployment soared in the clothing counties. By late 1616 exports through London were one-third down on 1614, the Dutch were finding new suppliers, and the king's customs on cloth had fallen correspondingly. To the relief of most concerned the old Merchant Adventurers were re-established in December 1616, though at further cost to themselves and consquently higher prices. Although by 1618 London broadcloth exports were back to their 1603 level, never again did they reach their 1614 heights. It was an object lesson in the risks to the economy of the government intervention which all thought proper.

The saga of scandal was, unfortunately, not limited to the Cockayne scheme. In 1615 the Howard edifice began to crumble, for the family's rivals, rather inappropriately led by Archbishop Abbot, introduced a beautiful youth named George Villiers to the king.

James was willing to be distracted, for the favourite, now lord chamberlain, had been taking their intimacy too much for granted. Sensing a change – as a Somerset supporter punned bitterly, 'The cat has found a new tail to play with' – the court promptly broke out into a new factiousness. When a rumour was heard that Frances Howard's marriage to Somerset had been eased by the murder of the latter's disapproving secretary Sir Thomas Overbury, Secretary Winwood and Chief Justice Sir Edward Coke pounced on the chance to destroy their enemies. Coke's investigations soon established a case against the new countess of Somerset and forced Somerset to part from James in October 1615. The following winter saw the scandal of the century go to trial, though Somerset shied away from fulfilling his threat to expose James's dirty linen as well as his own. Enormously relieved, the king commuted the death sentence on the couple, although Frances Howard's assistants in poisoning Overbury suffered from the prejudices of hierarchy and went to the scaffold.

The Howard debacle seemed to offer the chance of a major change at court. In 1616 the anti-Spanish group secured the release from the Tower, where he had been confined since the fevered plotting of 1603–4, of Sir Walter Raleigh, that doughty warrior against Spain. But the disunity of the Howards' enemies temporarily allowed the rest of the clan to survive Somerset's fall and protected James from pressure to change his policies further. In particular, the king resented Sir Edward Coke's excess of zeal, which had brought scandal uncomfortably close and besmirched the image of crown and court. Coke's professional rivals seized the opportunity.

Coke's chief claim to fame lies in his passionate commitment on the bench to the supremacy of the common law, a commitment which at times irritated the king who put him there. It is tempting to trace Coke's aggressiveness back to rivalries between the courts. Many common lawyers practising in the central courts feared that their position and their fees were being undermined by the economic changes and increasingly fluid land market of the sixteenth century, for which the outmoded precedents and procedures of the common law provided no remedy. The main beneficiary of the growth in business was the more flexible equity court of chancery, headed by Coke's enemy Ellesmere. But issues of principle were also involved. In the attempt to rescue the common law Coke and his fellow judges often wrenched precedents and statutes out of context; a good example is Coke's deployment of Magna Carta to damn commercial monopolies in his comments on the *Darcy v. Allen* playing-card case of 1603. To justify this bold approach – so necessary in a legal system based on custom as well as on statute – Coke and his colleagues articulated a philosophy of the 'artifical reason' of the common law. In a sophisticated version of the ancient notion that law was not merely custom but was also immanent in the universe, Coke argued that the common law, as law, embodied reason. The judges, skilled in the 'artifical reason' of the law, could see in the profusion of cases coherence and underlying principles.

Coke attempted both on the bench and in his immensely influential *Reports* and *Institutes* to make sense of the maze of legal precedents and to give the common law an appearance of certainty, the greatest desideratum to most contemporaries. That attempt seemed challenged by chancery. As keeper of the conscience of the king, who was the fountain of justice, the chancellor dispensed equity, by now a fairly defined blend of discretion and common law rules. In certain circumstances Lord Chancellor Ellesmere felt able to relieve parties against whom the common law courts had decided, and so seemed to strike at both the certainty of legal remedy and the coherence of the law. The assertiveness as chancellor of Ellesmere, though a common lawyer himself, drove the common law judges to confront the rival courts, hurling writs of prohibition barring further proceedings in cases which could be tried at common law. It was no wonder that Ellesmere and Archbishop Abbot – whose ecclesiastical court of high commission had also been challenged – joined eagerly with Sir Francis Bacon, Coke's jealous rival, when the chief justice overreached himself in a direct attack on chancery's jurisdiction in 1616.

The alliance against Coke succeeded because James himself had grown impatient. Repeatedly when on the bench Coke had treated the crown's discretionary powers with some reserve, and had not been cowed when in 1613 James kicked him upstairs from the main civil court of common pleas to the more prestigious but less remunerative king's bench. Coke's anxiety to preserve the judges' independence of the crown came to a head in the so-called '*commendams*' affair over ecclesiastical patronage in 1616, where he refused to swear to consult the king beforehand in cases involving the prerogative. Coke's belief that the law arose from the customs of the people over the generations, and not from the king's will, cost him his job. His dismissal, the first of a judge in over thirty years, ushered in a period of increasing royal pressure on the bench: in Charles's reign two other chief justices, Crew and Heath, and one chief baron of the exchequer court, Walter, were to follow Coke into the wilderness. James himself, suspicious of the role of common lawyers in the attack on impositions, lectured the judges on the grace of kings, and was echoed by Ellesmere and by the latter's successor as chancellor, Bacon. Judicial care for the king's interest was certainly justified by ancient convention, but the law was also supposed to protect the subject's rights. Too close a political identification of bench and crown could only bring the former into disrepute.

The upheavals at court did not end with the fall of Coke. Although James loved to balance the factions and thus preserve his own freedom of action, to others politics was an all-or-nothing business. Suffolk and his following had watched with disquiet as George Villiers cemented his position in James's bosom with his ennoblement in 1617 as earl and then marquis of Buckingham. Seizing the opportunity presented by the absence that year of king and favourite on the first royal visit to Scotland since 1603, the Howards schooled and beautified William Monson, the son of a client, to catch James's eye. They failed, but Buckingham noticed the threat and concluded that he must break his rivals.

Charges to level against the Howards were not lacking. The most visible fruit of their years in power had been mounting debts and burgeoning scandals. The one successful revenue device of Suffolk's treasurership, the sale of peerages, had worsened the odour surrounding the court. Marketing baronetcies had at first been unobjectionable, since they had been sold to men who on the whole warranted recognition and since there had been no old baronets to offend. But when in 1615–16 the list of vendible commodities was extended to include baronies at £10,000 apiece the vital concept of honour was sullied. The old nobility was understandably affronted when in 1616 a man twice indicted for sodomy, recently pardoned for murder and excluded from the commission of the peace for his delinquencies was created Lord Stanhope. Equally startling was the increase in the number of earls, from twenty-seven in 1615 to sixty-five in 1628. Although the most blatant courtier profiteering from the sale of peerages occurred during Buckingham's hegemony after 1618, the obloquy for its earliest manifestations fell on Suffolk. Buckingham was able to appear as the apostle of reform and attract to himself those like Cranfield and Bacon who hoped to purge the worst extravagance and corruption.

The fall of Suffolk before star chamber charges of embezzlement brought the reputation of James's court to its lowest point. The case against him, although political in origin, was damning. Like any treasurer he had had abundant opportunities for taking bribes, since with the crown so deeply in debt creditors competed fiercely for early payment. But in accepting £1,000 p.a. from the officers of the army in Ireland who had vainly hoped that their troops might be paid he had gone too far. By 1619 a contemporary could note with gusto that the Tower was occupied by a former lord chamberlain (Somerset), a lord treasurer (Suffolk), a secretary of state (Suffolk's client, Lake, who also fell in a massive sex scandal), and a captain of the gentlemen pensioners, or commander of the ceremonial attendants at court (Suffolk's son Lord Walden).

The sordid tale of corruption and decay which bulks so large in gentlemen's diaries and correspondence does not, however, justify those historians who have dismissed the Jacobean years as a steady decline into the crisis of the next reign. In the crucial financial field such a characterization is accurate enough. But elsewhere James's government continued to show inclinations to reform.

The king's intense interest in the judiciary in the summer of 1616, which led him for the first time to appear in the court of star chamber, reinvigorated the council's long-standing campaign to improve the efficiency of local government. The judges on their assize circuits were instructed, as they had been periodically since 1605, to note the performance of JPs. This time an extensive pruning of the commission of the peace followed in 1616–17. Furthermore, renewed tension in Europe, especially after 1618, caused the council to abandon its long unconcern for the militia; the spreading deployment of the more up-to-date, and costly, musket testifies to the success of governmental pressure.

The effort to consolidate and improve local administration was coupled with signs of a practical paternalism. At the end of the decade the council vainly urged JPs to avert dearth by establishing county granaries for the poor, while the new chief justice, Sir Henry Montague, urged parish overseers of the poor to subsidize the growing of the fashionable root crops.* More successful was the council's bid to curb the unpopular use of paid informers. Protests in the Commons in 1610 against one of the worst sharks, Sir Stephen Proctor, who had been granted a patent to suppress blackmail by informers and had then gone into business on his own account, had been reinforced by the council's anxiety to remove impediments to the textile trade in the aftermath of the Cockayne Scheme. Under the stimulus of Bacon, who was increasingly concerned about the government's image, official discouragement of actions brought by informers in the central courts soon spread. By 1619 actions by informers in the key central court of the exchequer were at one-sixth of the level they had been at in 1613, and continued to fall thereafter. The parliamentary campaigns of 1621 and 1624, which in the latter year barred most informers from the central courts, reinforced and prevented the reversal of a policy the council had already initiated.

*Norfolk and Norwich Record Office, Walsingham Mss. xvii/2, De Grey Letter Book.

The political prospects thus seemed much brighter after Suffolk's fall and as Buckingham consolidated his position in 1618–19. Even James now seemed moved. He had forced London to lend for his Scottish journey of 1617, and his default on both interest and principal ruined his credit in the City until the end of his reign. By mid-1618 the debt stood at the record level of about £900,000. The king's embarrassment encouraged those at court who saw retrenchment – ostensibly more feasible, and certainly more popular politically, than the alternative of discovering new revenues – as the only way to avert bankruptcy.

A first step was to put the treasury once again under commissioners, in the belief that they were more likely to resist temptation than a single lord treasurer had been. But the key to reform seemed to be Buckingham, who coveted a patriotic image and who yet had few of the patronage ties to officials which might deter him from stern measures. Commissioners appointed for the navy when the favourite replaced the ageing Charles Howard, earl of Nottingham, as lord admiral in 1618 uncovered a saga of corruption similar to that at the treasury. At one point there had been a mere seven ships in commission, while contractors, desperate for payment, paid retainers to officals and in return marked up the price of their supplies sometimes by 3,000%. This sad decline from Elizabethan days owed much to James himself who had twice refused to pursue Northampton's jealous complaints against the kinsman he hated. But now, thanks in particular to the diligence of John Coke, a future secretary of state, the commissioners both cut costs and built more ships. In the royal household too, where Cranfield took over as master of the wardrobe in 1618, economies were achieved. By rigorous accounting, checking how many cuts of meat could be had from an ox and ensuring competitive pricing, the former merchant trimmed the waste significantly; in the wardrobe he reduced expenditures by more than half. The combined savings, at the treasury, in the navy and in the household, were probably in the region of £120,000 p.a. Meanwhile expenditures continued to rise.

Even had determined support from James been available, there remained insuperable obstacles to further reforms which might have balanced the books. Only the revolutionary upheaval of mid-century was to provide favourable conditions for administrative reform, for to eliminate official corruption would have necessitated raising salaries, which would in turn have entailed a dramatic, and improbable, restructuring of government. The economist Maynard Keynes was undoubtedly correct when he argued that in many societies corruption is the most efficient form of taxation.

Furthermore, the strength of will of the reformers can be doubted.

To attack the pockets or jobs of courtiers was always a dangerous undertaking; and the reformers were themselves subject to temptation. The disastrous showing in the wars of the 1620s of the ordnance, or provisioners of artillery, was facilitated by Cranfield's readiness to halt his investigations once he had extorted land from the officers. Equally, the attacks in the parliament of 1621 on the delays and expense of justice in chancery suggest how little Bacon had done in his own court, to which he was appointed in 1617. The good intentions he trumpeted seem to have produced little more than self-righteous and unsolicited advice from the sidelines – the parallel with his vaunted scientific activity is striking. But most important of all, Buckingham in power did not regard attacks on patronage in the same light as he had when rising. Unlike Somerset, he was surrounded by a grasping tribe of relatives, provision for whom was both expensive and disreputable – as Cranfield and Sir Edward Coke amongst others discovered, advancement required a marriage alliance with the favourite's family. Moreover, the exhaustion of the royal treasury meant that the Villiers clan had to look for other support. Not only did the sale of titles increase, but a renewed flood of patents testified to the king's anxiety to reward Buckingham's friends as well as his own.

By the summer of 1620 the reverberations could be heard in the country. A public sermon to the assize judges in Norwich protested at the extortionate ways of the court, and a gentleman in Staffordshire reported that 'the country is much oppressed, so much, that . . . it is a grief to hear the cry of the poor: not a week is there, that some payments are not made, and what becomes of the money the Lord knows.'* Politically more dangerous were the resentments of lawyers and gentlemen as patentees were given arbitrary powers of enforcement, and as they trespassed on the traditional preserves of JPs through such patents as those for the licensing of inns and alehouses. But little would have disturbed the narrower world of court politics had not events overseas confronted James's dynastic and pacific policies with ruin.

*Folger Library, Washington, Ms. L.a.402

5 Wars, Parliaments and Buckingham 1621–1629

In the course of the 1620s the English polity was transformed, partly as a result of the succession to the throne of a man of very different outlook from that of his father, but partly too as a result of war. For the demands occasioned by war imposed further strains on assumptions of balance and reciprocity which, as we have seen, had already come into question during the Jacobean peace; while Charles's unyielding personality and his emerging religious tastes caused those demands to be construed by some otherwise than they might have been. Worst of all, the war that broke out was one which many insisted on interpreting as a religious war. It thus injected a dangerously ideological element into a body politic already disordered by the theme of corruption.

In 1618 the fuse was lit that sparked off the long-expected European conflagration. In that year Bohemian protestants rebelled against their elected Habsburg king, the future emperor Ferdinand, and then invited James's ambitious son-in-law, Frederick of the Palatinate, to accept their crown. The challenge was not one that the Habsburgs could ignore, but the key question was whether the king of Spain would go to the aid of his Austrian cousin – since the twelve years' truce between Spain and the Netherlands was due to expire in 1621 a German struggle could easily turn into a European one.

The crisis elicited very divergent English responses. To avert the destructive horrors of a pan-European war for religion James more urgently sought for his son Charles the Spanish bride whom the king had long seen as the foundation-stone of interdenominational harmony. Meanwhile, he berated Frederick for his intervention, and protested his own good faith to Madrid; as evidence of the latter he even executed in 1618 the long-condemned foe of Spain, Sir Walter Raleigh. There were soon rumours – at least some well-founded – that courtiers were learning Spanish and their ladies converting to Catholicism in anticipation. Yet the drift towards Madrid conflicted with the legacy of the long Elizabethan wars, which had contrived to define English patriotism as gut hostility to Catholicism and to

Spain. While James in 1618 could address the pope as 'holy father' when urging a joint mediation effort, Archbishop Abbot joined many of James's subjects in foreseeing the apocalypse in the gathering storm: 'The kings of the earth . . . shall now tear the whore [Rome] and make her desolate.' Incomprehension grew as James's friendship with Spain seemed to threaten his religion and his daughter – in the summer of 1620 Spanish troops entered the Palatinate. Nemesis came to Frederick that autumn when disasters in the Palatinate were matched by a crushing Imperial victory outside Prague, at the battle of the White Mountain. Frederick and his English queen fled into a life-long exile.

The catastrophe narrowed James's options as he had feared. However strongly he wished to succour his children – and indeed honour demanded he do so – the campaign of retrenchment had not yet yielded enough to fund the diplomatic efforts the crisis had forced him into, let alone any more forceful action. He was accordingly, and with manifest reluctance, driven in the winter of 1620–1 to turn to his people, in hope that parliamentary pressure for a protestant war might yet moderate Madrid. But his unease about the domestic response to the apparent collapse of European protestantism was clear in the proclamation against public talk of affairs of state he issued on the eve of the parliament. Almost as disconcerting was the fact that England was in 1621 slipping into the deepest depression of the century. Currency manipulations in the Baltic states had occasioned a drain of English currency as damaging as the devaluations' other consequence, the overpricing of English goods abroad. Coin, the 'driving money' to contemporaries, was essential when credit facilities were so primitive, and the catastrophic shortage created both economic bottlenecks and human hardship as people found themselves without the cash to pay for goods, even before falling exports increased unemployment. Any demand for taxes was bound to create alarm in parliament.

The history of any early-modern parliament provides invaluable insights into the state of what can without too much exaggeration be called public opinion. However unrepresentative the franchise the 'political nation', the local governors and their connections, was represented; furthermore, such men had to pay heed to those below them on whom their influence rested, all the more so in a time of depression. The parliament of 1621 proved that the long intermission of parliaments had not occasioned the build-up of dangerous political pressures. The polls were quiet, and the rivalries fought out overwhelmingly local, underlining once again the importance of parliament itself as the stage for debate. The number of courtiers in the Commons changed little overall, though some experienced difficulties in the more populous and prestigious county constituencies. If even the freeholder voters of metropolitan Middlesex preferred local gentry candidates to privy councillors on the grounds of the inaccessibility of the latter, the suspicion of distant Yorkshiremen that Secretary of State Calvert might be too unresponsive to local interests is hardly surprising. The Howard years had not been without effect.

Nevertheless, it took later storms to harden disquiet about scandal and corruption into outright discontent. The most noticeable feature of the members of the 1621 parliament is their conciliatory disposition. They listened carefully to the king's warning that if he were to secure peace he must prepare for war. Although the hints that their response would shape James's attitude to future parliaments failed to draw from them the blank cheque James dreamed of, the Commons did quickly vote two subsidies, or about £140,000. The sum would help cover immediate costs, and give substance to James's efforts to persuade Madrid that there was support for war. He had good reason to be pleased, since the Commons correctly foresaw hostile constituency reactions to the grant when there was so little money to be had locally. Their acquiescence is therefore as great a testimony to their desire to please as is their avoidance of the question of impositions when they turned to investigate the depression. The Commons realized as much as had the council in its revenue debates of 1615 that impositions could wreck a parliament: neither was eager for conflict.

The other prime cause of present woe, the shortage of money, presented fewer dangers. Monopolies and patents were a tempting scapegoat for everybody, and the attack on the patentees provides the best measure of this parliament. The campaign should not be seen as part of a developing confrontation between 'government' and 'opposition' or 'court' and 'country'. True, suspicion of some courtiers was evident both at the polls and in parliament itself. But many courtiers eagerly seconded country complaints against patentees in the hope of harassing private enemies, and the involvement of such court rivalries gave the parliamentary campaign its staying-power and success. Thus, while the attack on the patentees, which brought the downfall of Lord Chancellor Bacon, has often been seen as a stage in the growth of parliamentary control over the executive, at every point crucial initiatives came from within the court. Two privy councillors, Cranfield and Sir Edward Coke, redirected the complaints against minor offenders onto the 'referees', the king's legal and financial officers, who had approved the patents; in so doing the two councillors led the hunt after their private rivals, Lord Chancellor Bacon and Lord Treasurer Mandeville (formerly Lord Chief Justice Montague). And it was Coke who provided the means of destruction when he reminded the Lords of their long-disused judicial powers.

The attitude of the king is as revealing. James refused to intervene when Cranfield and Coke advanced the charge that Bacon had accepted bribes on the bench, for he insisted on the divine origins of the justice he and his servants administered. Bacon therefore paid the penalty for James's conviction of the moral, rather than the partisan, character of the political world. A similar commitment to the principle of harmony led the king to congratulate Coke for his demonstration of the Lords' powers. What was to be refined in later cases as the process of impeachment, unknown since 1450, thus emerged under the guidance of a privy councillor and with the blessing of the king. Equally revealing was James's replacement of the conciliatory, if politically ineffective, Bacon as head of chancery with an equally conciliatory cleric, John Williams, bishop of Lincoln. But although the attack on the patentees is no story of constitutional confrontation we should not assume that the court took all the initiatives. The hunt for patentees and referees, and the parliamentary support for impeachment, indicated both disquiet at the way the country had been governed in recent years and a sense – shared by Coke – that parliament was a necessary purgative.

However explosive its ending, the brief second session of the 1621 parliament does little to shake our estimate of the first. When members met again in November they harkened as the council once again turned them towards foreign policy, despite their anxiety to proceed with a confused mass of local concerns. Though fears had been voiced that 'we that go home may be made subjects of the people's fury, if not of disgrace', for having granted taxes and obtained no return in the form of beneficial statutes, members willingly set their duty to the king above that to their constituencies. But they showed some reluctance to become entangled in a European land war. This was to prove fateful for parliament and, ultimately, for the crown. It has led some historians to conclude that MPs were wilfully blind to reality when they protested in 1621 and again in 1624 their readiness to hazard their all for Frederick, his wife Elizabeth and the protestant cause, and yet steadfastly refrained from opening their pockets. But recent verdicts, that parliament was no longer a useful tool when it failed to provide for the wars which were its traditional duty to fund, are too harsh. MPs throughout the 1620s could validly question *which war*.

While James and Buckingham had been amusing themselves in the country for much of the summer and autumn of 1621 most councillors had become convinced that only by war could the Palatinate be regained. But despite the Spanish intervention no councillor would commit himself on the question of whether the war would be with Spain, for James had made his reluctance to engage with Spain too apparent. For their part, the baffled MPs knew only that Spain's life-blood flowed in the annual treasure-fleets from the New World, and remembered the Elizabethan privateering successes. When they heard councillors forecast that a Palatinate campaign would cost £1M. a year they understandably preferred the verdict of Sir Walter Raleigh in his *History of the World* that £200,000 p.a. would make the king of Spain 'swim in his own channel'. There was considerable support in the council too for the view that an Anglo-Dutch attack on Spain in the Low Countries and at sea would prove more effective as well as cheaper than a land war. Some MPs can be accused of sheer irresponsibility in the fiscal debates of the 1620s; nevertheless, the Commons' conduct also stemmed from a respectable, though flawed, strategic vision.

The immediate dilemma seemed to resolve itself when Sir George Goring, a known client of Buckingham, appeared to declare in the Commons for war with Spain. Goring's motion, which was certainly made with higher approval, probably aimed to elicit a parliamentary threat for use as a bargaining-counter against Spain. But the house was not well-suited to the consideration of subtle signals: it had not been fully briefed and it contained too many protestants fearful of the religious consequences should prince Charles marry a Spanish Catholic. Instead it called abruptly for preparations for war and, logically enough, for an end to the Spanish match negotiations. James reacted furiously to what he took as an attack on his dearest, dynastic, prerogative. Threatening to arrest over-bold members, he reminded the Commons once more that they held their privileges of the mere grace of kings.

James's reassertion of the position he had taken in 1604 at last brought constitutional issues to the fore. He provoked the Commons to stop business and to compose a Protestation consciously echoing the 1604 Apology in its insistence that parliament was 'the ancient and undoubted birthright' of Englishmen, an institution which had a continuous history and which faced a long-standing threat. The parallels with 1604 are indeed very marked, for in both instances the king was genuinely misinformed of the Commons' aggressiveness. The house had in reality shown considerable self-restraint, over impositions and in their refusal to become involved in several potential privilege disputes. Putting that conciliatory record behind them, the drafters of the Protestation insisted that without the privilege of free speech there was little future for parliaments – self-restraint was one thing, forcible restraint quite another. But had the future of parliaments depended on a policy of confrontation that future would have been bleak, for the king possessed the power. James reacted melodramatically by ripping the Protestation out of the Commons' journal and more practically by arresting a handful of MPs after the dissolution.

The legacy left by the 1621 parliament was complex. The cause of war, strong in November, now seemed hopeless, since James had swung against the arguments of councillors like Pembroke and Abbot. His irritation with the Commons was increased by their readiness to let bills for social and economic regulation, and for extending lapsing statutes, die at the end of the session while they sought to vindicate their privileges; moreover, the Lords had seen abortive attacks on Buckingham and also friction between the old aristocracy and the recent creations. But the Lords at least had made some gains, for the rediscovery in impeachment of the peers' judicial role helped to give them a new sense of institutional purpose. More important, perhaps, the Commons' sense of their own function was also changing. Dissatisfaction with the state of the kingdom had given rise to standing committees for grievances and for courts of justice; that development points to a growing conviction that members were to act together as the 'physicians of the realm', rather than merely as the spokesmen of local interests.

The failure of the parliament left James where he had been, with no money and contemplating an economy for whose ills he had no remedy. As it became clear during 1622 that the harvest to be brought in that autumn would be bad the depression intensified. Grain prices soared in the spring, eroding domestic demand for cloth and so worsening unemployment – London's broadcloth exports in 1622 slumped to about 40 per cent of their 1618 level. The next harvest was even worse, and the crisis became a disaster. One Lincolnshire gentleman reported in 1623, 'There are many thousands in these parts who have sold all they have even to their bed-straw, and cannot get work to earn any money. Dog's flesh is a dainty dish, and found upon search in many houses.' In isolated areas in the north-west it became a genuine subsistence crisis, with the death-rate doubling or tripling during the famine; many died also amongst those forced onto the road by hardship.

The crisis exposed the contrast between the aspirations and the reality of government for the council had of course neither the means nor the information to mount large welfare schemes. It pressed JPs to ensure that the markets were supplied with grain for the poor, and strove to minimize unemployment by keeping clothiers in business, especially by protecting them from their creditors: here, as so often, the council's concern for social stability overrode its care for private property rights. The reports of scattered rioting in the clothing counties undoubtedly stimulated these short-term responses. But the council's efforts were anyway of less importance than the energy of many JPs locally and the rapidly rising expenditures on parish poor rates.

More signally, the intensity of the depression encouraged a search for longer-term solutions. From the beginning the baffled council had sought to consult outside opinion, willingly turning to parliament in 1621, to merchants, clothiers and JPs. In 1622 these efforts culminated in the establishment of a standing investigatory commission, the forerunner of the board of trade. Most of the advice offered was predictably impotent, and reflected the range of contemporary prejudice. Nevertheless, the crisis prompted the elaboration of a body of thought which later ages labelled 'mercantilist'. Most contemporaries – understandably preoccupied with a 'balance of treasure' when coin was so vital in the economy – fixed on the symptom, the shortage of coin, and demanded exchange controls against the outflow of money. But one commentator, Thomas Mun, saw what the prolongation of the industrial depression was to make many others realize by mid-century, that the problem was one of a 'balance of trade', and that remedy lay only in a surplus of exports over imports. Not surprisingly, official action did not end the depression.

The government's energies were anyway divided by the diplomatic crisis. The failure of the 1621 parliament had determined James to intensify his efforts for a Spanish match for his son Charles, and in the summer of 1622 the judges were ordered to relax the penal laws against Catholics. Protestant opinion had long foretold that the Spanish match would lead to this, and worse: as John Pym, the future parliamentary leader, put it apocalyptically in 1621, 'If the papists once obtain a connivance, they will press for a toleration; from thence to an equality; from an equality to a superiority; from a superiority to an extirpation of all contrary religions.' The apparent threat to protestantism posed by the Thirty Years War, when the domestic Calvinist consensus was already unravelling in the universities, aroused fears which challenged James's early confidence that puritanism was a paper tiger. Accordingly in 1622 new instructions ordered that sermons be confined to the most uncontroversial matters of faith and obedience. The ban on the preaching of militant protestantism when the relaxation of the laws and the prospect of a Catholic queen were bringing recusants into the open inevitably bred rumours of an imminent alteration of religion.

But the negotiations at Madrid did not prosper, for Philip IV, the devout new king of Spain, was more hostile than his father to protestant heresy. In his frustration the naive and awkward Prince Charles fancied himself in love with reports of Philip's sister, the Infanta, and assumed that his presence in Madrid would cut through all knots. He was encouraged in this by Buckingham, who wished to ensure his own position in the next reign; furthermore, the favourite, who was often politically realistic, may have calculated that action might at least resolve the negotiations which had for so long preoccupied James. In February 1623 the two young men therefore set off quixotically for Madrid, disguised with false beards and with merely a single servant. They left the king distraught and the court in an uproar.

The Spanish journey rapidly turned into a comedy of errors. Half the English court flocked to Madrid, though that famine-stricken city could scarcely support its own population. The informality of Buckingham, newly created a duke, shocked the etiquette-ridden Spanish court, and his mere presence affronted the resident English ambassador, the earl of Bristol. As Charles discovered that Spain was not anxious for a marriage he was reduced to climbing walls to catch sight of his beloved and to enlarging his offers of religious concessions, although with little return in Spanish aid over the Palatinate. James, desperate for the safety of his son and his favourite, willingly agreed to underwrite any terms reached in Madrid. As these came to include something like a public toleration for all Catholics, the suspicions rampant at Whitehall intensified the usual deadly game of court faction. Buckingham's clients repeatedly warned him over the summer of the domestic risks he ran, and these promptings reinforced the duke's exasperation with the Spanish. In time even the more obtuse Charles appreciated that Spain was merely temporizing, to forestall any English military action.

The failure of the Spanish journey brought a turning-point. The return of the prodigal pair without a bride generated the clearest expression of public opinion before the Restoration, and for a few exhilarating months the prince and duke were popular heroes. It was an experience which, to his puzzlement, Charles was not to enjoy again. But for the moment it eased their task of defending Buckingham at court, allowing them to blame their concessions on Spanish duress and to accuse Bristol, who posed the major threat to their account, of treacherously urging Catholicism on Charles. The concerns of the court soon swung from marriage to war. The adventurous Buckingham, who had been brought up in France, was now again openly pro-French and anti-Spanish, while Charles came to see war as vital for his honour. But although James was physically deteriorating with age and illness, he was still opposed in principle to war, all the more so since a war would require another distasteful parliament.

The task facing the prince and the duke was therefore to assure the king that a new parliament would be placid. They had powerful assets. Charles's promise of future favour meant that few courtiers and officials were anxious to oppose them. Furthermore, the welcome prospect of war with Spain made some of Buckingham's enemies, particularly Pembroke, waver. Buckingham and Charles also seem to have negotiated an understanding with some of the Commons' leaders of 1621, notably Sir Robert Phelips, Sir Edwin Sandys and Sir Edward Coke: if the king called a parliament and broke off the treaty with Spain, these new 'undertakers' were to ensure that the Commons would not pry into the dangerous topics of impositions or their privileges. Reassured but still protesting, James was persuaded to revert to his policy of 1621, of using parliamentary anger against Spain. He therefore summoned a new parliament for February 1624.

The prince and the duke clearly counted on the anti-Catholic mood in the country to do their work for them. The excitement of the autumn gave them reason for confidence, and the Catholic threat was certainly an issue in several elections. After the relaxation of the penal laws Catholicism was, however, no longer merely an international spectre, and when Sir Richard Grosvenor as sheriff of Cheshire harangued the county's voters it was to a domestic danger to religion that he pointed. Moreover, the continuing slump encouraged members to put the concerns of their communities before the call for what must be an expensive war.

Still more of an obstacle was the resistance of the king. After their experience in 1621 the Commons could hardly be blamed for fearing to tread with at best an equivocal invitation, and James in his opening speech merely asked parliament's advice on what to do about the negotiations with Spain. Urged on by Buckingham, the Commons promptly requested that the 'treaties' be broken off. But James also made it clear that any war must be in and for the Palatinate, an undertaking which the Commons had been warned in 1621 must cost £1M. p.a.; furthermore, he also demanded that his debts – which by now amounted to around £1M. – be paid first. It was an offer that was easy to refuse, and Charles and Buckingham had to work furiously to avert such a refusal. In moves that were to create colossal future problems for themselves, they handed out informal undertakings that a war would be the one the Commons' strategists favoured, the tried Elizabethan way of action at sea and perhaps an Anglo-Dutch diversionary campaign in Flanders. Once they had dissuaded James from requiring aid with his debts the way was clear for the undertakers to prevail on the Commons to offer slightly under £300,000.

The house then turned to the other famous work of this parliament, the impeachment for corruption of Lionel Cranfield, now Lord Treasurer Middlesex. There were murmurings of suspicion in the Commons of Cranfield's intention to impose further duties on trade, but the major reason for his downfall was private interest. No treasurer who sought to counter James's generosity by withholding payment of pensions could hope to be popular, least of all when he combined arrogance with humble origins. His chief pursuers in the Commons were Sir Edward Coke, who felt he should have been treasurer and whose perennial delight in political trials reveals an elemental blood lust, and Sir Edwin Sandys, who had long been embroiled with the treasurer over the management of the Virginia Company. But most important of all was Buckingham's determination to destroy an enemy. Middlesex had been the moving spirit in a bid to foist Arthur Brett, another handsome young man, on James while the duke was in Spain, and not even the king could protect his servant against the consequences of such boldness. Once again, court animosities were critical in the development of impeachments.

Not surprisingly, then, if we ask whether England had yet entered on the high road to civil war we encounter only confusion. Simple polarities are distorted by the role of Charles and Buckingham, who were in a very real sense the leading opponents of the king. And the Commons as a whole were reluctant to challenge the royal prerogative in foreign policy. The constitutional innovation contained in the subsidy act, the requirement that expenditures be accounted for to treasurers appointed by parliament, resulted from an agreement between James and Buckingham, who both sought to persuade the Commons to pass a subsidy grant suitable to their different purposes. A similar lack of constitutional aggression is evident in the major measure of 1624, the statute of monopolies. In their awareness that the crown must be able to govern, the Commons deliberately left a large loophole, which enabled Charles in the next reign to declare that patentees were either technological innovators, royal officers, or corporations, and thus outside the statute. If the monopolies act was the product of an opposition, then that opposition was constructive to the point of ineffectuality. Appropriately therefore, this parliament's legislative record was extremely productive. The seventy-three statutes (albeit many had been prepared in 1621) were a record for a single session, and seem a testimonial to harmony.

Yet we should not follow the recent tendency to write off the Commons as myopic and submissive. That the Commons talked so little of foreign policy owed as much to the eagerness of Buckingham's supporters to conceal the extent of his divergence from the king as to narrow-mindedness. And while the suggestion that supply be appropriated to parliamentary treasurers came from the court, it would scarcely have been needed but for the widespread suspicions of what James wanted the money for. Indeed, the warning given by Sir Benjamin Rudyerd, a prominent client of Pembroke, that 'if this parliament fail, it will be the last of parliaments', sounded a common theme. This house was as fearful of the future as had been that of 1610, and that fear led it to take novel steps to increase its own numbers, and the numbers of voters. Systematizing and justifying in these terms some haphazard 1621 moves, the Commons in 1624 created several new constituencies by 'restoring' defunct ancient ones. They addressed the problem of the electorate by extending the vote from the corporation to the freemen in some thirty towns in all in 1624 and 1628, as local disputes brought elections for adjudication to the house. Surprisingly radical arguments were used in the Commons in 1624, and still more in 1628, about the need to involve as many men as possible in elections to withstand the threat from the great to parliament's existence.

In 1624 the Elizabethan body politic appeared capable of lurching along in its old ways. A year later that was much less the case, and not merely because of the succession of the inflexible Charles to his father's throne. The aftermath of the 1624 parliament was to prove disastrous. The Commons had pointedly shied away from any involvement in the morass of Germany, and had granted James a large supply on what they took to be undertakings by Charles and Buckingham. But James, ailing though he was, was still king and still controlled policy; the intense frustrations of the young pair with that fact provide a plausible background for the subsequent rumours that Buckingham poisoned him. No naval war came, nor even a public breach with Spain. Instead, by the time of his death James was committed to an annual expenditure of £720,000, most of it in support of foreign land forces in the central European theatre: to James the Palatinate, not Spain, was the key. The distrust engendered by the breach of Charles's word was to ruin the new king's relations with his early parliaments.

The failure of the Spanish match left Charles needing a bride of appropriate grandeur and with an appropriate dowry. France was the logical provider, all the more so since it was traditionally anti-Habsburg. The latter consideration was vital to Charles and Buckingham who recognized that only a Catholic ally, averting any prospect of religious war, would persuade James to engage against the Habsburgs and thus allow them to redeem at least some of their parliamentary credit. But to the surprise of the eager young warriors, Louis XIII was reluctant to sell his sister as part of a military package deal, and insisted on religious concessions as extensive as those Spain had demanded. Since both James and Charles had in the 1624 parliament publicly committed themselves never to make such concessions to gain a marriage this caused them to hesitate; but their strategic needs soon triumphed. The recusancy laws were suspended once again, and a public chapel, which would mean access for English Catholics, promised for Charles's future bride, the Princess Henrietta Maria.

The French entanglement determined the course of domestic history more than did any other diplomatic episode of the early-modern period. James, Charles and Buckingham made large concessions in religion and honour – matters of the utmost importance to kings – to obtain a marriage which they assumed would be the basis of a wider alliance. That Cardinal Richelieu, Louis's able chief minister, was only too happy to see England fighting Spain, but not to join in that cause himself, was a realization that only dawned late. The sole consolation for their failure to obtain a firm French alliance was Louis's agreement to join James in financing a proxy descent on Germany by the German mercenary Count Mansfeld. But even this small return was lost when a revolt by the Huguenots, the French protestants, caused Richelieu to turn his attention inwards. The luckless force of pressed English infantry which set out under Mansfeld in January 1625 wasted away on the Dutch coast as Anglo-French bickering grew.

Worse followed. As earnest of English good faith Richelieu had demanded the loan of English naval help to suppress what at first seemed a localized revolt by the Huguenot duc de Soubise, and James and Buckingham jumped at the chance to show their value as allies. But to their horror the revolt spread to involve most of the French protestant communities, and the awful prospect arose of English ships and sailors suppressing their co-religionists. In its anxiety to avoid handing them over, the government even sponsored a mutiny amongst the sailors. James's death in March 1625 left Charles facing political disaster with his marriage. French coolness had driven James, and then still more his young successors, to make repeated concessions in the futile hope of drawing France closer; in so doing they baffled those who had heard what seemed very different undertakings in the 1624 parliament. The growing frustration of Charles and the duke, inexperienced diplomats as they were, with what the latter once called the 'shitten mouths' of the French led eventually to war in the most catastrophic circumstances, in a yawning credibility gap.

Charles was ill-suited to cope with his plight, and must rank among the most inept of all English kings. Possessing none of the subtlety of his father, he shared to the full James's views on the divinity of kingship; he also had a total conviction of his own rectitude. While it would be foolish to conclude that the civil war occurred simply *because* Charles was king, it would be equally foolish to underestimate the part played by his personality. Not unadvisedly, Clarendon began his great *History of the Rebellion* with Charles's accession in 1625; so too, from a very different perspective, did the Commons' Grand Remonstrance of 1641.

Charles was brought up in an authoritarian fashion, very much in the shadow of his glamorous elder brother Henry. The diffidence of his youth may have been intensified by a habitual stutter; whatever the case, Clarendon was later to blame the king's notorious proneness to vacillation – which proved a major handicap to the royal cause in the 1640s – on his not 'trusting himself enough'. That awkwardness may also help account for Charles's insistence on the dignity of kingship. But while Elizabeth had seized any chance to use royal ceremony as a political instrument, Charles seems almost to have put on a show for himself – his inordinate fondness for the masque is suggestive, for the masque focused its visual perspective on the king as the prime spectator, and played to the relatively closed world of the court. The only *public* ceremonial with which Charles seems to have been genuinely concerned was that of the royal chivalric order of the Garter – which was played out in the small town of Windsor rather than in London.

Charles's attitudes had immediate political consequences. He failed to appreciate the need to explain his actions – never one of James's failings. His terse speeches from the throne to his parliaments reveal not only his awkwardness but also his vision of rule: the proper course was conformity, not argument. Charles's incomprehension that any could honestly differ from their king led him to mistake the functions of his councillors and to turn his Scottish council in particular into a body of yes-men. As Laud once despairingly concluded, Charles was 'more willing not to hear than to hear'. As damaging was the king's insensitivity to the mutual gratification entailed in that management of patronage which was perhaps the most vital of a king's tasks. Austere, reserved and private, Charles 'knew not the art to please', as Bishop Williams put it; or, as Clarendon observed, 'not in his nature very bountiful,' the king 'paused too long in giving, which made those to whom he gave, less sensible of the benefit.' Charles far preferred the private worlds of connoisseurship, hunting and family life.

The king's character traits led him, under stress, into what sometimes looks uncomfortably like sheer dishonesty. While he justified his weasel ways in the negotiations with his enemies in the 1640s as the only means to deal with rebels against God as well as God's annointed, no such explanation can be offered for his readiness to blacken Bristol in the winter of 1623–4. Charles can be accorded few accolades for statesmanship, and the distrust with which many of his subjects later viewed him is readily comprehensible. As disaster loomed even Laud sadly concluded that the king 'neither knows how to be, nor to be made, great'.

Charles found an empty treasury on his accession, and the royal credit almost exhausted. He was immediately forced to mortgage £216,000 in land to the City to restore the credit his father had damaged and to secure a paltry loan of £60,000. If he were merely to make good the commitments in Europe that his father had made, let alone act for himself, he had to call a parliament.

The timing of that parliament, which assembled in June 1625, was doubly unfortunate. When questions were already being asked at the polls about the 1624 taxes it was unfortunate that Charles had nothing with which to offset the disasters of the tolerance of recusancy required by the marriage, the charade of the loan ships sailing back and forth across the Channel, and the plight of Mansfeld's troops. The extravagant celebrations feting the arrival of the new queen in London, which exactly coincided with Charles's plea to the parliament for aid, did not help to quell scepticism. And worst of all, James's death was promptly followed by the outbreak of what was to prove one of the worst plagues since the Black Death. By the end of 1625 about 20 per cent of London's population was dead, about the same proportion in Norwich by the plague's end in 1626, and considerably more in Exeter. Besides its ill auguries for the new reign the epidemic disrupted the nation's economic life in the summer of 1625, as merchants, magistrates and even ministers fled. It was also politically damaging in that the standard protestant response to plague was to regard it as divine judgment for backsliding. The council's cessation of the prosecution of Catholics seemed to threaten the lives of all.

Charles's goal was, of necessity, speedy supply and then adjournment to a time more propitious for other business. But he was the prisoner of his own rash diplomacy. He needed to prepare a fleet for use against Spain, since England's worth to France as an ally rested on its navy. But were he to declare war on Spain and thus convince parliament to give money, France would see still less need to commit itself. Keeping the purpose of his fleet a mystery may have been a diplomatic necessity, but in the context of the 1624 misunderstanding and the affair of the loan fleet it was a disaster for domestic confidence. Furthermore, few protestants could understand how suspension of proceedings against recusants could accompany war against Spain, since their Elizabethan upbringing had led them to identify patriotism and anti-Catholicism. While Charles was assuring the Lords that his marriage would bring no privileges for English Catholics, locally 'papists' were coming into the open. The Scottish earl of

Kellie reported privately from London in late July on the suspicions generated by Charles's conflicting intimations to France and to parliament: 'You can not believe the alteration that is in the opinion of the whole world touching his majesty.' Despite the king's abrupt claim in his opening speech that parliament was morally bound to support him after 'engaging' for war in 1624, neither at Westminster nor at Oxford in August – where they were adjourned to escape the plague – would uncomprehending MPs go beyond their meagre offer of two subsidies, or about £120,000. The need to fight a war without support then forced measures on Charles which only compounded his problems.

Nevertheless, Charles's unfortunate inheritance of the French connection was not wholly responsible for the breakdown. Symptomatic is the fate of another revenue measure, the branch of the customs known as tonnage and poundage which was conventionally granted to a king at the start of his reign. Fearing that the usual statute might justify impositions for life, several members urged revisions, but since a plague time was unpropitious Sir Robert Phelips proposed a temporary measure. As so often, we must note how little the Commons' leaders were bent on confrontation. Phelips and Sir Edward Coke were ready to use the new climate of the new reign to give retrospective sanction in a tonnage and poundage act to the existing impositions, thus preserving the principle of parliamentary control while leaving the crown the revenue it needed. But their good intentions were disrupted by the beginnings of an attack on Buckingham with which they – disillusioned by the aftermath of the 1624 parliament and frustrated by their own failure to gain the reward they thought their due – were not out of sympathy. Tonnage and poundage was supposedly granted for protection of the seas, and it therefore seemed an appropriate weapon for striking at a lord admiral whose monopoly of office, extravagance and diplomatic failings were all resented, and whose ships were having little success against pirates. The insulting proposal for a one-year grant which emerged stood little chance in the Lords, and Charles was thus left without parliamentary authorization for a revenue he had to have if he were to go to war. Much of the constitutional crisis of the later 1620s can thus be traced back to the urgency of the plague year and hostility to the duke.

There were signs of a deeper malaise. Suspicions of impositions were present; and the Commons' acceptance of the one-year timetable for tonnage and poundage suggests the extent of unease at recent policies. Others too felt the body politic was not functioning as it should. Sir John Coke, shortly to become secretary of state, warned the Commons that if parliament would not pay for the war 'some new way' must be found. There is no evidence that any of the king's

servants were planning constitutional innovation. They were, however, encountering all those frustrations of organizing a modern war
effort on medieval conventions of financing against which Salisbury
had rebelled. Phelips's reminder that England was alone in Europe in
retaining its 'original rights and constitutions' was timely.

In beginning his account of the Civil War with 1625 Clarendon was
undoubtedly thinking of the unfortunate political style of the king he
had served; but 1625 was a turning-point in another way. Under
James English protestants had been able to assume that the church
was united in its basic beliefs, but Charles's views and ways soon put
an end to this happy state.

Within months of his accession the deeply ceremonialist Charles
was giving ominous support to the few clerical Arminians. So-called
because they were thought to follow the Dutch theologian Arminius,
in fact these came from a native English tradition, which the eirenic
James had carefully protected, of academic dissent from Calvinist
predestinarianism. But not until 1624 was there a public assault
on the fundamentals of Calvinist orthodoxy. In that year Richard
Montagu, a minor Arminian cleric, sought to exploit James's growing impatience with the Calvinist anti-Catholic stridency born of the
Thirty Years War by publishing *A New Gag for an Old Goose*, which
seemed to minimize the differences between England and Rome. This
caused some disquiet in the parliament of 1625, all the more so when
Charles took Montagu into his personal protection. The alarm drove
two leading Calvinist peers, the earl of Warwick and Viscount Saye
and Sele, to try to clarify matters, and at their request Buckingham in
February 1626 called a theological debate at York House, his London
residence. Up to this point Buckingham's ecclesiastical and political
patronage had spanned the whole theological spectrum, doubtless as
an insurance against every possible eventuality. But knowing which
way the wind from the throne was blowing, at York House the favourite leaned decisively against the Calvinists. It was a sign which intelli-
gent observers did not miss, especially as the influence and promotion
prospects of Calvinist bishops soon dwindled. For the first time since
the middle years of Elizabeth religion was to become a major issue.
Correspondingly, after 1625 we can talk of an ideological divide
between government – if not yet court – and country, as the differences in constitutional emphasis evident in James's reign were reinforced by increasingly emotive disagreements over religion.

Still more dangerously, the court as a whole grew more isolated.
Charles was intolerant of disagreement and Buckingham was, as
ever, selfish. Whatever his personal weaknesses James had balanced
his court as determinedly as he had his foreign policy, and had

protected those like some of his old Scottish friends or Lord Keeper Williams who were at odds with the favourite. His death secured the duke's final elevation. Buckingham's most astute move had been to recognize that the awkward prince Charles needed affection and admiration. The enormous charm with which he bathed the prince had its reward in a devotion even greater than James's: the duke's enemies were now the king's enemies. Charles's accession sent the Scots into eclipse, isolated the hapless Bristol and Middlesex more than ever, and allowed the duke to move against his other foes. Williams was dismissed after the 1625 parliament and the earl of Arundel put under house arrest early in 1626. Within a year of Charles's accession Pembroke was the only major figure independent of the duke left at court, and he was not the stuff of which determined opposition was made.

The monolithic court of Charles's devotedly ducal years had wide effects. When Buckingham turned his hegemony over the king's ear into a monopoly politicans were driven to employ new tactics when they found the normal means of influencing the king blocked. Although Pembroke had seen no need to join an early attack on Buckingham in the Lords in 1621, his clients in the Commons turned on the duke in 1626. More alarmingly, a distortion of central politics necessarily had repercussions locally, and might even upset gentlemen's sense of the paramount need to impress obedience on their inferiors. Thus, when Sir Thomas Wentworth, thrust out of his local offices in Yorkshire late in 1625, found there was no hope for him save by subservience to the duke he broke with convention and made a vindicatory speech at the Yorkshire assizes. Most dangerous of all, however, were the day-to-day consequences. Charles's patent incomprehension of the court's quasi-representative role in the body politic, his belief that a court served merely to glorify a king, meant that localities anxious to communicate their unease over some burden imposed on them had fewer contacts to whom they could turn for help. The corollary was a growth in mutual misunderstanding and mistrust.

The disruption of traditional politics went hand-in-hand with the accumulation of material grievances, since the active foreign policy of the 1620s brought more demands of all sorts. Parliament's intransigence in 1625 led the council to levy the equivalent of the two subsidies lost by dissolution in the form of a forced loan on the rich. The poor suffered too, since the forcible levies of men, for Mansfeld in 1624 and to serve in the 1625 fleet, had to be paid for and billeted locally, and repayment only came – and that slowly – after 1627. Furthermore, Charles's accession and war plans caused the council to pay ever closer attention to the militia, and detailed instructions were sent out in the summer of 1625 for the regular training and equipping of a 'perfect militia'. When fear of plague made men all over the country shun company, and when the consequent stoppage of trade caused grave hardship in the clothing areas particularly, these burdens were doubly objectionable.

Politically more damaging was the fate of this military activity. The fiasco of Mansfeld's expedition was compounded by the disaster which met Charles's forces when they finally sailed for Spain in September 1625. Their aim was to relive the glories of the Elizabethan raid on Cadiz, but the adventure was poorly planned and badly executed. The return to south-west England of the tattered remnant, starving, unclothed and disease-ridden, in winter conditions was an irreparable blow to confidence in the administration. One Dorset minister preached that 'the late repulse' was God's punishment on a land which 'was not governed by justice, but by bribery and extortion.'*

Charles's decision to call a new parliament for February 1626 appears in these circumstances at best quixotic and at worst suicidal. Recently, some historians have seen in Charles's willingness even now to work with parliament evidence that he almost instinctively accepted parliament as a part of an harmonious body politic. But his career on the whole shows that the role Charles accorded parliament was fairly circumscribed, and much more important were his practical hopes of it in the winter of 1625-6. Once again, foreign affairs held the key. The loan ships had eventually been handed over to the French in a lull in their civil strife; but to the anguish of Charles's council the revolt flared up again, and the ships were put to effective use against protestants. All the resentment against the French which had built up during the marriage negotiations broke out anew, exacerbated by the fact that relations between the king and his new bride were proving less than loving. But Charles could not simply abandon a diplomatic entanglement which had already brought him intense political embarrassment: his pride demanded that he restore his sister in triumph to Heidelberg. Accordingly, with royal patience exhausted, disaster threatening in any new parliament, and Buckingham facing likely destruction, a new foreign policy emerged in late 1625. England was to take its rightful place at the head of the protestant cause. Recusants were persecuted once again, and the council planned a firm allianke with the Dutch, renewed action against Spain, help for the suffering French Huguenots and therefore measures against France. Observers concluded that Charles would go to the

*J.H. Bettey, ed. *The Casebook of Sir Francis Ashley, JP* (Dorset Record Soc., 1981), p. 91.

new parliament asking for support for a godly war. However little
parliament had been able to determine James's foreign policy in
1624, financial and political desperation had led Charles to shape his
policy to parliamentary tastes.

Soon after the election writs went out, the French pulled the rug
from under him. Fearing war on too many fronts, Richelieu now
established a hasty peace with the Huguenots and left Charles without
a policy when the parliament opened. The prospects looked bleak.
Continuing depression in the traditional textile industry was intensified by the plague and another bad harvest in 1625; the foreign
entanglements had also had a large effect, for the one sector of the
textile trade not devastated in the depression had been the new
draperies, and exports of these to southern Europe were badly disrupted by the hostilities with Spain and the growing tensions with
France. When unemployment and hardship grew in the clothing
regions parliament-men were likely to find the plight of their neighbours overriding their concern for the protestant cause in Europe,
particularly since Charles had not yet shown much commitment to
that cause himself. For neighbours might make their views very
apparent. The magistrates of Bury St Edmunds in Suffolk, a badly
affected clothing town, declared during the 1626 elections that 'in
general they would give no voice [vote] to any courtier.'

The Commons' reluctance in 1626 to grant taxes is therefore scarcely
surprising. But no more than in any other 1620s parliament were they
wholly negative. Revealingly, even Sir John Eliot, who was soon to
take the lead in the onslaught on Buckingham, showed some sympathy for the crown's problems:

> Cut off the king's revenues, you cut off the principal means of your own safeties,
> and not only disable him to defend you, but enforce that which you conceive an
> offence, the extraordinary resort to his subjects for supplies, and the more than
> ordinary ways of raising them.

But the conservative formula Eliot advanced for getting the crown off
the people's backs, the resumption of grants of crown lands and pensions, had its chief attraction in its implication for Buckingham, the
chief recipient of such grants.

The attack on the duke had far greater support than in 1625. Corruption was as tempting a target as ever, privateer depredations were
increasing, and French retaliatory seizures of English ships could just
as much as the Cadiz disaster be laid to the lord admiral's door. These
back-bench themes were reinforced by the cries of jealous courtiers,
and Pembroke's clients in particular focused on the charge of 'single
counsel'; it was a Pembroke man who opened the way to impeachment

proceedings. The charge that the duke was the origin of all the nation's ills had considerable plausibility – England seemed to be lurching into conflict with both great powers, France and Spain, after English arms had twice been humiliated, and Buckingham had been the chief protagonist in the ill-omened undertaking of 1624. But to challenge the king's ministers was to confront the unavoidable fact that government was the king's government, and the impeachment foundered when Charles in mid-May declared that he personally cleared the duke of all fault. The next two decades were to underline the difficulty of controlling the policies of a king.

The attack on Buckingham reveals much of the state of politics. Its concern with abuse rather than ideology suggests that polarization had not yet come. Moreover, the focus on the malfunctioning of the council shows that the majority in the Commons clung to an ideal of a monarch well-advised by a privy council, and did not aim at any governmental role for parliament. But though Pembroke's men might have been content with Buckingham's abandonment of a few offices, and an Anglo-French alliance, the aristocratic patrons did not control the Commons. The anger and perplexity of Eliot and many others over the course of foreign policy since the parliament of 1624 could not be stifled. Nor could Pembroke's men obtain supply from those interests damaged by a pointless crisis, nor soothe the ordinary gentleman appalled by the reports of corruption and Catholicism at court, and particularly in Buckingham's family. Instead, with impeachment blocked, the Commons delayed their vote of supply, hoping to persuade the king to dismiss the duke.

That the parliament survived into mid-June needs explaining. The supply the sceptical Commons intended was only about £200,000, scarcely one-third of what Charles needed for the year even if hostilities did not expand to include France. Not surprisingly, in their last two months the Commons heard both councillors and king threaten 'new counsels' and 'other resolutions' of the sort which had led to the disappearance of parliaments in Europe. But Charles was never the most realistic of politicians, and until the end he seems to have assumed that parliament-men would do their duty. Furthermore, considerations of royal honour were also involved, and here for the first time in years the Lords dominated the stage.

Charles and Buckingham had sought to smoothe their path by excluding several of the duke's enemies from the parliament. The Commons had not challenged them for removing Coke, Phelips, Wentworth and a few others from the Commons by appointing them sheriffs, but the seclusion of the earls of Arundel and Bristol from the Lords provoked major storms. Bristol, tired of his long house-arrest, petitioned the Lords that he was being victimized by Buckingham because he had information against him; Charles then retaliated, in the hope that the Lords would drop the matter, by charging Bristol with treason committed in Madrid. But the Lords' sense that the sale of titles, and the Buckingham years, had besmirched the honour on which aristocracy rested made them at this point more conscious of privilege than were the Commons. They would not give way. Charles then put Arundel, an ally of Bristol and holder of several proxy votes, under house-arrest, only to generate another storm over privileges. Although the Arundel case soured relations, the Bristol affair was more serious. The charges and counter-charges, centring on who had tried to convert Charles to Catholicism in Madrid, involved the public washing of some very dirty royal linen. Charles insisted that his honour be vindicated, but not surprisingly the Lords were reluctant to proceed with such dangerous business. Only when it became clear that they would not condemn Bristol did Charles dissolve the parliament, throwing the blame on the Commons in an attempt to rebuild bridges to the peers.

The parliaments of 1625 and 1626 had had results exactly the reverse of those the institution was supposed to yield. Instead of restoring harmony between crown and country they had only exposed tensions. Those tensions might call the value of parliaments in question, all the more so if Charles could raise money elsewhere. But if the king was coming to doubt parliament's worth, others found dramatic confirmation of it. On the day after the 1626 dissolution Charles issued a proclamation forbidding, in the name of domestic tranquillity, public argument about sensitive doctrinal matters: this was widely and correctly interpreted as an attempt to restrain the preaching of orthodox Calvinism. It required no great political sophistication for Calvinists thenceforth to associate the survival of their religious truths with the survival of parliament. That coupling, and its converse – popery and absolutism – was to prove explosive.

As soon as the council was freed from the distractions of parliament to turn back to Europe it found a familiar world. The French had again duped Charles by making peace with Spain in the spring of 1626, thus destroying the central premise of his policy. Undaunted, Cardinal Richelieu still pressed Charles about the treatment of Catholics in England while maintaining his pressure against the Huguenot stronghold of La Rochelle. Mutual provocations at sea soon took Charles into a war in which remarkably few English interests were involved.

Only money would allow Charles to make a reality of that war, and the frantic attempt to substitute for parliamentary aid reveal both the strengths and the weaknesses of the early-Stuart monarchy. Financial strains were not, it should be stressed, unusual for belligerent nations in this period, and the kings of France and Spain also lurched from crisis to crisis in the liquidity shortage endemic to the whole of Europe. The difference lay in the greater failure of English govern-ments in finding ready sources of credit. The City of London now declined to lend, and Charles was reduced to trying vainly to pawn the crown jewels in Amsterdam. In the absence of funds as well as of a clear objective the fleet Charles assembled in the summer of 1626 wasted away almost as miserably as had Mansfeld's forces. The only alternative to a humiliating peace was therefore to make a reality of the threats of 'new counsels'.

The intentions at this point of those at Whitehall are hard to categorize. Charles, impatient of the contumacy of parliament-men, was reliably reported to have enquired as to how Louis XIII had eliminated the estates-general; the metropolis certainly abounded in the coming months with rumours of his intransigent hostility to any talk of a parliament. Buckingham for his part had little cause to relish the prospect of a parliament and good reason to hope for the sucess of any alternatives, while Charles's favourite clergyman, Bishop Laud, had concluded that a parliament would mean a challenge to his vision of the church. Nevertheless, probably a majority of Charles's council-lors still hoped for harmony; and undoubtedly, none had sufficient drive to create a new order. Symptomatic is the hesitation in the winter of 1627–8 of one councillor, Sir Thomas Edmondes, in face of innovatory proposals 'without either the consent of a parliament, or the hope of gaining the submission and conformity of the people thereunto.' Most councillors probably sincerely believed their public defence, that the new measures were temporary and emergency expedients. There was considerable support – especially in the church hierarchy, in the Lords in 1628, and even in the country too – for the king's claim to an absolute prerogative empowering him to secure the defence of the kingdom, and requiring the subject to assist.

Nevertheless, Charles's attempt in the summer of 1626 to collect as a 'benevolence' the subsidies lost by the dissolution of parliament was ill-judged. By summoning all the tax-payers Charles seemed to emphasize that parliament was deliberately being by-passed. That the 1626 benevolence failed abjectly suggests both that parliament had put down deep roots into popular opinion and that the king's explicit appeal to doctrines of necessity alarmed many. The frustrated council therefore turned to a more peremptory approach, to a forced loan. This, though like many of its predecessors a loan in name only, was less constitutionally provocative. But it was novel in its scope and in its systematic execution. Subsidy-payers were summoned to meetings where local commissioners, often reinforced by itinerant privy councillors, pressed them individually to pay, and this direct and unremitting approach proved remarkably successful. Few dared, or were willing, to withstand royal authority, especially when the council sensitively tempered coercion with the offer that counties could recoup their military costs from the loan monies. Over £260,000 – or just under the five parliamentary subsidies desired – had been raised by the end of 1627, in a much shorter time than a large subsidy collection normally took. The loan rescued Charles from immediate bankruptcy.

The yield of the loan is eloquent testimony to what the council could achieve by sustained effort, and to the deference which allowed an unpoliced society to function. While the 1628 parliament showed that many were conscious of the constitutional implications, few chose to voice them outside the legitimate arena. Nor was this because of the greater sanctions at the disposal of the crown. The council made few innovations, though Buckingham's purge of twenty-four opponents from local office in the aftermath of the 1626 parliament, and a subsequent purge of loan refusers, may have had some effect. More important was the general realization that the country had to be governed, and that the king alone had the right to govern. In the same way, the local élites cooperated voluntarily with the deputy-lieutenants who worked more or less diligently in 1624–7 at the thankless task of levying and billeting some 50,000 conscripted soldiers, or about 1 per cent of the total population. The men were often weak or unsuitable, and their arms only too often rusty cast-offs. Yet local self-government produced men and money for an unpopular cause through means which – as the 1628 debates showed – were wide open to legal challenge. Equally striking, humbler householders whose lot it was to provide billets acquiesced; the only significant disturbances occurred when Irish or Scots soldiers inflamed local xenophobia.

The council could not, however, capitalize fully on the readiness of the nation to conform, since it could not make all its commands felt. Its preoccupation with disciplining loan defaulters meant that it was distracted from the final objective, the military preparations. The drive for a perfect militia wound down; still more serious was the council's inability to oversee both the loan and the logistics of the war with France. The expeditionary force Buckingham took in 1627 to aid the Huguenots of La Rochelle found itself supplied with wheat but no means to bake bread, and with scaling ladders too short for the job; troops arriving at rendezvous found neither orders nor officers waiting, and commanders were left for weeks without instructions. The disorganization underlined the advantages of having the parliamentary gentry vote and collect taxes themselves; for the council did not have the resources to govern the country alone.

By the end of 1627 the crown's credit had proved unable to bear the strains of war. That winter Charles alienated to the City the last major body of crown lands, worth about £350,000, in return for the cancellation of past debts and the extension of another loan. He thereby ended the traditional role of land as a major source of royal revenue and with it, it might be said, the medieval monarchy. It became correspondingly more difficult to tempt the City to ignore the Stuarts' bad record as debtors and lend again. The withdrawal of the City explains the crown's subsequent total reliance for credit on the customs farmers, who used their own private credit and the security of their control of the customs to channel loans from merchants to the crown. But even the farmers could not finance a war, and they now seem to have refused to lend unless a parliament was called to grant Charles additional revenue as security.

The council was left badly divided in the winter of 1627–8. Yet another military humiliation – Buckingham's withdrawal with the loss of more than half his men from a fruitless siege of the Ile de Rhé off La Rochelle – had not quelled Charles's desire to vindicate his honour. Nor had it enamoured him any more of parliaments. The king's conviction that since 1624 parliaments had repeatedly failed in their duty to fulfil their alleged 'engagement' of that year had led him to question the worth of the institution. However, the majority of the privy council recognized that the gaoling over the loan of some seventy gentlemen and an earl and the dismissal of four leading peers from local office boded ill for further hard-line measures, and that a parliament would have to be called. Yet even as Charles was prevailed upon to summon one, to meet in March 1628, he took his most radical step yet by instructing his ministers to consider an excise tax, the prime means by which princely power was raised in Europe.

The burdens imposed in the prosecution of an unpopular war between 1626 and 1628 shaped political attitudes. The 1628 elections saw a stronger preference than ever in larger boroughs and in the counties for local members instead of the courtiers who might once have been chosen for their ability to do favours for the constituency. The dangerous implication, that the court was isolated from the country, was made explicit in the reports from several counties, from Lincolnshire to Cornwall, of popular support for newly released loan refusers. As the Suffolk clergyman John Rous noted in late 1627, 'Men be disposed to speak the worst of state businesses.'

Several historians have plausibly seen in essentially localist 'country' antipathy for the court and its multiplying demands the key to an understanding of the developing political crisis. Charles's desire to

fight an incomprehensible war – and a war that was fought badly –
during a depression strained the informal ties between governors and
governed which were so vital to the functioning of society. At the
same time the usual safety-valves were becoming less effective as the
court grew more introverted and less responsive. For Buckingham
seconded his purges from local office in 1626–7 by the promotion of
dependents, all too often as doubtful in religion as was his own family
– and the Catholic Earl Rivers was no match for the earl of Warwick
as a mediator in Essex. Yet 'country' sentiment became less simply
localist in the course of the decade. Ambiguities remained, clearly
enough in the cases of Phelips or Wentworth, whose influence rested
both on local standing and on favour at court. Nevertheless alarmed
accounts of events at Whitehall and on the continent appear increasingly in gentry correspondence in the 1620s. More striking still is
the way in which local opinion focused on parliament as the hope for
reform – during the decade many quite minor gentlemen like
William Davenport in Cheshire acquired manuscript copies of parliamentary speeches on major issues. They evidently did not see parliament as the place for local business alone. Neither was the news
they gathered locked up in the manor houses. In his address to the
voters at the 1624 Cheshire election and in his charges to local juries,
Sir Richard Grosvenor, a solid back-bench figure, eagerly communi-
cated national issues.

The roots of this awakening were various. The manifest corruption
of the court, first under James and then with Buckingham's hegemony, had crystallized a sense that the country was virtuous and
public-spirited. Further, the 'new counsels' of recent months confirmed suspicions evident in parliament since at least early in James's
reign that English liberties under law were not secure. But religion
too now played a part. Unease at the reports of Catholics at court and
amongst the newly promoted 'dukists', as some were beginning to call
them, had not been quelled by Charles's recent adoption of a protestant foreign policy. Although the chaotic shifts, and the cost, of his
policies, had undermined support for a holy war, the Catholic successes in Europe bred in many English protestants a deep sense of
insecurity. Some of the more alert, such as Pym, or Thomas Scott, the
thoroughly alienated puritan MP for Canterbury, saw in the favour
shown to Laud, Neile and Montagu evidence that the enemy was
already within the gates. Few went as far as to join John Winthrop
and his East Anglian friends in emigrating to New England; yet their
very departure shows a novel religious estrangement. The Mayflower
Pilgrims of 1620 had been separatists or congregationalists, beyond
the pale of normal religious life. But Winthrop was a reputable member of the Jacobean consensus: an orthodox Calvinist believer in a·

national church, and a gentleman, he feared England's fall to Rome.

Calvinists had other reasons to worry. To those who saw the world as the theatre of God's judgments, the disasters overwhelming England must be the result of sin – thus, a sermon to the 1628 Commons by an Essex minister, Jeremiah Dyke, saw in the recent calamities a warning that God was turning his back on England. And to a country gentleman like Walter Yonge in Devon counting the popish lords, or those brooding over the Overbury murder or the myriad manuscript copies of obscene poems about the duke, where was more sin found than at court? Both the Old Testament and the classics taught that politics was about moral actions and that the vice of rulers brought retribution on the nation. The focus of so much correspondence and debate on corruption and sin, rather than on constitutional crisis, is thus not necessarily the evidence of political naivety that some have thought it. Many assumed that one followed from the other.

And by 1628 that crisis was at hand, for it seemed that the subject could have little confidence in either his liberty or his property: as Sir Benjamin Rudyerd warned the Commons, this was 'the crisis of parliaments'. The council had gaoled without charge many who had resisted the loan, a levy made even more dubious by the dismissal of chief justice Crew for refusing to pronounce in its favour. As unnerving as the council's actions had been the failure of the courts in 1627 to give protection. To the distress of the revealingly small total of five knights who dared to challenge the king by sueing for *habeas corpus*, Charles refused to allow the legality of the loan to be tested in court. Instead, the attorney-general, Sir Robert Heath, argued narrowly that the crown must have an emergency power of arrest which it was trusted not to misuse. This the judges quite properly accepted, but the technical form of their order was not such as could serve as the binding precedent for future discretionary arrest that Charles clearly wanted. When Heath realized this he tried surreptitiously to amend the record. The subsequent revelation of the attempt, and, worse, of Charles's insistence on it, proved a severe blow to that trust in government to which the king appealed. Sir John Eliot's rhetoric caught the mood: 'Where is law? Where is *meum et tuum* [property]? It is fallen into the chaos of a higher power.'

The first priority for the asembling parliament-men was to keep parliament in being as the only hope of safety: as Thomas Scott noted in his journal, 'If free parliaments be gone, all is lost.' Charles demanded a speedy supply for war, and urged the Commons to trust him to govern by the laws for the future. But as the enormity of his conduct in the *habeas corpus* case became clear, the majority of MPs grew more intransigent. Charles's financial desperation gave them their chance. The king could ill afford to despise the Commons' offer of five subsidies, though the sum of about £280,000 involved was painfully inadequate to his war needs; with the grant tied up in committee and all local business thrust aside the house could proceed to uphold the rule of law.

The king shocked many in the Commons by resisting at every step. The most vocal MPs seem to have intended a statutory condemnation of Charles's recent practices and an affirmation of the subject's liberty. This he fiercely opposed, both for its reflections on his past courses and for its attempt to tie his hands for the future. An angry dissolution soon seemed likely, with unforeseeable consequences for a country whose king intended to continue at war. It was in a desperate attempt to dispel the tearful panic which beset the house that Sir Edward Coke seized on a suggestion of the more antiquated parliamentary form of a petition to the king. Such a petition, for a matter of right rather than of grace and favour, would, if sent from both houses and accepted by the king, be enrolled in the law courts; it would thus bind the judges while avoiding the appearance of novel formulation which Charles found so objectionable. The success of the king and duke in alienating even the crown's natural allies duly ensured that despite Charles's cynical creation of a spate of new peers before the session the Lords capitulated – many of them reluctantly – before the Commons' insistence. The king was thus left under enormous pressure, political now as well as financial, to accept the Petition of Right. But as so often his concession, when it came, was graceless – one witness to his performance in the Lords noted, 'Prince did never speak with less applause.'

The Petition's appeal to an 'inherited . . . freedom' showed its continuity with the abortive Apology of 1604 and with the Protestation of 1621. These too had declared that certain rights were as much guaranteed by law and as integral to the body politic as were the powers of the crown. In its attempt to maintain old barriers against abuses rather than erect new ones, the Petition reveals the sheer conservatism and hostility to innovation of the critics of royal policy. Yet though Coke and others conceded in debate that the provisions of the Petition of Right were only implicit, rather than explicit, in existing law, the Petition did not simply embody Coke's faith in an 'artifical reason' underlying the law. The *habeas corpus* case had bred suspicions that the law, 'fundamental' or not, might not be able to stand alone in face of power, and inclined members to accept the more novel arguments of John Selden and some of the younger lawyers in the house. For the Petition appears to insist – following Selden's very positivist view of law – that there ought to be statutory warrant for every executive action.

The public response was revealing of changing attitudes to parliament. In London bonfires greeted the Petition's passage; the Petition itself and notes of speeches circulated the country as never before, and the city of Bristol enshrined six books of the arguments in its records. Of the parliaments of the 1620s only that of 1624 had produced more than a handful of statutes, but that fact had evidently not diminished respect for the institution. The popular fervour of 1628 confirmed that parliament, not bread-and-butter matters of legislation, held a vital place in the heart of the body politic.

Despite the rejoicing, the passage of the Petition did not calm the Commons. During the winter of 1626–7 the government had promoted a small preaching campaign on behalf of the loan, and the sermons confirmed John Pym's suspicions that the Arminians intended to advance absolutism in order to bring in their forerunner of popery: parliament's intransigent protestantism must make any Catholic seek to subvert it. The 1626 proclamation against Calvinist doctrine had pointed to the connection, and had Pym known of it he would have found further proof in Laud's advice in the winter of 1627–8 against calling a parliament for fear of a religious storm. The most outspoken loan sermon, by Roger Manwaring, ironically no Arminian himself, had urged the religious duty of paying fiscal tribute to princes as Gods on earth, thus transforming what most would have accepted, the divine origin of kingship, into practical politics. The practicality of those politics seemed all the greater when Charles provocatively published the sermon under the title *Religion and Allegiance*. The Commons moved swiftly to impeach the author, as protestant English nationalism began to focus its alarmed gaze on a domestic fifth-column standing at the king's right hand. As early as the previous winter Thomas Scott had confided to his diary his conviction that the duke and his 'dukists' were the heart of a vast conspiracy to bring in popery and tyranny. The dawning suspicion that only parliament, and no longer the king, could be trusted to protect religion and liberty was to make civil war possible.

Apprehensions of an apocalyptic conspiracy took firmer shape during the long debates. Members learned that the king had early in 1628 considered introducing an excise tax, and in so doing had seemed to mock the Commons' conciliatory restraint on impositions. Anger flared in early June with the discovery that Charles had tried to raise cavalry in Germany – not all could believe that he intended it for service in France. Some members asserted that they were to enforce the excise, others that they were Buckingham's tools for a coup, 'praetorian bands' in Eliot's phrase, with all that that implied of imperial tyranny; indeed, by the civil war the German cavalry had

become part of the folk memory about Charles's despotic designs.*
An emotional response was therefore guaranteed when Coke named
Buckingham as the 'grievance of grievances', and members exploded,
crying 'It is he! It is he!' Charles had hoped for statutory backing for
the militia and his continued collection of tonnage and poundage, but
he was left little choice but to close the session by prorogation in order
to head off a remonstrance indicting his whole regime along with his
favourite.

For all parliament's hold on public opinion, Charles still held the
vital cards. The Petition of Right had claimed only to declare existing
law, and since it did not explicitly outlaw the crown's emergency
powers the judges readily concluded that those powers remained
implicit in the law; Charles accordingly accepted the Petition. That
he had not changed his views he made provocatively clear after
the prorogation by withdrawing the agreed text and publishing a
mangled version, with an assertion of his right to collect tonnage and
poundage. Undeterred by the Petition's denunciation of any levy
lacking parliamentary consent, he continued to collect tonnage and
poundage, only to be met by resistance from a number of merchants;
to their chagrin, their protests were rejected by the judges, who held
that the wording of the Petition was too general for application to such
a case. Worse was to follow when the judges – this time accepting the
Petition – allowed bail to Richard Chambers, a merchant whom the
council had gaoled for comparing English government unfavourably
with Turkish despotism. Charles promptly retaliated by having
Chambers heavily fined and gaoled by the prerogative court of star
chamber. The king showed the value of his control over the executive
again after the 1629 parliamentary session when several arrested MPs
applied for bail: by forbidding the gaoler to produce them in court he
prevented the judges hearing the application. The Petition had little
effect upon discretionary power.

If the courts and the merchants could not change Charles's course,
direct action could. As Buckingham was at Portsmouth in August
preparing for yet another expedition to La Rochelle he was assassinated by a disgruntled officer. The widespread rejoicing probably did
as much as anything to estrange the grieving king from his subjects.
The immediate effect was the disordering of the military preparations, although these were soon rendered unnecessary anyway by the
capitulation to starvation of the Rochellois. This new blow to
Charles's sense of honour – since he had in the spring of 1627

---

*See, for example, M.F. Stieg, ed., *Diary of John Harington* (Somerset Record Soc., 1977),
p. 16, and *Thurloe State Papers*, V. 787.

guaranteed the Huguenots' safety – must have seemed to him a further argument against reliance on parliament. It could, of course, equally be taken as an indictment of the rashness of Charles's policy.

The sudden vacation of Buckingham's many offices disordered the competitive world of the court, but politically the duke's death marked more of a turning-point. Although his hegemony had kept out some able men, like Bishop Williams, Buckingham was above all things a political pragmatist. There were signs that summer, most particularly in the appointment of the anti-war Sir Richard Weston as lord treasurer, that Buckingham had learned his lesson sooner than Charles and was contemplating a change of policy towards peace and retrenchment. He had certainly surrendered some of his offices and had been reconciled to enemies, such as Abbot, Arundel and Wentworth. Even after the York House conference he had through his Calvinist secretary Packer maintained his ties to puritans, including some officials like Sir Robert Harley who became staunch parliamentarians in the 1640s. But Charles's forte was not even-handedness, and at the time of Buckingham's death the king was already granting ecclesiastical promotion to Laud, Montagu and Manwaring. In an important sense, therefore, Charles's 'personal rule' began in 1628 with the duke's removal; thereafter he held 'in his hands the whole directory', as secretary Dorchester put it. The importance of Buckingham in preserving something of a balance was to become clearer retrospectively as the scales tipped steadily towards the Arminians in 1629.

A dazzling figure, immensely charming, an eloquent if sometimes incoherent orator, Buckingham was also not incapable as an administrator. As admiral he appreciated the value of small fast frigates in a way that Charles, preoccupied in the 1630s with ponderous hulks that would trumpet the glory of monarchy, did not. Furthermore, the duke used much of his huge income to bail out the king's war effort in 1626–8. But to compare him only with Charles is to distort the record. He was an impetuous lightweight, and the conjunction of his rashness with Charles's *idée fixe* of royal honour brought English foreign policy to disaster in the confused involvement with the French and in the unconcern with the limitations the Commons had sought to make clear in 1621 and 1624. His implementation of that policy was scarcely more creditable. The selection of Viscount Wimbledon to command the 1625 Cadiz raid was catastrophic, and whatever the duke's own bravery his failure to mount an effective rearguard during the withdrawal from the Ile de Rhé in 1627 contributed largely to the slaughter.

To judge by contemporary comments, Buckingham's rapaciousness did bring the court further into disrepute. His goodwill had to be purchased in all appointments, sometimes at enormous cost, as in the £20,000 that Sir Henry Montague, later earl of Manchester, paid to become lord treasurer in 1620. Moreover, peerages were sold faster than ever. Between 1615 and 1628 thirty English and forty Scottish and Irish titles were sold for about £350,000, of which the crown saw less than half. Buckingham received £25,000 from the sale of Irish peerages alone in 1618–22. The instability of early-Stuart politics can be tied to Buckingham in more ways than one, for the problems of precedence the sales created disturbed the Lords in 1628–9 and gravely disrupted county politics in Cheshire, Northamptonshire and probably elsewhere.

The removal of the duke coincided with a major diplomatic shift. With his only close friend dead Charles looked elsewhere for companionship, and there developed one of the great royal love affairs of history, that of the king and queen: Henrietta Maria's first confinement came nine months after the duke's death. The new relationship brought Charles closer to France again, particularly as the collapse of the Huguenots had removed his major reason for fighting. Peace with France came in 1629, and with Spain in 1630, in both cases very much on the basis of the *status quo ante*. The gains had been nil, and the material costs of war and diplomacy over the decade more than £2M.; the political cost had been incalculable. Those whose minds were running along apocalyptic paths and who saw Romish conspiracy at every hand were scarcely mollified by the peace. In 1629 puritan aristocrats headed by the earl of Warwick and Lord Saye were driven to found the Providence Island Company as the private-enterprise base for the privateering war against Spain in the Americas which they, like so many others, felt the crown should have conducted in the 1620s.

Although he remained deeply in debt, the curtailment of hostilities freed Charles from the most pressing urgency. His decision to meet parliament again in January 1629, after the hysteria of the previous June, is therefore something of a mystery. It can probably be explained more by reference to the commitment of the country to parliamentary ways than to Charles's. For the troubles with the merchants over tonnage and poundage, disorders over billeting, and continuing legalistic challenges to the militia in the provinces all underlined the advantages of statutory sanction. But Charles did little to encourage parliament to come to his aid. At the opening of the session he withdrew his aggressive declaration of the previous June and now asserted that he collected tonnage and poundage as a matter of necessity rather than of right, but the effect of this concession was undercut by the dishonesty of his printing of the Petition of Right and still more by his ecclesiastical promotions. Despite the strength of Calvinist convictions – Pym's half-brother Francis Rous had during the 1628 session denounced the Arminians as 'frogs from the bottomless pit' – a parliamentary complaint against a clergyman seemed the surest way to give him a bishopric.

The Commons initially concentrated on alleged breaches of the Petition of Right and the affair of its printing. In council proceedings over tonnage and poundage against John Rolle, a merchant who was also an MP, Eliot and Selden insisted they had to hand a case of breach of privilege by which to challenge the council's actions without directly confronting the king. But the house was divided, for Pym, Warwick's cousin Sir Nathaniel Rich, and a number of others feared that to oppose the king would be to break the parliament before they had vindicated the cause of true religion; they briefly seized the initiative. But they soon ran aground on the problem of defining true religion. Neither Pym nor Rich were radicals, bent on asserting the Commons' right to define truth by resolution; but they had no answer to the question of the origins and justification – whether historical, statutory or canonical – of the English church. They were unable therefore to show precisely how the Arminians had offended. In their confusion the initiative passed back to those frightened by what they saw as the weaknesses of the Petition of Right.

Eliot's tactics in leading the challenge to tonnage and poundage were as unrevolutionary as those of Pym over religion. His position, revealed in his attack on Buckingham in 1626, in 1629, and in his writings in the Tower before his death, was that nothing was fundamentally wrong in the state. Rather, Charles had been misled by evil counsellors, who must be purged. To the anxious conservatives in the Commons the case of Rolle seemed the safest path to this goal – since Rolle's goods had been seized by the customs farmers, private contractors, it should be possible to question them as private men and to deter any future evil counsellors while avoiding awkward questions of fundamentals. But Charles had no wish to see the erection of a tribunal outside his council to which his officers must answer, and accordingly declared that his servants acted on his orders. On this rock the political and intellectual conservatives in the Commons stuck, as many were to do again in the 1640s. By the last week in February the house had degenerated into confusion and division, from which Charles rescued it by adjourning for a week, to the second of March.

If the Commons found themselves bankrupt, the same could be said of the Lords, whose behaviour seemed more ineffectual than it had at other times in the 1620s. Admittedly, once the Commons determined to focus on Rolle's privilege there was little the Lords could do, though they might have tried to find a compromise on religion. Instead, with attendance significantly down, the parliamentary diary of the puritan Lord Montague noted 'little done of any note.' After the failure of their brief effort to mediate between Commons and king over the Petition of Right, most peers showed little eagerness to try again.

In such conditions, Charles's attempt to reach an understanding over tonnage and poundage in the adjournment was doomed, and he assembled parliament on 2 March only to adjourn again. The suspicion that there was no more to hope for probably accounts for the low attendance in the Commons that day, since so many dreaded a confrontation. This duly came when Eliot and his friends, certain that there would be no more parliaments, determined to appeal to the people with Three Resolutions against Arminianism and tonnage and poundage. But still Eliot's fundamental loyalism, and his desperate anxiety to blame evil counsellors rather than the king, showed through. In an unlikely, but revealing, flight of fancy, Eliot denounced the new lord treasurer, Weston, 'in whose person all evil is contracted'.

Eliot's denunciation of Weston made sense, however, insofar as Weston was a crypto-Catholic and thus brought together in his own person the twin threats of popery and arbitrary rule. Rous now feared 'Romish tyranny and Spanish monarchy', and the Commons' Three Resolutions, which attacked both Arminianism and tonnage and poundage, implied a smiliar coupling. But if those threats existed the Common were poorly placed to confront them. The notorious climax to the parliament, the holding down of the Speaker to prevent another adjournment, was a futile gesture. Although the Three Resolutions implied a new crime of treason against the state rather than against the person of the king, and although they invited a taxpayers' strike, at least in the short run the future belonged to Charles. The low attendances in parliament were symptomatic, and several MPs were privately critical after the dissolution of Eliot's 'very faulty' tactics, which had jeopardized the struggle against Arminianism. Charles promptly arrested Eliot and eight other ringleaders – all but one were to spend long years in gaol, and Eliot to die there – and declared that there would be no more parliaments until the nation understood him better.

Just as important, though, was that the king should again see some value in parliaments. While by the winter of 1627–8 he had recognized that he could not fight a war without parliamentary supply, the ensuing parliament, which failed to give statutory confirmation either to the militia or to tonnage and poundage, convinced him that he could not rely on parliaments for constructive action. He might gain supply, if little else, but the Petition ofRight had shown that the cost could be high. If parliament were no longer useful, there was little point in calling it. The late-medieval constitution, with its assumption that the subject would aid the king in wartime and that the king would 'live of his own' in peacetime, had been found doubly wanting. The king must now develop other sources of revenue, and think hard on the wisdom of wars.

6 Order in Church and State 1629–1640

The eleven years after 1629 have no unchallengeable claim to be regarded as a coherent whole. True, no parliaments were called, but to stress that feature is to exaggerate the importance of consultation in government; after all, there had effectively been no parliament between 1610 and 1621 either. Although the 1630s did witness repeated attempts to by-pass the assumption that consent was needed for extraordinary levies of money, the same frantic quest for new fiscal devices had been evident between 1626 and 1628, when several of the most notorious measures of the 1630s were considered seriously. In religion too, 1629 was no watershed, since Charles's ecclesiastical appointments had taken a revealing turn in 1628. If, as seems indubitable, the character of Charles was critical in the troubled history of his reign, then 1625 may have been the real turning-point. Yet there was a unity to the period. The absence of parliaments and – until the late 1630s – of wars left the government some freedom to do more than merely react to crises. The fatal attempts to bring a new uniformity to Scotland, Ireland and the church were the result.

One modern label, 'the eleven years' tyranny', sometimes applied to the period is misleading. While Charles was in 1631 contemplating plans to establish a permanent force of 1,000 soldiers, and while in 1633 he confiscated the records when the clerk of the Commons died, he had little idea of how to give effect to his dreams and his dislikes. On the contrary, the fiscal measures of the 1630s were founded on a careful exploitation of the letter of the law. More satisfactory is the common alternative, 'the personal rule', which stresses the role of the king himself. His council contained no truly dominant figures. Serving in the north and Ireland, Wentworth was excluded from power, despite the legends, until 1639. Laud certainly had enormous influence – he served on all the key committees, he gained the appointment of his protegés Francis Windebanke as secretary of state in 1632 and Bishop Juxon as lord treasurer in 1636, as well as the dismissal for religious dissent of Sir Robert Heath, now chief justice, in 1634. But he had neither the interest in nor the time for secular affairs that he did for ecclesiastical. Lord Treasurer Weston, earl of Portland from 1633, was the leading councillor until his death in 1635, but he was at odds with Laud and others, and increasingly beset by illness. Thereafter, Charles's closest ally was probably the queen, who was not herself a councillor. Indeed, Charles's tendency to ignore his council helps explain the speed of its demoralization and collapse in 1640. He was far more adept at creating lasting friendships with a handful of intimates than at selecting and trusting his advisers. With neither chief minister, nor, after Buckingham's death, favourite, to turn to, Charles ruled personally as well as reigned. Not only did he attend fussily to detail, worrying over the trivia in Laud's reports on the state of the church and involving himself in all the ship money proceedings; to the confusion of foreign ambassadors he also reversed the normal order of proceedings by insisting that he see them for discussions before his ministers did.

The central importance of Charles in the politics of the 1630s accounts for much of the history. His authoritarian temperament seems to have concealed a fundamental insecurity which became clear as his repeated vacillations in the crisis of 1639–40 disrupted the English military preparations. And his cold aloofness was almost certainly as closely related to the increasing introversion of his court as was his domestic bliss with Henrietta Maria. The latter was itself dangerous, for the queen's religious tastes and political views were ultimately more disastrous than Buckingham's flamboyance had been. Furthermore, Charles's distrust of men of independent judgment like Wentworth led him to turn away, in his choice of advisers, from men with solid landed bases in the country. The death of Pembroke in 1630 removed one of the few front-rank figures who was also a local magnate. This had a significance beyond narrowing the range of advice the king might receive, for it also diminished the numbers of those who might act as bridges to the country. As Sir Thomas Lucy, the leading gentleman in Warwickshire, lamented in 1633, Secretary of State Sir John Coke 'is the only councillor left I have had the honour to be acquainted with'. Few of his neighbours were better placed.

The religious character of council and court heightened their isolation. After Pembroke's death there were few who could quell the growing misgivings about popery in high places, as the earl's funeral sermon, with its remarkable premonition of religious war, made painfully evident. Weston, or the earl of Portland as he was soon to become, and his subordinate at the treasury, Cottington, were rightly suspected as crypto-Catholics; they were in 1632 to have a co-religionist in the new secretary of state, Windebanke. The religion of Laud himself caused widespread unease, while too many gentlemen of the bedchamber were, or were feared to be, papists. Charles's Italianate aesthetic tastes undoubtedly made conversions fashionable, and he was insufficiently concerned about them: to him the purity of his own motives was sufficient guarantee.

That insistence on his own rectitude was perhaps Charles's most unfortunate characteristic. It bred in him a fatal stubbornness and indifference to public opinion, best revealed in his crowning error of admitting papal agents – Gregorio Panzani in 1634 and George Con in 1636 – to court to please his wife and further his diplomacy. It led him too to the unwise assumption that his ends justified his means. So long as his ultimate intentions were honourable – and to him preserving the position of the crown was a religious duty – deception and the manipulation of the law, as in the *habeas corpus* case of 1627 or so many of the fiscal expedients of the 1630s, seemed well warranted.

Charles made his concern for order and majesty clearest in the area where he could have most impact, the regulation of his court. Impressed by what he had seen in 1623 in Madrid – the model for pre-Versailles Europe – he issued new orders in 1629 and 1631 minutely regulating the conduct of courtiers, particularly in the areas near the royal presence. Lucy Hutchinson, scarcely a sympathetic witness, paid well-deserved tribute to the improved moral tone of Charles's court. Charles had abandoned the sale of peerages on Buckingham's death – to resume it again only in the financial exigency of the onset of civil war – and took care to strengthen the public image of the nobility which ought to reflect grandeur back onto the monarchy. He may of course have felt such action was needed when so many of his peers were upstart new creations. Charles discouraged duelling even more insistently than had his father, frowned humourlessly on sexual escapades, and cultivated the principle of hierarchy both in private and in public. Considerations of degree were to govern admission to proximity to the king, and aristocratic display found a carefully regulated outlet, and an outlet oriented towards the king, in the ceremonial of the Order of the Garter. More revealingly, Charles moved toward granting the nobility novel legal privileges. Massive damages awarded by star chamber to the earl of Suffolk in 1632 in a case of undeferential behaviour constituted, it was reported, 'the bravest sentence for poor lords that ever was heard of'. The following year Charles invigorated the nobility further by declaring himself 'willing that all his subjects should find his courts of justice open to all men alike; yet when a man of mean quality shall prosecute against a noble man for an offence of heat or passion,' that liberty was not to be allowed.*

---

*W.S. Powell, *John Pory* (Chapel Hill, 1977), supplement, pp. 223–4: *Cal. State Papers, Dom., 1633–1634*, p. 339.

Equally suggestive of the importance Charles attached to the principles of monarchy and degree are the court masques of the 1630s,
with the composition of which he was closely associated and in which
he and the queen often appeared. The masques' themes are an
insistent elevation, to the point of an apotheosis far greater than that
of the Jacobean masques devised by Ben Jonson, of the royal couple
and their court. Fairly typical is the contention of *Coelum Britannicum*
['the British heaven'] of 1637 that Charles's court was the pattern of
perfect order and the model for Jove's heaven. There was philosophical point to the praise, for the guiding spirit of the masque, the
great Italianate architect and designer Inigo Jones, maintained a
fashionable neo-Platonic position. Contemplation of the Ideal would
necessarily elevate the beholder's thoughts and ultimately reform his
actions by making him desire to emulate it. The exaltation of king
and queen provided exemplars for the courtiers and thus ultimately
for the country. The repeated denouements of the masques, where
the mere appearance of the king or queen established order, offer the
clearest insight into Charles's intensely hierarchical vision, in which
the lower members took directions from the head.

The confidence of the masque contrasted sadly with the difficulty of
ensuring that orders were obeyed in the unpoliced state of England.
Illusion parted company with reality in other ways. The imperial
affectation of masques like *Britannia Triumphans*, and the heroic
imperial stance in which Charles had himself portrayed in Le Sueur's
notable equestrian statue commissioned by Portland in 1630, still
more in Van Dyck's triumphant equestrian portraits of 1633 and
1638, look odd in the context of such a cloistered court. They also
make Charles's eventual nemesis in Scotland less surprising. The
huge imperial palace at Whitehall he was planning with Jones in
1638, which might have made London the wonder of Europe, shows
the scale of his delusions. More fittingly, the cultural achievements of
a court whose head justly prided himself on his aesthetic taste were
remarkably superficial. Apart from Charles's magnificent art
collection – to be scattered in the whirlwind of the 1640s – and additions to work begun under James on the Whitehall banqueting house
and the queen's house at Greenwich there was little to show. The
classical west front Jones imposed on the old Gothic cathedral of
St Paul's, the classical façades Laud added to St John's College,
Oxford, and Wentworth to the King's Manor at York, are a telling
comment on the substance of Charles's rule.

The façades, and the failure to start anew, also throw light on the
fashionable argument that 'two cultures', the cultures of court and
country, diverged under Charles. The claims have been taken too far.
It was of the essence of royal courts at any time to set styles, and

Charles was not being necessarily 'popish' in following Italian models, particularly since the latter largely derived from anti-papal Venice rather than from the more advanced Baroque of Rome. Nor was the splendid realism of Van Dyck's portraits inherently unEnglish, different though it was from the rigid blacks and whites of so many country 'limners'. Staunch parliamentarians of the future – Warwick, Arthur Goodwin, Lord Wharton's family – could sit for the fashionable Flemish painter as eagerly as could the queen; equally, the list of purchasers of Charles's collection after his execution – the regicide Colonel Hutchinson bought many bargains – indicates the unwisdom of using culture to mark a political divide. So too with the theatre: John Milton could still write, in *Comus*, a non-court masque; and the puritan lawyer William Prynne gained remarkably little public attention when he had his ears mutilated by star chamber in 1633 for his virulent attacks in *Histriomastix* on the sinfulness of stage plays and players, including by implication the queen. Plays such as Massinger's *Believe as you list* of 1631, or the lost *Cardinal's Conspiracy* of 1639, critical of courtly values and performed at the popular London theatres, the Red Bull and the Fortune, suggest that the theatre had not degenerated entirely from the universal appeal of Shakespeare to the sycophancy of the masque on the one hand and popular bawdy and violence on the other.

The only respect in which the claims that two cultures were polarizing are valid is in the field of religion. Too many of the Titians and del Sartos Charles pursued so energetically while building up his art collection were works of Roman Catholic devotion. And the revelling cavalier poetry of the likes of Thomas Carew contrasted dangerously with the desperate certainty of puritan sermons that God was turning his back on England.

The man most puritans held responsible for their despondency was William Laud, promoted to the archbishopric of Canterbury on Abbot's death in 1633. They were to learn only slowly that it was Charles's own concern with hierarchy, order and reverence which drew him to Laud, and that the archbishop was only the agent, rather than the origin, of their woes.

Laud's aims have been aptly characterized as the reversal of certain major aspects of the Reformation. He sought to restore the church to the respect and influence it had lost at the Reformation: only thus, he felt, could true religion, the monarchy and society be preserved. The determination with which he challenged the prevailing patterns of worship and relations between church and laity established over a whole century makes it plausible to see Laud, and his royal ally, as the real innovators in early-Stuart England; the puritan gentry and clergy were speaking no less than the truth when they claimed to defend old English ways. The scale of the attempt, moreover, casts doubt on the assertions of some recent historians who, in their concern to emphasize the contingent nature of the collapse of 1640, argue that religious polarization had been greater in the 1580s than the 1630s. Certainly the overt presbyterianism of Elizabeth's reign was dead, and anti-episcopal agitation only grew with the failure of reform in 1640–1. Nevertheless, alienation does seem to have been far greater in the 1630s. The presbyterian spokesmen under Elizabeth had had prominent defenders at court in Leicester and even Burghley. Laud's enemies had none to look to at Charles's court. Warwick, Lord Saye, Lord Brooke and John Pym not only contemplated emigration but also took up legal cudgels; some of their associates at least *talked* of other forms of action. Such estrangement was both remarkable and dangerous.

Although Laud was no major theologian, and is most famous for his ceremonialism, the key to his position was theological. While Calvinists accorded a large role to edifying sermons, Laud attached the greatest importance to the sacraments. For him the altar rather than the pulpit provided the means to salvation – reverence replaced engagement. His private book of devotions reveals a Lutheran, and very non-Calvinist, sense that in the communion service the believer received Christ's 'blessed body and blood' – as he gratuitously added, 'I quarrel not the words.' All else flowed from that sacramental position. Laud's sacerdotalism, the elevation of the dignity of the priesthood which so offended anti-clericals, made sense if the clergy were mediators at the altar between God and man, rather than merely expounders of God's word. So too his ceremonialism: all to do with the altar must be seemly, and the clergy must wear distinctive vestments. As his opening sermon to parliament in 1626 showed, with its vision of the tribes coming up harmoniously to Jerusalem to worship, his concern for religious reverence reinforced, and was reinforced by, his political objectives. Like Charles, he vehemently believed in the existence of a divinely ordered hierarchy in the universe, on which both church and state should be modelled.

Laud's preoccupations dictate caution when talking of Arminianism. Although the archbishop was almost certainly himself an Arminian, and although Calvinists everywhere bewailed the undermining of what they saw as orthodoxy, Laud did not, as did Bishop Montagu at Chichester or Wren at Norwich, strive to control the kind of doctrine preached. Instead, Laud was ready to suppress Arminian as well as Calvinist works as destructive of the unity of the church, and concerned himself primarily with the 'beauty of holiness'. The altar was to be raised and railed off, while dignified church buildings

and ornaments would induce a reverence which might make wor-
shippers receptive to the grace of the sacraments. Despite protestant
aborrence of 'idolatry', stained glass, bowing at the name of Jesus
and to the altar, were to be restored. Even the illiterate, used to white,
barn-like churches, might understand the attacks on such 'creeping
popery'. Equally if not more alarming to Calvinists who saw in
sermons the hope of mankind, Laud set limits on preaching. His ideal
was one sermon a week from the pulpit, to be delivered by orthodox
parochial ministers – not nonconformist unbeneficed lecturers –
prepared to observe the full ceremonial of the prayer-book service;
the rest of the sabbath should be given over to catechizing or to the
legitimate pastimes enjoined in the book of sports of 1633. Accordingly, to the dismay of those who saw Satan's hand in impediments to
preaching, Bishop Wren forbade afternoon sermons in his diocese.

There were certainly grounds for Laud's campaign. Reports spoke
of dogs fouling unprotected altars and birds flying through dila-
pidated churches; his old cathedral, St Paul's in London, had become
a squalid thoroughfare. But the price of uniformity was high. Wren's
campaign in Norwich in 1636 deprived the city of five of its most effective preachers, for whom the corporation vainly vouched. And the
book of sports, with its apparent invitation to desecration of the sabbath, outraged mainstream sabbatarian opinion, occasioning the
largest number of suspensions of ministers since the enforcement of
the 1604 canons. William Prynne's response, the recording in his
Divine Tragedy of the sad fate of sabbath-breakers, helped lose him
what was left of his ears and gain a branding in 1637.

Laud aimed too to restore the clergy to a financial independence
suited to their elevated standing as ministers of God and defenders of
obedience. To this end, in his court of high commission he harassed
lay impropriators of livings to persuade them to pay higher stipends to
their ministers; he took on a still more intractable problem when
he addressed the matter of advowsons, or patronage rights over
parish livings, about one-third of which were owned by laymen. Lay
advowsons, Laud felt, carried with them the risk of corruption as
ambitious clergymen strove for appointments; they also diminished
the control of the ecclesiastical hierarchy. But property rights
were property rights, protected by the common law, and Laud's
campaign was on the whole supremely ineffectual. He erred all the
more in making it noisy, as when he unwisely told Sir Arthur Haselrig,
soon to be one of the radical parliamentarian leaders, that he
hoped 'ere long not to leave so much as the name of a lay fee in
England'.

Others shared Laud's conviction that the parlous finances of the
ministry must be reformed. But whereas Laud sought to strengthen

the established parochial structure, puritan reformers directed their energies first towards endowing lectureships in market towns, where they could be sure of large audiences. When the York House conference of 1626 convinced the well-informed that the battle to win over the church's hierarchy was lost a group of London merchants, lawyers and clergy came together as the feoffees for impropriations, with the aim of using charitable gifts to buy up impropriations in order to endow godly preaching. But Laud only saw puritan subversiveness in their organization – however limited its thirty-odd grants – in their concentration on towns, and in their aim of extending their activities to the purchase of advowsons. In 1633 he had the feoffees dissolved. If York House had been a milestone, for some the dissolution was the end of the road, and John Davenport, one of the clerical feoffees, emigrated to New England.

As early as his 1626 sermon to parliament Laud had revealed an unfounded belief that puritanism was a conspiracy against church and state. The few signs of genuine organization, such as the feoffees or the network which distributed the books of Prynne and other dissidents, convinced him that he had found the tip of the iceberg, and drove him to idiosyncracies like setting a spy on the Calvinist Bishop Morton. More notoriously, he also inflicted brutal punishments, such as the ear-cropping of the pamphleteers Prynne, Burton and Bastwick, thus creating martyrs. The vehemence was to be amply repaid, for despite its provocativeness his campaign made little headway. The church courts, even those of Canterbury diocese, were ineffective, since they were clogged with other business, which was often more attractive to fee-hungry officials; charges laid against dissidents therefore often bogged down. A further obstacle was that lay role in the church which Laud sought to eliminate. Nonconformity in worship had to be presented for prosecution, and this required the co-operation of churchwardens, who might themselves be puritans. Accordingly, the hard-line Bishop Wren's attempts to catch puritans in his new diocese of Ely in 1638 failed because he could not find out from the churchwardens who his targets were. Above all, lay patrons could be counted on to protect 'their' ministers; thus, Warwick provided a refuge for the radical Hugh Peter, while powerful gentry like Sir Robert Harley in Herefordshire could usually protect their clients.

Whatever impact Laud had stemmed from his political position, for Charles was his firmest prop. The king's motives appear to have been mixed. During the 1640s he readily abandoned Laud himself to his fate and showed little concern for the prayer book, while in his years of power he interested himself far more in the prestige project of rebuilding St Paul's than in the refurbishment of the church in the localities. Nevertheless, the potential conflict between the king's

statutory position as governor of the church and Laudian claims that
the church existed *iure divino*, by divine right, independent of the laity,
seems not to have perturbed Charles. After Portland's death in 1635
the archbishop was the king's leading councillor, and when Laud's
nominee Bishop Juxon of London became lord treasurer there were,
with Archbishop Neile of York, three bishops on the council, the
highest total since the Reformation. Furthermore, the rise of the
Laudians at Whitehall was reflected in the localities, as senior clergy
were added to the commission of the peace. By the end of the decade
the Kent commission included eight clergy, again the highest total
since the Reformation. As one of Wentworth's correspondents commented, 'We begin to live here in the church triumphant.' But by
enlisting the state so closely in pursuit of ecclesiastical goals, Charles
and Laud ensured that any attack on the clergy would also involve the
crown. James's Hampton Court dictum, 'No bishop, no king,' might
yet come true.

The reciprocated passions were all the more heated in that Laud's
programme also had a social dimension. His own humble origins,
matched elsewhere on the episcopal bench, helped earn Lord
Brooke's sneer that the Laudians were '*excrementa mundi*', the refuse of
the world. And to local élites the 'pomposities' of assertive and low-
born Laudians seemed like an assault on hierarchy rather than the
affirmation of it that Laud claimed. Town corporations whose elevated pews in municipal churches bishops removed in the name of
'decency' resented being levelled with the multitude, understandably
enough when, like the Norwich aldermen, they were deliberately
jostled by their new pew-mates. It is not inconceivable therefore that
aspects of Laudianism may have been 'popular' in a sense which we
rarely consider. Historians have often noted that the Laudian 'beauty
of holiness' cost money, and that money demanded for alterations
which many churchwardens saw as idolatrous and popish was not
easily gathered; thus, by 1640 only one-quarter of Somerset parishes
had obeyed Laud's injunctions over the communion table. Yet we
have only recently been made aware of how much support, often
semi-pagan and superstitious, there was in the countryside for a
ritualist and ceremonialist church. To the godly élites it must have
appeared that Laud and his allies were gratifying the baser instincts of
the meaner sort.

Most dangerously of all, the Laudians were operating in a context
of the king's and not of their own making. Despite the archbishop's
protests, Charles allowed successive papal agents to operate at court,
and to make some spectacular converts in the later 1630s. He did little
to stop ostentatious displays at the chapels of foreign ambassadors, or
even Catholic processions through neighbouring London streets.

Laud's determined bid to change the face of the church, in alliance with a group of theologians who challenged the central tenet of English Calvinist orthodoxy, therefore magnified and gave point to the popery in high places. Apocalyptic fears of a popish plot had been evident in the Commons in 1628-9; a decade later they were much more widespread. Foxe's *Acts and Monuments*, with its ideal of the emperor Constantine, the godly prince, had made the protection of true religion the ruler's chief duty. The growing evidence that Charles was in default could not help but colour the response to other demands he made.

The experience of the Jacobean peace suggests that the Elizabethan attempt to establish a national church subservient to the crown was by no means bound to fail. But by the late 1630s the local alliance between church and state had been fractured. The magistrates of Chester feted Prynne on his way into exile after mutilation in 1637; by 1638 the Sussex magistrates' bench had become a sounding-board for denunciations of Laud's reforms. The catastrophic nature of the alliance between Charles and Laud was becoming clear.

New departures were far less evident in Charles's secular policies than they were in Laud's campaign in the church. Just as in the Jacobean peace his father had been able to think of little beyond survival, so Charles during his years of peace gave few signs of seeking to establish new forms of rule. His first priority after the recent turbulence was simply the establishment of stability and security.

The end of the 1620s had brought a combination of high food prices and industrial depression as grievous as that of 1623. Exactly one-third of the twenty-four known incidents of food rioting in Kent between 1558 and 1640 occurred in 1630-1. And in the south-western forests the so-called 'Western Rising' flared intermittently from 1626 to 1632 as poor commoners strove to protect their livelihoods against royal efforts to raise money by selling tracts of woodland to speculators for disafforestation. Ironically, the cause of much of the social malaise – insofar as it lay outside the atrocious weather and another plague outbreak in 1630 – was political. The earlier textile crisis had never wholly eased, and the vulnerability of the economy was soon revealed as the new draperies faltered. Privateers from Dunkirk made exceptionally deep inroads into the trade in 1629-30, despite the imminence of peace; the merchants' actions against tonnage and poundage increased the disruption. By the spring of 1629 there was mass unemployment in Essex, Suffolk and other new drapery regions, with occasional reports of demonstrations for work and isolated bread riots. The lot of the poor worsened catastrophically when the harvest brought in in 1630 was as bad as that of 1623. As usual, when food prices soared domestic demand for cloth fell and unemployment spiralled.

The response of the governors, both central and local, was as characteristic as that of the poor. With the exception of a single incident in Maldon in Essex – which reaped a savage governmental reaction – the crisis did not see faceless mobs rising to help themselves to what was not theirs. Instead the poor asserted the duty of the rich and powerful to protect their just rights to life and sustenance. And in their turn, local magistrates helped prevent economic ills turning into social conflict by stepping up relief and by regulating the activities of food traders. This response to rising prices had the full support of the privy council, which echoed the poor in blaming high prices on exploitative middlemen: thus, in 1631 it publicized widely a star chamber judgment against a speculator, in hopes, presumably, of maintaining order as much as of lessening suffering.

The crown's response to the socio-economic crisis of 1629–31 was, however, much broader than a mere hunt for profiteers. The programme which emerged, culminating in two books of orders in the winter of 1630–1, was a catch-all, linking market and vagrancy regulations with remedies for plague and attempts to control the rate of building in London. It has often been thought symptomatic of the Personal Rule. To an older generation the government's policy seemed almost to embody christian socialist paternalism in its protection of the weak from the economically strong; more recently, several local historians have seen such intervenionism as the offensive peak of early-Stuart attempts at centralization.

The regulations may indeed have been characteristic of the crown's policy in the 1630s, but that is hardly because they revealed any novel goals. The government was essentially traditionalist in its approach, responding to crisis by instructing local authorities to enforce existing regulations for providing work for the poor, suppressing alehouses and vagrants, and so on. JPs were instructed, as so often since 1605, to report on their activities to the assize judges, and diligently to hold petty sessions every month to ensure the good governance of the countryside. And in many respects the books of orders accorded with the intentions of JPs, who could recognize symptoms of social distress as well as could the council; indeed, much of the programme, characteristically, attempted to systematize existing local initiatives. Not surprisingly there is no sign of any local protest against unwonted interference in local ways. Anyway, only a minority of counties submitted reports at all regularly, and scarcely any after 1633. Most tellingly of all, despite another plague epidemic and more abysmal harvests in the later 1630s, the council showed little concern at such backsliding. As a disciplinary system the book of orders left much to be desired. Historians' association of the 1630s with 'Thorough', determined rule from the centre which broke through self-interested obstructionism, results primarily from the survival of the correspondence of Laud and Wentworth. It does not reflect the ramshackle edifice of Charles's rule, or even probably of his intentions.

No more does economic policy yield clues to the long-term aspirations of the crown. Some historians have seen in an alliance with the City, through the customs farmers, the coalition between monarchy and merchants which is held to have built absolutism in Europe. Others have seen Charles heading a feudal reaction, striving in the books of orders to bind the poor to the land through service in husbandry, maintaining a profitable feudal dependence through the court of wards and granting economic privileges out to courtiers as earlier kings granted out land. There is some truth in each characterization, yet each grossly exaggerates the crown's ability to formulate, let alone pursue, distant objectives. The enduring feature of royal policy was its susceptibility to short-term fiscal considerations.

Claims that Charles was bent on a fruitful alliance with the merchants seem particularly suspect. Royal dependence on the credit of the customs farmers was indeed so great that the crown was unable to extract from the farmers any major increase in rent. This was despite some recovery in trade during the 1630s – Dover built up a substantial re-export trade, convoying supplies from Spain to the Spanish armies in Flanders, while imports from the Mediterranean, East Indies and Americas all rose. The constraints were made cripplingly clear when in the new customs lease of 1638 Charles found that a higher rent only decreased the amount that the farmers could lend him for his efforts against the Scots. But such dependence does not mean that the government was in the pocket of the great merchants. While Charles in 1634 confirmed the privileges of the Merchant Adventurers, in 1635 he licensed an interloping merchant, Sir William Courteen, in association with the courtier Endymion Porter, to break into the East India Company's monopoly of trade to the Indian Ocean. Money in his pocket could pull him in either direction. Still more revealing are his dealings with the City government, the collective voice of the great merchants. In pursuit of minor pickings from the fees of those wishing to trade free of City restrictions, Charles in 1636 dismayed the City fathers by incorporating a new body, the corporation of the suburbs, outside their jurisdiction. Most provocative of all, Charles hounded the City corporation and the City companies throughout the 1630s in hope of fines and confiscations over the administration of the great 1627–8 transfer of crown lands, and of the City's estates in the Ulster plantation. Since these were both ventures into which the crown had coerced the City in the first place there were good grounds for resentment. A policy conceived cynically with an eye to short-term gains was hardly ground for a long-term alliance.

Casting the crown as a feudal reactionary is equally inappropriate. Certainly the council appreciated the stability of agricultural employments, yet even here mercenary motives deprived its policies of any consistency. Despite Laud's moralist concerns, the commission established in 1633 to protect the midlands poor by limiting enclosure and depopulation soon degenerated into a mere fiscal device which sold licences to enclosing landlords. Even its intentions – let alone its effects – were countered by the crown's own disruptive record as a speculative encloser and depopulator in the southwestern forests and the fens. Certainly, too, Charles distrusted the unrestricted growth of London, and like James and Elizabeth disapproved of the capital's growing role as a social centre; he therefore proclaimed a ban on new building, and, more innovatively, sought to bring the spreading suburbs under closer control. But these ventures too were soon corrupted, for the council was primarily interested in the fines to be raised from new buildings and the fees to be had from tradesmen.

Nowhere is the cynicism to which policy was liable more apparent than in the 'popish soap' monopoly. The soap patent, granted in 1632 to a syndicate which included some of Portland's Catholic clients who claimed – spuriously – to have discovered a superior means of making soap, did much to discredit Charles's government, not least through the 'trials' used to judge which soap washed whiter. The extent to which all of Charles's administration was contaminated is suggested by the sardonic comment of one Kentishman that the book of sports of 1633 would be a good device for making money. 'Moral bankruptcy' may be too strong a consideration of the regime, but Wentworth certainly, if piously, thought in 1637 that some projectors ought to be hanged, to take 'the reproach off all [the king's] upright and well-meaning ministers.'* The opportunism which runs through the economic policies of the Personal Rule suggests the wisdom of looking for motives not in any long-term objectives but in the immediate gain which might help those in power escape from a morass of debt. Even the degree to which there was a specifically royal policy can be questioned. Pym calculated in 1640 that the crown received about 10 per cent of the profit on a patent for licensing wine sellers, and a modern estimate is that the crown received about 13 per cent of the proceeds on monopolies overall. The courtiers and contractors scooped the rest.

*Cal. State Papers, Dom., 1635, p. 301; W. Knowler, *Strafforde's Letters and Dispatches* (London, 1739), II, pp. 77, 117.

Similarly short-term were the fiscal devices developed by Portland and his successors. The council's stock response to its need for money was to look to the past for inspiration, and the tired collection of precedents for benevolences and forced loans that Attorney-General William Noy listed in a 1634 enquiry into how to raise money by the king's 'absolute prerogative' was not the stuff of which Richelieu's rule in France was made. Devices such as Portland's exploitation of the anachronistic statute of Henry VIII for compulsory use of the longbow* were more likely to scandalize than to threaten.

The obstacles to new departures were certainly great enough, as both Salisbury and Cranfield had variously found. But while the French crown was currently forging a new order by a determined policy of creation and sale of new offices and the taxation of office-holders, none of Charles's ministers thought of such changes. The financial crisis was not deep enough, the political dangers too obvious, and their own instinctive conservatism too rooted. His council did nibble at administrative reform, which might have been the means to a new pattern of government. Commissions on fees were sporadically active in 1629–31 and again in 1637–8, charged with investigating corruption, revising fee-levels and fining offenders. The later commission in particular uncovered massive fraud, scarcely surprisingly when the household accounting officials alone were cheating the crown out of about 1 per cent of its income throughout the early seventeenth century. But this was not the start of any restructuring; neither did it yield any appreciable dividends, for only about £35,000 in fines was levied. Charles was indeed not the king to carry through the major reform needed to establish absolutism. Symptomatic was his refusal to appoint Wentworth, whom he distrusted for his assertiveness, treasurer on Portland's death in 1635. For Wentworth at least saw the attractions of a salaried bureaucracy that was both more efficient and responsible to the king. Charles, typically, had the worst of all worlds, for in harassing his officials pointlessly he helped ensure that only half the office-holders sitting in the Long Parliament would ultimately side with him.

Such an outcome, of gains inadequate to warrant the resentment provoked, was the result of too many of the fiscal devices of the 1630s. Perhaps the most glaring example of royal fiscal antiquarianism as well as of its political short-sightedness was the campaign to fine landlowners for alleged encroachments on long-forgotten medieval boundaries of royal forests. Thus, one forest court, or eyre, extended the limits of Rockingham forest in Northamptonshire from six to sixty miles; in so doing it alienated the crown's natural allies, for the earl of

*Cal. State Papers, Dom., 1635, pp. 45, 244.

Westmorland was fined £19,000, the earl of Salisbury £20,000, with scant justification in equity in not in the letter of the law. And almost incredibly, Charles believed that to impose such large fines and then to remit the bulk of them would both affirm his power and display his magnanimity, thus generating gratitude. Instead, it bred only distrust and anger. Furthermore, the king's practical gains were small, probably only about £20,000 for the whole ill-advised campaign. The rest was skimmed off by courtiers and officials.

One short-term device did, however, yield an appreciable revenue. In 1629–30 the council began to fine landowners worth the now trifling sum of £40 p.a. for ignoring their ancient duty of presenting themselves to be knighted at the king's coronation. The council's concern was manifestly with revenue rather than with the number of knights – the corporation of Leicester was advised to compound at the high rate of five subsidies for its eligible citizens.* But although many delayed payment few were willing to withstand a demand that, however obsolete, was undoubtedly legal. By 1635 almost 10,000 landowners, or probably half the non-knighted gentlemen in the country, had paid in a total of over £173,000. But such extraordinary ventures were no formula for solvency: as the observant Venetian ambassador commented, they were 'false mines for obtaining money, because they are good for once only, and states are not maintained by such devices'.

More remarkable was the transformation of the crown's ordinary account, its regular incomings and outgoings, which was in the black by 1635–6. That the king arrived at this unusual and happy state was due most of all to the customs – the fears of so many of the Commons' speakers in the 1610 and 1614 debates proved justified. Peace and its accompanying expansion of trade, further impositions, and Portland's revision in 1634–5 of the book of customs rates to take account of the increasingly valuable colonial imports, raised the customs revenues from abut £300,000 p.a. to almost £500,000 p.a. during the decade. Total annual income from all sources, including extraordinaries like knighthood fines, rose from just under £750,000 to over £1M., and the larger picture is revealing. Crown revenues almost doubled in real terms, allowing for inflation, between 1603 and 1639; furthermore, the royal debt, which at just over £1M. in the mid-1630s was the rough equivalent of one year's total income, was hardly terrifying. The crude figures indicate that the financial auspices for the crown on Portland's death in 1635 ought not to have been grim. That fact, of course, has a bearing on the long-term prospects of rule without parliaments. Had Charles not blundered in Scotland, might parliaments have gone?

*H. Stocks, *Records of the Borough of Leicester* (Cambridge, 1923), pp. 256, 263.

The king's decision to replace Portland as treasurer with the honest but unimaginative Bishop Juxon is revealing. As in his handling of the administrative reform commissions, he showed that whatever his hostility to talk of parliaments he had no stomach for the action that would be needed to secure any permanent change. Accordingly, while Charles balanced his ordinary account the 1630s saw little reduction in the debt; instead the king limped along by courtesy of the customs farmers. Even before the Scottish crisis broke he was regularly 'anticipating' or spending in advance, over £300,000 p.a. of the following year's revenues – a level similar to that of the strife-torn 1620s. Although Charles was by no means as profligate as his father, he had already made his priorities clear when in 1627, in the financial crisis accompanying Buckingham's expedition to La Rochelle, he spent £27,000 acquiring the fabulous art collection of the duke of Mantua. Not surprisingly, the increased income of the 1630s was soaked up by increased expenditure – the queen's palace at Greenwich cost £133,000. Since he was already drawing to the full on the credit of the customs farmers through anticipations, Charles allowed himself little margin for emergencies. His huge sale of crown lands in 1627–8 had left him little to offer as security to other lenders; and his cavalier treatment of creditors – he let his main prop of the 1620s, Sir Philip Burlamachi, go bankrupt in 1633, and harassed the City in innumerable ways – was to gain its reward in 1640 when none would lend to him. However much the Scottish debacle was the unnecessary product of his own folly, Charles's finances were not sound enough to give him much safety in the troubled Europe of the 1630s.

And complications were not unlikely since, particularly as his finances stabilized, Charles aspired to the position in Europe which he felt his due as king of so many kingdoms. Historians have assumed that once Charles abandoned parliaments his policies hinged wholly upon peace, and there is contemporary warrant for their belief. Clarendon's famous tribute to the halcyon – and insufficiently appreciated – Caroline peace of the 1630s was not simply nostalgic, for panegyrics to the king in verse and masque throughout the decade celebrated the peace and plenty which England alone in Europe enjoyed. Yet the fanciful pastoralism of so many of the masques did not tell the whole story, since as we have seen it was repeatedly balanced by presentations of Charles as an heroic figure, as one who had not drawn in on himself. More concretely, throughout the early 1630s – even before the ship money years – Charles continued to spend on the navy and on harbour fortifications.

The king's great hope remained the retrieval of his family's and his country's honour by the restoration of his sister to the Palatinate. Although his likely course varied with the changing conditions in Europe, Whitehall buzzed insistently with rumours of alliance and the journeyings of diplomats. Unfortunately, neither the rumours nor the diplomats were for much of the decade comprehensible to many of Charles's subjects. Sharing his father's distaste for the Dutch as republican rebels and trading rivals, and believing equally that Vienna danced to Madrid's tune, Charles inclined away from those around him who urged a protestant alliance. He indicated his distaste for such a policy, and his attitude to Gustav Adolf of Sweden, a protestant hero whom many Britons idolized during his phenomenal wave of successes between 1631 and 1633, by banning in 1632 the circulation of corantoes, the early newspapers which detailed the war's events. But new possibilities seemed to open in 1635 when France's entry into the Thirty Years War offered the prospect of an anti-Habsburg alliance which was not simply and disreputably protestant, all the more so after Vienna coldly rejected Charles's proposals for a settlement the following year. High-placed courtiers grew confident of a change in alignments, and the arrival in London in 1636 of Charles's nephew, the young heir to the Palatinate, seemed to strengthen their suspicions. But to the despair of some of his protestant councillors, the furthest the king would go was to permit the Providence Island Company to engage in some minor privateering against Spanish shipping in the Caribbean. Although his hopes of an active alliance with Spain to dismember the Netherlands and regain the Palatinate dwindled after detailed negotiations in both 1631 and 1636, Charles on the whole maintained a benevolent neutrality. Spanish troops and supplies were convoyed up the Channel and, in 1639, Spanish soldiers were even allowed to march across English soil.

Charles's unwillingness to commit himself may have stemmed from a proper sense of the paucity of England's resources and of the dangers from the parliament which a war must bring. If so, his realism had its limits, for it did not in the end deter him from a fatal aggressiveness towards the Scots. Nor did it amount to a coherent policy. Charles asserted his naval dignity in the most flamboyant fashion, naming his flagship *The Sovereign of the Seas* and giving his fleets in the 1630s little else to do but force others' ships to recognize his claims to maritime sovereignty. In 1639 Charles was given a golden opportunity both to maintain his posture and to apply pressure to Spain one way or another when Dutch ships attacked a Spanish fleet just off Dover. But instead of acting, Charles left his fleet to stand by without clear instructions while the Dutch destroyed their enemies in English waters. Such blustering vacillation earned the contempt of many European rulers while running a real risk of provoking one of them to call the English bluff. Laud and Wentworth had some grounds for fearing, before the Scots brought him down, that Charles's activities would drag him into some crisis, necessitating a parliament. That a parliament would be critical was apparent in the mob assaults on the survivors of the Spanish ships attacked off Dover.

Ship money must be seen in this international context, for the most famous project of Charles's 'personal rule' stemmed from his desire for action to redeem the failures of the previous decade. It was no would-be absolutist attempt to bolster his general revenues, for ship money genuinely was spent on an enlarged fleet. Neither was its administration the new departure that might have ushered in absolutism. True, the post office was reorganized in the mid-1630s, and there were some improvements in the council's book-keeping; but remarkably little attention was paid to obtaining reliable local officers. Sheriffs, made the key to the system on the assumption that a single officer would be more responsive and responsible than the multiple commissioners who otherwise ran local government, were increasingly taken from the highest levels of the county gentry. This indicated the council's sense of the importance of the task, but it did not guarantee the sympathy of those selected. In contrast to the period of the forced loan, the county commissions of the peace were left substantially intact, with only a minor pruning of the inactive – rather than the disloyal – in 1637. The process of government in the 1630s looks very much like the mixture as before.

Ship money was one more product of the council's fiscal antiquarianism. The ports had long been compelled to provide ships, or money in lieu, when required for defence of the realm, but in 1634–5 the council progressively extended the convention to the whole country, on the plausible argument that the prosperity of all suffered from the still troublesome pirate raids. With this expansion went an increase in the sums demanded, from *c.* £80,000 in 1634–5 to almost £200,000 p.a. for the rest of the decade, with the exception of 1638–9, when plague, a disastrous harvest and political crisis persuaded Charles to reduce the levy to *c.* £70,000. These figures contrast with the total of about £1M. levied by parliamentary subsidy and forced loan in the whole previous, belligerent, decade. The novelty became still more apparent with the increase in the taxed population – in Essex about four times as many were assessed for ship money as for the 1628 subsidy. For the first time the country was being asked to pay regularly to its government.

And the money came in, to a degree remarkable by seventeenth-

century European standards. The characteristic deference to justifi-
able commands meant that as late as the 1636–7 levy the shortfall
was only 3.5 per cent. Conformism was reinforced by more tangible
considerations. Where there was a genuine threat of piracy, or of
enemy raids, tax-payers seem to have accepted the legitimacy of the
levy: thus, the vulnerable south-coast counties of Hampshire and
Sussex paid right to the end. Furthermore, the strength of the old *quid
pro quo* rule of politics was clear in, for example, the relative success
of ship money in Cheshire. There both the county and the city of
Chester vied for a hearing from the council, and each strove to bolster
its claims against the other by responding with alacrity to the council's demands. Whatever the climate of suspicion, the practical links
between court and country had to be maintained.

Yet there was opposition, and its character is revealing. Much of
the earlier resistance took the form of rating disputes, challenges to
the distribution of the burden between areas. A myriad such disputes
eventually ground collection to a halt in many counties, for the majority had to be settled by the catastrophically overburdened council:
thirty disputes from Essex alone reached it in 1637. Several recent
historians have argued that the prevalence of rating disputes indicates
the sheer conservative localism of the gentry, rather than constitutionalist fervour. Yet localist friction does not tell the whole story,
even in the context of an overburdened council and of a court which
had too few contacts in many areas to allow it to smoothe ruffled
feathers effectively. Challenges to the equity of assessments were
clearly in at least some cases camouflage. Thus, when the earl of
Warwick, the leading articulator of constitutionalist opposition in
Essex, was threatened with an attack on his local power base, he
promptly switched to challenging the validity of the local rates; again,
rating disputes in Somerset were suspiciously concentrated in the
neighbourhood of that old trouble-maker, Sir Robert Phelips. The
sheriff of Rutland in early 1637 was not alone in sensing refusals on
'matter of conscience', and even areas of Lincolnshire devoid of resident gentry evinced articulate opposition. The final crystallization
and diffusion during the 1620s of a coherent sense of how England
was to be governed, and of the legal limits on government, was doing
its work.

Ominously too there were signs of organized resistance. An extensive puritan cousinage, based largely in East Anglia but stretching
out to include the Buckinghamshire gentleman John Hampden, Lord
Saye in Oxfordshire and the earl of Bedford farther west, had been
able to maintain contact in the 1630s in meetings of the Providence
Island company; and by the later 1630s they were eager to challenge
the government on ship money. Emboldened by a judicial resolution

in his favour, Charles at last decided in 1637 to allow a test case to be brought. John Hampden's counsel, notably Oliver St John, who was also legal adviser to the earls of both Warwick and Bedford, argued that the regularity of ship money payments meant they constituted not an emergency levy but a tax, for which parliament ought to have been summoned. The case had plausibility in the manifestly non-emergency character of the ship money fleets, but seven of the twelve judges took the legally sound view that the king was the only judge of emergencies, and of the action required. Doubts about the crown's intentions were, however, increased by provocative judicial asides in the packed courtroom. Judge Berkeley's off-hand remark that the king was '*lex loquens,* a living, a speaking, an acting law', was in the circumstances fiery stuff; so was chief justice Finch's declaration that 'no acts of parliament make any difference' to the crown's power to raise money for defence of the realm. Finch's views suggested the very extension of the prerogative that the Petition of Right had striven to block, and he caused further alarm by expounding them in the counties in propagandist charges on the assize circuit. *Hampden's Case* failed to settle the matter as Charles had hoped it would.

Time still seemed to be on the king's side, for despite the huge public interest in the trial the yield of the 1637-8 levy fell eventually only 9 per cent below target. And in the immediate aftermath of defeat the earl of Warwick, Lords Saye and Brooke and John Pym were all contemplating emigration to America. But the reassuring yield concealed ominous strains. Although the Scottish crisis was probably crucial in persuading the leading dissidents to remain, the trial itself had not been without effect. The arguments of the five judges who sided with Hampden gained a wider circulation in the country than did Finch's, and in Kent gentlemen debated the issues with learning and sophistication – although in an ominous pointer to future developments both sides found supporters. Furthermore, the high yield of 1637-8 had only been obtained by intense, and unrepeatable, conciliar pressure. When in the following year the Scottish crisis divided the council's energies and emboldened the discontented, chastisement of defaulters wound down and non-payment soared. One-third of the much lower demand of 1638-9 could not be collected. The limits on the government's assets were to be fully exposed by the new military demands of the summer of 1639, coat and conduct money and the rest.

By early 1640 collection had all but collapsed. The council responded to the deteriorating situation, which saw frequent local violence against collectors, by heaping blame on the sheriffs, forty of whom had been threatened with star chamber proceedings by February 1640. Charles's characteristic isolation from reality is best summed up in the tone of the council's reply in March 1640 to the sheriff of Northamptonshire's report on his problems, which included a grand jury presentment against ship money: 'We have had the patience to read your tedious letter', which it then condemned as a tissue of excuses.

If the heterogeneity and insubordination of the English were distasteful to a king whose watchwords were unity and order, the disunity of his other realms was bound to be all the more displeasing. The religious divisions in both Scotland and Ireland were an affront to the dignity of a powerful monarchy and, Charles and Laud were confident, to God. Their political intractability had also prevented Charles from calling on all their resources in the wars of the 1620s. If he were to take his rightful place in the world and do his duty to God he must reduce them to order. Unfortunately, Charles even more than James was oblivious to the political risks of attempts by the core kingdom of dynastic states to impose its religious forms or heavier fiscal demands, or both, on neglected and resentful regions.

The larger task lay in Ireland. Although English objectives had for generations been Anglicization and the spread of protestantism, the prospects had grown fainter since the arrival of Catholic missionary priests in the 1620s. The crown and church of England were ill-placed to respond. Protestant energies were divided, since many Scottish presbyterians had settled in Ulster after the flight of the earls. The English church in Ireland had been ruthlessly plundered by generations of protestant settlers, and could not attract clergy to cater to the old-established Anglo-Irish inhabitants, who were thus left open to the Catholic missioners; still less could English ministers preach in Irish to the Gaelic inhabitants. And the crown itself had difficulty in securing the increasingly divided island, since its own lands and revenues had been ravaged.

Charles's most important step came at the beginning of 1632 when he appointed as lord deputy Wentworth, who had made a name for himself by his forceful government at York as president of the council of the north. Wentworth's goals were summed up in the slogan he shared with his great ally Laud, 'Thorough', the restoration of the position of crown and church – and, not incidentally, the building of his own – despite all obstacles. There were other similarities between Wentworth and Laud. Both were domineering, both had a total sense of their own rectitude and an equally total inability to sympathize with the motives of others; and both believed from the first that danger and destruction lay all around. Wentworth saw himself in an heroic mould, and to some extent his characterization, if not at first his sense of crisis, was justified. He was a brilliant manipulator, a bold strategist and, as he had shown in his parliamentary attacks on maladministration and the follies of war in the 1620s, a commanding speaker. But even Wentworth was no absolutist. Like others at court, he seems to have concluded that harmony with the nation could only be achieved if passions were allowed to subside and if the king met parliament with his pressing debts removed and thus no longer desperate for supply. The Irish administration's part in this was to contribute to the English exchequer instead of running at its usual loss; this would also of course give Wentworth a strong claim to promotion in England. Peace was the vital factor in his strategy, since it would allow Irish trade with the continent, and thus customs dues, to recover.

The novelty of Wentworth's rule lay in the way he struck out against all groups, not just the usual target of the native Irish. He was dazzlingly successful at profiting both the crown and himself by playing off against each other the two major political groupings, the 'Old English', that is, the Anglo-Irish, and the 'New English', the recent protestant settlers. By careful manipulation of the Irish parliament he called in 1634, Wentworth was able to gain a lavish grant of taxation and power to vet titles to land. He then used his new position with utter self-confidence. Adapting the legal process to 'a little violence and extraordinary means', as he put it, he strove to undo the effects of generations of equally extraordinary plunder by Old English and New English alike. By judicious intimidation of juries, he upheld the crown's claims to four-fifths of the land in county Galway. Of the next, equally intimidated, jury in county Clare he wrote, in apparent seriousness, 'in all my whole life did I never see. . .men with so much alacrity divesting themselves of all propriety in their estates.' He had almost equal success in forcing several New English landowners, including his enemy and the greatest protestant magnate, the earl of Cork, to disgorge church lands. The more hamstrung Laud watched from England in grateful appreciation.

The application of Laudianism to Ireland was, however, particularly dangerous, though Wentworth deemed it especially urgent in view of the rooting of Scottish presbyterianism in Ulster. Protestantism in Ireland identified the dominant colonial class and anti-Catholicism was a necessary buttress to its superiority; the Irish church before Wentworth had therefore been more uniformly Calvinist than had the English under Abbot. In this context the importation of ceremonialism, even more than the recovery of church lands, seemed to threaten the whole protestant ascendancy. The Ulster Scots and their mainland compatriots in particular took notice of Wentworth as the man most likely to overturn the protestant cause.

Neither was Wentworth without English enemies. The full extent of the loathing, particularly amongst northerners who had suffered under him, can only be appreciated if his arrogant declarations of high-mindedness are remembered. Part of the historians' charge against him, that of being a political turn-coat, can be dismissed as an anachronism. The only political career was in the king's service, and many of those who hounded him to death had themselves been prepared to take office. It is clear that his attitude to legal process did change when he entered office, but his commitment to efficient administration and to peace as the prerequisite for political harmony and prosperity does suggest a basic continuity in his career from the 1620s to his death. More damaging are the allegations of crude hypocrisy in one who seized the ill-gotten gains of others and yet raised his own income, through office, from £2,000 p.a. in 1628 to £23,000 by 1639. These gains did not, however, wholly conflict with 'Thorough' or his sense of official ethics. The New English plunderers, or the popish soap monopolists, made their fortunes by defrauding the crown, the people, or both. Equally, an empty English courtier like the earl of Holland made perhaps £10,000–12,000 p.a. simply through being the king's friend and waiting for gifts to fall into his lap. Wentworth consistently made money for the crown as well as himself. Even while strengthening the Irish army he put the Irish treasury in the black, enabling it to contribute to the English exchequer for the first time in decades. Furthermore, unlike Charles's other servants he was prepared to risk everything for the king in 1639–40.

The enormous short-term success of Wentworth's government in Ireland points to a perennial feature of early-modern politics, the importance of a clear commitment at Whitehall. Earlier deputies had all been forced into bidding for the support of local factions by their vulnerability to intrigue at court. Wentworth had before he left browbeaten Charles into giving him a free hand, and his friends Laud and Cottington ensured that Charles on the whole stayed firm to his undertaking.

The contrast with Scotland could not have been greater. Consistency and clarity of aim were as lacking at Whitehall as was determination amongst Charles's servants in Edinburgh. Whereas Wentworth divided and ruled in Ireland, Charles united highly diverse elements in Scotland and in so doing created an irresistible opposition. Forgetting his father's caution, he drove quasi-nationalistic aristocrats resentful at the reduction of their country to the status of a frontier province to make common cause with religious zealots. The combination of aristocratic and clerical protest had torn apart France and the Netherlands in the sixteenth century, and was to prove equally destructive in Britain.

From the start of his reign Charles's actions in Scotland seemed calculated to excite hostility. In an act of revocation in 1625 Charles declared, on the flimsiest of legal grounds, the cancellation of all grants of crown or church lands made since 1540; although he made little effort to enforce the revocation, the gesture was unsettling enough. Aristocratic susceptibilities were not soothed by the nature of Charles's government. Scottish visitors to Charles's increasingly formal court were ostracized as uncultured boors, while the Scottish council at Edinburgh was almost equally out of touch with local feeling. Notoriously more interested in obedience than advice, Charles placed nine bishops, most of them suspect also for their Arminianism, on the council, on the assumption that unlike lay magnates they would be wholly dependent upon him. Noble members of the council soon dissociated themselves from what they came to see as a pointless exercise, leaving the council largely in the hands of bishops and officials, and incapable of withstanding royal pressure.

Charles's religious objectives made his inheritance of separate kingdoms doubly unfortunate. His concern for uniformity was affronted by the dominance in Scotland of ways of worship he and Laud were endeavouring to root out in England. Besides challenging their own belief in the divine warrant for their chosen forms, the presence of presbyterianism in the Scottish kirk, or church, could only encourage puritan dissidents in England. When in 1633 Charles profited from the tranquillity in England to make a grand entry into his Scottish kingdom for his coronation there he indicated his intent to reduce his northern church to the English pattern. Affronting legalist prejudices too, he then used the crown's dominant position in the Scottish parliament to force through an affirmation of the king's powers in religion. Suspicions of his trustworthiness grew when he had Lord Balmerino sentenced to death – although the sentence was not carried out – merely for possessing a petition against his actions.

The heralded campaign for uniformity reached its peak in 1637 when Charles introduced a new prayer book in Edinburgh churches. Imposed by prerogative, and without reference to the general assembly of the kirk or to parliament, it threatened rule that was arbitrary as well as from London. As if that were not enough, the form of communion service it provided proved to be even closer to Laud's semi-Lutheran position than was that of the English prayer book. When Edinburgh burst into rioting in July Charles's Scottish council showed itself less determined than the bishop of Brechin, who read the prayer book over loaded pistols pointed at his congregation: the council promptly withdrew the book and went into recess for a month while it consulted the king.

The prayer book provided both a focus and symbol for the discontented. Resistance to what many saw as flat popery – even the earl of Montrose, soon to be a devoted royalist, saw the book as 'the brood of the bowels of the whore of Babel' – revived memories of the bloody sixteenth-century troubles over religion, and of what had then been done. In February 1638 almost one-third of the parish clergy and still more of the nobility met in Edinburgh to subscribe a national covenant to defend the kirk. Although the wording of the covenant was loyal, it was manifestly a gesture of defiance. Moreover, its claim to be a covenant with God heightened the Scottish protestant sense of being God's chosen nation; thereafter, the prospect of an imminent struggle with the popish Antichrist steadily subsumed the more familiar alignments of a factious nobility. Compromise might have been possible in 1637 had Charles withdrawn the prayer book. But his sense of a religious duty to impose uniformity, and an equally religious duty not to admit any derogation of his kingship, allowed the kirk to discover its divine mission. Many nobles were to live to regret the advent of the kirk militant.

The Covenanters' passion was of course reciprocated. Charles's determination to use force was clear in his characteristic instructions to his cousin the marquess of Hamilton, whom he sent north in June 1638 to buy time: 'flatter them with what hopes you please. . .until I be ready to suppress them.' Charles saw war as essential not just to restore his royal dignity and to stop the contamination spreading to England: his inability to comprehend the views of others also led him to echo his father's Hampton Court dictum, that presbyterians were in reality republicans. As he told Hamilton, 'the number of those that are against episcopacy who are not in their hearts against the monarchy, is not so considerable.' The conviction never left him, and seriously curtailed his range of options over the next decade.

No less deep-rooted, and perhaps less irrational, were the Covenanters' suspicions of popery. They knew that a distressing number of the Scots at Charles's court were Catholics and that the queen's Catholic confessor was a Scot: the advice Charles received was therefore bound to be hostile. Indeed, though they were unlikely to have known it, long before Charles broached the Scottish crisis to his English council he discussed it with the papal agent, who assiduously fostered the common court argument that Catholics were better subjects than were puritans. But the Scots did learn of Charles's most foolhardy project, the so-called Antrim Plot, which aimed to destroy the Calvinist Campbells of south-west Scotland by means of their hereditary Irish, and Catholic, clan enemies. The immediate consequence was that the chief of the Campbells, the earl of Argyll, the most powerful nobleman in Scotland, was driven off the fence into the arms of the Covenanters. The more important result was the final crystallization of the most influential belief of the 1640s, that a monstrous popish plot existed.

The speed of the collapse of Charles's position showed how limited had been the gains of the 1630s. He had been lulled into his aggressive policy by servants reluctant to shake the royal vision of power and peace so confidently reflected in the masques; by anticipating the revenues of future years they had contrived to assure him that all was well. But reality soon intruded, and in the summer of 1638 Charles was driven to postpone military action – even after years of peace he had been unable to build a financial reserve, and long carelessness about royal credit now reaped its reward. But in 1639 the king's position was little better, and he found that the credit of the customs farmers alone was no more capable of supporting a war than it had been in the 1620s.

Not only did the crisis entice Charles into a financially ruinous policy. It also dangerously highlighted in English as well as Scottish eyes the religious complexion of the court. The queen had long provided an alternative pole in Whitehall politics, for her person offered the prospect of a French alliance, and she loved factional politics for their own sake. Accordingly, despite her Catholicism she had attracted protestant courtiers who dreamed of a more 'Elizabethan' anti-Spanish, and thus pro-French, policy. Her friendship with the earls of Holland and Northumberland and the elder Sir Henry Vane helped reassure more estranged 'country' figures like Holland's brother Warwick. But a decisive shift had occurred when Charles in 1637 turned his back on a French alliance at the very moment when he was embroiling himself with France's old ally Scotland. More than ever excluded from the making of policy, Holland and his friends watched in alarm as the papal agents, Panzani and Con, pressed Henrietta Maria to act out the uncomplicated role of the 'good Catholic'; Con's efforts were energetically seconded by the disastrously coincidental arrival of the queen's mother, Marie de Medici, a bitter enemy of the French government of Cardinal Richelieu. While Con blackened the more overtly protestant courtiers as sympathizers with the Covenanters, the queen set herself against France. The hostile caricatures of the court, as Catholic and pro-Spanish, became increasingly appropriate.

Charles foolishly added to the rumours. Despite his desperate need for money he was unwilling to persuade the highly expensive, and provocatively Catholic, Marie de Medici to depart; worse, despite the growing religious tensions he failed to banish Con from court, or to curb the dangerously public activities of Catholics there. Almost as public, and certainly as dangerous, were Henrietta Maria's ill-advised efforts to raise money from English Catholics to put down the rebellious Calvinist Scots. Perhaps the crowning folly came when the earl of Arundel, whom Charles had appointed commander of the 1639 expedition, rode conspicuously in Con's coach, adorned as it was with the papal insignia. For those who believed in an international popish threat it was only too easy to draw the worst conclusions, all the more so when Charles that year allowed Spanish troops harassed by Dutch raiders to march across English soil. Even the king's councillors wondered: as Charles drove on in his bid to crush the Scots without calling a parliament or changing his policies Lord Admiral Northumberland confided helplessly, 'We are as great strangers to all proceedings as if we lived at Constantinople.'

The quality of Charles's forces might be inferred from his readiness to appoint that unhappy aesthete Arundel commander on the revealing grounds that he was the senior English peer. A neo-feudal summons in 1639 to English landowners to do their duty underlined Charles's isolation. Over a half of the gentry summoned made excuses or did not trouble to reply, and while the bulk of the nobility made some response to the call on their allegiance the court's character was not such as to breed much enthusiasm – even the earl of Bridgwater, president of the council of Wales, found half his complement of ten horsemen amongst local drunkards.* Equally seriously, horses proved in as short supply as were decorative plumes. The council's efforts to raise infantry from the trained bands of selected counties also ran into difficulties, since many saw the struggle as an extension of their own, and the rest lamented it as occasioning one more burden. Further, since the militia was supposedly for home defence to march it northwards was legally questionable; it was politically unwise too, as anti-Catholic scares always brought with them fears of Spanish invasion. Too often, ineffective substitutes were provided for those levied for service, and the money to equip and transport them was not forthcoming. The earl of Manchester, one of several privy councillors who were to defect from their master in the coming storm, took comfort in the belief that such a motley force would be 'but a show', and that Charles intended merely to test the obedience of his subjects. If so, the answer was unnerving. The ill-clothed, ill-armed and ill-trained men smashed church ornaments, the symbol of the cause of the war, on their way northwards, and helped enclosure rioters pull down hedges. Charles for once recognized reality, and in June 1639 signed the treaty of Berwick, putting an end to the so-called First Bishops' War. He then proceeded to prepare for the next.

*Huntington Library, San Marino, El. Ms. 6602.

The Scots had less need to buy time, but their contacts with the English aristocratic opposition must have led them to hope that Charles's domestic position would soon disintegrate. The soundness of their calculations was revealed that same June when the City of London, judging Charles's credit wanting, rejected his request for a loan of £100,000. Indeed, the nation had grown if anything even less prepared for a war than it had been in the spring. Many of the returning English soldiers had abandoned their weapons on the way; many more died of disease. Perhaps more damaging, the gathering of nobility and gentry in the north had allowed them to talk, an activity which had been impeded since the last parliament. The views of radical peers like Lords Saye and Brooke were guaranteed a hearing.

Correspondingly, the papers of councillors and officials show increasing signs of demoralization and a sense of isolation. Early in 1640 Northumberland lamented, 'it grieves my soul to be involved in these counsels.' The ordinary functions of government began to be affected, and as early as July 1639 Attorney-General Bankes declared his reluctance to issue a proclamation, for 'the times were ill for proclamations.'* This is not to say that government was crippled by a general revulsion against its activities, for there is little evidence that local governors were seeking to dissociate themselves from the government as a whole. Whatever the unease of petty constables facing occasionally violent resentment at the levying of troops and of ship money, their superiors were either more quiescent or realized more clearly how much they had to lose from a collapse of government. Although historians once thought otherwise, JPs appear to have continued to serve as efficiently or as inefficiently as ever, and the deputy-lieutenants worked hard both in 1639 and in 1640 at the thankless task of raising the forces demanded.

There was still therefore some hope when in October 1639 Wentworth returned from his isolation in Ireland to take control. Characteristically, although the lord deputy deplored the prevailing chaos, he was soon justifying Charles's desperate summons to him by making plans for a new political future: to the dismay of some who learned of them, these included the standing force of 1,000 cavalry of which Charles had dreamed in 1631. But in the short term, he concluded, a parliament would have to be called.

* J. Bruce ed., *Letters and Papers of the Verney Family* (Camden Soc., 1853), p. 266.

7 The Crisis of the Three Kingdoms 1640–1642

The overwhelming majority of the political nation in 1640 sought to recapture an idealized vision of an Elizabethan harmony in church, state and the localities. Yet civil war came, and it is only by dint of a careful study of the rush of events that we can understand just how men for whom unity and harmony were watchwords in 1640 could find themselves fighting each other, some more, some far less, eagerly in 1642. The puzzle centres not simply on the ability of a king who had stood virtually alone in 1640 to find the support to fight, and almost to win, a civil war. Equally complex is the process by which his opponents overcame their concern for obedience and consensus.

The solution to the puzzle lies in the fact that to a considerable extent the Englishmen who strove for harmony were not in control of their own destiny. Events and aspirations in Scotland and Ireland, two polities much less committed to polite assumptions of consensus, imposed their own momentum, to more devastating effect than had the European struggle of the 1620s. The outlying kingdoms at last took their revenge for decades of subordination.

In the short term, however, the crisis of 1640 revealed how fragile had been the apparent tranquillity of the 1630s. The crown had little left to pledge as credit, and any storm was bound to rock the ship of state. Charles's determination to punish the Scots brought on that storm.

Wentworth, now made earl of Strafford, encouraged Charles in his wrath. Either, he felt, English dislike of the Scots could be manipulated to draw from parliament-men the means to rescue the king's war effort; or, if they failed in their duty, that fact would justify sterner measures. That he was not entirely building castles in the air is evident in the forced loan levied on courtiers and office-holders, which yielded £232,000 between December and May, not far short of the £300,000 which had been hoped. But that sum was only collected on the understanding that a parliament would redeem the king's commitments, and the king's isolation was clear in the refusal of any save those who depended on the survival of his regime to lend to him. It was no wonder that that winter the last court masque, *Salmacida*

Spolia, took as its theme Charles as king of an ungrateful nation.

Equally worrying was the immunity of most of the political nation to anti-Scottish urgings. The northern counties might turn their eyes fearfully northwards; but when elections at last gave Englishmen as a whole the chance to express themselves after eleven years of silence they showed themselves far more conscious of domestic grievances than of external threats. The election in Lincolnshire probably reflected the temper of other areas in its mixture of local and national issues: a widely circulated doggerel urged voters to 'Choose no ship [money] sheriff, no court atheist, no fen drainer, nor church [that is, covert] papist, yet though the number of contests had doubled since 1628, this was no revolutionary situation. In many constituencies the elections still conformed to traditional patterns of gentry factional alliances; and while towns largely, as in the 1620s, preferred men with local ties, they might not absolutely insist on rejecting courtiers. Thus, while Laud failed to get his secretary elected at Canterbury he was successful in his home town of Reading. As one courtier judged perceptively, the Commons were neither as good nor as bad as they might have been.

What was to be the Short Parliament was therefore open to persuasion. But the government was clearly taken aback by the deluge of country petitions of grievances, and Charles dealt himself an equally serious setback. Characteristically, his brief opening oration on 13 April offered no justification of the Scottish war but merely demanded money to help end it. Strafford must have winced at the unfailing tactlessness of a king who promised that if the Commons would proceed with supply 'they should have all their just favours'. This stood in unhappy contrast with the Commons' conviction that their privileges were rights, and caused 'a great hum'. But there was encouragement in the Lords, where the loyalty of all the bishops and most of the peers in what could be presented as a wartime crisis seemed to put the two houses on a collision course. Furthermore, John Pym, who was fast emerging as one of the leading critics in the Commons, proved unable to dominate the lower house. Resentments were certainly strong – 'a general humm' of sarcasm greeted Lord Keeper Finch's opening platitudes about respect for the ancient constitution, and Sir Francis Seymour angrily and disrespectfully denounced the treason of the king's advisers who had 'betrayed the king to himself' by telling him 'his prerogative is above all laws'. But few wished to challenge the king directly. One well-informed puritan newsletter-writer even reported that during the closing stages of the parliament, a short three weeks after it began, the Commons were ready to ignore Pym's protests and accept Charles's offer to abandon ship money for the high price of twelve subsidies. Strafford's hopes of exploiting the old animosities for the Scots may not therefore have been altogether far-fetched, while Charles's decision to dissolve the parliament looks all the more rash. The charitable explanation may be his plausible fear that Pym, who with his aristocratic friends had for some time been in contact with the Covenanters, was about to call for support for them. Scotland was already having its effect on English politics.

A great danger in analysing political breakdown is the assumption that long-term causes explain everything. The mood of the Short Parliament shows that neither the 1620s nor the 'personal rule' led directly to a determined onslaught on the king's government. Instead, Edward Hyde, then a critic but later a leading councillor of Charles I and his son, thought that by dissolving the parliament Charles threw away his best chance of working with moderate opinion. Certainly, the very different mood of the autumn was to show that the arousal of hopes of reform and then the sudden calamity of the dissolution on 5 May had dramatically intensified distrust. One Kent member, Sir Thomas Peyton, was sure by 6 May that the situation had deteriorated, since parliament as so often had made men think beyond their petty local grievances. They now knew that these were widely shared; worse, that realization could not be confined, for the common people 'received a diffusive knowledge from the dispersed house'. Politics were no longer to be a polite preserve, and London apprentices and artisans, already smarting from economic depression born as much of political insecurity as of harvest failure and plague, greeted the dissolution with riots against Laudian targets.

The rebuff left Charles undismayed. He remained determined to confront the Scots, though his finances were in ruins and the City still refused to lend. Strafford, ever the gambler, and confident of his Irish army, supported him in the belief that the failure of parliament reflected the breakdown of the ancient constitution in a wartime crisis. He now argued strongly that Charles was 'loose and absolved from rules of government', and should resort to extraordinary measures; the lord lieutenant's advice was to be remembered against him, though it probably revealed less of arbitrary intent than of present desperation. Charles anyway lacked the resources to act on it, and was driven instead to a flurry of fruitless devices. Though Spain was equally wracked by domestic and international pressures, Strafford looked there vainly for repayment – in the form of a loan, or even military aid – for Charles's naval assistance in the 1630s. More damaging were other expedients, the seizure of merchants' bullion deposited in the Tower and a projected debasement by 75 per cent of the coinage. Although merchant outrage forced the council to abandon these ventures, the insecurity they engendered only intensified the depression and bred further unemployment; they also confirmed the widespread sense of the crown's insensitivity. The paralysis boded ill for further military adventures.

Recent historians have largely attributed Charles's defeat at the hands of the Scots to localism and foot-dragging in the counties. These factors cannot be denied. The failure of earlier parliaments to provide statutory backing for the militia left a catastrophic opening for legalists to obstruct Charles's attempts to raise forces for Scotland from the militia. As the Shropshire deputy-lieutenants protested, they had a 'persuasive but no compulsive power'. But as in so many early-Stuart failures, much of the responsibility for the second fiasco in the north must rest at the centre, with the indecisive Charles and his advisers. Although in several counties deputy-lieutenants acted promptly to implement the council's directives, repeated changes of plan at Whitehall saw the men and their supplies dwindle. The result was beyond doubt. Almost one-fifth of the men who had arrived at Selby in Yorkshire by August were unarmed, and the equipment of many more was unserviceable. Equally disturbing was the behaviour of men who, as their new commander, Northumberland, observed, were 'readier to draw their swords upon their officers than against the Scots'. The troops raised in the 1620s had been disorderly enough, but the disturbances of 1640 were very different, and testify to the growing arousal of the ordinary populace. The state of popular opinion in 1640 can probably be gauged less from the elections than from the trail of broken and burnt altar-rails left by the troops as they marched north; or from the lynchings of two Catholic officers, perpetrated with revealingly little hindrance from bystanders. The horror shown by the earl of Bedford at this volatile anti-Catholicism suggests how rapidly the safe 'puritan' cause of the conservative gentleman might fracture.

The Covenanters meanwhile were handicapped by few problems of morale. When under the guise of petitioners they entered England in August 1640 Charles's army disintegrated after token resistance at Newburn on the Tyne. The Scots, who had not expected quite such demoralization, found themselves possessors of the two northernmost counties and of Newcastle, perhaps the fourth city of the kingdom. They had no intention of proceeding further, though there was little to stop them, since Strafford's vaunted Irish army was only slowly assembling across the Irish Sea. Conscious as was Charles of the British ramifications of their position, the Covenanters hoped to make common cause in a parliament with disaffected English puritans and magnates.

Charles for his part was now desperate enough to turn to his people, since his two northern expeditions had cost him £1M., and yielded nothing but humiliation. But he had no intention of changing course. He seems to have assumed that the presence of rebellious Scots on English soil would at last persuade his English subjects to rally to him, and to prepare the way he determined on a neo-feudal appeal to the peers. They had in the Short Parliament given him some support; might they not now recall their traditional role as king's councillors and, in a Great Council, underwrite a loan or in some way support his military efforts? But once again Charles showed his ignorance of sentiment in the country. Although he opened the Great Council at York in September 1640 with an announcement that he would call a parliament, he also made clear his continuing hostility to the Scots. Unimpressed, the earl of Bristol and many other peers made no secret of their belief that the king should accept his defeat, make peace, and use a parliament to heal the wounds of the body politic. Charles's council could suggest no better. Laud urged his colleagues that month that they should 'put to the king, that we are at the wall, and that we are in the dark, and have no grounds for a counsel.'

Still uncomprehending, Charles went ahead with his plans for a new parliament. The Great Council had, at the king's request, appointed commissioners to negotiate a peace, which he hoped would leave him room for further manoeuvring. But the Scots appreciated the strength of the British card in their hand. All they wanted of the new treaty, of Ripon, was a truce, with payment of their expenses – the colossal sum of £850 a day – and the postponement of negotiations until parliament met. The union of the crowns was proving Charles's nemesis, for the Covenanters appreciated that their kirk could not be safe while militant Laudianism reigned in England. The new burden on his finances allowed the king little escape.

The treaty of Ripon left Charles mortgaged to the forthcoming parliament. Nevertheless, his opening speech was to show him determined as ever to maintain his course against the Scots, and staggeringly unpersuaded of the need for domestic concessions. The king had little support in his intransigence. Most councillors seem to have joined the rest of the political nation in assuming that he would climb down from his high horse and restore harmony: to that end the council began emptying the gaols. Furthermore, some councillors' nerve had failed. Although both Laud and the earl of Holland had obtained seats for their nominees at Reading in the spring, in the autumn neither tried; indeed, Laud avowed his anxiety not to involve the town in his own unpopularity. Such restraint played a part in the reduction of courtiers and office-holders in the Commons to about 15 per cent of the total, in contrast to the level of over one-third in 1614.

As important was the growing political awakening. The number of election contests soared again, with between a third and a half of all constituencies being fought, the highest level ever. While contests testify primarily to gentry activity, the meaner sort could not help but be involved when, as in Worcestershire, the mustered trained bands heard one candidate repeatedly denounced as 'fitter to break parliaments than to serve in parliament'. Rarely, as at Marlow in Buckinghamshire where the simply-dressed carrier Toucher Carter urged Bulstrode Whitelocke to stand to vindicate the Commons' rights, popular involvement was more direct. The character of the elections was equally noteworthy. The defeated courtier who concluded that 'the opinion is grown general that whoever is not Scottishly must be popishly affected' did not wholly exaggerate, though he ignored the localist tone of most of the elections. But while the sights of most of the MPs who assembled on 3 November 1640 for what was to become the Long Parliament were set on visible evils, Laudianism in local churches, ship money in the neighbourhoods, they shared a concern to lead England back into its ancient ways and to purge it of its recent corruptions.

Those concerns were soon to be given shape, for as one new backbencher wrote home, 'God be praised, here want not skillful agents.' Too often the parliaments of the 1620s had dissipated their energies by failing to establish priorities. The relative cohesion of the two houses in the first months of the Long Parliament, which allowed pressure to be put on the king, stemmed not just from shared grievances. It also arose from fruitful contacts between peers – Essex, Warwick, Pym's patron Bedford, Saye, Mandeville – and in the Commons men like Pym, the earl of Clare's son Denzil Holles, Saye's son Nathaniel Fiennes, and Hampden and St John of the ship money case. The sprawling East Anglian cousinage linked many of these men with religious radicals such as Oliver Cromwell. Understandings forged in the 1630s through the meetings of the Providence Island Company in particular had been bolstered by connections with City puritans trading to America; these proved invaluable in the spring of 1641 when Pym wished to apply pressure to wavering peers. The leadership could also tune other strings. A favourite device was the selection of sympathetic clergymen to address the Commons on their ceremonial fast days. Thus, on 17 November 1640 the preachers were Stephen Marshall, Warwick's client and the most influential preacher in the coming revolution, and Cornelius Burges, an ally of Bedford. Their theme in these first fast sermons was the need for common action against the 'Nimrods' – that is, tyrants – who had perverted religion and the laws; Burges later testified that he and

Marshall met weekly with the parliamentary leadership.

The workings of politics cannot, however, be reduced to the ties of patronage and of cousinage. There were some striking groupings, though families and friends often divided for civil war and Charles I was a distant cousin of John Hampden. Bedford did indeed find pocket borough seats for Pym and St John, but in many cases the magnate merely supported an appeal by a gentleman to the more or less independent choices of voters. Thus, Warwick was alleged to have deployed preachers such as Marshall, as well as bailiffs, to secure victory for his allies in Essex. Once in parliament, and particularly in such a long parliament as this was to be, the cohesion of most aristocratic connections was much less apparent. Bedford's clients, St John and Pym, differed over financial matters, and in the wider grouping Pym and Holles clashed repeatedly. Still more outside parliament, Pym was to find in 1641 that the City's purse could no more be opened at the will of his friends than it had been at the king's: aristocratic connections could at best guide, not dominate.

Politics had of course never been merely an aristocratic pastime. MPs were subject not just to the agitation of factional leaders but also to lobbying, whether by constituents or by clergy – 'the black-coated walkers of Westminiser Hall', as the Kent MP Sir Edward Dering called them in disgust – trying to stir godly consciences. Most of all they became subject to petitioning. The prominence accorded both by localities and the Commons to petitioning on all manner of business suggests the importance politicians attached to being able to represent, or to misrepresent, the sense of the country. It also points to the involvement of a wider public in the political process. The coming revolution was to be a battle of books, or rather of ill-printed pamphlets, as much as of bullets. In 1642, and again in 1643, 1647 and 1648, over a thousand books – excluding newspapers – were published on political or religious topics; and while the 1620s had seen the genesis of the English newspaper, the 1640s were to see its flowering, with on occasion over ten journals a week appearing. Printed copies of parliamentary speeches testified to a politically as well as commercially inspired desire to gratify the popular appetite for news. Influence in parliament in these circumstances could not be based on factional discipline alone.

The most urgent concern of all at Westminster was to ensure that this parliament did not go the way of the last. The presence of the Covenanters in the north made that goal easy to attain. The central fact of the first session of the parliament was Charles's need to pay the Scottish army and the remaining English troops until such time as a settlement brought disbandment. The soldiers' hungry bellies were the wall behind which parliament sheltered, for only parliament could supply taxes, which in turn provided the vital security for loans for army expenses.

Nevertheless, despite its security, parliament was strangely halting in its labours. Moves came swiftly against those deemed responsible for all the grievances – and particularly the religious grievances – of recent years. Laudian clergy were eagerly hunted down, while the houses expended considerable time cataloguing the military burdens laid on the north, and various other ills. Yet however widespread the conviction that Charles's government had constituted a general threat to the religion and liberty of the subject and to parliamentary ways, the only *reform* to emerge in the first six months was the triennial act, making provision for the holding of parliament every three years; this, furthermore, was passed primarily as a device to give security for loans for the soldiers' pay. All the other measures which historians have celebrated as the inevitable fruit of the houses' reformism waited until the autumn of 1641. Redress had to compete with the concerns of normal parliaments, with bills to regulate light-houses or the watermen on the Thames; equal energy had perforce to go to often frustrating and exhausting, but vitally important, fiscal measures, the securing of loans and the supply and regulation of the troops. Parliamentary committees were also involved in the negotiations for peace – which were all the more drawn out by the opposition leaders' reluctance to see the Scots' army speedily disbanded.

Reform competed too with the continuing political crisis. However much Charles seemed isolated and deprived of anything which could be called a royalist party he might still be tempted to try a sudden stroke against his opponents. Strafford, likened by St John to a 'beast of prey', was clearly the only man with the drive to rescue the king, and the opposition leaders therefore moved to destroy him. Within a week of the opening of the session Pym had co-ordinated what was to become an impeachment for treason. Strafford's vulnerability lay not in his conduct in Ireland, for few Englishmen objected to harshness to Irishmen. Rather, the impeachment went ahead because the army in Ireland could be seen against a backdrop of leniency to court papists and priests in England, and of the Laudian corruption of the church. The lord lieutenant was an early victim of the dread of a popish plot. But though the very formulation of the impeachment charge gave firmer shape to the rumours of popish conspiracies the opposition leaders were still not safe. Preparing the case would take considerable time, and the animus against Strafford might drop amid the minutiae of legal proceedings.

Pym and his friends therefore sought to maintain that atmosphere of excitement which, paradoxically, was scarcely conducive to the

quiet work of reform. Here they had assets in the tense expectations
of a purge which the summoning of the parliament had aroused in the
political nation. Almost from the beginning, reports of popish plotting trickled in from the constitutencies and Pym – whose belief in
them cannot be doubted – exploited them brilliantly. The developments on the northern frontier and Charles's stockpiling of arms in
the Tower had heightened fears to which the king had unwisely given
dangerous focus when at his insistence the ecclesiastical convocation
which met in the spring of 1640 had required all clergy and graduates
to swear that the church hierarchy, listed with an ominously vague
'etc', accorded with the word of God. To those who smelled a popish
plot, 'the etcetera oath' was final proof that Laud, 'the sty of all
pestilential filth', as the moderate Harbottle Grimston called him,
intended to introduce the pope surreptitiously. In December the Commons voted to impeach the archbishop as 'an actor in the great design
of the subversion of the laws. . .and of religion'. The acceptance of
the full conspiracy thesis threatened not only Strafford but also any
chance of compromise, for no compromise could be taken at face
value.

With Laud sent to join Strafford in the Tower, the parliamentary
leaders pressed on, aiming not just at vengeance but also at providing
object lessons to future servants of the crown. Into a frightened exile
fled the crypto-Catholic Secretary of State Windebanke and the new
Lord Keeper, Finch; the courts too, where the king had chosen to
fight so many of his battles, felt the rod of the new justice. Charles's
mistaken fondness for exploiting the letter of the law earned its reward
in the impeachments begun over the winter of 1640–1 against all but
one of the surviving judges of the 1630s. Yet for all the noise, the
Commons did not press home their attack, either on Laud or on the
judges. Equally, although a myriad grievances were investigated few
measures were brought to a conclusion. Indeed, even the triennial
bill, the one early success, owed at least as much to the pressure of the
Scottish presence as to the general conviction that ancient rights could
only vindicated by parliaments and that frequent parliaments were
therefore essential.

The reasons for such slow progress are various. Other business
– the case against Strafford, the raising of money – was more urgent.
Other business was also more complex and time-consuming, and
even before the end of 1640 a committee on committees was considering which of the Commons' rapidly multiplying committees ought
to be dropped. It was the story of the 1620s all over again, and as in
the 1620s MPs found the pressing financial business not the most
exciting of matters. By January 1641 the Commons were occasionally
finding a quorum of forty difficult to attain. While the two houses

were unwilling to trust the king with the means of governing, few MPs had yet any sense of their own mission to govern.

But the mundane record, of attention to business as trifling as the fixing of rates for landing coal and wood at Westminster, casts light both backwards and forwards. The houses' ability to do business and to act in practice, if not in theory, as an executive suggests that when purposes were largely agreed in time of crisis parliament might behave in a more positive fashion than it had during an unpopular war in the 1620s. Moreover, the houses were also to find, when civil war came, that the expansion of their activities had been invaluable, for it had given them an administrative training, and it had accustomed those they dealt with to obeying their orders. But the emergence of a *de facto* parliamentary administration also reveals much of the state of politics in 1640–1. In particular, it raises the problem of the motive of the *de iure* government, the king and his council, in acquiescing in such apparent affronts to the prerogative.

The corporate morale of the council had been shattered by the autumn of 1640, and the ensuing turmoil did little to restore it. The clerk of the council, Edward Nicholas, commented in 1641 on the emptiness of the council's role, and the two houses were therefore filling a vacuum. Nevertheless, not all councillors had fled or fallen. Whatever Charles's own views, many of his councillors, particularly those who leaned towards the 'French' rather than the 'Spanish' side, had in the 1620s and even the 1630s shown a commitment to harmony and dreamed of working with parliament. With the body politic so wracked, it was no wonder that they now sought to restore relations with the political nation. The Scottish disaster had anyway hardly strengthened their faith in Charles's judgment, and his secretiveness must have left them resentful. Some perhaps had baser motives. Warwick's brother Holland feared an attack on his role in the forest courts, and the secretary of state, Sir Henry Vane snr, had a family feud with Strafford. But their co-operation, and that of Northumberland, the lord admiral, of Leicester, the former ambassador to Paris and Strafford's successor as lord lieutenant of Ireland, of Manchester, the lord privy seal, as well as of the king's legal officers – non-Laudians all – with the growing parliamentary government is suggestive. Like others, they appear to have felt that Charles had tipped a balance. Their aristocratic constitutionalism parallels markedly that of the *frondeurs* who were soon to challenge French absolutism.

The impossibility of talking at this juncture of a 'government' and an 'opposition' suggests perhaps the most important reason for parliament's limited legislative achievements in its first six months. Few of the purgative measures eventually passed in the summer of 1641

involved particularly complex drafting, and they proved uncontentious in parliament when they finally emerged; it may therefore be
that the leaders of what is often called the 'opposition' may not have
wanted to do too much. For the constant castigation of the 'evil counsellors' who had misled the king is one side of a coin of which the other
is the intense efforts of a group who were soon to be called the 'good
lords' to enter office. If they were to become the king's servants they
might not want to see the reins of government mangled.

The fate of the Petition of Right could have left the parliamentary
leaders with few illusions about the strength of statutes. An angry
king who had power in his hands and who had harkened to judges
preaching the inalienability of the prerogative could always evade
them. Not surprisingly, Essex, Bedford, Pym and the rest seem to
have had another safeguard in mind. They had long been interested
in office, and indeed, Pym had for years been a minor revenue official. They now intended the traditional safeguard of aristocratic
dissidents, the taking of control of the council. But since magnates no
longer led bodies of armed retainers, Bedford and his friends willy-
nilly shared with a wider public the conclusion that parliaments were
the way to check untrustworthy kings. Pym for his part had shown by
his eagerness for financial reforms in the 1620s that unlike more
localist parliament-men he was not averse to effective government: he
merely insisted that it be sound in religion and less devoted to 'new
counsels'. As early as December 1640 there were reports of negotiations for office, which predicted that Bedford would gain the lord
treasurership and Pym the chancellorship of the exchequer. Their
insurance would be their control over the purse strings. For not only
did they seem able to open the parliamentary purse but they also
intended to take over the customs farms, the major source of royal
credit.

Charles himself initially had few objections, since he saw office as a
means of winning men over. His determination to chastise the sinful
and rebellious Scots had not waned, and since he patently had no
other solution co-operation with Bedford and Pym must have seemed
the only means to that paramount end. Accordingly, early in 1641
Charles made some largely honorific appointments, of peers such as
Bedford, Essex and Saye to the council, and of St John to the solicitor-
generalship. Nevertheless, his feelings still revealed themselves in
carping: thus, his assent on 16 February to the triennial bill was a long
complaint that parliament had 'taken the government all in pieces,
and I may say it is almost off the hinges.' They revealed themselves
too in an insistence that Bedford and Pym show that they could and
would do him service by sparing Strafford and gaining him funds.
Hyde in his *History* condemned Charles for destroying perhaps the

last hope of reuniting king and country by means of Bedford's scheme for bridging appointments. Yet by demanding delivery in advance Charles was not merely displaying his usual incomprehension of the *quid pro quo* rule of politics. However similar Bedford's objectives may have been to those of his continental equals, the English opposition leaders did not owe their standing to territorial influence. Should they prove unable to lead their followers there was little point in the king turning to them. And there were ominous tensions. Revealingly, Sir John Hotham saw Pym as a new Strafford that spring, and likened his schemes for reforming the subsidies to a Turkish despotism. 'Country' hostility to an expensive central executive had helped hamstring Charles's war effort in the 1620s, and now it subverted Pym's hopes of a political accommodation. Charles would probably have found a rapprochement with his critics repugnant on various grounds; but it also proved open to practical objections.

The question of Strafford underlined the imbalance in the equation. Charles felt bound in honour to protect him, and not only because he had promised to do so. Yet the fear of the lord lieutenant was strong, particularly outside parliament, amongst the Scots and their London paymasters. The Covenanters hated Strafford for his attempt to obliterate the presbyterianism of Scottish settlers in Ulster; they abhorred too the project – though it was not Strafford's – for using Irish Catholics against the Scottish mainland. The London aldermen for their part remembered all too well Strafford's advocacy of stern measures against them after the Short Parliament. The spectre these intransigents raised, of troops rampaging unpaid as loans were withheld, was a powerful stimulus, especially to northern MPs like Hotham. Desperate for a settlement, and therefore for the preservation of Strafford's life, Pym replied by proposing that the Londoners be compelled to lend, in fine disregard for the Petition of Right. But there were too many who feared that Strafford might yet rescue the king, and for that reason, as the earl of Essex put it, 'Stone dead hath no fellow.'

Strafford's fate hinged on notes, surreptitiously obtained, of the council meeting of 5 May 1640 at which he had argued that the king was 'loose and absolved from rules of government'. He had then gone on to point out that the army in Ireland could be used to 'reduce this kingdom' – whether Scotland or England was left fatally unclear. When the impeachment opened on 22 March 1641, the managers, notably St John, responded to the difficulty of trying the king's servant by alleging what has been called 'constructive treason' against the king: Strafford's individual acts may not have been treasonous, but cumulatively they amounted to a design to subvert the constitution. Precedents certainly existed for the approach, but its weaknesses were enough for Strafford. In a magnificent performance he tore apart the charges, humiliated the Commons' spokesmen, and gained numerous supporters amongst his judges, the Lords. It was a Pyrrhic victory. The majority in the Commons responded by abandoning the uncertainty of legal proceedings and opted instead for the simpler, and more arbitrary, way of a bill of attainder, which would merely declare Strafford guilty.

Strafford's trial indicated the weakness of Pym's position. The abandonment of impeachment would impugn the judicial capacities of the Lords, on whose co-operation hopes for accommodation depended, and Pym and Hampden vainly opposed the shift. Dangerous gaps were opening in the Commons' ranks too, as the bored and the less conscientious voted with their feet. The momentous final vote on Strafford mustered – at 204:59 – a bare half of the Commons' members. It also revealed other strains, for the intensity and scale of the attacks on the king's government, and the arbitrariness of the destruction of Strafford, appalled some conservative members, as did the publication of the names of the 'Straffordians' in the Commons who had opposed attainder. The breach of parliamentary secrecy was symptomatic of the frightening new tone of politics, and Lord Digby for one, a stalwart of the early opposition, became further estranged from his former friends. But the growing fear of violence – by early April one prominent Welsh family, the Wynns of Gwydir, had begun to stockpile arms for 'if the times prove bad' – also helps explain the extent of support in the Commons for the violent measure of attainder.

Convinced that the Commons would never do anything substantial to aid him against the Scots, the resentful Charles soon gave shape to the rumours. It seems clear that during April he was actively seeking a loan from Catholic sources abroad to allow him to break with parliament; more rashly, he also contemplated using the discontented remnants of the English army to release Strafford from the Tower. News of the latter scheme, the army plot, broke on 3 May.

The discovery of the army plot was a major turning-point. Pym's claim that a popish conspiracy surrounded the king seemed less than ever irrational, and the frightened Commons joined at last in Pym's long-cherished dream of a national covenant before God. The Protestation of 3 May 1641 was an attempt to identify the popish enemy among the non-subscribers; but it was also an oath of association to counter a coup.

Some needed little stirring. On 3 and 4 May mobs surged around the house of Lords, intimidating into absence those peers who had not been thoroughly alienated by the plot; ultimately, perhaps only nine voted to save Strafford. The crowds then turned on the king, and throughout 8–9 May huge demonstrations massed outside Whitehall calling for Strafford's head. On the 10th a shaken Charles conceded, fearing for the lives of his family, and released by Strafford from his promise that he would protect his servant. The lord lieutenant was executed on 12 May, sacrificing himself to preserve that unity between crown and people which he still, as much as Pym, saw as the only preservation of society. His death may have allowed some, both in and out of parliament, a sense of security, but the reverberations of the plot soon dispelled any hopes of calm. Pym and his friends now knew that Charles was prepared to use force.

The death on 9 May of Bedford, around whom the bridging plans had revolved, was less significant in the collapse of accommodation than the fact that Pym now genuinely feared for his life. His goals changed accordingly. Like many others in both houses he would probably have seized with relief on the medieval solution to ill-advised kings, an enforced regency, had there been a suitable candidate: certainly, in not many months he was to show great familiarity with precedents drawn from the periods of Edward III's senility and Henry VI's insanity. But the lack of English princes of the blood forced him into more difficult waters, as that summer he turned to attempts to render formal the growing parliamentary control over the administration. He may not have intended a permanent constitutional departure, for as they emerged in 1642 his proposals would have altered the balance of power for the likely length of Charles's life; but he certainly sought to take power away from this untrustworthy king. The essential foundation was laid on 10 May, when Charles was panicked into signing not just Strafford's death warrant but also an act declaring that parliament could not be dissolved without its own consent. Although, like the triennial act, this originated in the desire to obtain political security for loans, the measure gave parliament some protection against the rude fate of so many earlier assemblies. And not coincidentally, the summer months also saw the rushed passage of the great reforming statutes whose progress during the winter and spring had been so slow. The constitutionalist revulsion provoked by the measures of the 1630s was at last given focus by a leadership whose own hopes of office had been dashed and which was now fearful of a royal counter-attack. June and July saw the abolition of ship money, knighthood fines and the extension of the forests. The courts of ecclesiastical high commission and star chamber also went down, the latter widely disliked for its involvement with the Laudian church and for its harassment of sheriffs over ship money. Fears of arbitrary rule equally accounted for the condemnation of some of the privy council's judicial powers, a move which effectively doomed the provincial councils in the north and in Wales, whose prime function had by now become judicial. The failure of accommodation had brought a constitutional revolution, which placed large limits on royal power.

Perhaps the most remarkable feature of that revolution was its uncontested nature. By the summer parliament was far from unanimous, yet none of the reforming legislation occasioned a division in the Commons. No clearer sign could have been given of the extent of the conviction that Charles had been systematically tipping the constitutional balance.

But Pym was unable to effect his reforms undisturbed. The collapse of the bridging scheme in the spring of 1641 accelerated the rate of change in the ecclesiastical as well as the secular sphere. It was this above all which rent the consensus at Westminster, and in the country too.

Hyde in his *History* castigated Pym and others bitterly for the encouragement they gave the radicals by failing to advance positive reforms. Yet Pym was by no means in full control. He and his friends recognized from the outset that parliament was far from unanimous on the issue of church reform, and that long debates might fragment the unity that was so vital. Accordingly, and in revealing contrast to his conduct in 1629, Pym took little part in the debates on the church in the spring of 1641. While he did not hesitate to heighten the animus against Laudians and popery, he strove to divert the energies released to the more immediately pressing matters of Strafford and of finance. He was to find that many, both inside and outside Westminster, were more single-minded than he. On 11 December 1640 a petition allegedly signed by 15,000 London citizens called for the abolition 'root and branch' of episcopacy, and petitions from thirteen other counties in January echoed the cry.

Willy-nilly the Commons were dragged into the religious fray. While inconvenient, religious debate ought not have imperilled moderate reform, since in London in early 1640 there had probably been only about a thousand actual separatists from the national church, and even fewer convinced presbyterians. But the speed of events generated a new consciousness, as the completeness of the Laudian collapse convinced many that the hand of God was at work. Nonconformists returned from exile and made new beginnings in the provinces as well as in London: in Cheshire one former New England minister was in January 1641 denouncing all organized forms of worship as 'loathsome unto God'. Reports came in from the counties around London during the spring of sporadic attacks on the prayer book, on the grounds that ceremonies and set forms encouraged idolatry; indeed, all regions felt the strain, for with the fall of Laud and the demoralization of the church courts at the end of 1640 had come the collapse of press censorship. A flood of broadsides followed, often selling for a few pence, condemning episcopacy in their call for reformation. The political risks were apparent in the warning of one Kent gentleman that 'the monstrous easy receipt of petitions' by the Commons 'makes authority decline', and not surprisingly the debates on the church in February and March 1641 brought a strong conservative response from MPs. Laud's estrangement of moderate opinion had been so complete that scarcely any spoke in favour of the church as currently established. But Digby was not alone in expressing concern about Scottish pressure and about the levelling implicit in the attack on ecclesiastical hierarchy. As the poet-MP Edmund Waller was soon to put it, if the bishops went down, 'the next demand perhaps may be *lex agraria*, the like equality in things temporal.'

Yet despite Hyde's allegations, the opposition leaders intended something more than mere destruction. The ideal of a large majority of parliament-men in the spring of 1641 was the substitution of 'primitive' for 'lordly' episcopacy. Decentralization of ecclesiastical authority would overthrow episcopal tyranny while preserving the office and continuity of bishops, which even many of those whom Laud had thought 'puritan' deemed essential; likewise, redistribution of ecclesiastical wealth would strengthen the preaching clergy which parochial poverty enfeebled. This indeed seemed the heaven-sent moment to realize the dreams of generations of protestants. The wide appeal of such proposals early in 1641 can be seen in the range of their sponsors: the universally respected Archbishop Ussher, Calvinist primate of Ireland and in close touch with John Pym; Laud's enemy Bishop Williams, soon to become archbishop of York; and puritan clergy like Marshall, Burges and Calybute Downing, who were shortly to forget their moderation. Associated with these schemes, and made more urgent by the Lords' doubts over Strafford's trial, was a bill aimed at excluding the bishops from the upper house. To the dismay of leading Covenanters, who dreamed of presbyterian uniformity, the programme made rapid headway as its conjunction with Bedford's bridging scheme seemed to promise a broad settlement. But the goodwill of the Commons and probably of most of the articulate clergy was offset by the peers' resistance to any attempt to alter the composition of their house. They were probably encouraged in this by Charles, whose love of hierarchy coincided with his desire to retain his episcopal supporters in the Lords. The hopes for primitive episcopacy dimmed with the failure of the exclusion bill.

Further fragmentation now became almost inevitable. One

response to the frustrations of the spring was the introduction into the Commons in June of a bill for the abolition of episcopacy 'root and branch'. Yet though 'root and branch' was for some merely a means to press the Lords to exclude the bishops, it did attract widespread sincere support. Some sought more freedom for the godly – Sir Arthur Haselrig and the obscure East Anglian back-bencher Oliver Cromwell shared the radical sympathies of Sir Henry Vane jnr, who had journeyed to New England in the 1630s. And many more, such as St John and perhaps Pym, were slowly coming to the conclusion that more direct courses were needed to deal with an entrenched evil. Theirs was a pragmatic awakening, rather than a principled conviction of the utter unlawfulness of episcopacy. But although most of its parliamentary supporters saw 'root and branch' as merely facilitating purer reconstruction, to appalled conservatives it seemed a long and dangerous way from primitive episcopacy.

Historians have sometimes talked of a 'functional radicalism', a non-ideological response to circumstances. But the substitution of 'root and branch' for the exclusion of bishops also showed that some members were being swept along in a rising tide of excitement. The apocalyptic potential inherent in puritanism had been inflamed by the growing spectre of a popish plot and still more by the upheaval of 1640-1. The dramatic shift from persecution to the prospect of godly rule was one of the most important developments of the seventeenth century, giving rise as it did to the millennialist fervour which was to dominate the following years. To some it seemed clear that the Holy Spirit must be at work, no longer simply affirming interpretations of scripture but now bringing new illumination to the souls of men. As Lord Brooke declaimed in 1641, 'The light still, will, must, cannot but increase.' It is no accident that some 70 per cent of the religious material published in the 1640s was millenarian in its bent. And while, in 1641, only a few looked to an imminent apocalypse, many thought that a godly commonwealth could at last be erected to hasten that event. Preaching to parliament on the eve of the summer's recess, Stephen Marshall was driven by the fall of Laud to see 'such hopes and beginnings of a Jubilee and Resurrection', and his belief that this was the 'time of times' carried increasing numbers of his parliamentary audience along. Sir Simonds D'Ewes looked hopefully to the imminent abolition of atheism, profaneness and blasphemy. Indeed, the surprisingly peaceful disbandment of the armies in the late summer strengthened hopes that the instruments of Antichrist had been broken. In what was to prove a brief respite, some moved from eager rhetoric to drawing blueprints for transforming men and the world. Three foreigners, the Czech intellectual giant Jan Amos Comenius, his Scottish ally John Dury and the Prussian Samuel

Hartlib, now published various proposals for educational and socio-economic reform. Encouraged by figures as diverse as Bishop Williams and Pym, they linked their call for educational expansion to dreams of peaceful protestant enlightenment which would unify the European churches and, perhaps, herald the approaching millennium.

The new awakening was still more evident outside Westminster, if only because those outside had previously been unheard. And while parliament-men might strive towards an orderly, national reformation which would preserve distinctions of degree, others dreamed other dreams. Even that cultural élitist John Milton prophesied that the imminent return of Christ would 'put an end to all earthly tyrannies', and not merely that of bishops. Thomas Goodwin, preparing to return from exile in the Netherlands to his London pulpit, noisily accorded priority of place in God's battles to 'the meaner sort of people'. The costs of religious enthusiasm were becoming clear, boding ill for hopes of moderate reform.

The parliamentary leaders were trapped between increasingly vociferous radicals on the one hand and alarmed social conservatives on the other. Despite almost a year's sitting the houses had failed to secure religious reform, and some of the godly were taking matters into their own hands. It was probably in an attempt to redeem parliament's standing amongst the faithful that Pym pushed through a thin house on 8 September, on the eve of the recess, an order for the destruction of relics of Laudianism in the churches. The order was remarkable in that not only did it conspicuously fail to enjoin respect for prayer book worship, but also in that the Commons took it upon themselves to give such a command. The Lords retaliated the following day by ordering that services should be conducted as the law provided.

The gulf between the two houses over the September orders on religion suggests how far Charles's position was from lost. Dwindling attendances in the Commons during the summer testified to a growing unease, and to weariness with this unprecedentedly long parliament. Moreover, however uncontentious the passage of the constitutional reforms, the few divisions on other issues revealed a surprisingly close balance of opinion. A royal policy of tact might yet have isolated Pym, since the indoctrination of orthodox protestants with the model of Constantine, the godly prince leading godly people, guaranteed the king a deep reserve of loyalty. Charles had made some well-timed moves when in late May he appointed various non-court peers to minor offices, and even gave the embittered Lord Saye the lucrative mastership of the court of wards. He maintained his posture of conciliatoriness yet more assertively in the following months, accompanying his assent to the destructive bills with ringing declarations of his readiness to sign whatever his loyal parliament sent him – a safe enough boast in view of the growing tension between the houses.

But that posture of conciliatoriness was not the only royal guise that contemporaries detected. The constitutional reforms had not addressed the central question of trust which underlay the crisis, and in June Secretary Vane concluded gloomily, 'We are here still in the labyrinth and cannot get out.' For just as Pym had in May abandoned thought of bridging schemes, so Charles was duly shutting the door: the good effect at Westminster of his moderate stance was quite offset by rumours that he was looking abroad for aid in restoring his divinely entrusted position. Although the news was not to break until the autumn, Charles in a second army plot in June seriously considered using the English army in the north to overawe parliament; and, unknown to the opposition, in July he sought military aid in Ireland. More public were his plans for Scotland, where he had long hoped to exploit the resentment of noblemen like Montrose at the growing influence of Argyll amongst the Covenanters. In May 1641 Charles announced his intention of going north to settle peace. In reality he probably sought support in hope of somehow himself playing the British card.

Charles's plan to go north changed the tempo of politics. The possibility that he might try to break parliament once he found himself near soldiers gave the final push to the two houses' legislative efforts that summer, and reform measures at last emerged from committee. A measure of the disquiet Charles had aroused lies in Pym's success on 24 June, in the first major display of his new stance, in gaining passage through both houses of ten propositions whose most notorious clauses called for a purge of papists from the king's entourage and the appointment of counsellors in whom parliament could trust. Suspicions increased further when Charles's eventual departure in August came the day *after* the completion in London of the peace treaty with the Scots, conceding most of their demands for a pure kirk and regular parliaments, which was supposed to be its justification.

The heightened crisis saw a remarkable increase in parliamentary power. Since the council was moribund, the king's departure from London left the two houses the *de facto* government: as Secretary Vane revealingly reported in August, 'The affairs of state are now in his majesty's absence in the parliament.' But the two houses were not now simply the executive. The erroneous labours of Sir Simonds D'Ewes, an indefatigable antiquarian, satisfied them that they had in the past made good law without the king by issuing ordinances – a term reminiscent of the Lords Ordainers who had long ago usurped the government of Edward II. Reassured, the houses in the three weeks before the scheduled recess in September took a series of precautions against popish disorder, culminating in the establishment of a joint committee which was to prepare for any military contingencies during the recess. Royal officials duly co-operated with the committee as they had with the two houses throughout, and Pym's role in it began to acquire him the nick-name 'King Pym'. Yet those who accorded him the title did not see him ruling over a united nation, and it would be a mistake to see the summer's developments as wholly pragmatic. The same distrust which produced the call in the ten propositions for trustworthy ministers manifested itself more glaringly in the houses' dispatch of a committee of four northwards to watch the king and to counter his efforts amongst the Scots.

Despite the encroachments on government the late summer and autumn of 1641 was an unnerving time for Pym, for the parliamentary coalition crumbled as apathy and disillusion set in. Fear of the plague and desire to go home had reduced attendances in the Lords to around a dozen by the end of August and to less than seventy in the Commons, as even that stern radical Sir Arthur Haselrig went home early. And while divisions opened in parliament, the peace with Scotland brought with it the disbandment of the army which had been Pym's surest guarantee. The paper security of statutes gave little reassurance, for the army plot had shown Charles's willingness to use force, and that message was dramatically underlined during the visit to Scotland. In the notorious 'Incident' of early October some of Charles's new-found Scottish supporters, jealous of Argyll and Hamilton, determined to settle matters in their own way. But though their bid to seize the pair was botched, it was damning enough for the king's reputation. Charles compounded the damage by going to the Edinburgh parliament surrounded by hundreds of armed supporters to deny the existence of any plot.

The Incident ensured that the second session of the Long Parliament, which opened on 20 October, would resume where the first ended. On the one hand stood those who now strove all the more to deprive Charles of his power. To that end Pym and his friends desperately needed the co-operation of the Lords, and they promptly renewed their campaign against the bishops in the upper house. But on the other hand Charles still had much to hope for, since while Pym's fears had hardened so had the rather different apprehensions of others. The peers still held firm over the bishops, while growing numbers – typified by Bristol in the Lords and Hampden's counsel

Robert Holborne in the Commons – saw the grievances of the 1630s as mistakes which were being rectified or as the work of evil men who were now gone, and in mounting anti-popish fervour and Pym's mounting demands the real danger. To strengthen such misgivings Charles had in the first session coldly left Laud to his fate and politely assented to the destructive measures of the summer. In the autumn he at last moved to reinforce those who should have been his natural allies. In letters from Scotland he urged Bristol and other supporters to aggravate the friction between the two houses; and five new, non-Laudian, appointments swelled the bishops' bench in the Lords as he emphasized his abandonment of his Laudian past.

Charles could count on an increasingly responsive audience. Parliament-men had been able to go home during the recess and talk to neighbours who had been less exposed than Londoners to the constant pressure of rumours and demonstrations. Many countrymen were perplexed as they saw old ways undermined. Parliament had sat long but had gained little; the crying need, church reform, was still neglected, as were long-standing problems like the scale of administrative fees and all the local matters so prominent in the letters MPs received from their constituents. The only tangible fruit of parliament's sitting had been taxes, all the more unwelcome in that a new plague epidemic in the summer of 1641 intensified the economic dislocation which political instability had brought. Although the need to pay the armies was obvious, the burdens of 1641 weighed heavier than ship money had done. Parliament first imposed a tax of six subsidies, and these were followed by a 'poll tax', to fall on every householder, as Pym edged towards tackling the problem of chronic under-assessment. Taxpayers and tax-assessors who had objected to the novel devices of the 1630s soon showed by delays and evasions that being part of a 'country' reaction against the crown did not always make them followers of Pym. As the disgruntled Yorkshire gentlewoman Margaret Eure was soon to complain, 'I am in such a great rage with parliament as nothing will pacify me, for they promised us all should be well, if my lord Strafford's head were off, and since then there is nothing better, but I think we shall be undone with taxes.' Although the puzzlement at events seems to have been greatest in areas remote from London, closer to home Sir Thomas Barrington wondered at the 'strange tepidity' and 'present spleen' in Essex in the summer of 1641.

During the recess the consequences of the Commons' religious policy, and especially of the September order against Laudianism, became clear. Disorders in Kent churches drove Sir Edward Dering to abandon his earlier support for Root and Branch; the city marshal had to protect the altar of St Paul's cathedral during service, and the sheriff of Herefordshire reported that after a fracas in Leominster church some were laying in muskets to kill puritans. Men now found it much easier to see bishops, whatever their faults, as an essential link in the chain of order and property. Sir Thomas Aston's *Remonstrance against Presbytery*, one of the most vehement of the new secular defences of episcopacy, found eager readers.

Despite the blunder of the Incident time was now on Charles's side. With the safeguard of the Scottish army gone the prospects for the parliamentary leaders looked bleak, the act against dissolution notwithstanding. The overwhelming likelihood at this point was that Charles would gain sufficient support to dissolve parliament with its own agreement, rather than that he would break it by force – an alarming sign of Pym's altered standing was the appearance in London that autumn of hostile flysheets and slogans. Fearing isolation and destruction, for his protestant cause no less than for himself, Pym in late October sought some means to heighten the excitement. A strongly oppositionist committee, established the previous November to survey the state of the kingdom, was ordered to produce its work, and thus emerged the Grand Remonstrance, with its sweeping retrospective indictment of the king's evil and popish counsellors. Even in the enormously intensified crisis of November 1641 this was to split the Commons down the middle, and Pym's decision in October to tell the story of old battles testifies to his desperation.

Just as the Scots had reprieved Charles's critics in 1638-40, so the Irish did in 1641. The news that reached parliament on 1 November of the outbreak of the Irish revolt doomed Charles's hopes of exploiting a return to normality. The need to suppress the revolt raised with new immediacy the question of Charles's own trustworthiness, for the two successive army plots and the Incident disinclined many to trust him with troops. But most damaging of all, the revolt gave terrifying substance to the popish threat. The rebels' not entirely empty claim to be acting in the king's name lent credibility and urgency to the opposition's charges that Charles was the tool of a Catholic conspiracy.

The revolt yet again demonstrated the dangers in an inheritance of separate kingdoms at a time of religious division. The triumph of aggressive puritans in Westminster and Edinburgh could not but threaten the Catholic Irish, for the colonial subjection of Ireland invited the former to export their religion. The danger of a reaction was the greater in that Strafford's recall created a vacuum which offered the native Irish, particularly in Ulster, the chance to regain their inheritances. But the revolt was a Catholic revolt rather than a

Gaelic revolt, and the behaviour of the Old English was more fateful. The Old English recognized as much as did their Gaelic co-religionists the threat from across the Irish Sea, but they saw them-selves as loyal Englishmen. Charles's quest for support in the spring and summer of 1641 seems to have given them the vital sense of legitimacy which allowed them to provide much of the leadership for the rebellion. By offering concessions to all the Irish groups, and ordering a halt to the disbandment of Strafford's Irish army, Charles invited Old English dissidents to think that they had the king's blessing – and even a forged royal commission – for resistance to the domi-nant English puritans and their New English and Ulster Scots allies. The rebels' claims of loyalty to the king could not have come at a worse time.

The initial rebel objectives were probably similar to those of the Scots – seizure of the centre of government and then negotiation from a position of strength for the ending of plantations and for religious guarantees. To that extent it can be argued that even this most alienated of all groups in the British polity sought to work within largely legitimist channels. But the attempt on Dublin Castle failed, and as the rising spread through Ulster and beyond the leaders lost control. The best estimates suggest that perhaps 4,000 protestants died immediately and another 8,000 when they were thrust from their homes in winter. But objective analysis was impossible for those at Westminster, even had full details been available. To English protes-tant opinion, the atrocity stories of the Irish Revolt confirmed every bloody stereotype of aggressive Catholicism. Undoubtedly, the scale of the suffering was exaggerated by some with a vested interest, since damning all Catholics would open all Ireland to confiscation and settlement. Undoubtedly also, protestants in turn committed atrocities, leaving the balance hard to determine even when it is divorced from its Cromwellian aftermath. But however convenient the revolt was for Pym, and however skilfully he used it, there is no reason to doubt his horror, or that of the majority of his countrymen. Rumours of, and precautions against, a popish rising spread over fifty miles in a night along the Welsh border; messengers from every direction brought reports of popish disturbances to Leicester; in Dorchester watch was kept from the church steeple. The national alarm had tangible consequences in the declining incidence of fiscal obstructionism when a major new tax of £400,000, much of it intended for the reconquest of Ireland, was voted in the spring of 1642.

The more obvious impact of the revolt was on parliamentary poli-tics. The new atmosphere of plot and murder – the Commons were regaled with fresh rumours almost weekly – rescued Pym. In an undoubted instance of functional radicalism the crisis persuaded members, as Pym's oratory had earlier failed to do, that they must limit the king's ability to turn to disreputable advisers. On 5 November, the anniversary of the Catholic Gunpowder Plot of 1605, Pym responded to the problem of the control over the force necessary to put down the rebellion by proposing his famous 'additional instruction': unless evil counsellors were removed, the Commons would be 'forced, by discharge of the trust which we owe to the state, and those whom we represent to resolve upon some way of defending Ireland.' For the Commons to involve themselves pragmatically in military affairs was no longer remarkable – councillors had gone straight to parliament with the first news of the revolt, and the houses had responded by issuing precautionary orders. But to declare openly their readiness to proceed without the king, and to justify such a move by an appeal to a responsibility to the nation was a different matter. The additional instruction passed an angry house by 151 votes to 110, in contrast to the unquestioned passage of many of the earlier measures of parliamentary administration.

These weeks saw an upsurge of partisanship, perhaps even of parties. In the attempt to browbeat the growing resistance in the Commons and the solid conservative majority in the Lords, the opposition leaders introduced the Grand Remonstrance into the lower house on 8 November. Although the Irish Revolt had seemed to confirm its allegations of monstrous popery, the Remonstrance only passed by the narrow margin of 159:148 after two weeks of angry debate which culminated in the drawing of swords in the house. It was a political watershed. While the unity of the Commons had begun to fragment far earlier, even the assumption of consensus was now breaking down. Preoccupied with unity and harmony as most men were, they were congenitally averse to proceeding to a vote, which by definition recognized the existence of disunity. But after the recess divisions occured in increasing numbers. The drawing of swords, and still more the threat by Hyde and others in December to make formal protestations against any vote to publish the Remonstrance, shows that a 'royalist' party was being born, a party more committed to the cause of order than to parliamentary unity.

On the other side too 'fears and jealousies' were doing their work. The votes on the additional instruction and on the Remonstrance had shown over 150 MPs rallying behind Pym, yet men who were coming to see themselves as politicians, with causes to advance or careers to make, probably made up at most fifty or sixty of Pym's following. About a hundred puritanical country gentlemen, lawyers and merchants were therefore sufficiently convinced that a popish plot surrounded the king to take steps which a matter of months before they would have found intolerable.

Nevertheless, the Grand Remonstrance, for all its denunciations and for all its demands for parliamentary approval of the king's ministers, was more a product of fear than an act of aggression. A horrified Sir Edward Dering thought its aim was to 'remonstrate downward, tell stories to the people, and talk of the king as of a third person.' But it reads as a very defensive document, and not merely in its assertion that Romish agents were subverting English religion and liberties. Its authors clearly feared isolation before the wrath of a vengeful king. Not only were parliamentary attendances unnervingly low – although the Remonstrance brought one of the half-dozen best-attended divisions of the parliament, over two hundred MPs did not vote. More alarming was opinion in the country, where the danger-ous conviction that the lower house was in the grip of a sectarian fever was clearly gaining hold. At the end of the Remonstrance comes a revealing series of clauses insisting that parliament did not intend 'to let loose the golden reins of discipline and government in the church'. It was manifestly to allay the gathering anger of religious conserva-tives that the opposition leaders recounted their mortal struggle against popery.

The alarm of Pym, Holles and the rest was well-founded. Despite the intensity of the recent shock, the lull in its wake brought a return to a semblance of normality, which in turn brought a real prospect of a royal triumph. For much of the traditional political nation was, what-ever its concerns about Irish papists, now desperately anxious for stability.

The changing mood was apparent in the enthusiastic reception – 'our wives conceive with joy', declared York's recorder – given Charles on his journey south from Scotland. He received further encouragement in London's lavish welcome on 25 November. Aldermanic memories of sordid money-grubbing by crown and court in the 1630s were steadily fading in face of other grievances: a City committee had reported in October that the privilege of immunity for debt enjoyed by members of both houses and their servants had already cost £1M., more than ship money. Equally disturbing were the disorders in the metropolis, which the parliamentary opposition seemed to exacerbate with its appeals for support. The mayoral elec-tion in September 1641 had brought a reassuring conservative triumph, and Charles eagerly seized his chance. Assuring waverers of his devotion to protestantism and the ancient ways of government he made material concessions to the City, and cast the blame for recent strains between king and City on 'the meaner sort of people'.

There followed a noisy campaign of moderation, skilfully crafted by Bristol and by new royal advisers, those quintessential moderates, Hyde, Lord Falkland and Sir John Colpepper. Charles followed his appeal to the City with a conciliatory proclamation on religion on 10 December, which was given plausibility by his appointments to bishoprics that autumn. Most important of all was his very measured rejection of the Grand Remonstrance on 23 December. He reinforced his denial of its conspiracy thesis with a major new initiative when he on the one hand offered concessions to those offended by religious ceremonies while he at the same time enjoined use of the prayer book. Charles was deftly appealing to all those who doubted the houses' good intent in religion, and that he had caught the mood was apparent in a surge of petitions in December in favour of episcopacy: that from Somerset claimed 14,000 signatories. Had the king then gone on to announce the appointment of the earl of Essex, widely respected and as experienced as anyone else at his disposal, to command in Ireland he might have done much to dispel the climate of fear in which Pym survived. But despite his rhetoric, Charles was now bent on confrontation. Seeing only the insubordination of his enemies and the growing numbers of his own supporters, and judging further surrenders both anathema and unnecessary, he let it be known that he would go to Ireland himself. Dismissing the conciliatory Secretary Vane, he left few doubts that his objective was not compromise but the building of sufficient support with which to regain his powers.

In that cause in the weeks after his return the king seemed to be successful. The Lords held firm while, as the Commons got down to practical matters, raising money for Ireland and such long-overdue measures as bills against piracy and scandalous ministers, Pym's hold weakened. As he had done in October, Pym turned desperately to a hunt for scapegoats, in hope of raising the temperature again. Early December saw him lead futile bids to exclude Bristol and Digby, Charles's new confidants, from the Lords; equally vainly, he also renewed the campaign against the bishops. The vulnerability of the opposition's cause is reflected in the violent and excited demonstrations that thronged around Westminster in these weeks. Not only were the tumults a sign of desperation. The sometimes bloody clashes with discharged army officers also showed that the king too had acquired some impetuous, and less reputable, supporters.

The mounting passions in the streets and alleys of the metropolis were the key to what was to prove the opposition's preservation, the London revolution of December–January. Marxist historians used to assume that London's support for parliament revealed the natural hostility of merchant interests for an exploitative crown and aristocracy. The discovery that the bulk of the City's merchant élite was, if not royalist, then certainly not parliamentarian, challenged this analysis. Some historians have since argued that the City was divided between the 'ins', those to whom economic privileges had been awarded, and the 'outs', but this of course oversimplifies the complexity of commercial groupings and attributes too much coherence to Charles's policies. Domestic patentees and the customs farmers did indeed tend to support the king but they were a minority in the City's government, and Charles had in the 1630s offended the major merchant groups and the City corporation indiscriminately. Nevertheless, despite the affronts much of the City's élite rallied in the course of 1641 to the king and the cause of order.

But the merchant princes in the court of aldermen no longer ruled the City. The survival of elements of civic democracy allowed other groups in the gathering crisis to overwhelm their superiors. Among the second-rank merchants who plied the North American trades vested interest was less likely to restrain the puritanism which had often drawn them into dealings with the colonists, or to soften their resentment at the recent royal measures. Furthermore, probably the bulk of the colonial merchants were also involved in retail trading, especially in tobacco and sugar. They thus had more dealings with the London populace than did the aldermanic élite, and were better placed to organize politically in the metropolis – colonial merchants in fact provided the leading radical parliamentarians in London throughout the revolutionary years. And below these clamoured the freemen at large, many of them genuinely poor artisans and journeymen, who had probably been milked, proportionately, more than their betters during the 1630s, whether by the patentees in the various new corporations or by City magistrates passing on the burden of ship money to their inferiors. But the bitterness of artisans and shopkeepers stemmed even more from the deepening depression which had set in with the Scottish crisis. Probate inventories, as well as the papers of Nehemiah Wallington the turner, indicate that they kept most of their resources in stock, items for trade; and Wallington's persistent cash-flow problems left him chronically dependent on credit. Not surprisingly, he was suffering gravely by late 1641 as political insecurity led merchants to curtail their activities. It would be folly to assume a crudely materialist explanation of London radicalism – London mobs rabbled the separatist congregation of Praise-God Barebone as well as bishops in December 1641. But hardship, as well as the Irish Revolt, does seem to have given a sharper edge to Wallington's puritan convictions, and to have made him and his fellows a ready audience for Pym's appeal against the bishops and popish lords in the upper house.

London was crucial to Pym's fortunes throughout the crisis. Utilizing parochial and ward organizations in the closely governed City, and calling on the enthusiastic aid of puritan ministers like Cornelius Burges, the radical London MPs Isaac Penington and John Venn had been able to orchestrate weighty petitions and demonstrations. But the greatest success of the opposition came on 21 December 1641, when municipal elections brought a revolution in London politics and halted the most critical element in the drift towards the king. In an impressive display of popular feeling, the voters – all the freemen in the wards – changed almost half of the common councilmen. The emergence of a radical majority in the common council, threatening the control of the mayor and aldermen, had immense implications. In early January the City's militia was put into new hands, giving parliament the hope of physical security. Equally important, however, was the question of control over the City's money bags. Ireland would only be reconquered – and, as it proved, a civil war fought – with the aid of City loans; much would hinge on whether king or parliament were lent the means to raise troops.

The king's appeal to the City fathers, and the opposition's success amongst the lesser citizens, suggests that the political nation was now embarked on a sequence of action and reaction that was to lead directly to civil war. But such an assumption ignores the peers. Had the Lords held firm on a middle ground Pym would have been unable to apply the pressure of both houses on the king.

Once again Charles destroyed his own position. Previous crises had seen him hesitate between conflicting courses of action, reaping the worst of both harvests. He had failed equally to support or to block both the army plot and the Scottish Incident; so too now, though he was overtly following Hyde's constitutionalist advice, he gave his ear to the hot-headed Lord Digby, the champion of the discharged officers thronging the court. On 22 December, the day after the opposition's triumph in the London elections, Charles justified the suspicions entertained of him by appointing as Lieutenant of the Tower of London a harsh professional soldier, and convicted felon, Colonel Lunsford. He could not have signalled his thoughts of a coup more clearly, and his move precipitated days of yet more intense rioting around the houses. But although Charles soon capitulated to London merchant pressure and replaced Lunsford, the Commons could not feel secure. The majority in the Lords still held out, and the demonstrations risked generating a dangerous reaction. As John Dillingham, a newsletter-writer close to St John, wrote gloomily after Christmas, 'in case we fall out' it would not be only 'the religious in general but even parliament-men' who would be held up to vengeance as sectaries. The desperation of the Commons' majority is reflected in their order on the 30th that MPs' servants should bring pistols to defend the house – many at Westminster now recognized what they could not have conceded a year before, the possibility of war. 'There is now nothing sought for so much as guns', reported Dillingham that day. But although the appointment of Lunsford suggests such apprehensions were well-founded, the king gave his enemies a temporary reprieve. He seems to have been jolted into precipitate action by the angry response of both houses to the bishops, ill-advised attempt to challenge the validity of parliament's proceedings when the mob was at the door. Fearing the loss of the Lords, and fearing too the impeachment of the queen, Charles was vulnerable to Digby's promptings.

Opening one of the great melodramas of English history, the king on 3 January 1642 sent to the Lords charges for an impeachment of treason against Viscount Mandeville and against the 'five members', Pym, Hampden, Haselrig, Holles and William Strode. The inclusion of Strode, prominent in the debacle of 1629 although rather less so to date in the Long Parliament, shows how much Charles's beliefs mirrored those of the opposition leaders, for the Grand Remonstrance too traced conspiracy back into the 1620s. But whatever his memory, Charles lacked foresight. The bishops' challenge in the previous week had fatally offended the dignity of the peers, and instead of ordering arrests, as they had done when Pym complained against the bishops, the Lords temporized. Facing humiliation, the king took several hundred armed men to Westminster the following day in search of his quarry. But his 'birds' had 'flown', forewarned by friends at court, and instead a shaken king confronted a house of Commons silent but for mutterings of 'Privilege, privilege'. The Commons were equally alarmed, surmising from Charles's guard of 'papists, ill-affected persons . . . panders and rogues', as one member called them, that the king would have used force if necessary. Accordingly, both houses voted to adjourn to the safety of the City, where angry crowds lined the king's way when he tried to fetch the five members from their refuge. Fearing mob assaults, on 10 January Charles left Whitehall, never to return until he was brought back in 1648 to face trial and execution. He had lost London in more ways than one.

Thwarted at Westminster, Charles was now probably coming to contemplate civil war rather than the coup at which he had aimed while still in London. Mid-January saw abortive royal attempts to seize the huge northern arsenal at Hull and other supplies of arms at Kingston-on-Thames and Portsmouth; by the end of the month the queen was preparing to depart for the continent to find aid. But civil war could be only a distant prospect while the king had no more than

200 men with him. The attempt on the five members was proving as disastrous for Charles's standing amongst the waverers in parliament, still more in the country, as the army plot had been. In order to repair the damage he therefore turned once more to the appalled Hyde, who swallowed his own doubts to write descants upon the theme of harmony. In a tone reminiscent of his answer to the Grand Remonstrance, on 20 January the king declared his readiness to co-operate with parliament in measures necessary for the safety of the kingdom and of protestantism. In further attempts to win over the Lords, in the next three weeks he indicated his willingness to work with the houses over militia appointments, to accept the Grand Remonstrance's proposal that a synod of divines prepare a religious settlement, and to withdraw the charges against the five members.

It might have worked. The revolutionary implications of the events of December and January may have seemed less clear to contemporaries than they have since. There could be no better indication of the fluidity of politics than the career of the earl of Newport, who had actually sided with the Commons over the religious orders of September 1641 but who yet became a royalist. There were many more such waverers, and had Charles allowed himself to be guided by Hyde the eventual outcome would have been very different. Even at this late date, the king's enemies owed much to the largely pragmatic growth of parliamentary government: thus, they had been able to exploit the growing habit of obedience to their commands when they ordered local militia officers to block the royalist efforts in January 1642. Similarly, fear of papists and of the Irish, as well as of the king, had finally extracted from the majority in the Lords in the aftermath of the attempt on the five members an endorsement of the new London militia and a still more reluctant co-operation in the Commons' plans for the disposition of the nation's militia as a whole. Charles's declaration of 20 January caused many peers to think again, and had he held to such a stand before the attempt on the five members the Lords – and perhaps the Commons too – might never have been lost.

Although many yearned to hold a middle ground of moderation and conciliation, that ground could be sapped by extremists on either side, especially when one of the extremists was the king. In the Commons ineffectual moderates like Sir Simonds D'Ewes and Framlingham Gawdy left the chamber in despair when the going grew too rough, while the London mob turned out in force to stiffen those inclined to smile upon Charles's conciliatory messages. The new campaign of intimidation thinned the numbers in the Lords from around sixty to some forty by the end of January; it thereby left the ground distinctly stonier for Charles's further efforts at conciliation in early February, when – in his fear lest the prince of Wales be held hostage – he accepted at last the exclusion of the now impotent bishops from the Lords. The king's hopes of the upper house finally crumbled with the interception in mid-February of a letter from Lord Digby, which showed that some prominent royalists thought Charles's concessions a sham. When, after seeing Henrietta Maria set sail later that month, Charles turned northwards instead of back to the vicinity of London it became obvious that he thought more of force than of politicking in his capital. The Commons meanwhile were subject to a barrage of reports of Catholic plotting and Catholic arming, and on 5 March they passed their 'declaration of fears and jealousies', the quintessential product of these months, which reveal-ingly traced the crisis of trust back to Charles's 'popish' preparations against the Scots in 1639–40. On the same day the houses passed an ordinance regulating the militia which omitted even a nominal role for the king.

It took several months for the mutual 'fears and jealousies' to persuade a sufficient number in the country to take sides. At Westminster the few with a clear sense of purpose were able to drag along an unhappy majority which was left floundering by the king's refusal to be as conciliatory as they wished him to be. In mobilizing the militia, a defensive arm, the houses saw themselves as defending England against a 'popish' malignant' enemy which by no means all members yet identified with the king; they were accordingly far better placed at first in the quest for support than was Charles as he began to seek volunteers. The pragmatic nature of the houses' activity is underlined by the fact that several of their nominees for militia commands that spring were eventually to join the king: when the future parliamentarian stalwart Sir William Brereton could support the appointment of the future royalist activist Lord Strange, it is clear that many found the ordinance a non-partisan means to put the sword in reliable hands. Correspondingly, many officials continued to answer to the two houses as they had done for months. The houses were, after all, moving to defend a working government; conversely, in seeking to raise troops the king was not only attempting to regain his capital but also an executive which had not, in practice, been his since at least the summer recess. Perhaps the most telling comment on Charles's position is the readiness of Sir Edward Littleton, lord keeper of the great seal, the primary symbol of government, to sup-port the militia ordinance in March 1642, before he belatedly joined the king two months later.

Yet the houses' pragmatic assertion of control over the adminis-tration does not explain how men nerved themselves to fight. The parliamentary resistance to the king was not simply an unthought-out reflex. However unpartisan the intentions of many of those who supported the militia ordinance, it had been brought into the Commons on 7 December 1641 by men who were thoroughly partisan, by Haselrig and by Strode. Those who firmly believed in the existence of a popish plot grimly took steps to confront it, and pulled behind them others who were less certain of the meaning of their actions, or who could present no alternative solution to the crisis. The account given in the Grand Remonstrance of the monstrous growth of conspiracy since Charles's accession is the most important single piece of evidence for an understanding of the outbreak of the civil war.

The political process had proved unable to contain the novel tensions of three kingdoms. The gravest blow to Charles's position had been the Irish Revolt, which not only brought to the fore the crucial question of the disposition of force, in control over the militia, that was to be the occasion of war; it also aroused the passions in parliament's supporters that were to make civil war possible. But there were domestic strains too which diminished the prospects for a solution to the enveloping crisis of mutual mistrust. When fears grew of a self-willed king and popery on the one hand and of parity and mob rule on the other parliament proved incapable of acting as the mediator, as the 'point of contact' between king and country. The 'root-and-branch' petitioners who had raised their voices inopportunely, the London merchants who had hurried Strafford to his death, the 'country' members who disrupted Pym's financial efforts and thus lessened his usefulness to the king, the church disturbances which accelerated the drift away from Pym, the London freemen voters in late 1641, all gave warning that the political equation now contained alarmingly independent variables. Even before Charles began to look for armed support, national politics had opened out to include the country, in part at least because of public pressure, as the spate of petitions shows.

And it was above all the religious issue that drove men on, outside Westminster now as well as in. Whatever the incomprehension during the summer of 1641 about the nature of the crisis, alarm at the popish threat had soared with the Irish Revolt and the Grand Remonstrance. One measure of public arousal – as significant in its way as the London revolution – is the soaring totals of Catholic recusants presented in county after county in 1641: the hundred of Thirsk in the North Riding of Yorkshire alone achieved the remarkable total of some 2,000 presentments. Another measure is the surge of petitions in 1642; parliament received petitions from thirty-eight of the forty English counties. While a majority of petitions to king as well as parliament called for accommodation, the religious crisis proved to have polarized the nation – over half the counties petitioned in support of the established church against the sectarian challenge. The fears the parliamentary leaders had shown in the Grand Remonstrance about the state of public opinion were well-founded. Although it took months for the parties to overcome Englishmen's preoccupation with unity, when they appealed in earnest to the consciences of their countrymen they found a sufficient response to enable them to take the field.

8 Civil War 1642–1646

Recent historians have justly pointed to the paradox of the English civil war. 1647–9 brought revolutionary developments, yet the aspirations of most of those at Westminster in 1642 centred on preserving the gains of 1641 and securing moderate religious reforms. Such men, scholars argue, were insensibly drawn by threats and by circumstances into taking the minimum steps needed to avert total defeat, and would have been horrified to learn what the future held.

There is much truth in this account of conservatives who were forced reluctantly onwards. But it reacts too strongly against the implausible views of other historians who have seen, far back in the 1620s, a self-conscious, deeply motivated opposition bent on a radical restructuring of church and state. Had all parliamentarians been intransigent conservatives, it is difficult to see how they could have steeled themselves to act. Granted, the Commons' chamber had in 1628 and 1640 rung with anthems on the rule of law; yet the popish threat, and in particular the Irish Revolt, soon convinced many that the ways of their fathers could only survive if protected, that necessity existed and must be confronted. Within a surprisingly few months, therefore, John Pym was able to persuade enough of the gentlemen left in the Commons, and of the still more uneasy peers in the Lords, to create an administrative machine which, in order to fight a war, broke dramatically with cherished 'country' ways. Long before the catastrophes of 1647–9, parliament-men who believed they were fighting God's battles had shown themselves capable of responding to the dictates of necessity.

Nevertheless, the quest for the middle ground dominated 1642. Such was the king's isolation that only two peers went north with him to York in March 1642; though shocks like Sir John Hotham's repulse on 23 April of Charles's second attempt to seize the arms at Hull did speed the trickle of supporters a little, not until June did the king's entourage swell appreciably. Few relished the prospect of civil war, or association with the extremist views of the adventurers and younger sons – and perhaps of Charles too – at the small royal court-in-exile.

In June the earl of Lindsey, soon to be commander of the first royalist field army, urged the king to accept parliament's uncompromising Nineteen Propositions; and if the gloom of the earl of Dorset is at all representative, some 'royalists' at York feared a royal victory as much as a parliamentarian, and desperately hoped for an accommodation.

Charles's propaganda reflected his dilemma. On the one hand he intensified his efforts to win Anglicans to his side, declaring his devotion to the Elizabethan church and pouring scorn on the sectarian rabble who threatened the social order; meanwhile Hyde and his friends reminded constitutionalists that their proper home was with the king. Their finest hour came with the royal answer, drafted by Lord Falkland and Sir John Colpepper, to parliament's Nineteen Propositions. Stressing that government was mixed – neither simply regal nor parliamentary – the answer concluded with a magnificently rhetorical reminder that the parliamentary leaders' populism threatened all property-owners and gentlemen. But the contention clashed with the central royalist claim that allegiance to the king was indivisible, that obedience was due 'unto the natural person of the prince', rather than to his office as parliamentarians claimed. It also clashed with simpler verities, dear to Charles, purveyed by clerical supporters such as the Calvinist bishop Joseph Hall, who claimed that the king held power in trust not from the people but from God and that resistance was therefore a sin as well as a crime. The brilliant Dudley Digges was soon to develop a parallel and almost Hobbesian argument for an unchallengeable royal sovereignty.

The two houses were similarly ambivalent. Charles I was not the first English king to persist in being ill-advised, and long before 1642 men had sought to distinguish between the crown and the person of the king. However confusing to the unsophisticated, the houses' claim throughout the war to be defending 'king and parliament', and the powers if not the person of the king, cannot be dismissed as a disingenuous appeal to a conservative nation. It underlay their practical demands, spelt out in the Nineteen Propositions, that they retain effective power for twenty years, a period which exceeded the presumed life-expectancy of this king. And it fit the facts, since the houses remained in the capital attempting to conduct a government from which Charles had withdrawn. Yet some of parliament's spokesmen embraced necessity enthusiastically rather than apologetically. As the controversy over the militia reverberated in the summer of 1642 amidst widespread fears of popery the houses steadily elevated their status as the 'representative body of the kingdom' into a claim to possess, in the last resort, supreme executive authority. Henry Parker, client of Lord Saye, eagerly elaborated this new thesis of the sovereign power of parliament in his *Observations upon Some of His*

Majesties Late Answers and Expresses; in this he argued forthrightly that since parliament represented 'the whole community in its underived majesty' it must by the law of nature take the steps necessary for self-preservation. It was the mirror image of the king's position in the ship money trial.

Still more striking, and undoubtedly more effective, were the out-pourings of the pulpit. The providentialist claim that God had put man on earth for a purpose was scarcely original to Calvinists, but they certainly maintained it more strenuously than did most of their contemporaries. In face of a king corrupted by popish conspirators, a king clay in the hands of the queen and thus of 'the Romish vice-god', in Parker's words, some found it easy to argue that their duty to resist Antichrist transcended all other obligations. In February 1642 the Commons, and then a wider audience, heard Stephen Marshall apply the frightening Old Testament text of the cursing of Meroz to all those who withheld their hands from shedding the blood of the popish enemy. Anti-Catholicism had gained an apocalyptic edge. After the Irish rebels' flaunting of their royal 'commission', Parker's advocacy of parliamentary self-preservation made sense.

Parliament's hopes of isolating Charles hinged on its insistence that the danger was popish. But Pym could not conceal for ever the fact that the militia ordinance was to defend the nation against the king's friends as well as other foes. When Charles condemned the ordi-nance, and then in June issued commissions of array to local notables to secure their counties, the scale of the crisis dawned even on those who tried to shut their eyes to it. In Kent Henry Oxinden wept that he was 'between Scylla and Charybdis', and prayed for the emergence of an unchallenged authority. Alarm increased as disorder threatened: the business of the Whitsun fair at Chard, Somerset, fell by a half, scattered rioting against enclosures warned that peasants might profit from disorder, and religious zealots intimidated one another. Although the rival propaganda machines called for support, a flood of local petitions in the summer called for accommodation.

Everywhere, men sought an escape in neutralism. The ruin of Ger-many during the Thirty Years War, and the scattered agrarian unrest that had broken out all over the country in 1640–2 as political controls began to fracture, only reinforced the natural human prefe-rence for peace. Even those whose loyalties were clear, such as the parliamentarian Fairfaxes in Yorkshire, could recognize how much they had to lose and strove to neutralize their own areas – Sir John Hotham's fear lest 'the necessitous people. . .set up for themselves to the utter ruin of all the nobility and gentry', was widely shared. In county after county gentlemen shunned both the militia ordinance and the commission of array: the extreme case was Staffordshire, where the gentry tried to raise a third force to resist outsiders. Towns like Leicester shut their gates, and most ordinary countrymen infinitely preferred to follow the plough rather than the drum.

If neutralism was so prevalent, how was civil war possible? Why did fortress Staffordshire fall, and all the other neutrality pacts collapse? The haphazard beginnings of the Civil War illuminate both the strengths and the weaknesses of the endemic localism. For the neutrals found that their counties and towns were by no means autonomous, and that pressures existed both within and without. The conflicting principals acted as magnets to the areas around them, a fact which helps to explain the well-known geographical division into a parliamentarian south-east and a royalist north and west. Parliament easily disarmed neutrals in neighbouring Kent and Hertfordshire; conversely, the movements of the king undermined the efforts of many in the north to stay out of the fray. In other areas, paradoxically, the need to preserve the social order did the work of the belligerents. Thus, anti-Catholic disturbances amongst industrial workers suffering from the deepening depression drove frightened gentry to collaborate with the regionally dominant power, whether parliamentarian in Suffolk or royalist in Staffordshire. Indeed, such considerations of prudence rather than principle – who was most to be feared locally? who was likely to win? – probably determined the allegiances of the majority of the population throughout the war.

But zealots could be found everywhere, and the neutralists could not build quarantines against them. The Worcestershire minister Richard Baxter gave a moving account of how royalist violence against otherwise peaceful puritans drove many to parliamentarian garrisons for refuge, and thus willy-nilly to align themselves. As Lucy Hutchinson in Nottinghamshire observed, 'every county. . .had the civil war within itself.'

The hesitations of some of Baxter's godly neighbours suggest that this was by no means solely a war for religion. The mixture of motives that could lead participants on was most apparent at the humblest level. Most recruits on both sides fought for pay and plunder, a prospect rendered all the more attractive in a depression. Amongst those prompted by principle, the ordinary countrymen in Somerset who believed that the king intended a general onslaught on 'liberty and property' were not alone in their secular concerns. Oliver Cromwell's later judgment, that 'religion was not the thing first contested for', is often cited; while he then had in mind a specific form of religious settlement, his verdict remains plausible if his 'religion' is interpreted more widely. Mrs Hutchinson noted of her husband, a future regicide, that 'though he was satisfied of the endeavours to. . .subvert the true protestant religion,. . .yet he did not think that so clear a ground of the war as the defence of the just English liberties.'

There were two parliamentarian causes in the Civil War, one of which was certainly the crusade of the godly against Antichrist. But the other was a more secular struggle for parlimentary and legal liberties, for the Petition of Right and against the arbitrary fiscalism of Charles's years in power. The war against the king was after all fought in the name of parliament, not of the godly people. The two causes might be completely separate. The most radical MP was the thoroughly ungodly Henry Marten, and the equally ungodly lawyer John Selden the most cogent constitutionalist. The continuing support of Selden, and of other such distinguished lawyers as Henry Rolle and Mathew Hale, for increasingly radical parliamentarian regimes suggests how wrong it is to accept the claim of Clarendon's *History* that all constitutionalists joined the king. More often, though, the godly and the legalist causes dwelt together in the persons of the puritan property-owners who largely composed both houses. In that conjunction lay parliament's tragedy. The harsh demands of fighting a war steadily brought the causes of godly rule and of legal liberties into inexorable – and by 1648 violent – conflict as many parliamentarians baulked at the measures they were driven to set their hands to. Their concern for property led such men as Holles, or, still more, back-benchers like Sir John Holland from Norfolk, to cry out for peace as the war progressed.

Yet the importance of religion cannot be underestimated. Sheer anti-Catholicism drove on many conscientious followers of parliament – as Baxter said, it was religion that 'put the resolution and valour' in parliament's soldiers. The parliamentarian battle-standards of 1642, with their slogans such as 'Antichrist must down' and 'Sacra Scriptura', tell the story graphically, and when Sir Robert Harley's Herefordshire castle of Brampton Bryan fell to the royalists his tenants cited Marshall's vituperative *Meroz Cursed* as the reason they took up arms. The legend of the popish plot proved as destructive as that which had defeated the king in Scotland. What could be made of the Grand Remonstrance's thesis of a jesuited conspiracy was revealed in the bloody tract *Anti-Cavalierisme*, published late in 1642 by the radical London minister John Goodwin. Its call for an all-out war against Antichrist, and the whoremongers, blasphemers and papists around the king, in the opinion of some made the breach irreparable. A Shropshire royalist complained bitterly that autumn of the parliamentarian propaganda: 'They beat us more in the impression of fables. . .beloved among common people, than any open force can prevail.'* The outcries were, however, not mere fables. Although, to avoid exciting further hostility, probably the majority of Catholics stayed neutral, a disproportionate number did support the king. Almost two-thirds of Lancashire royalist gentry were Catholic, about a half in Suffolk and over a third in Yorkshire; one-third of the officers of Charles's northern armies were Catholic. The traditionalism of their outlook as well as their hostility to parliament's militant protestantism probably helped account for their alignment.

It was a war of religion on both sides. Despite the prominence of Catholics in their ranks, royalists claimed to be fighting for the true protestant religion no less than did parliamentarians. The twin constants of Charles's declarations were his devotion to law and to the protestantism of Elizabeth, and others joined him in fulminating against sectarian excesses. Rural husbandmen as well as clergymen willingly suffered persecution in the 1640s for using their fathers' forms of worship enshrined in the prayer book; their loyalties may not have been Laudian, but they can certainly be called Anglican. And their hatred of parliamentarian puritans curiously mirrored their enemies' loathing of Catholics, for each saw in the other blasphemous advocacy of rebellion and subversion of the social order. Both sides saw chaos as the inevitable outcome of religious deviance. The violence of the sermons of Goodwin, or of Henry Burton, was abundantly matched by royalist broadsheets blasting roundheaded cobblers in the pulpit, and by sermons urging parishioners to protect the prayer book. Many itched for the opportunity to pay off old scores, and the sheriff of Herefordshire predicted in late 1641 that his neighbours 'if the times would serve. . .would show as little favour to those that they call puritans as any English or Irish papist would do.'

The social patterns of alignment have proved harder to discern than the religious. Historians have understandably concentrated on the gentry, who provided the bulk of the parliamentarian leaders. Yet it is doubtful whether the results have justified the time spent in identifying those who were rising and falling economically. At Westminister each side – before the royalists left – had a broadly similar profile; the parallels held true throughout the war. And while the steady decline in the social composition of the leading parliamentarians has led some historians to discern an inherently radical vehicle for social mobility, on both sides cautious magnates with much to lose were displaced during the course of the war by harder men. Parliament's self-denying ordinance of 1645 can be matched by a piecemeal edging out of most of the royalist notables in the regions by 1644. Indeed, perhaps half of the king's field officers during the

Huntington Papers (London, 1926), V, 52.

war were from the blurred area where lesser gentry merged into plebeians, and a disproportionate number were younger sons; the former drayman, and parliamentarian colonel, Thomas Pride, had his match in the former Warwickshire 'cowgelder', and royalist major, Thomas Jennings. English peacetime society allowed only limited social mobility, and wartime service presented welcome prospects, on both sides. With fewer ties of neighbourhood, and less reason to observe social niceties, the upwardly mobile were notoriously prone to efficiency and enthusiasm. A royalist victory won by such men as Jennings, and under such a king, might have changed the world as dramatically as did the New Model army's triumph.

Yet some contrasts are evident, most obviously in the fact that about twice as many peers eventually fought for the king as for parliament. Like those ill-fated kings, John, Edward II and Henry VI before him, Charles had repeatedly offended the nobility. Not only had he failed to act as a 'good lord' to those who counted, but he had also been defeated in his wars. The wonder is, not that he found so many aristocratic opponents but that he found so many supporters. For that, Charles could thank the long elaboration of the cult of monarchy, which was at last found to have done its work; he also owed much to the peers' recognition that they were the major beneficiaries of the hierarchy of order of which the crown was both the pinnacle and the symbol. Furthermore, the family traditions of the nobility often centred on service to the crown. Such considerations applied to all the magnates, and not just to the peers, for a significant majority of the richest gentry who committed themselves sided with the king. The promptings of honour and tradition are clearest in the famous case of Sir Edmund Verney, Charles's standard-bearer at Edgehill, whose sympathy for parliament's complaints was outweighed by his sense of honour.

Such concerns were not absent on the other side. Some parliamentarian peers, such as the all-important Lord General Essex, were probably angered by Charles's failure in the 1630s to treat them as they had felt their due. More generally, most peers, on either side, were aristocratic constitutionalists. They believed that true monarchy rested on, governed through and was limited by a strong nobility: Northumberland probably had peers as well as people in mind when in 1642 he identified parliament's cause as 'laws, liberties and privileges'. The nobility's sense of its due place played a crucial part in giving substance to the central parliamentarian claim that *both* houses were withstanding a misled king, and in lending some social respectability to the cause. Not for nothing did the twenty colonels of parliament's first field army include ten peers.

That commitment to a hierarchy of degree meant that – with the

exception of religious radicals like lord Brooke or hotheads like Lord
Digby – few noblemen or greater gentry ranked amongst the militants on either side. In June 1642 the earl of Dorset, with the king at
York, commiserated with the unhappy earl of Salisbury, currently
with the parliament, on the lot of 'those that enjoy such a portion
of honour and such a proportion of estate', and concluded disapprov-
ingly that the radicals on either hand were 'men only either of
desperate fames or fortunes', whom their betters must strive to
check. The political consequences of such attitudes were apparent in
the distrust for the wealthy Colonel Hutchinson shown during the
war by the Nottingham parliamentary garrison, who 'thought it
scarce possible for any one to continue a gentleman and firm to a
godly interest'.

If the bulk of the activists amongst the great supported the king,
why in a hierarchical society did they fail to carry the country with
them? The extent of their failure has probably been exaggerated, for a
resident lord could be remarkably effective. The alignments in
Leicestershire, behind the Hastings and Grey families, echoed those
in the Wars of the Roses two centuries earlier, while the earl of
Newcastle's northern whitecoats, and on the parliamentarian side the
early loyalty of the men of Essex to the earl of Warwick, point to the
continuing importance of the magnates. But too many of the aristocracy had become remote courtiers or rentiers, thereby undermining
traditional ties. Moreover, they had become unused to leading men.
Decades of peace had encouraged lord lieutenants – and here
Warwick is a suggestive exception – to abdicate their local militia
responsibilities to gentlemen deputies. Lesser men were therefore left
freer to decide, or to stay neutral, in this crisis.

In a few areas, where there had been a particularly aggressive
landlord – like Charles himself in the fens – there is something to be
said for the Marxists who see rural and urban middling sort lining up
against oppressive (although scarcely 'feudal') superiors. But such an
argument has its limits, for as we have seen the economic profiles of
the leaders of both sides were broadly similar. A case can be made for
the parliamentarian sympathies of some of the rural middling sort,
but it must see them reacting against a threat from below rather than
from above. The reappearance in Essex in 1640, after a lapse since
1629, of parish petitions from godly ministers and the 'better sort of
householders' for moral reformation suggests the identification of
parliament with the puritan concern for disciplining the poor. Seeing
parliament as the means to godly rule nationally as well as locally such
groups – although contracted by disillusionment – formed much of
the 'honest party' which remained ready in most counties to do parliament's increasingly unpopular bidding throughout the war. The

godly Major-General Worsley was able to find support in such quarters in the north-west in 1655–6 for his moralist crusade.

Related factors may help explain the distribution of royalism. The higher incidence of resident gentry in the lowland arable belt of southern and central England, and the more frequent coincidence of manorial and parochial boundaries, probably had some bearing on allegiances, whether royalist in Wiltshire and Berkshire or parliamentarian in Lord Saye's Oxfordshire neighbourhood. Elsewhere, as in parts of the north and of Wales, where social polarization was less advanced, and where neighbourly ties still bound middling sort and poor, the need for disciplinarian puritanism might be less felt. Puritanism was anyway less likely in outlying regions, where the poverty of most parishes offered few attractions to able graduate clergy – all the more so in Wales, that most 'dark corner of the land', with its language barrier. Godly zeal therefore offered less challenge to older, hierarchical imperatives, of honour for the gentry and of deference for their inferiors.

Whatever the state of the countryside, contemporaries agreed that towns were the heartland of parliamentarianism. Support for that assumption can be found in, for example, the port towns' tendency to follow the lead of London, on which they so often depended. But this was no urban revolt. Even in cosmopolitan London and Norwich urban oligarchs were primarily neutralist, and eager only for peace and profits. Popular commitment to a wider cause was often – as at Newcastle or Maidstone – simply a weapon against local superiors, just as much earlier electoral activism in the towns had been. Easy assumptions also founder on the royalist leanings of market towns in arable areas of Somerset and Wiltshire, with their economic dependence on mainly royalist landowners. But anti-Marxist scholars have yet to explain the parliamentarianism found in textile areas in the west country and in Yorkshire. The relative infrequency of masterman relations in the cottage-based textile industry may have fostered independent attitudes in a work-force which, as Richard Baxter noted, could read and talk at its work. The metallurgical industries varied. Lead seems largely to have been worked, as in the parliamentarian Somerset Mendips, by small independent masters, as was iron in the equally parliamentarian west Midland woodlands; conversely, the coal mines of the north-east, an area which provided more royalists, often needed more capital and may have generated a more dependent labour force. There does seem some correlation between industrial organization and popular alignment, but far more research needs to be done.

Social determinism cannot, however, sufficiently explain allegiance. Alignment in the villages was as complex as in country mansions, and godly poor or ungodly yeomen might be found any-where; above all, areas outside the close control of the gentry were unpredictable. Inadequate religious provision could perpetuate a kind of pagan irreligion which fostered anti-puritan recruits for the king, as in parts of Richard Baxter's homeland along the Welsh borders. More alarmingly, the burgeoning industrial areas could also generate something close to class anger when the political controls fractured in the midst of a deep depression. Gentry of all persuasions were horrified at the anti-Catholic rioting and looting in 1642 in the East Anglian clothing villages of the Stour valley. The fierceness of the rebuff to the earl of Derby's attempt to raise Manchester for the king, and to the marquess of Hertford's bid for the clothing towns of Somerset, led many to ponder the prospects for social subordination in a war. Had industrialization progressed further, noblemen and gentlemen might have been still less willing to risk the social peace in a civil war.

Visible proof of the importance of the middling and meaner sort came in the dark days of 1642–3 when royalist cavalry threatened to carry the country. A novel propaganda campaign during a depression sparked a response in some very untraditional communities. Popular support in 1642 helped win for parliament the pastoral and industrial areas of Somerset, parts of the textile-working north, and the wooded north of Warwickshire; most importantly, eager recruits rallied from the City and its suburbs. The civil war was no social revolution. But it was equally clearly not merely a division within the élite. As Baxter observed, 'The war was begun in our streets before the king and parliament had any armies.'

It is easy to assume that parliament held the trump cards. Ensconced in London, it could tap an unrivalled source of loans which alone ensured its financial survival. It gained control of the fleet, which proved critical in tipping European powers into neutrality no less than in keeping coastal garrisons such as Hull and Lyme supplied, thus tying down royalist forces in long sieges. Yet in the short term at least Charles possessed enormous assets. His own person provided an invaluable device for raising funds and volunteers. And in contrast to the plethora of parliamentary committees he gave his cause an undivided source of command – though in this context his habitual indecisiveness was to prove of more significance than his enjoyment of soldiering. Furthermore, the wealth of his noble supporters at first gave him the money to pay his troops: the earl of Worcester was reported to have contributed over £300,000, a phenomenal sum, by the end of the war. And perhaps most important, he had an experi-enced officer corps, for perhaps 90 per cent of the English professionals serving abroad joined the king when domestic employment opened up for them. Charles also had easier access to vital supplies of cavalry horses through his princely relatives in the Netherlands. The consequences were clear in the succession of parliamentarian disasters in the first year of the war. Not surprisingly, the king's strategy centred on a rapid strike on London, while only slowly was parliament able to reap the benefit of its greater reserves.

Yet the nature of the two causes did give parliament a vital advantage. The king proclaimed the loyalty owed by his subjects to his person, and honour-bound gentlemen responded to that call by rallying to his standard. They thereby left their neighbourhoods open to those who wished to stay at home and organize – which the two houses, with their insistence in the militia ordinance on defence, encouraged. The earl of Derby, trying to consolidate the north-west for the king, saw many of his allies rush south to join Charles; a similar efflux allowed parliament to acquire a secure heartland in East Anglia, a vitally important source of regular revenues. Conversely what were to become the royalist counties of the west midlands were constantly disturbed – and administrative routine disrupted – by raiding from the parliamentarian garrison in Gloucester. Not for nothing were the frustrated cavaliers more likely than their opponents to rely on the sword as a fiscal arm.

The greater royalist propensity for the abuses of power was intensified by the way the two sides made decisions. The royalist council of war was generally subordinate to the wishes of the king, who increasingly tended to side with one or other of his commanders. It was therefore even more ill-suited to mediating local disputes than the already overburdened pre-war council had been. The hallmark of the evolving parliamentarian war machine, on the other hand, was a ramshackle committee system, the necessary fruit of a legislative – in which attendances in the Commons still ran at the unwieldy level of just under 200, and in the Lords at around thirty – slowly transforming itself into a full-time executive. But proliferating committees rarely permit a clear chain of command. Even the establishment in July 1642 of a supposedly dominant executive, the committee of safety, brought the houses little relief, for this was handicapped not only by its size – eighty, drawn from both houses – but also from the congenital reluctance of parliament-men to surrender ultimate authority. Consequently, the houses, the committee and the lord general all vied for control over strategy. There was, however, considerable compensation. While the clumsy parliamentarian administration obstructed speedy military action, it saved parliament from the worst excesses to which royalists fell victim. Military commanders on both sides inevitably tried to consolidate their grip on local resources; but the existence of overlapping parliamentary committees to check and balance, and the survival at Westminister of at least some MPs from most areas, both gave the aggrieved in the localities an outlet for their resentments and helped limit the reach of the sword. Charles in contrast was dangerously ready to allow his officers a free hand – a hand which they were the more ready to take, since their ethos of service above all to the king's person seems to have imposed fewer restraints on them than did the parliamentarians' greater stress on service to the country. And although the soldiers could extract money readily enough, only civilian co-operation allowed a viable political cause to survive.

The early months of the war are a story of previously civilian bodies adjusting uneasily to the fact of war. Each side believed that the other would collapse when it saw the drawn sword, and each insisted that it was fighting not to innovate but to conserve. Both therefore grasped reluctantly at those instruments which might make a war possible. King as well as parliament aimed to use local forces to consolidate the counties, while raising mobile field armies for strategic victory. The king's main field force, at first under the earl of Lindsey, was shadowed by the parliamentarian field army under its lord general, Essex; these were supplemented by regional contingents under royalist magnates like Hertford and Newcastle and parliamentarian notables like Lord Brooke and Sir William Brereton. And volunteers filled all these mobile forces; not until late 1643 did parliament dare breach legalist values by openly introducing impressment. Again, parliament echoed the king's strident respect for law by striving to support these volunteers on a voluntary basis, making 'propositions' to the country in the summer of 1642 for 'loans' on 'the public faith', rather than through fiscal innovation.

Until the end of the war parliament had as many men in local garrisons and local forces as in its field armies, and the local dimension of the war remained of critical significance, not least in providing the necessary logistical base for wider efforts. And in the localities as well as at the centre the war brought great changes. A sweeping royal remodelling of the commission of the peace in 1642 effectively deprived parliament of the services of those work-horses, the JPs. The houses were accordingly driven to turn to the county committees of deputy lieutenants appointed under the militia ordinance. If a revolutionary consequence of the war was the dramatic concentration of power, then revolution appeared first in local administration, where the houses thrust upon many county committees the duty of raising money, first upon the propositions of 1642 and then with the new fiscal ordinances of 1643. Worse, there was no appeal save to the houses themselves, since the actions of the committees were expressly put outside the jurisdiction of the courts. Only the plethora of competing authorities both in the regions and at Westminister prevented the county committees, with their expanding civil and military functions, appearing at the beginning of the war as the tyrannous monster that they were to seem at the end.

Charles too awoke to the military unserviceability of a legalist posture. His administration creaked from the start, since even more than did parliament he failed to specify the relations between military commanders and the local civilian authorities for which he had little patience. He intensified his problems when, lacking a parliament to legitimise his demands, he at first looked for a show of consent in unwieldy county assemblies; he also initially strove to maintain the appearance of civilian justice in the areas under his control. But Charles soon followed his enemies in introducing compulsory contributions and impressment. By 1643–4 he was also replacing the unhappy magnates, like Hertford in the south-west, who commanded his regional forces with hardened soldiers, often followers of his homeless nephew, Prince Rupert of the Rhine. Even more than parliament, which delayed its great reorganization until the winter of 1644–45, he thereby signalled his appreciation that war demanded the triumph of national priorities, which only forceful outsiders, untrammelled by local loyalties, could ensure.

The two camps mirrored each other politically as well as administratively. Although the divisions amongst the parliamentarians are the more notorious, Charles's followers differed just as deeply about the war and the way to end it. Indeed, the cavaliers' tendency to think that they were fighting primarily for honour and loyalty often gave their disputes a more bitter and personal edge, and helps account for destructive gestures such as the decision of the earl of Newcastle to go into exile after Marston Moor in 1644. More generally, the queen, Prince Rupert and his bitter enemy Lord Digby, and Charles himself, saw the destruction of rebellion as the only solution, and were eagerly seconded by the young men who hoped to ride to fortune on a victory. Others, regional magnates such as Hertford and politicans like Hyde, the earl of Bristol and Lord Falkland, thought a political settlement based on some middle ground the only hope of permanency, and genuinely feared a total royalist victory. They watched in dismay as the prolongation of the war, and Charles's own sympathies, gave the military men the upper hand. Their unease is perhaps clearest in the dilemma of the earl of Sunderland who, shortly before he died fighting for the king at Newbury in 1643, was contemplating exile should the king win the war.

The roots of controversy at Westminster were much as they had been in 1641 – disagreement over the extent to which terms could be forced on a king. Four major divisions can be discerned. Over a half of those remaining were quintessential back-benchers, often localist, infrequent speakers, but puritan in a non-doctrinaire sense. In addition, the 'peace party', the 'war party' and the 'middle group' were composed of perhaps thirty members each in the Commons, loose clusters of friends and allies associated for limited political ends. The strength of the peace party lay in the many lords and gentlemen who distrusted Charles and yet bewailed the need to fight him, fearing – in the words of the influential Denzil Holles – lest 'servants should ride on horses' when they saw what rebellion could achieve. Their defensive war aims centred on the hope that a demonstration of force, or a stalemate, would persuade Charles to moderate.

The war party, whose most vociferous members included Henry Marten, the younger Sir Henry Vane and Sir Arthur Haselrig, almost mirrored the views of royalist extremists like Lord Digby. It saw security only in the destruction of Charles's power to do ill. Indeed, distrust for Charles so worked on the republican values imbibed in a predominantly classical education that Marten and a handful of others soon showed an ominous unconcern for the preservation of monarchy. Others, like Vane, sought a radical godliness in England. Nevertheless, at least until 1645 the occasion of division was not religion or the constitution but the question of how much Charles could be trusted, and accordingly whether negotiations or military measures were most appropriate.

Straddling that question stood the middle group. Unlike the war party this included several important peers, notably Warwick and Saye; but its main pillar was John Pym, 'the director of the whole machine', as one perceptive observer called him. Backed by the politic John Hampden, by Oliver St John and by Oliver Cromwell too, Pym pursued a negotiated settlement, but insisted as he had all along on security, on control over Charles's counsellors and the militia. Accordingly, in the seasonal flux which brought politicking in the winter and military preparations in the spring and summer, the middle group worked with the peace party to keep negotiations open and yet joined Haselrig and Vane in strengthening parliament's war effort. The measure of Pym's success lies as much in the fact that the two wings of the uneasy parliamentarian alliance did not fly apart as in the passage of his vital fiscal measures through the houses.

The unhappiness of so many of the parliamentarians almost brought disaster in the early months. In the first major engagement of the war, at Edgehill in Warwickshire on 23 October 1642, the earl of Essex's army managed only a very shaky draw with the king's forces.

Plunged into gloom, the earls of Northumberland and Holland led a successful peace party push for negotiations; unfortunately they pulled in their wake Essex, who had managed to race the royal army back to London. Prince Rupert shared no such scruples, and on 12 November he attacked Brentford on the outskirts of London. Confronted by the prospect of a sack, the City militia rallied with Essex's forces to suburban Turnham Green and there outnumbered and outfaced the royalists, thus foiling Charles's dash for London and with it his hopes of an immediate end to the war. Characteristically, Pym ran with both war and peace party during the crisis, and managed to salvage something more than the simple stalemate at Turnham Green. While supporting those who pushed for peace talks, he had also harkened to another response to the shambles at Edgehill, one typified by John Goodwin, whose *Anti-Cavalierisme* found an apocalyptic meaning in the bloodshed. Exploiting the heightening zeal of the London godly, and the exposure of Charles's cynicism about negotiations, Pym managed to persuade the two houses to embrace at last the principle of fiscal coercion in the form of compulsory weekly assessments on London. Later steps towards a viable war effort were to prove similarly anxious.

Cold feet were not the only impediment, for equally damaging was the prevailing localism. Each county looked for help from elsewhere and little thought to yield any return, since each threat to a neighbour too often seemed to demand that local defences be strengthened. Thus, when parliament finally passed national fiscal measures in the spring of 1643 most county committees determinedly and improperly held on to the money they collected: it has been estimated that only 2 per cent of the money collected before March 1645 in Cheshire – admittedly a distant and contested region – ever left the county. But if passionate attachment to old ways led men to shy away from the measures necessary to win a war, they could after Edgehill and Brentford at least see the need for defence. Both royalist and parliamentarian gentry soon recognized that the administrative frontiers of the counties were strategic nonsenses, and in late 1642 leaders of many neighbouring counties 'associated' for common defence. Such moves gained ready approval at both Oxford and Westminster respectively, though in themselves the associations could promise no great military contribution. Anticipating only a single campaign, both Charles and parliament allowed anomalies to multiply. While the parliamentarian Eastern Association, centred on East Anglia, was geographically rational, the East Midlands Association stretched from Derbyshire to Buckinghamshire; by mid-1643 Shropshire was listed in five parliamentarian associations, giving an open invitation to evasion and disputes. In their confusion, neither parliament nor king gave their associations much financial or organizational substance; nor did they specify the relations between the new associations, the colonels of the earlier regional volunteer forces, and the respective generals. Long feuds reverberated in the localities and at Westminster between association commanders, such as the earls of Denbigh and Manchester (formerly Viscount Mandeville), and regional colonels, such as Sir William Brereton and Lord Willoughby, who vied with them for rank and resources. Such feuds were parallelled at the royal court at Oxford where Charles failed utterly to reconcile interminable and vicious quarrels, either between his advisers – particularly Digby and Rupert – or amongst his field officers, such as that in 1643 between Rupert and Lord Wilmot.

The ramshackle associations did little to alter the strategic balance. 1643 therefore opened with the royalists maintaining the initiative which their superior liquid assets and professional experience had given them in 1642. Although parliament over the winter consolidated its hold on most of East Anglia, the south-east and Somerset, elsewhere gloom prevailed. The royalists advanced in the south-west, the north, the west midlands, and raided the surrounding counties from Oxford. Royalist risings were every day expected in the surlily neutralist counties of Norfolk and Kent, while Londoners resented their own disproportionate burdens. The parliamentary response to imminent disaster in the spring was as it had been in November: some urged sterner measures, but others pressed for peace.

The spring of 1643, so agonizing for those at Westminster and their supporters, was a watershed for the country. Despite the fulminations of king and parliament, neutralism had until now been a perfectly logical response to the war. Did not both sides protest their devotion to the same ideals in church and state? But the failure of new negotiations at Oxford that spring, in face of the understandable refusal of the victorious Charles to make further concessions, showed that whatever their rhetoric the two sides were far apart. There was now no escaping the conclusion that civil war had to be fought out. The last flickers of neutrality pacts in Cheshire and elsewhere therefore died out, while polarization proceeded apace at Westminster. There the discomfiture of the peace party at the Oxford failure was intensified by Pym's discovery of contacts between unhappy moderates in both camps. Weaving fact with fiction, Pym in May used 'Waller's Plot' to tar the advocates of peace with worse than defeatism.

On the growing awareness of the reality of the royalist threat Pym erected the measures needed to continue the fighting. Inded, his genius was never clearer than in the way he repeatedly exploited crises – in the autumn of 1642, in the spring of 1643, and then again in the summer of that year – to refurbish the tottering parliamentary machine. While allowing peace talks to go forward at Oxford, in the spring of 1643 he worked with the anxious Lord General Essex to avert another such fiasco as that at Brentford by securing the passage of ordinances which laid the basis for the enduring parliamentary fiscal system. These at last shifted the burden from parliament's friends, and provided for the sequestration, or confiscation for the duration, of the property of 'delinquents'. Additionally, in a signal instance of the way war overcame constitutionalism, the ordinance for 'the fifth and twentieth part' imposed a massive forced loan on those who had not lent voluntarily on the contributions. Most important of all, compulsory assessments were extended from London to all the parliamentarian territory. And instead of relying on out-dated valuations as did the old subsidy, the new tax – ironically modelled on ship money – required a specified sum from each county. To their misfortune, the royalists never systematized a tax as effectively as did the committees at Westminster.

But the fiscal measures of the spring could bear little immediate fruit, and Essex's field army was therefore paralysed for lack of supplies. It managed to take Reading on the road to Oxford in April, but then bogged down in the rain and mud of the Thames valley. By mid-summer the lord general, unable to risk another engagement, had seen his 13,000 men dwindle, through typhus and desertion, to a mutinous 5,500. Harried by royalist raids, perhaps his greatest loss was the death in June of Colonel John Hampden, his increasingly effective aide and an invaluable link to the Commons' leaders. There were few consolations elsewhere. Although the cavalry of the Eastern Association, under the inexperienced Oliver Cromwell, proved surprisingly successful in sweeping its region – not least because even localist county committees saw the danger from the royalist earl of Newcastle – even this force was reluctant to act beyond the Association's frontier. Meanwhile the war in the midlands turned into a formless struggle for the countless minor garrisons which sought to secure an area and its resources. And despite early successes in Yorkshire by Lord Fairfax and his son Sir Thomas, most of the northeast had by June 1643 fallen to the earl of Newcastle. In the west the news was grimmer still. Sir William Waller had been the most successful of parliament's early commanders, and was lionized in the City for his gains in the south and south-west, while Essex was lampooned. But in this as in any war success depended on logistics as well as on skill, and Waller could not consolidate his hold. Crushing royalist victories in July at Lansdown in Somerset and Roundway Down in Wiltshire gave virtually all the south-west to the king. But the greatest blow came later that month when Prince Rupert stormed Bristol. The second port of the kingdom, Bristol gave Charles access to supplies from the continent and from Ireland, and to customs revenue.

The gloomy summer shattered parliament's morale. The western disasters coincided with anti-war revolt in Kent and rumblings in Norfolk, and most ominously of all, with a growing peace movement in London. Seeking scapegoats, the war party blamed Essex's inactivity, and almost drove him to the point of resignation. But Pym, desperately needing the lord general, for the social respectability he brought, for his standing with the Lords, and not least for his huge popularity with the soldiers, as so often made huge gains from apparently imminent defeat. Placating militants as well as the frightened City oligarchy by strengthening Waller's position, at the same time he conciliated Essex by gaining for him a vitally needed impressment ordinance to swell his forces. All this had to be paid for, and that gloomy July Pym gained his greatest and most lasting triumph over the peace party and its supporters. The 1628 debates had revealed the virulence of constitutionalist hostility to an excise, or sales tax, which was seen as a vehicle for arbitrary rule; but now the houses agreed to an excise on such widely consumed items as beer and tobacco.

The lurching sequence of military crisis and belated administrative reform was thus played out again, but it was no way to fight a war. That the parliamentary coalition managed to survive owed less to the increasing discipline of Cromwell's famous 'Ironside' cavalry in the Eastern Association than to the grim determination of garrisons under siege.

Unlike his enemies, Charles had something which could be called a strategy. Although his habitual diffidence in face of his generals left too much of it a dream sometimes committed to paper, his thinking in 1643 centred on a junction of the northern and western armies with his own at Oxford. Together they would then – in the respect for the City's militia Turnham Green had taught Charles – blockade London in hope of occasioning an uprising in the already hard-pressed capital. The plan was plausible enough, for the citizens' distress would certainly have swelled to a crescendo had Newcastle driven south to link up with rebellious anti-parliamentarians in Norfolk, or had Charles struck at the Eastern Association. But the enduring strategic reality of this war was the consolidation of territory, and sieges could therefore be as crucial as rapid movements and set-piece battles. That two of the three royalist forces turned aside to try to protect their rear – Newcastle to confront the Fairfaxes' refuge at Hull, Charles to Gloucester – probably testifies less to their timidity than to their concern for their supply lines in what must be a long campaign. The reprieve allowed both Manchester in the Eastern

Association and Essex to build up their forces, and indeed enabled Essex to win an unusual moment of glory. Reinforced by the London trained bands, who were sufficiently stirred by the urgency of the situation to leave their homes, the lord general briskly relieved Gloucester at the end of the August. He then caught the king at Newbury in Berkshire on 20 September. It was Edgehill all over again, with Charles once more racing for London; this time Essex out-generalled him.

The autumn of 1643 was a major turning-point. Gloucester was preserved, impeding Charles's access to his recruiting-grounds in south Wales, and London was safe. The war must now be prolonged, straining further the pockets of the king's supporters, while the parliamentarians were able to exploit the undisturbed south-east and East Anglia. But parliament's greatest gain that summer had been political, not military. Its fruit was the 20,000-strong army of the Covenanters which in January 1644 re-entered the northern counties it had left two years earlier. By relieving the pressure on the parliamentarian heartlands the Scots dramatically altered the strategic balance.

Many Covenanters had wished to enter the war from the beginning. They had sought both to extend their cherished presbyterianism southwards and to prevent Charles revenging himself on those who had first risen against him. But though they had then been dissuaded by the English parliament's belief in the rosier days of 1642 that it could stand alone, by mid-1643 the Scots would probably have intervened even had Westminster not invited them. Their discovery in June 1643 that Charles still dreamed, as he had in 1639, of using Irish Catholics against the west coast of Scotland effectively sealed the Anglo-Scottish alliance, for the mainly Lowland Covenanters dreaded – and with good reason, as events were to show – lest the Catholic clans of the Highlands unite with their Irish kin. The further spur of Newcastle's 'popish' army across the border was scarcely needed.

The chief obstacle to an Anglo-Scottish alliance was religious. The Covenanters' cause was almost wholly ecclesiastical, whereas the English parliamentarian leaders had long played down the religious issue in fear of its destructive potential, and accordingly sought a purely civil league. Once more Pym gave in order to gain. On 12 June 1643 the houses established the Westminster assembly of divines, which first met the following month – 120 carefully picked, wholly Calvinist English ministers, with thirty lay assessors from both houses and eight Scottish commissioners, were to advise parliament on reform of the church. Pym thereby hoped to satisfy Covenanter zeal and at the same time to give some substance to parliament's tired protestations of its godly goals, while yet containing any threat to the domestic religious peace. But despite his mediatory skills, the treaty with the Scots met fierce opposition at Westminister. Peace party fears of any broadening of the war merged with long-standing anti-Scottish sentiment and with widespread contempt for Covenanter claims that presbyterianism was sanctioned *iure divino*, by divine right. Even the conservative Sir Simonds D'Ewes, whose hostility to episcopacy as well as to disorder might have made him a natural supporter of the Scottish form, was soon to denounce the 'tyrannical power' implicit in it. Although the summer's military disasters made the need for allies undeniable, it took the deletion of any *iure divino* reference to ease the Solemn League and Covenant through the two houses in early September. Even the diluted document seemed bad enough to English conservatives. By publicly committing parliament to the extirpation of episcopacy and implying a presbyterian alternative it appeared to change the character of a war which had previously been cast as defensive. A war avowedly for religion was a frightening prospect; and the presence of the Scots must disrupt any future peace talks, since their sole demand, presbyterianism, was not one that Charles thought negotiable. Not surprisingly, the Scottish alliance brought renewed calls for a peace which would pre-empt the calamities that must ensue.

Pym never did more to earn his reputation than in the way he emerged from the appalling summer of 1643 strengthened not just militarily but also politically. Capitalizing on the widespread recognition that capitulation could be the only outcome of negotiations at such a troubled time, he deftly blocked the new peace initiative. In their despair, and probably too in fear of a traitor's death should the royalists win their expected victory, several peace party leaders promptly abandoned the struggle. The earls of Holland, Bedford and Clare left for Oxford, while in the Commons Denzil Holles and several others lapsed into demoralized inactivity. But Pym did not seek to dismember the parliamentarian coalition, and that August he reassured conservatives at Westminister by obtaining the expulsion and imprisonment of Henry Marten for his outspoken republicanism. He thus gained on every hand. The war party lost its most troublesome figure, the peace party was again tainted with treachery, and permanently weakened in the Lords where its main strength had lain.

The victory was short-lived, for Pym, worn out, died on 8 December after a long illness. His stately funeral testified to the magnitude of parliament's loss. More than anyone, Pym had ensured parliament's survival. Although his new Scots allies were eventually to prove a two-edged sword, he had dissuaded the houses from tearing themselves apart, and he had placated Essex. More important, he had established the financial machinery by which parliament was able to wear down the royalists in a war of attrition. The royalists too had had their losses that year: in particular, the death of Falkland made moderation still more of a lost cause at Oxford, since Charles revealingly replaced him as secretary of state with the extremist Digby. But the losses to parliament were far more serious. Pym, Hampden and Lord Brooke, another casualty, had all been able to work with both radicals and conservatives. That quality was to be sorely needed as the strains of a spreading war polarized opinion still further.

As he had done so often before, Charles cemented Pym's political achievements. To widespread royalist despair, the king frowned on the defecting peers, who were in his eyes traitors, and thereby discouraged others from following. Still more damagingly, in September he retaliated against parliament's Scottish alliance by arranging the 'Cessation', a ceasefire with the Irish rebels. He claimed to seek the services only of the English troops tied down there, but rumour soon obliterated the distinction. There was a world of difference between dealings with presbyterian Scots and with Catholic Irish, and Charles's undoubted military gain from the reinforcements – especially in securing the Welsh borders – was at least partly offset by the political loss. For some unhappy royalists, like Sir Edward Dering, the Irish cessation merely underscored the prominence of Catholics at Oxford and in the king's armies, and drove them to defect. More than ever now this was becoming a religious war, and brutality and intransigence increased.

The cessation was symptomatic of Charles's attitude at this stage in the war. As rapid victory eluded him he turned to hard-line solutions, and seems to have intended to couple the importation of fresh troops from Ireland with an attempt to dissolve parliament unilaterally. Appalled at such a breach of the non-dissolution act of 1641, Hyde persuaded the king instead to use his undoubted prerogative of summoning parliament to meet at Oxford, in hope of the breakthrough which had eluded the soldiers. In the anger provoked by parliament's insatiable demands and by the Solemn League and Covenant the king might attract not only unhappy neutrals but even some peace party waverers.

Once again Hyde was too late. The cessation, and the treatment of the defecting peace lords, demonstrated that Charles pursued victory, not peace. Although in January 1644 the Oxford 'parliament' mustered perhaps three times as many peers as did Westminster and just over half as many of the MPs elected in 1640, the political reality was less impressive, since its preponderance of peers stemmed largely from Charles's efforts since 1642 to raise money and reward his supporters by selling titles. It soon gained an air of vacuity, since parliamentary legalism was out of place at Oxford. Charles, who increasingly turned to the professionals whose instinct was, like his, to win the war, was now more than ever impatient with 'country' complaints. Although the Oxford 'parliament' began by trying to call to account corrupt royalist officers and officials, it was soon reduced to tamely approving Charles's demands for supply and to condemning the parliamentarians. While it did lessen the apparent arbitrariness of Charles's actions it held little attraction for those weary of Westminster. Nor did it divert the attention of moderate royalists from the military dominance and cavalier roystering, feuds and corruption rife at Oxford. By the end of 1644 one visitor could comment on the 'cyphers of the other Lords and Commons, few and poor', he found there. The key to the decline lay in the king, who refused to contemplate the negotiated peace in hopes of which many had initially assembled at Oxford.

Pym's death therefore embarrassed Westminster less than might have been expected. Instead of having to watch further desertions, his successors were able to profit from the renewed unity brought by Charles's Irish policy and devote themselves to integrating the Scots into the alliance. This they did to impressive effect.

Although the Scots commissioners in London were to lament the frustration of their religious hopes in the interminable text-mining of the assembly of divines, they found it easier to reshape the political arena. Parliament usually dealt with any novelty by appointing yet another committee with circumscribed powers. But such treatment was manifestly inadequate for the cold and hungry Scottish army. The situation provided a welcome opening for those in the war party and the middle group who had long hoped to remodel parliament's ramshackle structure of command; more immediately, they longed to displace the peace lords and the now less than militant Denzil Holles who had been appointed to the committee of safety in the very different days of 1642. It needed little genius to see in the Scots a means to a variety of ends, and the non-aligned majority in the Commons could readily accept the arguments of the men of war. Few could ignore the disorganization which had contributed to the disasters of 1643, nor the back-biting and recriminations of the various commanders during the winter's lull in campaigning. Regional factors too provided powerful incentives: even conservative MPs whose estates were threatened by royalists in the north or west might be ready to diminish the power of the equally conservative, but lacklustre, Essex in the

Thames valley. Exploiting these sentiments in the spring of 1644, the new leaders of the middle group, Saye in the Lords and St John in the Commons, in alliance with the more militant Vane, deftly swept aside the old committee of safety and replaced it with the committee of both kingdoms, whose appeal lay both in its joint Anglo-Scottish composition and its greater executive powers.

Reform was not to be won so easily again, for the winter of 1643–4 widened the rifts in Westminster politics. Even though Pym had been the supreme mediator, his goals had been closer to those of the war party than of the peace party; he had simply known better than, say, Haselrig, the importance of compromise. The middle group moved a little further off the fence after his death, for St John, while a skilled conciliator, was temperamentally closer to the war party; and as Charles's intransigence became clearer, so anyway did the importance of winning the war. But the Scots alliance and the committee of both kingdoms inserted a further wedge. The ever-more sensitive Essex interpreted those developments, and the strengthening of the regional forces under Manchester and Waller upon which the committee promptly embarked, as criticisms of himself. He accordingly moved closer to the more unhappy, and pacific, of his colleagues in the Lords, who were themselves further aggrieved by their sudden loss of power. Tensions between the two houses mounted.

The reorganization therefore brought little apparent gain. Instead of marching north to protect London against Prince Rupert, who was rapidly mopping up the parliamentarians in the midlands, Essex spent the spring of 1644 politicking against the committee and in support of the Lords' demands for peace talks. And while the Scots certainly helped neutralize the earl of Newcastle's army, they could not be persuaded to march southwards: instead, they settled down to an embarrasingly long ten-month siege of the town of Newcastle. Beset too by the continuing regionalism of Manchester's Eastern Association and Waller's South-Eastern Association forces, the parliamentarian armies failed to generate an effective offensive, and a half-hearted advance on Oxford by Essex and Waller in late May 1644 petered out in squabbling. Charles's advisers now saw a chance of beating his enemies piecemeal as Essex turned west. Catching up with Waller, the king's forces bested him in a hard-fought encounter at Cropredy Bridge in Oxfordshire on 29 June, and then slowly moved off in pursuit of the lord general. Even after six months of Scottish aid the fortunes of war still ran against parliament.

But there were grounds for hope. When the London militia contingent seconded to him deserted after Cropredy Bridge Waller claimed in frustration that 'an army compounded of these men will never go through with their service.' All field commanders who had to do with local forces would have sympathized. But although localism was certainly a perennial impediment it was by no means the barrier to military proficiency which some historians have claimed. The London militia was parliament's most effective infantry in these years, proving decisive at Newbury in 1643; on the other side too, the morale and discipline of Sir Ralph Hopton's Cornishmen had proved formidable at Lansdown. And when so much of the war was siege-work, local forces were not inappropriate. Waller's gloom was in fact ill-founded, for by now both officers and men had acquired experience to match that of the royalists; furthermore, Pym's reforms had recently secured slightly more regular pay for parliament's 'marching armies' at least – garrisons tended to live off their neighbourhoods. The difference in the armies lay in the cavalry, at Cropredy Bridge and elsewhere often the critical arm in engagements. The royalists had at the beginning had a marked advantage in the equestrian upbringing and military experience abroad of many of those who flocked to the king's standard. But training and discipline, where there were good officers, had by 1644 gone some way to make up parliament's deficiencies, particularly since the royalist cavalry also had its handicaps. Often reared on the hunting-field, and too often interested in plunder, Prince Rupert's horsemen were unstoppable in more ways than one. Even when the parliamentarian horse far outnumbered the royalists, as at Naseby in 1645, they found it difficult to stand up to Rupert; but despite his charisma, Rupert found it as difficult to rally his men after their first charge. Cromwell, an equally inspired leader of men, taught the cavalry of the Eastern Association the value of a 'pretty round trot,' and the importance of shunning plunder until commanded. His troopers could thus reform for an often decisive second encounter.

The Eastern Association had a second solution to the problem of morale. Both Manchester and his cavalry commander Cromwell were godly men who treasured soldiers who could pray; they also agreed, at least up to the summer of 1644, in wanting to win the war. Accordingly, if not enough gentlemen were willing to lead, they would promote others: 'better plain men than none', as Cromwell put it. The contrast with other armies, whether parliamentarian or royalist, was of course not absolute, for efficiency was valued everywhere. But more than most generals, Cromwell could contemplate with equanimity the political consequences of promoting men from the ranks. If such men were religious radicals, then Cromwell would defend the 'plain russet-coated captain that knows what he fights for and loves what he knows'. Not surprisingly Holles and the alarmed Lords sought throughout the spring of 1644 to subject Manchester's command to that of Essex. It was, however, money as well as zeal that ensured that by late 1643 Cromwell's 'Ironside' cavalry could at last withstand the royalists. Throughout the first half of 1643 the officers of the Eastern Association army had protested vainly to a divided parliament that they could only fight if the various county committees were forced to look beyond their local priorities and to support the association. It took the ominous advance of Newcastle's army into Lincolnshire in 1643 to secure frantic ordinances in July and August of that year giving the association's commander, Manchester, and his local allies extensive powers. The rapid emergence over the next six months of the army of the Eastern Association points to the limits of localism. Only division and uncertainty at the centre allowed localism to flourish; and in the case of the Eastern Association, the houses eventually willed that one of their armies should be effective.

Charles had grounds for concern by the summer of 1644. The worth of the parliamentarian foot had been shown at Newbury and of its horse on the borders of the Eastern Association and in some of Waller's engagements in the south. Royalist hopes of profit from Ireland were dashed when the Yorkshire forces of Sir Thomas Fairfax destroyed the biggest 'Irish' contingent in January 1644 at Nantwich in Cheshire. Worse, at the end of April a Scottish detachment joined the Fairfaxes in bottling up Newcastle in the city of York. Faced with the imminent loss of his northern army and capital, Charles dispatched a relieving force north under Prince Rupert. The prince rapidly did all that was expected of him by drawing off the besiegers in a brilliant manoeuvre and relieving York; but he was not one to avoid a fight, even though the parliamentarian forces, now joined by Manchester and Cromwell, numbered 28,000 while even with the addition of Newcastle's tired and resentful troops Rupert had only about 18,000. On 3 July at Marston Moor the royalist army was destroyed in the biggest battle of the war. At first it looked as though it would go the other way until the Ironsides reformed after their first charge and broke in on the royalist centre, annihilating Newcastle's superb 'Whitecoat' infantry. York surrendered a fortnight later and the earl left in despair for the continent.

Marston Moor was a turning-point, if perhaps less militarily than politically. Although Charles had lost the north, his forces were to win further victories. But to the puritan, God spoke through dispensations in this world, and while the Scots tried to claim the victory for the kirk, Cromwell was equally emphatic. To his fervent mind, 'it had all the evidences of an absolute victory obtained by the Lord's blessing upon the godly party principally.' Religious animosities were to become increasingly important, and were to blunt the military edge gained at Marston Moor.

The fall of the old order in 1641 had ushered in what was for some a new age. The dereliction of the church courts and of most censorship too had put an end to the clerical monopoly on the exposition of the gospel, and suddenly the laity gained an unprecedented freedom to speak out. Calvinist orthodoxy began to crumble as characteristically lay beliefs gained an airing, especially in London. The primacy of the scriptures, with all their learned apparatus of interpretation, was challenged as unlettered layfolk claimed personal illumination – all the more urgently in the case of the many who believed that the age of the spirit had dawned. Necessarily following on that challenge came a questioning of the claims of the clerical estate, and indeed of the very principle of an established church with its support in compulsory tithes. Equally unnerving were the doubts increasingly heard about the fundamental tenets of Calvinism, and of Christianity too. Challenges to the doctrine of predestination were perhaps not surprising in view of the moralist strain in popular religion; but these were joined by an alarming scepticism about the more arcane points of Christian belief, particularly the nature of the Trinity and the existence of hell. Alarmed conservatives had more practical grounds for concern too. As radicals 'gathered' churches regardless of parish boundaries they undermined not only ecclesiastical order but also civil administration, most obviously in the form of parochial poor relief.

The most dangerous sect seemed to be the Baptists. Divided into two quite distinct strains, the particular, or Calvinist, and the general, or non-Calvinist, the Baptists carried the typical radical revulsion at the idea of a national church to the extreme of confining membership of their church to believers whose exclusiveness was sealed by adult baptism. In their frontal challenge to the principle of unity, and in their insistence on a personal experience of religion – an experience which was to spawn all manner of enthusiasms during the Interregnum – the Baptists seemed the very fount of excess. But though Baptists were in the later 1640s very active in the struggle for freedom for godly consciences, and although Baptist officers figured prominently in the radicalization of the New Model Army, as a group the Baptists were fairly quiescent: they had an embarrassing inheritance to live down, in the German Anabaptist outrages of the 1530s. Nor were they very numerous, for by 1660 there were only about 250 Baptist churches in the country, with membership largely drawn from the middling ranks of society.

More significant were the Independents, so-called from their demand for congregational independence of any superior discipline. Like the Baptists, they reacted against the legalist emphasis so characteristic of puritanism after Perkins and demanded instead evidence of conversion, of the work of grace within the soul. And like many – although not all – Baptists, many Independents shared with other radical puritans the sense born in 1641 that the Holy Spirit was at work in the world. Far more than earlier protestant dissenters, therefore, both groups maintained that truth was to be found in the spirit as much as in institutions and formal creeds – though more extreme radicals were soon to drive them to a more conservative stance. But in the early 1640s the insistence of Independent ministers such as Philip Nye and Thomas Goodwin that God might yet grant further illumination, and that liberty for tender – protestant – consciences was essential, appealed to undogmatic temperaments.

The importance of the Independents, and their insidiousness in the eyes of contemporaries, lay in their church order. Independents were at least semi-separatists, restricting full membership of the church and access to the sacraments to voluntary rather than parochial associations, to those 'visible saints', in whom grace was apparent, who covenanted together to walk in the ways of the Lord and found a church. But that outline of a congregationalist gathered church was blurred by their continuing commitment to the old puritan ideal of godly rule, of national regeneration, and therefore of a national church as a discipline for the ungodly. Independent clergy were accordingly ready to act within that church if called, and thus catered to the anxiety for a national framework of gentlemen like Oliver Cromwell, Nathaniel Fiennes or his father Lord Saye, while providing the satisfaction of spiritual exclusiveness. To the disgust of those who sought to pin them down, Independent pastors ranged from the London leather-seller Praise-God Barebone to the immensely learned Nye, an ordained minister of the church of England. As pressure mounted, the handful of Independents in the Westminister assembly were finally driven in February 1644 to break the London clergy's self-imposed ban on public controversy by publishing the *Apologeticall Narration,* a somewhat evasive defence of their practices. The offence this gave to conservative neighbours was compounded by developments in the important City parish of St Stephen's, Coleman St., where John Goodwin had duly succeeded as minister, only to swing to Independency. By early 1644 he had gathered a church in St Stephen's from all over London and was soon refusing the sacraments to any but these select 'saints', thus effectively 'unchurching' the bulk of the parishioners from their own parish church. The danger of Independency seemed clear to those who had eyes to see it.

The extent of the fragmentation can be exaggerated. Such was parliament's anxiety to leave the issue open for negotiation with the king that the national church remained in law, if not in practice, episcopal until October 1646. More important, the face of worship often changed little. Most puritans remained loyal to the idea of a national church, and only a very small minority deserted their parish churches in the 1640s in favour of separatist gatherings. Piecemeal simplification in the liturgy, and sometimes the expulsion of unpopular ministers, probably sufficed to satisfy most of the godly. There seems to have been only scattered enthusiasm, at least in the countryside, for the anti-ritualist directory of worship parliament finally published in January 1645, and most communities probably made do with modifications of the Anglican prayer book, which the directory officially replaced. Similarly, parish records suggest that 'Anglicanism' survived widely as parishioners and minister clung to the celebration of Christmas and Easter despite parliament's 1647 prohibition on 'superstitious' observances. But the decline of discipline and the turmoil of war did bring some disintegration. Essex's MPs were exercised by the inability of even godly ministers in that county in 1643 to collect tithes. Purges by both sides, and the flight of many ministers from violence, emptied pulpits and in the ensuing vacuum sectarianism and crude irreligion often seemed indistinguishable. Alehouse cynics who mocked those fighting a holy war were matched by well-publicized sectarian outrages – iconoclastic saints urinating in Canterbury Cathedral, an Eastern Association troop baptizing a horse in urine, the usual horrified rumours of sexual immorality in secret gathered church meetings. The fears of puritan gentry and clergy poured out in the torrent of outrage that greeted Milton's *Doctrine and Discipline of Divorce* of August 1643. Learnedly championing in the name of Christian libery the right of divorce – for men – where affection was lacking, Milton denounced the 'tyranny' of the arranged marriage, and thus seemed to challenge the foundation of society, paternal authority. Sheer 'blasphemy' was bringing dissolution in its wake.

Although parliament periodically fulminated against excesses, the distractions of war made it no more anxious to tackle the problem of religious order than it had been in 1641. Save for its reluctant establishment of the Westminister assembly of divines, parliament's actions in the ecclesiastical field were effectively limited to ordinances for the destruction of images and sporadic purges of clergy variously deemed 'scandalous'. It was, however, equally reluctant to let others take the lead, and it carefully confined the Westminister assembly to an advisory role: having defeated Laud it had no intention of allowing another set of assertive clerics to claim independence. If power were left in the hands of the two houses reform would take time. Yet to many of the godly, the disasters of 1643 were proof that God was judging a nation which had sinned by not pursuing reformation. They must therefore hasten the work of the Lord.

The way of the Lord was not equally clear to all. Influenced perhaps by the Scottish example, Edmund Calamy and several other

London ministers had even in 1641 seen in the strict discipline of the presbyterian order the only non-episcopal means to preserve a godly nation in face of the signs of separatism in London and amongst the exiles in the Netherlands and New England. By late 1643 the differences amongst the London clergy were emerging into the open. The entry of the Scots into the war certainly heartened the presbyterians; but independently of Scottish pressure, a majority of the sixty or so regular attenders of the Westminster assembly had grown sufficiently fearful to support presbyterianism as the sects in London dispensed with hierarchical structures and any but voluntary discipline.

Of all the disciplinarians frustrated with the endless arguments of the Westminster assembly, the most impatient were the Scots. The strife-torn history of the Scottish reformation had left them more committed than the English to ecclesiastical independence from the state. The vision of a church *iure divino,* and in particular of a hierarchical presbyterian church with the power to discipline sinners, seemed self-evident to the Scottish commissioners in London. They were left baffled and angry as the assembly debated while sectarianism grew and seemed – to their inflamed eyes – likely to contaminate Scotland if not speedily crushed. Still more puzzling to them was the inability of a divided parliament to do their work for them. It took the Covenanters a year to appreciate that though their 'dear friends' Vane and St John had worked eagerly for their entry into the war, a majority of their war party allies – the 'cloudy' Vane in particular – had more tolerationist views than Scottish stomachs could bear. But even by the spring of 1644 the Scottish commissioners were coming to the conclusion that only the swords of their soldiers would put an end to the disregard for their, and God's, wishes. The outcome of battle came to seem almost as important in the struggle within the parliamentarian coalition as in the war against the king.

That any victories should be Scottish was all the more important given the character of the allied forces. The availability of rich livings in vacant parishes left the parliamentary armies chronically short of chaplains, and as Baxter later perceptively noted, opened the soldiers to whomever would exercise his talents among them – be he a returned New England clergyman like Hugh Peter, whose radical zeal could triumph over the discomforts of camp life, or a layman. For all their professional differences, both Essex and Waller did try to restrain officers and soldiers who thought they could preach. But the attempt of Manchester and Cromwell to build a godly army in the Eastern Association had ensured that by early 1644 that force, and particularly Cromwell's cavalry, had begun to acquire a reputation for sectarianism and Independency. Any victory it won might embarrass its allies.

Although conservatives were hamstrung by parliament's divisions, in the localities, away from the London spotlight, it was easier to respond. Through the winter of 1643–4 Colonel Edward King, Manchester's subordinate in Lincolnshire, persecuted and imprisoned Baptists and Independents; at a higher level, Manchester's Scottish major-general, Crawford, commanding the infantry, strove to purge Independent officers, to the fury of Cromwell, who like Manchester had hoped to achieve a union of the godly. It is in this context, and that of the unyielding presbyterianism of the Scots he encountered in the Marston Moor campaign, that Cromwell's triumph at the victory there of the 'godly party' assumes its significance. After Marston Moor Cromwell replied in kind to Crawford, promoting Independents and purging the presbyterian officers who threatened those who believed as he did.

The Association's army, parliament's most successful force, was reduced to paralysis in August and September. Manchester failed to resolve the recriminations of his subordinates, while the committee of both kingdoms was scarcely more successful. But Manchester's efforts at mediation did not last long, for the Marston Moor campaign had been a watershed for him as well as Cromwell. For all the godly zeal which had made that 'sweet, meek man' the darling of the war party, Manchester remained a propertied nobleman who thought twice when insubordination threatened. The conflicts within his own command, and the hostility between Cromwell and the Scots, now led him to conclude that victory might be followed by something even worse than the tyranny of king and bishops, and that a negotiated peace was the only hope. Manchester's swing to the peace party had immediate military consequences – he even threatened to execute Lieutenant-Colonel John Lilburne for seizing a royalist garrison on his own initiative. There was little doubting his 'continued averseness to all action', of which Cromwell came to complain bitterly, as the committee of both kingdoms deluged Manchester with unheeded orders to march westwards to rescue the lord general.

The late summer of 1644 was disastrous for the parliamentarian high command. Essex was the first to fall. He had ignored the orders of the committee of both kingdoms and set off in quest of the glamour which had so long eluded him in a campaign into the south-west, in hope of relieving besieged Lyme in Dorset, a major obstacle in the path of the triumphant western royalists. Only success could have justified his disregard for the committee, and this signally eluded him. Although he relieved Lyme, he then allowed himself to be bottled up by a surprisingly decisive Charles in the Cornish peninsula, and while his cavalry broke through the royalist encirclement, he himself only managed to escape in a small boat. The surrender of his infantry and artillery at Lostwithiel on 2 September offset the moral, if not the strategic, effects of Marston Moor. But the war party was unable to revel for long in Essex's discomfiture. None of the available parliamentarian forces could on its own block the return eastwards of the victorious royal army, and accordingly the slow-moving Manchester – handicapped, it should be admitted, by the perennial reluctance of the eastern counties to send supplies outside the Association – was detailed to command a joint force. Effective co-operation was unlikely amidst such friction, and when the two armies finally met, on 27 October in the second battle of Newbury, the parliamentarians could only gain an inglorious draw. Further humiliation followed when on 9 November Charles returned unchallenged to retrieve the artillery he had left in the neighbouring Donnington Castle, although in full view of the combined parliamentarian army. No parliamentarian general in the southern theatre survived the autumn of 1644 unscathed. Essex was blackened by Lostwithiel, and Manchester and Waller, and Cromwell too, by Newbury. The Scots alone and at last had achieved something when Newcastle fell on 22 October; but their success came too late to save them from the contempt of the war party.

Waller and Cromwell moved quickly to salvage their reputations by blaming Manchester for Newbury, but in late November the earl counter-attacked. Painting an alarmingly detailed picture of Cromwell as a dangerous subversive – purging presbyterians, contemptuous of the nobility and of the Scots – he attributed his subordinate's backwardness at Newbury to his reluctance to see any but an Independent army win a victory, in hopes of extracting toleration from parliament. None of the accusations was implausible, and Cromwell's conduct in the western campaign remains baffling – the only charitable explanation is that his cavalry had been, as he claimed, exhausted. Cromwell countered by stressing the hesitancy and doubts reflected in Manchester's gloomy argument against action at Donnington: 'If we fight a hundred times and beat him ninety-nine times, he will be king still . . . But if he beat us but once, or the last time, we shall be hanged.' But although many subordinates supported Cromwell's complaints, it was he whose career was most at risk. The Lords jumped at the chance to destroy the most radical of the generals, and pressed the Commons for a hearing. Others too joined the fray, and in early December the Scots commissioners made overtures to the peace party.for concerted moves against Cromwell as an 'incendiary'. It was the first sign of the momentous political shift of 1645, when the disillusioned Scots turned against their old war party allies; and it dangerously strengthened Essex, allowing him to hope that he might emerge unscathed from the graveyard of reputations.

Political crisis rather than innate radicalism thus occasioned the self-denying ordinance, perhaps the Long Parliament's most famous break with the past. Sensing political, and consequently military, disaster, Cromwell on 9 December dramatically changed tack, and acknowledged that he like others had erred. In a startling extension of this new disinterestedness, he then called on all commanders to sacrifice private concerns to the public good, lest the already war-weary people 'enforce you to a dishonourable peace'. Hoping to extricate something from the morass by taking others down with him, Cromwell picked up widespread support. The extent of that support, in parliament and press, surprised many. What became the self-denying ordinance looked like a war-party ploy, prepared by Cromwell, moved by the intransigent Zouch Tate, warmly seconded by Vane: why should others fall for it, when Manchester might yet succeed in eliminating Cromwell?

Self-denial had the merit of appealing to all. Unpartisan MPs were as capable as the war party of recognizing that Charles intended to fight to a finish, and that it would therefore be folly to leave the architects of Lostwithiel and Newbury in command. The Commons' army committee had already been considering reducing the bloated officer corps of the three southern armies, and Cromwell's suggestion of a clean sweep at the top seemed to open a path to a more rational military structure. Furthermore, if self-denial was a war-party ploy it succeeded because the war party had stolen the peace party's clothes. The political nation was unaware of the realities of life in a full-time, war-time parliament, where lawyer-MPs were unable to practise and landowners were cut off from their estates; the peace party readily encouraged the belief that but for the many members of both houses who held lucrative military or civilian posts the war would long have been over. Cromwell's plea for self-sacrifice might help appease the weary cynicism in the country. And perhaps most important, that plea, upon which Tate built his proposal that members of both houses should lay down all their offices, drew not only on the language of the peace party but also of mainstream puritanism. God's judgment on sinful self-seeking might be seen in the failures of a manifestly godly cause; Cromwell was therefore guaranteed an almost religious hearing.

The self-denying ordinance is inseparably associated with the formation of the New Model army, and in the conjunction many have since seen a radical new departure, and the seeds of victory. Yet the remodelling did not immediately invigorate the troops. It brought no change in the rates of pay, which for foot soldiers remained no better than day labourers', and certainly more irregular. Disease and desertion were therefore high, and even in early June 1645, the month of Naseby, several foot regiments in the New Model were under strength and several more mutinous. This was not the proud army of later years. Nor was it an entirely new army, for it had been formed by merging existing under-strength forces; furthermore, anomalies continued, since some regional forces, particularly those of the northern association and of Edward Massey, commanding the western association from Gloucester, continued to operate more or less independently. The New Model's mixed origin left its unity in doubt, and many royalists relished the prospect of engaging with the 'new noddle'. In hopes of limiting the upheaval, most parliamentarian politicians agreed that existing regiments must be kept together, and the formation of the New Model therefore saw less of a purge of the officers, and more pragmatic horse-trading than used to be believed. On the whole the foot regiments kept their old officers, as did the horse. And whatever new political fire the New Model possessed hardly flowed from its commanders. The new lord general, Sir Thomas Fairfax, former cavalry commander of the northern army, was no sectarian radical but a middle-of-the-road puritan and the most effective, and respectable, general available who did not sit in parliament; much the same could be said of his major-general, 'honest' Philip Skippon, who had been Essex's infantry commander.

But the New Model did break with the past. Although the large majority of its officers were indeed gentlemen, none owed his position primarily to his social status. The emphasis on proficiency certainly helped make the New Model a more effective fighting force. Furthermore, the problems of localism which had beset Waller and Manchester in the vital southern sector were mitigated by the creation of a single field army. The rapidity and scale of Fairfax's marches in 1645 testify to the benefits of freeing an army from a narrow regional base.

That the New Model did break with the past was nowhere clearer than in the response of the peers. To them the self-denying ordinance seemed the most grievous in a long line of slights. True, they still possessed their institutional role as one of the two houses, and in men like the dignified Essex, 'old subtlety' Saye, or even Northumberland, an inveterate swimmer with the tide, they included politicians of the first rank. But their self-confidence was sapped by the pressures of war. Distaste for unpleasant decisions forced on them, and for the increasingly prominent radicals who took such decisions willingly, had shrunk their numbers embarrassingly; twenty had by now become a respectable attendance in the upper house. For men who had so much to lose disengagement was a tempting course, rendered all the more attractive by the treatment they received from the Commons, who repeatedly relied on their control over money matters – inevitably of critical importance in wartime – to shoulder opposition aside. By 1644 Lord Willoughby, witness to continuing pressure by City and Commons on the upper house, 'thought it a crime to be a nobleman'. The peers' one consolation had been the military prominence of many of their number, and this self-denial would remove. If its aim was self-sacrifice, then peers would rank disproportionately among the victims. Not surprisingly, they dug in their heels.

But a significant number in the Lords, as in the Commons, recognized that the war had to be fought. Critical in breaking down conservative resistance to remodelling was the inexorable failure during these months of the latest peace negotiations, the treaty (so-called) of Uxbridge.

Each winter's lull in campaigning brought serious politicking, and the Scots had long sought a chance to convince Charles of the virtues of presbyteries. Others were willing to give them their head. Scots talking peace held few terrors for the war party, since Charles's loathing for the kirk was well known. Furthermore, the hardest of military men could see the need for gestures about peace since popular discontent with the war continued to grow, not least in London. Parliament's inability to estimate the costs of war, and its greater inability to ensure that all taxes were paid, left it as dependent as ever on the City for loans; and there the old conservative élite had regained some of the power it had lost in the London revolution of 1641. Should the Scots be thwarted over peace negotiations, they might be expected to apply politically devastating pressure through the control over London's coal trade which the capture of Newcastle had brought them.

Similar pressures operated at Oxford. The increasingly hard-line character of the royalist cause, so different from the more aristocratic days of 1642, suggests that a royalist victory in the latter stages of the war might have had more arbitrary consequences than a victory won in 1642-43. Not all new men were tyrants, and the greatest of them, Prince Rupert, who ruled Wales and its borders, used his rank to obtain deference as deftly as did Manchester in the Eastern Association. Nevertheless, Charles's policy amounted to self-help by the soldiers; furthermore, while parliament was no more able than was the king to specify chains of command, Charles was certainly readier to use harsh commanders, like Lord Byron and Sir Michael Woodhouse, who were involved in some ugly incidents. When the Oxford parliament assembled for its second winter session in 1644–5 Charles heard a wave of protests, and of demands for peace talks. Whatever his own contempt for negotiations – in a letter to his wife in the spring of 1645 he voiced intense distaste for criticism even from the loyal Oxford parliament, the 'mongrel parliament', as he revealingly termed his own creation – he too had reason to go through the motions.

Undaunted, the Scots grew more hopeful that winter. They saw themselves, and presbyterianism, as allies of monarchy and supporters of order; and the chances for presbyterianism seemed rosier. Both houses had at last succumbed to Scottish promptings and sent Arch-bishop Laud to the scaffold on 8 January 1645, attainted – since the failure of the impeachment managed by Laud's own victim of the 1630s, William Prynne – for his part in the great popish plot to which Charles's recent Irish policy added a new dimension. While that sym-bolic blow against episcopacy was unlikely to persuade Charles, parlia-ment appeared ready to present him with a presbyterian *fait accompli*. Although the Commons had set their face against a *iure divino* presby-terianism, most MPs sought discipline more eagerly than ever. In January 1645 they resolved in principle that the future government of the church would be presbyterian; and both houses passed without a division the Westminster assembly's directory of worship, a directory which was far simpler than the Anglican prayer book but still provided a structured form of worship. Both separatists and episcopalians were left in little doubt that they would find no place in the sun.

Parliamentary support for presbyterianism did not, however, mean that the houses agreed with the Scots that a proper church order was what the war was about. At Westminster the trustworthiness of Charles was the issue, as it had always been. The peace terms finally sent to Uxbridge therefore amounted to a demand that Charles surren-der his powers indefinitely, accept presbyterianism, and see dozens of his supporters excluded from pardon. Charles saw little reason to con-cede. He hoped for fresh troops from Ireland, and recent reverses for the Covenanters in Scotland might yet undo the results of Marston Moor in the northern theatre; in the south, Lostwithiel and Newbury spoke for themselves. Furthermore, the disarray of the parlia-mentarians had been underlined not just by the self-denying ordinance but also by the manoeuvrings over the Uxbridge terms, in which two of the peace party leaders, Holles and Bulstrode Whitelocke, had engaged in almost treasonable dealings with the king. And like the most anti-papist parliamentarian, Charles would have no truck with ungodly enemies, whom God would surely overthrow.

The grim pointlessness of the talks at Uxbridge in January and Febru-ary 1645 showed that the war must go on and Charles must be beaten. It brought its reaction in parliament's commission for Fairfax as new lord general, which omitted the pious declaration that parliament and its armies were fighting to preserve the person of the king. The pressures of war were stripping away the old verities.

In April the protesting Lords at last accepted the military reorganization. But the ironic result of the winter's efforts, to which many had agreed in the hope of removing Cromwell, was that Cromwell was left in service. This may indeed have been a war-party ploy, as some alleged both then and since; but the Lords' obstructionism drew their fate on themselves. The usual rhythm of war was politics in winter, fighting in summer, but the Lords haggled over the list of officers so long that by the time the New Model was on the point of meeting the king in battle there was still no agreed cavalry commander. Fairfax's urgent request that he be allowed to keep Cromwell, as the best available commander, won for the latter a grudging three-month commission.

Fortunately for the parliamentarians, they were not alone in their disarray. Feuding amongst Charles's western commanders, Lord Goring, Sir Richard Grenville and Sir John Berkeley, brought to nothing his hopes of consolidating that region to balance the loss of the north; and the tetchy Rupert was once more bitterly at odds with the unstable Digby, Charles's main adviser. Rather than resolve the squabbles, as parliament had spent the winter doing, Charles turned his gaze north in the spring of 1645. Chester, vital as the entry-port for reinforcements from Ireland, was under siege. Beyond, a motley force of Irish clansmen and their Highland kin, led by the dashing ex-Covenanter Montrose, had capped a string of lightning victories by slaughtering Argyll's Campbell clan at Inverlochy in February 1645: the three kingdoms might at last bear fruit. Two tempting courses lay open to Charles. He could relieve Chester *en route* to join Montrose, and then restore his position in the north; or he could destroy the fledgling 'new noddle' by catching Fairfax's weary men on their way back towards Oxford from their first, ill-planned foray into the west. There was much to be said for either plan, so Charles characteristically opted for both. He thereby left each of the divided royalist forces smaller than those under Fairfax.

The chance of trapping Charles in the north between the New Model and the Covenanters did not appeal to the armchair strategists at Westminster. Conservatives still thought more of the defence of the parliamentarian heartland, while many in the war party dreamed of Oxford, now stripped of most of its defenders. But when Rupert, the royalist commander-in-chief, sacked Leicester on the edge of the undefended Eastern Association all awoke to the dangers of leaving the main royal army unattended to.

Divided commands determined both the occurrence and – almost

– the outcome of the battle at Naseby in Leicestershire on 14 June. Fairfax's approaching army badly outnumbered the royalists, and that the indecisive Charles fought at all must be attributed to the insistence of Digby, who was anxious to spite the more careful Rupert. Yet Rupert almost won, a fact which owes something to the composition of the New Model as well as to its weariness. The cavalry wing which broke was of mixed origin while that which held was purely Eastern Association, suggesting how risky remodelling had been. Rupert's own cavalry once more proved unstoppable; but Cromwell kept his under tight control and brought it round decisively onto the royalist infantry in the centre, destroying Charles's major field army and the remains of his reputation. The king's captured correspondence, published by parliament as *The King's Cabinet Opened*, revealed to the world his contempt for peace negotiations and his attempts to gain aid from all and sundry, including the Catholic Irish and the pope; one leading Welsh royalist, Sir Trevor Williams, promptly changed sides. Meanwhile Cromwell and others grew more confident that the hand of God was with them.

The political coup for the war party was as great as the military victory, and both were sorely needed. Despite the failure of the Uxbridge treaty the war party's standing in the mire at Westminster had weakened. Messy disclosures about dealings with Oxford tarnished both war and peace parties during the summer, and the ensuing attempts on both sides to use treason charges against political opponents underlined just how explosive would be the making of the final peace. Indeed, the appalling political problem of a likely military victory over an intransigent king was helping reduce the remnants of Pym's old middle group to what has been called little more than a state of mind. But perhaps the most alarming development for all but the peace party was the growing pressure outside parliament for peace.

In the country most of the passions of 1642 had been drowned in suffering. The civil war may have begun amateurishly, but by 1643 there were probably 110,000 men in arms, some 10 per cent of the adult male population – a proportion not to be reached again until the French Revolutionary Wars. Although such concentrations brought in contracts for clothing, food and equipment, they also disrupted both economy and society. True, the fighting remained localized. Although one-fifth of Gloucester was demolished to strengthen its defences in 1643, two-thirds of Taunton destroyed in the 1645 siege, and Birmingham, Bolton and Leicester brutally sacked, areas like East Anglia and Cornwall rarely heard the tramp of the marching armies. But all had to pay.

The official burdens were bad enough. The parliamentary weekly assessment, parallelled in the more orderly royalist areas by the 'contributions' to Oxford, was the equivalent of an income tax of 10 per cent or more, or almost one old parliamentary subsidy every two weeks. Most counties paid more in assessments every month than they had paid in ship money every year. And while little may have made its way from the counties to the opposing capitals, the soldiers saw to it that the money was collected: after the chaos of the early months of the war counties on both sides made it common practice to make groups of parishes responsible for the support of small detachments. Not surprisingly, yields in both parliamentarian and royalist counties approached 100 per cent. And while it was not until the partial restoration of order after 1645 that the excise had much impact outside London, other rates fell heavily. In some counties the money 'loaned' by householders in 1642–5 on the propositions, and whose non-repayment so damaged 'the public faith', equalled the return on the assessments.

Localized conflict meant far heavier burdens, imposed less officially. The failure of Oxford and Westminster to draw money away from the counties meant that unpaid soldiers had to live at free quarter. That is, they were billeted on householders, who were given promissory notes – only occasionally redeemed – in return for room and board. Estimates are problematic, but the parliamentary accounts committee in contested Buckinghamshire suggested that free quarter cost more than all forms of taxation; and most regions suffered since the bulk of the men served not in the main field armies but scattered in local forces and petty garrisons. These might extract their pay by sword's point, and far more men were fighting for a living than for a cause, with predictable results. The damage is impossible to quantify, but what it meant for the individual is clear: one Cheshire gentleman was pillaged three times by each side. It was during this war that the word 'plunder' entered the English language.

War also had indirect consequences. London's coal-less winter of 1643 was only the most dramatic of the shortages inflicted by the fighting. The industrial depression which had set in with the political crisis of 1640 worsened, despite the military contracts. Not only were big merchants reluctant to commit their capital, but inland traders suffered from marauding troops of either side. Rents fell as farmers whose horses or cattle were seized, or whose corn was trampled, were unable to pay, or abandoned their holdings. By 1646 it was generally agreed that rents were at one-third of their pre-war levels; in contested areas like the Thames Valley often nothing was collected. The business of the central courts similarly declined, by perhaps 50–75 per cent, during the war years. Partly this was because much of the country was lost to parliament, but probably equally important was the reluctance of parties and witnesses to travel. Assizes brought little relief, since parliament refused to allow the unreliable judges to go on circuit in 1643, and thereafter assizes were unusual in both parliamentarian and royalist territories; the clogged judicature of the house of Lords offered litigants little consolation. Injustices therefore multiplied without redress. Although in more settled royalist areas quarter sessions survived as Charles sought to use them to sanction his demands, in other regions this key institution of local government collapsed. The Warwickshire quarter sessions failed to meet for three years, and although the county committee did much of the work, considerable day-to-day business was left undone. By the end of the war in many parts of Yorkshire local officials such as constables and churchwardens had not been replaced and rates for road repair or the upkeep of the poor had not been collected; while in Dorchester the workhouse for poor children closed from 1643 to 1646. The human consequences of such social dislocation are hard to grasp, but they may be apparent in the unprecedented activities of the 'Witch-finder General', Mathew Hopkins, in East Anglia in 1645. Exploiting the disorganization, and the silence, of the local authorities, and playing on the cultural disturbance and yearning for scapegoats that the war had caused, the very non-puritan Hopkins was able to bring dozens to their deaths.

Local administration certainly continued to function. Towns tried to pretend that it was business as usual, although many of their old powers were eroded: most were steadily subordinated to the county governments, while those that were garrisoned found petty dictators in their governors. In parliamentarian counties the county committees were invariably disliked for their novelty and the apparent arbitrariness of their methods. While most historians who have studied the committees have commented favourably on their industry and probity, those who suffered at their hands were unlikely to agree, and there were a few petty tyrannies, most notably in Kent. The inclusion amongst the committees' functions of the sequestration of the estates of royalist 'delinquents' had alienated many local notables, who were often unwilling to act against men to whom they might be related. The committees therefore co-opted new men, who carried no prestige in their names and who were perforce more reliant on the troops. Sometimes the new men were the humble townsmen of outraged legend – Sir John Oglander's sneers at the pedlar, baker, apothecary and farmers on the Isle of Wight committee are typical – but more often they came from lesser gentry families, in the larger pool of which men radical enough, or hardened enough, could be found; and in areas which had been royalist there was naturally a cleaner sweep of the old governors. Furthermore, the complexity of wartime government bred a strange new species, the minor local bureaucrat. The agent of the county committee or of the excise commissioners probably saw his position as a step on the social ladder at least as often as he saw it as service to a cause, and he behaved accordingly. Every revolution throws up its own bureaucracy.

The county committees were still more distasteful in the methods they employed, which created an uncomfortable resemblance to star chamber. Abandoning jury presentments, the committees sequestered royalists' estates, with no appeal other than to the central parliamentary committee for sequestrations; they had summary power to fine and imprison for non-compliance, and they also set the rates for fiscal levies. Often too the committees intervened in ecclesiastical affairs by removing 'scandalous' ministers. As one disgusted Essex clergyman, Richard Drake of Radwinter, complained in 1645, 'The is the glorious ''liberty of the subject'' they used to set forth'. Predictably, the royalist counties followed a similar path away from the ideals of 1628. Charles's increasing reliance on outsiders with both military and civil authority in the regions, such as Prince Rupert in Wales and Prince Maurice in the south-west, brought to power men who have been likened to war-lords.

The strength of local resentments makes it as unwise to confine discussion of the war to high strategy as it is to overlook the confusion of its outbreak. Parliament's consciousness of its increasing political isolation provided much of the impetus for the self-denying ordinance, and for the Uxbridge treaty. Local sentiment in its most obvious manifestation, sullen hostility to the unprecedented tax burdens, constantly deprived the armies of supplies and hampered their movements. Equally damaging was the perennial aversion of county authorities on both sides to anything other than the local use of resources, which forced all the armies into prolonged periods of inactivity as funds dried up and soldiers slunk home. Even the previously energetic committee of the Eastern Association could be contaminated: facing the submergence of its army in the New Model in the spring of 1645 it petulantly declared, 'The safety of the kingdom . . . was not our work'. Humbler officials too were torn between the commands of external authority and the ties of neighbourhood, and to equally damaging effect.

Hostility to war sometimes took a more active form, piecemeal at first – as in isolated revolts in Kent in 1643 and 1645, or in sporadic vigilante attacks on straggling troopers – and then more widely, particularly as the king's finances steadily broke down. Charles's efforts to build a new army after Marston Moor imposed further strains on the Welsh borders, and local garrisons whose supplies were diverted therefore increasingly turned to living off the land. In some of the poorer, less 'gentrified' uplands of Herefordshire and Worcestershire village 'clubmen' banded together in the winter off 1644–5 in futile attempts to resist the marauding soldiers. But it would be unwise to rank the protests of 1645 alongside the activities of 1642 and to conclude that popular political activity was primarily simply neutralist. Some of those who resisted military incursions still saw themselves as part of a national cause. The same winter, angry gentry in several counties along the Welsh borders came together in short-lived 'associations', seeking to curb the violence of the royalist soldiery by taking on themselves the business of tax collection and supply: had similar indigenous royalist organization emerged in 1642, the king's party might not have fallen victim so soon to military abuse. More strikingly, at least some of the countrymen who associated in Dorset and Wiltshire in May 1645 to halt plunder and preserve the peace were inflamed by parliament's recent prohibition of the prayer book, so much a part of the Anglican fabric of life. As Fairfax marched west after Naseby he was confronted by huge and threatening demonstrations, though rural protest proved a broken reed before a disciplined force. The anti-parliamentarian bias of these groups suggests that popular opinion had not yet concluded that a parliamentarian victory was inevitable.

Those clubmen who did lean towards parliament may not therefore have merely sought to end the fighting by supporting the winning side. In western Somerset countrymen aided Fairfax in his pursuit of the last royalist field army under Goring after Naseby, and the location of these groups in the same upland wood/pasture zone which had rallied for parliament in 1642 suggests an ecological interpretation. For the anti-New Model demonstrations occurred in the contrasting arable region which stretched east through Dorset and Wiltshire. Such an analysis needs qualification, since the eastern belt alone had suffered from the parliamentarian foray westwards in the spring of 1645. However, the occurrence of more violent club activity, independent of gentry leadership, in the uplands along the Welsh borders suggests something of underlying social realities. The fielden zone was generally more closely manorialized, with more resident gentry and more parish churches; settlement in the wood/pasture zone was both more scattered and less hierarchical. It seems no accident that the clubmen of the former region accepted the leadership of the gentry and clergy, even of those who had earlier been in arms for the king, and issued anti-puritan as well as anti-war protests. In contrast, the clubmen of the wood/pasture belt, strident in their opposition to popery, opposed gentry attempts to incline the movement towards the king, and were instead capable of throwing up their own leaders, such as the Somerset yeoman, Humphrey Willis. The woodlands clearly had native traditions of political activity, stretching back at least to the riots against deforestation at the end of the 1620s.

But despite the widespread anguish, each side could normally find willing agents, whether adventurers or zealots. Anyway, although local alignments may have been critical in 1642, by 1645 they could not halt veteran forces. The tide had turned decisively in favour of a military solution.

That that solution would be imposed by the New Model became ever more likely. When Fairfax's army at last caught up with Goring on 10 July near Langport in Somerset, the outnumbered royalists had taken up a commanding position on a hill approached only by a lane wide enough for four horsemen abreast. To the godly officers around Fairfax there could be only one explanation for a victory won in such circumstances. As he watched the royalists break, the sectarian Major Thomas Harrison 'with a loud voice [broke] forth into the praises of God with fluent expressions, as if he had been in a rapture'. And Cromwell, always elated by battle, concluded in awe, 'To see this, is it not to see the face of God?' Two months later the parliamentarian control over the south-west was confirmed when, with too few troops to man the walls and a quarter of the population dead of plague, Rupert surrendered Bristol on 10 September. The city had been the king's last claim to credibility in Europe, and Charles, often slow to show gratitude for past service, never forgave his nephew for the shattering defeat.

At this point the God of battles seemed to be speaking unambiguously everywhere but in Scotland, where Montrose's tiny army was repeatedly humiliating the Covenanters. But three days later came the effective end of all the king's hopes. The charismatic Montrose had crowned his career at Kilsyth in August 1645 when victory left him master of both Edinburgh and Glasgow, but instead of consolidating his position he had obeyed the king's command to move south towards the border. Unable to keep his clansmen together as he moved further from the hills, he was routed at Philiphaugh on 13 September by Covenanting forces hotly returned from England. The subsequent slaughter was warmly approved by both Scottish and English Calvinists as the just judgment of God on a campaign which had been scarred by tribal atrocities on both sides. Charles still dreamed of fresh Irish troops, but all that was left for parliament to do was mop up the remaining royalist garrisons.

With victory must come settlement, and it was becoming clear just how difficult that would be to reach. Charles had few qualms about prolonging the struggle, or looking in the most forbidden of all quarters for aid, for his sense of the divine mission of monarchy was as driving as was Cromwell's very different God-given mandate. In a letter to Rupert shortly before the fall of Bristol Charles had indicated that whatever the outcome he would never submit, for 'God will not suffer rebels to prosper, or His cause to be overthrown'. In pursuit of whatever means God might put into his hand, Charles had for some time been seeking access not just to the soldiers of the old government army in Ireland, the avowed object of the cessation of 1643, but also – as his letters captured at Naseby had shown – to those of the rebel Confederation. But the Confederate leaders' control over most of Ireland put them in such a strong position that they refused to let him recruit their troops without major concessions. By October 1645 the desperate Charles was offering to make Catholicism the official religion in Ireland, with Catholic bishops in the Irish house of Lords and a Catholic lord lieutenant. Agreement came too late to do him anything but the harm which came with the capture of the correspondence, for even the most conservative amongst his enemies were appalled by the king's readiness to favour those they saw as Antichrist.

Charles's dreams of a dash to a popular reception in a war-weary London crumbled in the spring of 1646. Facing instead the sordid likelihood of capture by an angry army and an equally angry majority in parliament, he turned to the Scots. Encouraged by his more flexible wife and by the French government, Charles saw hope in the Scots' greater willingness to let him retain his civil powers, and thought to exploit Anglo-Scottish hostilities which had grown with familiarity. But his elevated sense of kingship proved an insuperable obstacle. No more than in the late 1630s could he comprehend the convictions of the Covenanters, and he expected that they, not he, would make religious concessions. He was genuinely surprised at the taunts to which he was subject when in April, having slipped out of besieged Oxford, he surrendered himself to the Scottish army besieging Newark.

The Scots' position was awkward. Possessing the person of the king they possessed the prime bargaining card in any settlement, and with it the chance to avenge themselves on their contemptuous allies. Even an agreement which at Westminster seemed a sell-out would probably hold, given the general longing for peace. But success depended on speed, for suspicions of Scottish intentions were bound to grow, and with them the risk of a new war. Withdrawing to the greater safety of Newcastle, the Covenanters deluged Charles with godly sermons in hope of his conversion; but although in his later English captivity Charles was to show a surprising personal unconcern for the

Anglican prayer book he never wavered in his hatred of the Covenant.

The Scots' failure to propagate their gospel gave the English parliament its chance. In the harsh climate created by Charles's Irish undertakings the ultimatum the houses sent to Newcastle in July 1646 promised to extend indefinitely the parliamentary control over the militia and government from the twenty years demanded at Uxbridge the year before. The Newcastle propositions also rested on the newly enacted parliamentary form of presbyterianism,* which the Scots despised as insufficiently rigid. Charles found the whole even more unpalatable than did the Scots. Confident that his English subjects loved presbyterianism and the parliament as little as he did, he had every reason to play for time, in the well-founded hope that his enemies might fall out, and in hope too that Henrietta Maria might find aid in France. Frustrated by such disingenuousness, and not daring to take him back to Edinburgh – where he would become a rallying-point for the anti-Covenanter sentiment evident after Montrose's last victory at Kilsyth – the Covenanters in August 1646 opened negotiations for the transfer of the king to parliament. They were assured by their few friends at Westminster that a safe and moderate, even if not a more presbyterian, peace could be extracted from the goodwill that would well up once Charles was safely in England.

All members of the parliamentarian coalition had assumed that Charles would at last come to terms. To the peace party that point had seemed likely to be when stalemate had been reached, and to the war party, when the king had been beaten; few had appreciated that in no circumstances would Charles concede. The Scots found others to take Charles from them, but his new gaolers might not be so lucky. That August, Dr Baillie one of the Scottish commissioners in London, predicted gloomily of 'that mad man' that 'he will [take] down with him all his posterity, and monarchy.'

*See below, pp. 265, 280–2.

9 Reaction and Revolution 1646-1649

The ending of the fighting solved nothing, and peace soon proved far more inflammatory than war. As both the stakes and tempers rose one strategically placed observer, Georg Rudolph Weckherlin, secretary to the dominant parliamentary committee in Derby House, concluded gloomily in the summer of 1647 that he lived in a fallen world: 'There is nothing but falsehood, speciously trimmed and adorned with robes of piety,* but Weckherlin was perhaps unfair to the ever-growing number of players in a political poker game where all the red cards ran wild and the most malevolent joker was the weather. Any settlement depended on both Scots and English armies being paid off and sent home. This required money, and the already constricted wartime economy was convulsed by post-war harvests almost as disastrous as those of the 1590s. The consequence was mounting pressure from below, with resistance to taxation and social unrest making a settlement both more urgent and more inaccessible.

Any hope that Charles's surrender would lessen the country's burdens soon crumbled. Fears that a vengeful king might yet return at the head of a Scottish army to regroup the defeated cavaliers and impose a presbyterian settlement which would leave him the sword meant that for the parliamentary majority the New Model must remain on foot. Moves towards disbandment came slowly, and expensively. In September 1646 the Commons reluctantly, and over the bitter protests of those who felt that the Covenanters had hardly earned their keep, agreed to pay the Scots £400,000 towards the support promised them in 1643. But it was not until February 1647, and with Newcastle housewives' cries of 'Judases!' ringing in their ears, that the Covenanters handed over the king to their paymasters and went home. In response, parliament that same month voted to reduce the military establishment of over 40,000 men to a standing force of 5,400 cavalry and a few minor garrisons; a larger contingent was to be dispatched for the reconquest of Ireland.

*Marquess of Downshire papers, Trumbull Mss., Weckherlin papers 1613–61, f. 127v. (Library of Congress microfilm).

The vote for disbandment came too late to bring internal peace, let alone to provide a stepping-stone to agreement with the king. Relations with the country strained to breaking-point as parliament remained on a war footing. Early-modern Englishmen had had no prior experience of regular national taxation, but at its later 1640s level of £120,000 a month parliament's monthly assessment was the equivalent of at least eighteen pre-war parliamentary subsidies every year; and the novel excise had, like most sales taxes, an inequitable impact on poor consumers. Moreover, the proud hopes that the reorganization of the spring of 1645 would enable the New Model to pay its way had taken a mere six months to prove vain. Thereafter the new army took free quarter like all the other forces, and added one more broken promise to a long list. The burden of the soldiers was intensified by their own discontent. By the end of the war the pay due to all parliament's armies was almost £3M. in arrears, a sum which needs to be compared with the pre-war royal revenues of around £1M. p.a. Although the New Model was pacified throughout 1646 with intermittent funds, the soldiers in the scattered regional forces fared much worse. In consequence, about half the English counties had reported incidents of military disorder or mutiny by the spring of 1647, even before the great army revolt of that year. In the country discontent flared as both rents and rain fell, food prices rose, depression deepened and a devastating plague outbreak came on the heels of the assorted diseases spread by the ragged armies. Clubmen grew active again, especially in the south-west.

Desires for a return to the old order were reinforced by the continuing activities of the county committees, for some time now the object of press broadsides. Even where the grosser abuses were absent, the committees symbolized the long breach with the old ways of quarter sessions and JPs. Whether in county or parish, objectionable measures were enforced by objectionable men, and the noises of protest were too loud for the houses to ignore.

The fervour of the demand for a restoration of normality was a mixed blessing for those politicians who most sympathized with it. On the one hand it strengthened their position, but on the other it risked carrying them faster than was politic.

The most obvious consequence of the post-war mood was the resurgence of the old peace party led by Essex, Holles and their ally Sir Philip Stapleton. With peace to be pursued rather than the distasteful necessities of war, conservative absentees from both houses slowly drifted back. An even more dramatic change occurred in the Commons when the house held new elections to seats vacated by death or purge. Its aim in thus 'recruiting' its numbers was to protect itself in the coming negotiations against royalist attacks on its claims to be representative of England; by the end of 1645 there were nearly a hundred 'recruiter' MPs, and 235 by the end of 1646, almost half the total membership. Although the elections were, as in the past, primarily local in their concerns they reflected prevailing political realities. The 1646 recruiters tended to be far less militant than those of 1645, particularly since in 1646 elections were held in pacified, but still largely royalist, counties like Cornwall. The peace party was accordingly reinforced.

Holles consolidated his position through his dominance of the Derby House committee. This had been created to oversee the reconquest of Ireland but it soon assumed all, and more, of the executive powers of the now lapsed committee of both kingdoms. Aided by the Covenanters' respect for his conservative credentials, Holles moved swiftly to pay them off. He then prepared for the disbandment of the English force whose rationale for existence now seemed ended.

Sending the soldiers home was the core of Holles's strategy. Disbandment would pacify country resentment, neutralize men whom he suspected of dangerous radicalism, deprive the parliamentary intransigents of their military allies, and thus permit a less uncompromising stance towards the king. There lay the road to a lasting peace, based on something like the the *status quo* of 1641. Although this was in the context of 1646 a conservative programme, in one respect – the final abolition of episcopacy – even Holles was a victim of the pressure of events, of functional radicalism. While by preference probably a moderate episcopalian, Holles saw in the lands and wealth of the bishops and cathedrals the only way to pay off both English and Scottish troops and reconquer Ireland. 'Country' hostility to taxation, and the exhaustion of parliament's credit during the war, precluded any other solution. But however realistic Holles's appreciation of sentiment in the country and in a parliament whose composition was steadily changing, his was hardly a consensus programme. The old war-party minority doubted more than ever that Charles could be trusted to abide by any settlement, and feared that disbandment would allow a vengeful king to appeal to a weary nation. They suspected Holles of intending a sell-out and fought bitterly if fruitlessly against his proposals, dividing the house on the disbandment of each petty garrison. During the war politicians had sought to preserve at least a semblance of unity, but in late 1646 divisions were called as often as in the tumultuous days of late 1641. The struggle for a settlement saw the breakdown of the parliamentarian coalition.

Understanding of the nature of post-war politics is unfortunately hampered by the terms used to describe it. The inappropriateness by 1646 of the old labels, 'war' and 'peace' party is apparent. It might be accurate to refer to the Essex-Holles-Stapleton clique on the one hand and the Vane–St John–Haselrig–Cromwell–Lord Saye group on the other, but it would hardly be elegant. Historians have therefore adopted the only contemporary taxonomy on offer, that of the Scots, who steadfastly assumed that politics centred on religion. They identified their enemies and their allies accordingly. Since the threat of sectarianism had driven them into the arms of the peace party they myopically associated the war party with their other bugbears, the Independent divines of the Westminster assembly, and wrongly assumed that the peace party were presbyterians like themselves. Some of the war party were indeed religious Independents, and Cromwell concluded his announcement of the victory at Naseby with a plea for liberty of conscience. But Zouch Tate, for example, a hard-liner whom the Scots classed as 'Independent' for his politics, was in fact a rigorous religious presbyterian. Similarly, the Scots saw the New Model as an Independent army, primarily because their enemies had always preferred it to their own; in reality the army's concerns throughout 1646 remained overwhelmingly professional. Parallel problems attach to the Scots' identification of the 'presbyterian' party. Although many conservatives did see presbyterianism as the only remaining path to order, others longed for a limited episcopacy.

To many the distinctions and labels anyway seemed as irrelevant as to others they have been incomprehensible. Parliament's faltering steps in late 1645 towards the establishment of a presbyterian church had been relatively uncontentious, while preparations for a political settlement in the winter of 1646–7 proved highly divisive. Few English politicians used religious labels to explain politics in 1647, still fewer in 1646. Most MPs saw the few dozen active speakers on either side as simply the 'Juntoes', in the phrase of Clement Walker, the Jeremiah of the back benches. Even to the zealous the religious issues did not always seem the most divisive: thus, a godly Independent like Saye's son Nathaniel Fiennes could see the ecclesiastical differences as 'inconsiderable' compared with the common goal, 'the kernel' of true reformation. Nevertheless, provided we remember that when we talk of the presbyterian party we mean active politicians mainly from the old peace party, political allies of the Scots but scarcely full sharers of their ecclesiastical views, then the term is useful as a shorthand. Equally, if we identify the Independent party as the former war party and middle group, deeply distrustful of Charles and hostile too to Scottish efforts to settle for religious terms alone we are on firm enough ground. But those parties by no means coincided with religious presbyterians and religious Independents.

Holles's strategy found justification in the speed with which uncommitted MPs swung behind the efforts to reduce the armies. The February 1647 vote on disbandment was followed by a Commons' resolution on 8 March to rescind exemptions from the self-denying ordinance and to reduce the officer corps. But while such steps could be seen as necessary economy measures and a return to legal propriety, they could also be interpreted as partisan moves against Cromwell, who had remained an MP, and those of Fairfax's subordinates, like Harrison, or Commissary-General Ireton, Cromwell's son-in-law, who had been elected as recruiters. And whatever Holles's discretion, others were being swept along by the tide of resentment. Petitioners in East Anglia in the early spring feared being 'eaten up, enslaved, and destroyed' by the army; more ominously, the fiery MP William Strode boasted back in Somerset, 'We will destroy them all . . . Sir Thomas Fairfax will be deceived, for part of his army will join with us, and besides the Scots are very honest men and will come to assist us.' Some at least of the presbyterian party militants could already contemplate using force against the New Model.

Not surprisingly, disquiet grew in the army as well as amongst the parliamentary Independents. The soldiers' unease was at first directed largely at the material prospects facing them. Although the pay of the cavalry in particular was over a year in arrears, several regional forces had been disbanded piecemeal in 1645–6 with a few weeks' pay in hand, and promises for the rest: disbandment of the New Model need not therefore have caused mutiny. But Fairfax's soldiers received scant encouragement in the development of a tax-payers' strike as sweeping as that of 1639–40. The City of London was 72 per cent in arrears on its monthly assessments from June–September 1646, and parliament itself gave a disturbing signal when in its eagerness to gratify the country it allowed the assessment to lapse for the following six months. The excise was no more fruitful: anti-excise riots in London and Norwich in the winter and spring gave violent point to what can be deduced from the army's failure to receive any excise money between November 1646 and June 1649. If left to the goodwill of a country which had had enough of payments, the soldiers would have a bleak future. Thrust back onto free quarter on householders made surly by the rise in food prices and unemployment, the soldiers were left in no doubt of their unpopularity. Worse, the return of peace had allowed JPs, grand juries and assize judges to resume some of their normal duties, and to pay off civilian scores against the military. Reports circulated early in 1647 of soldiers being hanged for having seized horses or supplies for war service. Accordingly, in mid-March the soldiers, aided by equally disgruntled officers, prepared to petition Lord General Fairfax about their grievances.

This was not yet a revolutionary army. No army fitted the hierarchical model of society, if only because common troopers bore
swords, the badge of gentility. All armies offered 'new' men opportunities for advancement, and all armies, whether in royal, parliamentary, Scottish or Spanish service, periodically mutinied over
their material grievances. But in March 1647, and for some time
thereafter, the soldiers were silent on the score of religion. Amongst
the more prosperous and literate cavalry troopers there were indeed
many 'saints', godly volunteers impatient of the religious discipline on which parliament seemed bent. Some were encouraged to see
themselves as about God's great work by fiery chaplains, John
Saltmarsh, Thomas Collier, and above all Hugh Peter. In the dangerous inactivity of peace others among the rank-and-file and junior
officers needed – or, in the largely unprovided army, were given –
little clerical encouragement. Their readiness to preach alarmed
conservatives all the more when conversions to the sectarian exclusiveness of Baptism increased, while the spreading conviction that
a new age was dawning as God's army went from victory to victory
brought to the surface the antinomianism always latent in radical
protestantism.* Cromwell was not alone in the certainty he voiced
after Marston Moor that the army was God's chosen instrument in
the crusade against Antichrist – in his short service as an army
chaplain in 1645 Richard Baxter was horrified to encounter soldiers
who believed themselves on that account above all ordinances.
Nevertheless, some half of the New Model's soldiers were conscripts
or royalist turncoats, and Baxter in 1645 worried about the army's
irreligion as much as about its incipient radicalism. Furthermore, the
many moderate or presbyterian officers appointed in 1645 were still
in their posts, while, like all generals, more radical commanders such
as Cromwell and Henry Ireton favoured discipline.

The army would therefore in the early spring of 1647 probably have
acquiesced in a settlement, even a presbyterian one, which made
some provision for its genuine needs. One of the most militant regiments later testified that payment of a mere four months' of its
arrears, instead of the eight weeks' pay offered, would have persuaded it to disband. Spread throughout the New Model that would
have required about £200,000, by no means beyond the lending
powers of a City of London which feared and hated the soldiers. But
while parliament's plight deserves sympathy – for the taxpayers'
strike made renewed civil war a real possibility should major new
burdens for the soldiery be imposed – Holles erred disastrously. By
challenging the army directly he gave it a political cause. Here,

*See above, p. 72, for a discussion of antinomianism.

Essex's death in late 1646 proved crucial, for the earl's concern for his fellow-soldiers might have restrained Holles's gut conservatism. Instead, alarmed by the warnings of City oligarchs and county petitioners that London and army radicals were about to make common political cause, Holles over-reacted. On 30 March the Commons published a 'declaration of dislike': the soldier petitioners to Fairfax were 'enemies of the state and disturbers of the public peace'. In the following weeks both houses galloped intemperately towards disbandment.

The radicalization of soldiers who had expected the thanks of a grateful nation for all their sufferings and met instead public denunciation was not long in coming. The alternative of penurious disbandment or equally penurious service in Ireland was scarcely attractive, and at the end of April cavalry regiments quartered in East Anglia led the way by electing 'agitators' or agents to act for them. Even this was not necessarily a radical step: the concerns voiced by both agitators and junior officers throughout most of May remained overwhelmingly professional, and the election of representatives was a common tactic of discontented soldiers throughout Europe. Nevertheless, several of the agitators were Baptists, a fact which suggests that religion moved at least some of the leaders; moreover, there were signs of political awakening. Speedy disbandment would leave the soldiers vulnerable to vengeful local authorities, and when the houses were also remodelling the London militia by putting it in safe conservative hands it was easy to detect a plot to create a counter-force and then sell out to the king. In May some agitators came to speak of 'tyrants' amongst Holles's Derby House clique, and their suspicions were confirmed when, in predictable reaction, the frightened parliamentary leaders rushed to dismember the army. On 31 May, the day before disbandment was to begin, two regiments mutinied, refusing to disband until justice had been done on men who not only planned a new war but who had also slurred the army's honour in the declaration of dislike. Although the desperate houses quickly voted virtually all the army's material demands, it was too late.

The character of the army changed dramatically in the days around 1 June. Most momentously, the troops gained a secular ideology to buttress the certainty of many that they were God's agents. Convinced that their opponents in parliament were selfishly working to divide the army and gain an insecure agreement with Charles, the soldiers concluded that they alone stood for the public interest – which an increasingly influential minority also identified with God's interest. The unity and altruism of the army therefore became a fundamental tenet, shaping the actions of radical subalterns – by restraining their intransigence – as much as it was often to have the reverse effect on the more famous career of Cromwell. But the agitators' new demand for a purge of a corrupted parliament was not the only obstacle facing Holles. Equally dramatic was the change in the army's composition as almost one-third of the New Model's officers, largely conservative and 'presbyterian', dutifully accepted parliament's invitation to volunteer for Ireland. Many of their replacements were not only more radical but also socially more disreputable. Although the casualties of war had brought promotions for many of the godly London volunteers of 1642, in 1647 the proportion of gentry amongst the New Model's field officers fell from five-sixths to two-thirds. The colonelcy for Thomas Pride was one consequence of Holles's intemperacy.

The army's emergence onto the political stage proceeded apace. The increasingly self-confident agitators seem to have aimed to put a new guard on Charles to avert any conjunction between him, the Scots and parliament against the New Model, but Cornet Joyce, a subaltern leading a body of cavalry to Charles's quarters at Holdenby House in Northamptonshire, exceeded his instructions in fear of a counter-attack; on 3 June he seized the king and transferred him from parliamentary to army custody. Fairfax and Cromwell then acquiesced in the actions of others as they had done in face of the mutinies of 31 May and as they were to do again. Both dreaded disorder in the army, and both, staunch puritans as they were, could explain Joyce's action as the hand of providence. Furthermore, the far more politically sophisticated Cromwell must have seen the political advantages in possession of the king.

The final stage in the army's arousal came in the following days. At a general rendezvous on 5 June the regiments espoused the *Solemn Engagement* of the army, drafted by the cool hand of the lawyer and general Henry Ireton, who was to prove the army's finest politican. Modelled as it was on a religious covenant, the *Engagement* affirmed the unity of the soldiery, declaring that the army would not disband until its honour was vindicated and justice done; it also sought to maintain that unity by calling for a general council of the army, containing both officers and agitators. For the first time a declaration spoke resonantly of the rights of 'freeborn Englishmen'. And on 14 June, in face of threatening moves in parliament and City, the army issued its famous *Representation*. Ringingly asserting that the soldiers were no 'mere mercenary army' but had instead been raised to secure the nation's freedom, Ireton outlined a political programme. In unpartisan fashion the *Representation* sought an end to self-interest, by a purge of corrupt MPs – the Derby House clique – and county committees, and by audits of all financial accounts. More ominously, it also sought to end tyranny over body and conscience, demanding parliaments of fixed duration and toleration for tender consciences. The hostility to arbitrary rule, and the commitment to a wider cause, indicated that the explosive influence of the Levellers had begun to be felt in the army.

In their possession of a party treasury and in their payment of dues, the Levellers were the first political party. They have not surprisingly been the subject of intense interest. While this may be out of proportion to their direct political significance it is justified by the reaction they provoked and by what they reveal of political radicalism in the period.

The Levellers owed their name to their enemies, who wrongly saw in them a threat to property, and much of their prominence to the propagandist flair of John Lilburne. But they owed their sophisticated tactics to the experience in the petty offices of local government that so many Londoners had, and their support most of all to the social and religious ferment in the metropolis. The Baptists, Independents and other sects who congregated in the teeming alleys had watched in fear as City magistrates and ministers pressed parliament to erect a sterner ecclesiastical discipline. Having overridden their inherent centrifugal tendencies and mounted a counter-campaign for toleration of the godly, the sects soon came to question the nature of political authority when they saw their petitions burnt by the developing presbyterian majority in parliament.

The religious impulse remained central to the Levellers. Their pamphlets and petitions resound with demands for liberty of conscience, for an end to coercion by the state church and to compulsory tithes. But the sectarian outlook also informs the more secular elements in their programme, with its insistence on 'equity', moderation and equal dealings towards all, and its characteristic sectarian assertion that the spirit transcends the letter of the law. Yet the Levellers could never have turned out tens of thousands in demonstrations had their appeal been solely to the sects. They spoke for the many who had thought the houses in 1642 promised a new order, only to find them deliver high taxes, abuses of power, and economic depression. The Leveller petitions spoke too of the anger of artisans suffering while the contractors and monopoly companies made fat profits, and of the bitterness of countless Londoners who in their early enthusiasm had lent to parliament on 'the public faith', only to lose interest and principal as the public treasury dwindled. Although Leveller petitions in 1646-7 attacked the mercantile monopolies rather than the craft restrictions of the guilds, and thus spoke for master craftsmen and shopkeepers rather than employees, their rhetoric was often of a different order. The Levellers' virulent attack on exploitation was all-encompassing, and exposed a nerve which looks remarkably like class hostility. The dislocation and suffering brought by war seem to have shaken the ties of deference.

Nevertheless, the Levellers little deserved their name, with its hint of enclosure riot. Of their leaders, Lilburne was certainly of gentry stock, and Richard Overton may have been; William Walwyn was a prosperous merchant and the grandson of a bishop. Their secular causes, law reform, electoral reform, the abolition of monopolies, were all the concerns of those who had something, who might vote or go to law. While agrarian discontent was to well up in 1649, the London leaders showed little concern with it, or with the subordination of women, although women were very prominent both in their demonstrations and in their organization. They were men of their time and place rather than visionary thinkers.

The genius of the Leveller moment was Lilburne. Restless, irascible and egocentric, he cast his sufferings for his conscience at the hands of every authority from Laud onwards into vivid prose for all the commons of England. Like the Old Testament prophets, he was suffering in God's name for His people: his autobiography became a political cause. Appealing, like so many of his contemporaries, to the warrant of the Holy Spirit, Lilburne demanded 'equity' in the application of the laws; for all men were equal before God. His pamphlet salvoes drew not just on the Bible but also – in a testimony to the diffusion of legalist thought – on Magna Carta and Sir Edward Coke. Citing to embarrassing effect the houses' declarations, he asked how parliament had come to oppress the people. At last there was a rebuke to parliament for its failure to consider who were 'the people' whom it claimed to represent.

His allies were more thoughtful. Overton and Walwyn poured scorn on the unrepresentativeness of England's constitution, the inequities of its laws – particularly those exacting the death penalty for a range of offences against property and those condemning debtors to gaol – and the costs of its legal procedures. Their demands ranged from the stock call for the disestablishment of the church and the abolition of tithes to the decentralization of the legal system and election to all local offices. The parallel with the conservative clubmen, who manifested an equal distaste for arbitrary power and an equal concern for the legal rights of the individual, suggests that the rise of a bureaucratic and forceful state was breeding a fierce reaction across the political spectrum. Yet the more rationalist Overton and Walwyn went far beyond the respect for the common law shown by Lilburne as well as by the Clubmen. By 1647 Overton was voicing what was to become a pregnant theme, the sovereignty of the people as a bar to the sovereignty of parliament; that sovereignty necessarily entailed a more democratic franchise. Elaborating the common Leveller claim that the laws were the product of the 'Norman yoke' of William the Conqueror and his tyrannical lords, Overton saw them as 'unworthy a free people', while Walwyn chided Lilburne for his faith in that 'mess of pottage', Magna Carta. In their readiness to transcend the letter of the law the Leveller leaders drew from a well which was the source both of much of their own support and of that of far more radical groups too. The fracturing of political authority had encouraged many saints to conclude that the law was being superseded by the spirit – in that lay the warrant for the freedom of the godly. Antinomianism was to prove a powerful stimulus to thinking about liberty.

As in so many revolutionary situations, events became a rush of action and reaction on various fronts as the political stage opened out to include new actors. On the counter-revolutionary side the leading role was taken by the City.

To be fair, we should recognize that London's presbyterianism did not simply stand for self-interested conservatism. In the 1640s presbyterianism had come to seem the only way to the national reformation so many puritans craved: as the Covenanters proudly boasted, when backed by the civil power the kirk was the means to stamp out sin. Yet the integrity of the parishes to which City merchants and clergy fiercely clung also undoubtedly mattered for reasons of social and political as well as moral order. The oligarchs and their clerical allies accordingly deluged parliament between 1645 and 1647 with cries for a rigid discipline to fill the vacuum left by the collapse of episcopacy and its courts, and to avert the chaos threatened by the sects. The intensity of the concern at sectarian excesses can be gauged from the publication in 1645–6 of three weighty catalogues of error, Daniel Featley's *The Dippers Dipt*, Ephraim Pagitt's *Heresiography,* and Thomas Edward's remarkable and vituperative *Gangraena*.

Not surprisingly, the City gave strong support to Holles in the crisis. City loans were to finance disbandment and the reconquest of Ireland, and the powerful City militia, newly remodelled, was to serve as the conservative counter to Fairfax's ill-supplied forces. Equally important, the increasingly royalist City mob turned out repeatedly in June and July 1647 to stiffen the faint-hearted in parliament as a resentful New Model army moved slowly closer. Whatever popular opinions had been in 1641, disillusionment had hardened in the long wartime depression. Bitterness at the ecclesiastical anarchy, when compounded with the consequences of parliament's appalling credit record, helped generate that prominent feature of the next century and a half, the 'church and king' mob.

But the City was ill-placed to head a counter-revolution. Its leaders constituted a party of order, yet they were instigating mob violence and preparing for renewed civil war. Furthermore, the overthrow of the New Model would bring the speedy restoration of Charles, with little hope for the repayment of war loans the City had made to parliament. In later June and again in July the City fathers' resolve weakened; simultaneously, the trained bands began to disintegrate as Fairfax and Cromwell gradually and reluctantly moved the army closer to London. The nerve of the less intransigent in both houses broke too, for there were few attractions in the rioters around and even inside parliament. The New Model was, in contrast, reassuringly disciplined, its political demands were by no means outrageous – Cromwell the country gentleman never sounded more conservative than when in July he angrily told agitator-saints bent on a coup, 'Have what you will have, that you have by force I look upon it as nothing' – and in the king it held the key to a settlement. The flight of fifty-eight MPs, not all of them Independents, several peers and the Speakers of both houses contributed to the moderate mood, for it allowed the army to claim, and to believe, that it was not imposing its will but merely restoring freedom to parliament. On 4 August Fairfax entered the City without resistance, and Holles fled, with the rest of the 'eleven members' whose impeachment the soldiers had demanded.

The crumbling of the City's counter-revolution allowed other actors to take centre-stage. Even while the City was organizing, negotiations had been under way between Charles and the army's political leaders, Cromwell and Ireton – for Fairfax, their superior, while a superb inspirer of his men, was no politician. The generals' proposals, drafted by Ireton and Fairfax's brilliant young colonel, John Lambert, were presented to the king on 2 August as the *Heads of Proposals*. Far less harsh than parliament's Newcastle propositions, these would have allowed Charles to retain the royal legislative veto, deprived him of his control over the militia for a mere ten years, and permitted the survival of a non-coercive episcopacy. But the 'grandees', or generals, could no longer talk to Charles in isolation – they had to watch their rear. Suggestive of the new realities were the assurances given to suspicious agitators that the grandees were not seeking to be bought off. In addition to the barriers that the grandees erected against coercion in religion, moreover, the *Heads* also provided against arbitrary parliaments, through biennial meetings of limited duration and – in the first major linkage of the potent theme of taxation and representation – electoral redistribution in accordance with the distribution of taxation.

Despite his assertions of honest intent, Charles was unlikely to agree. According to Sir John Berkeley, one of his attendants, he could not trust Cromwell and Ireton since they asked for nothing for themselves, and to Charles – more influenced by his beliefs than perhaps any other politician – obedience, gratitude, place and profit were the only respectable political motives. There were practical problems too. Even though the list of royalists to be excluded from pardon had shrunk from the fifty-seven of the Newcastle propositions to five, that was too many for a king whose conscience still bore the scars of Strafford's death. As reluctant as ever to surrender the militia, Charles continued to look for a change in his fortunes: the Scots, the French or perhaps the Dutch would intervene, or – most likely – his enemies would fall to blows.

Others besides the king were unconvinced of the grandees' good faith. Although radical pressure diminished as the army council returned to the mundane but satisfying business of redressing material grievances, the march on London had brought no gains for the London Levellers. The presbyterian party in parliament had not collapsed, and there had been only minor changes in the City's government. Worse, the gathered churches, the Levellers' allies in the presbyterian hey-day of the spring, began to fall away in the autumn as the grandees' victory seemed to promise the liberty of conscience which the sects had always set higher than the Levellers' political reforms. In hopes of fomenting unrest amongst the soldiers, the Levellers therefore mounted the first direct challenge to the high command with *The Case of the Army Truly Stated* of October 1647.

For all its meanderings, *The Case*'s attempt to weave the grievances of the soldiers into a wider cause had a dangerous plausibility. The self-seeking grandees were, the Levellers claimed, preparing for disbandment with few guarantees against future abuse; the king might be left free to take revenge and the people thwarted of the liberties which – *The Case* insisted – the army had intended all along. Moreover, the soldiers had not yet secured indemnity for acts committed in war, and their arrears were growing as the taxpayers' strike continued. The generals were left little option but to respond. However much Fairfax sought to ease the country of its burdens, he was equally committed to retaining the trust of his men; he could not help but be concerned. Moreover, if not he, then certainly his subordinates could see the political need to preserve the unity of the army. They therefore moved swiftly to summon a general council, which began its meetings in a parish church on the outskirts of London on 28 October. The Putney debates are one of the most revealing and famous encounters in English history.

The debates centred on the Levellers' *Agreement of the People,* their attempt to provide a new constitution for England. Drawing on the ideas of Overton, and adapting the early parliamentarian claim that all power was in trust from the people, the *Agreement* argued that the people were the supreme power. Parliament ought therefore to be representative, and barred from acting in certain reserved fields. This preoccupation with fundamental law as a barrier to the state reveals as much as does Lilburne's rhetoric the continuity between radical Levellers and the conservative legalists of the 1620s parliaments; it also underlines the Levellers' political weakness, since those who aim to limit the state rarely make effective revolutionaries. Nevertheless, the grandees saw danger enough in the antinomian claims to personal inspiration which allowed some of the agitators to demand that constitutions and past agreements be dispensed with in the quest for security and freedom.

The Putney debates are chiefly known for the arguments on democracy. These saw Levellers argue variously for a wide franchise, while Colonel Rainsborough went as far as to speak for 'the poorest he that lives', urging that men (significantly he had no word for women) were only bound by their own consent. In reply, Ireton contested the apparent individualism of the Leveller case, defending a constitution rooted in history and in valid laws and agreements: the vote, he insisted, should be vested in property-owners, those with a 'fixed interest in the kingdom'. But the franchise was a peripheral issue to the Levellers, a means to godly reform in a variety of fields – the proposal of successive *Agreements* that political rights be granted only to signatories smacks more of the covenants of gathered churches than it does of democracy. Perhaps the greatest historical significance of the debates lies in what they reveal of Cromwell's painful ambivalence. The conservative gentleman who grimly retorted that Leveller antinomianism 'must end in anarchy' could yet speak long and passionately of the mind of God, and concede that forms of government were but 'dross and dung in comparison of Christ'. That tension, between the property-owner's yearning for order and the godly officer's belief that the army was somehow a gathered church of the saints, was to dominate Cromwell's career, and the history of England for the next decade.

The Leveller threat did not simply interrupt the larger drama. Although the grandees managed to conciliate the agitators at Putney, and then to impose discipline on mutinous soldiers declaring for the *Agreement* and 'England's Freedom, Soldiers' Rights,' Charles used the crisis to justify his escape from Hampton Court on 11 November. Thanks in part to the pens of Clarendon and of the poet Andrew Marvell, this has become an episode in the legend of Cromwell the Machiavellian. It certainly brought Charles nearer to the block; but

Cromwell was no republican, and had worked steadily that autumn for further negotiations. That Charles headed to new captivity in the Isle of Wight, where Cromwell's cousin, Robert Hammond, was governor, was more the result of misplaced hopes of aid, from both Hammond and nearby France, than of Cromwellian guile.

Charles's plans centred on his enemies falling out. As unable as most of his contemporaries to imagine that a settlement could be made without him, he expected to sell his support to, and then exploit, the highest bidder. The differences between Holles and the City on the one hand and the army on the other, and the improved terms offered him in the *Heads of Proposals,* only seemed to bear out his strategy; on 24 December they emboldened him to reject with biting sarcasm parliament's latest proposals, which were only marginally less harsh than those offered at Newcastle. His boldness stemmed from that constant source of confusion, the British dimension. The Scottish nobility, angered almost as much by the domineering clericalism of the militant kirk as by events in England, harkened readily to Hamilton's plans for redeeming national pride by restoring their king to his own. On 26 December a delegation of largely Hamiltonian Scots secretly concluded the Engagement with Charles, by which they agreed to help him impose a settlement on England: presbyterianism would be established for a mere three years, except in the royal household, and an assembly of divines, of whose support Charles was probably justly confident, would then give final shape to the church. The royalist-Scottish alliance which Charles had vainly sought in 1641 was finally consummated.

Charles's intransigence bred an equal and opposite response, and on 3 January 1648 a revealingly broad coalition in the Commons voted that no further addresses be made to the king. Exasperation was far from republicanism, for even now only about thirty radical MPs could see any alternative to a monarchical settlement. But some key figures who had earlier insisted on negotiations now left their options open. While Ireton declared that Charles had broken his contract with the people, Cromwell was inscrutable, as he so often was when on the verge of great events. He now declared his continued support for monarchy, 'unless necessity enforce an alteration'.

As instrumental in the drift towards renewed bloodshed as the tortuous diplomacy in the Isle of Wight was the suffering which wracked the country. Famine persisted as the rains fell, and the depression showed no sign of lifting. The anxious Essex clergyman Ralph Josselin noted early in 1648, it was 'a sad, dear time for poor people . . . money almost out of the country'. The cry for a return to normality could not be ignored, as the taxpayers' strike widened.

The discontents that welled up in 1648 were not simply material. Even as committed a parliamentarian as John Milton thought a cause had been corrupted, and yearned to see 'Public Faith [parliament's early borrowings from its supporters, who now despaired of repayment] cleard from the shamefull brand of Public Fraud'. The absence of either reform or settlement in the many months since the end of hostilities cast a tawdry light on the broken promises of 1642. That so many of the revolts of 1648 occurred in formerly parliamentarian counties reflects the growing realization of property-owners that what many had taken to be a godly cause was not worth the sacrifices it entailed.

The causes of disillusion were legion. No civil war could foster those liberties, especially to due legal process, minimal taxation and unhampered local government by men of local influence, for which many gentlemen had taken up arms. The steady replacement in office of the disenchanted by harder men in turn brought further centralization, as newcomers sought to compensate for their own lack of weight; and while peace in 1646 had partly reinvigorated the purged commissions of the peace, the hated county committees retained their punitive powers.

Still more alarming to many in the country was the plight of the church. As early as 1646 the Essex grand jury had received complaints from Great Burstead parish of antinomian outrages; but as yet the sects were localized, generally confined to the towns and – worrying enough – to the army. Perhaps more distressing, and certainly more glaring in their contrast with the hopes of 1641, were the signs of dereliction. Although some northern provincial courts still acted in the name of the archbishop of York as late as 1648, the church courts had on the whole fallen with the bishops; so too had the means of ordaining new clergy, while at the same time war and purge had created many gaps. About one-third of the parish livings in the new presbyterian province of London were vacant in 1648, and there were deficiencies aplenty elsewhere. Meanwhile Anglicanism retained its vitality, most visibly in the forcible restorations by parishioners of ejected royalist or Anglican clergymen against which parliament fulminated vainly in August 1647.

Parliament had attempted to fill the void. During 1645–6 the houses had laid the foundations of a presbyterian church, although they signally failed to build a clerical disciplinary structure. The majority in both houses had as little love for sectarianism as did the presbyterian rump of the Westminster assembly, and they had in 1644 remained singularly unmoved by Milton's *Areopagitica,* with its ringing cry that truth could only be advanced by free discussion. But a widespread erastian conviction of the supremacy of the secular power, of which John Selden was the most devastating advocate, was reinforced by a gut anticlericalism which disposed them against the strict presbyterianism urged by clergy and Covenanters. The moderate Sir John Holland probably spoke for many when he confessed that he would as readily 'live under the tyranny of the Turk as the tyranny of the clergy'. Such feelings were encouraged by the endless clerical bickering, which demonstrated to most that there was no scriptural blueprint for a national church and thus no grounds for clerical *iure divino* claims. Accordingly, when the houses coupled their promulgation in August 1645 of the Westminster assembly's directory of worship with ordinances in the following months establishing a hierarchical disciplinary structure of *classes* and presbyteries they reserved to themselves ultimate control. The essence of the scheme was the 'presbytration' of the old parish churches. Each parish was to elect lay elders, to assist the minister in disciplining the congregation; they were also to play a part in the election of representatives to the next level in the disciplinary hierarchy, the *classes*, which covered parts of counties. Above the *classes* were to be ranked county and national assemblies, all subordinate to parliament. As the redoubtable Scottish commissioner Dr Baillie concluded in disgust, it was but a 'lame erastian presbytery' – which was precisely what the houses wanted.

But despite its neatness the scheme was flawed. Not least, many gathered congregations had even by its inception formed outside the parish churches and thus outside the presbyterian system. A graver problem was presbyterianism's lack of appeal. In London and in south-east Lancashire – isolated as the latter was in a sea of anti-puritanism – many ministers and lay notables went promptly to work. But all told only eight of the forty English counties made any real effort to implement the scheme; even in London, only three-quarters of the scheduled *classes* appear to have operated, and often limply at that. Even discipline-hungry clergy had their doubts, for professional sentiments were involved. Some refused to associate with lay elders for whom they could see no more scriptural warrant than they could for parliament's new ecclesiastical supremacy: thus, a minister offered the living of St Margaret's, Fish St., London, in 1648 stipulated that before he accepted 'you which be elders shall wholly lay down your offices.' For their party, many laymen shunned an office which required them to scrutinize their neighbours' conduct and therefore guaranteed them unpopularity – and conversely, as one 1649 pamphlet observed, few parishioners would ever 'submit to come before the lay elders'.

With presbyterian discipline still-born, and episcopal dead, parish ministers were left struggling alone to reform their congregations, and many baulked. Exclusion from the communion service, the major sacrament, was the chief instrument for the correction of sinners which ministers possessed, and many were given pause when they found neither episcopal courts nor presbyteries to shelter behind. Too frightened to try to chastise his parishioners alone, Ralph Joselin ceased offering communion altogether at Earl's Colne in Essex in the later 1640s, and to the dismay of the large numbers of the laity who treasured the sacrament, Josselin was not alone. The widespread alternative to cessation appeared to be the abandonment of any attempt at discipline, and the offering of communion to all, including sinners. It was no wonder that the value, let alone the prospect, of godly rule seemed open to question, or that so many favoured a return to old ways.

Appropriately enough, the first sparks of renewed civil war flew over a religious festival. In a bloody fracas in the streets at Christmas 1647, Canterbury townsmen challenged parliament's 1644 ordinance against Christmas; later, and still more divisively, they extended that challenge into an assault in the courts on the whole structure of parliamentarian rule in their county. Bloodier, if short-lived, affrays followed in London and Norwich in April, and by the end of the month it was clear that a nation-wide upheaval was under way.

Ironically, the houses were themselves partly to blame. Recognizing their isolation, the political Independent leaders had solicited support in the country for the 'vote of no addresses'. As the self-declared 'honest party' used packed grand juries to vent their manifestly unrepresentative views, outraged gentry and clergy in county after county swung back into the political activity they had abandoned after the army's triumph of the previous summer. A spate of petitions in the spring of 1648 called for a treaty with the king, and for disbandment. They were given dangerous support when in Pembrokeshire Colonel Poyer, commanding a garrison which faced an unrewarded disbandment, threw in his lot with the petitioners. More ominously still, the crypto-royalist Engagers amongst the Sctos were at last raising troops to defend their king.

The imminence of further bloodletting galvanized the army. Believing that divine providence had determined the outcome of the first war, Fairfax's officers searched the grimmer books of scripture in an emotional three-day prayer meeting at Windsor at the end of April. Abasing themselves for their 'politic' dealings with a king now sacrilegiously intent on once more defiling the land, they apocalyptically identified Charles as 'that man of blood' foretold in prophecy. They vowed vengeance accordingly. But despite the vote of no addresses, the officers could not count on the support of the two

houses. Emboldened by the enthusiastic petitions, a resurgent conservative majority in the Commons of almost two to one abandoned
the vote of no addresses and passed a stern blasphemy ordinance,
directed primarily against the Baptists. In June the 'eleven members' of 1647 were allowed to resume their seats. Nevertheless, while
the two houses eagerly resumed their course of a year earlier they
were not yet ready to surrender to the king, especially to a king
imposed by the Scots.

In the first civil war the political nation had split down the middle;
the second can justly be called a revolt of the provinces against a hated
centre. Old cavaliers were active, in Cornwall, in Wales, in Yorkshire
and the far north; closer to London the weathervane earl of Holland
joined royalists in a futile bid to raise the Thames Valley. But in the
main the royalists were demoralized by defeat and by sequestration.
More typical protesters in 1648 were the rebellions sections of the
Kent and Essex trained bands, or of the fleet, for except in a few
puritan havens like Rye in Sussex enthusiasm for the godly cause had
largely evaporated. This did not necessarily breed a wholehearted
royalism – the south Wales forces, and the fleet, defected from parliament at least in part in fear of the material impact on themselves of the
remodelling parliament and Fairfax had set in train in late 1647. But
as the impressive petitions from around London showed, many former parliamentarian activists were desperate to persuade moderates
at Westminster of the need to return to old ways while they still could.

The key to the resolution of the crisis lies in the word 'persuade'.
Many counties, like Surrey or Dorset, issued strident petitions and
then stood back to watch their effect. In the fleet the return of the old
sea-dog, Warwick, to command calmed much of the storm, and ultimately all but ten ships returned to their allegiance. More revealing
still are events in Kent, where some seven thousand took up arms,
probably aiming to coerce by demonstration rather than by violence
– as of course had been the case with many in 1642. The bulk of the
county's gentry united in May in a scarcely disloyal petition to
parliament against the county committee machine of the quarrelsome
Sir Anthony Weldon, which they had so long resented; neither was
there any compelling reason why their other demand, that parliament
negotiate with the king, should have occasioned violence. They were
driven to arms by the efforts of the county committee and of a frightened parliament to block their petition by force; nevertheless, the
'rebels' remained in essence petitioners, and their leaders strove to
distance themselves from opportunist cavaliers. It was, not surprisingly, contingents led by ex-royalists who finally fought it out with
Fairfax in the streets of Maidstone.

The Kent rebellion illustrates the weakness of localism as a political force in its own right. The rebels compounded their hostility to the centre with a fatal deference to it: they were acting for Kent, and were unwilling either to push their protest to extremes or to co-operate with other malcontents. Their attitude appears to have been common, and the rather different developments in neighbouring Essex provide little in the way of an exception. The local focus of gentry resentment in puritan Essex was much less significant, for there the pre-war élite had survived more or less intact. The county leaders were therefore less willing than those in Kent to risk unleashing the welling popular discontent in an unprecedentedly rainy famine summer. Their restraint allowed royalists to take the lead and gave a harder edge to the revolt, which endured a long and bitter siege in Colchester.

The rebels' lack of co-ordination permitted the government's forces to pick them off piecemeal. London, wary anyway after the 1647 crisis, and Norwich were quelled before Kent rose; the troubles in Kent were collapsing when rebellion flared in Essex; and the upheaval there was contained, and Colchester safely besieged, when the Scots at last entered England. The isolation of the Scots was probably not accidental, for many English rebels hoped to achieve a treaty with the king before the hated Scots could bring their own views to bear; furthermore, many northern royalists so despised them as 'judases' for 'selling' the king in the winter of 1646–7 that they refused to collaborate.

The Scots had troubles enough. The collapse of the alliance of kirk and nobility deprived the insufficiently godly Engagers of clergy willing to preach a holy war. Delayed by recruitment problems and by political squabbles, the Engager army did not cross the border until July, and it was then hampered by appalling weather as it straggled south into Lancashire. The lethargy and indecisiveness of Hamilton compounded his followers' woes, for it allowed Colonel Lambert's small Yorkshire force to delay him until Cromwell came up, fresh from quashing the south Wales revolt. In a brilliant running fight, from 17–19 August, Cromwell destroyed the much larger Scottish force around Preston. With the fall of Colchester to Fairfax ten days later the Second Civil War was virtually over.

The fighting confirmed the army's mood of the April prayer-meeting at Windsor – even the normally courteous Fairfax had two of the Colchester royalists summarily shot, and Cromwell was transformed. Seeing 'nothing but the hand of God' at Preston, he now concluded that justice must be done upon those who had questioned God's 'outward dispensations' of 1642–6 and – almost as great a crime in Cromwell's English eyes – sought 'to vassalize us to a foreign nation' by bringing in the Scots. But should justice extend to the king, as

some of the godly demanded? Cromwell was unsure, and characteristically turned aside to pacify the north and to await further guidance
from providence. 'Waiting on the Lord,' he left the nation's destiny
in the capable and relentless hands of his son-in-law, Henry Ireton.

The problems facing Ireton were awesome. Amongst the least was
that of shepherding Fairfax in a direction to which the latter was
temperamentally averse. He showed still greater dexterity in dealing
with the Levellers, who might yet have disturbed soldiers whose
inchoate militancy had hardened in the turmoils of 1648. Fortunately
for Ireton, the Levellers showed considerable concern for the common cause, and when in August – and probably with malicious intent
– the Commons released Lilburne from one of his many imprison-
ments 'Freeborn John' assured Cromwell of his goodwill. Accordingly, during the crucial winter months Ireton was able to sidetrack
the Levellers' demands for the freedom of the people into lengthy
committee discussions on general principles.

Ireton orchestrated the army with a watchful eye to parliament's
rush to settlement. Even during the fighting the houses had been
preparing for fresh talks with Charles, and on 15 September their
commissioners arrived at Newport on the Isle of Wight. Former
middle-groupers such as Lord Saye, who had hotly supported the
'vote of no addresses', now clamoured for an agreement; whether or
not they found regicide too awful to contemplate, they could share the
aversion of the younger Vane for the growing prospect of army rule.
But the negotiations dragged in face of Charles's habitual evasiveness, as he sought to set his enemies at odds. He confided to
friends that this would be but a 'mock-treaty', to buy time; perhaps in
consequence, he appeared willing to concede control of the militia for
twenty years. But the sticking-point was his refusal to surrender
episcopacy for more than three years – the Anglican martyr's crown
he thus gained would have seemed unlikely when he abandoned
Laud, or when he neglected the prayer book during his captivity in
1646–7. He presumably still felt as he had when facing the Covenanters in the late 1630s that without episcopacy monarchy could
not stand. But despite the rebuff, parliament would undoubtedly
have come to a settlement, if left to itself. Although it is hard to believe
that many thought Charles could ever be trusted, they saw even
greater dangers in their own allies than in the king.

Parliament was not, however, to be left to itself. On 20 November
the army presented to the Commons its *Remonstrance*, in which Ireton
argued forcefully that the people were the origin of all power, the king
had repeatedly broken his contract with them, and God had repeatedly witnessed against him. In the name of the safety of the people,
the supreme law, justice must be done against 'the capital and grand

author of our troubles'. Then followed proposals for electoral reform, which may not wholly have been sops to the radicals. But Ireton stopped short of advancing a republican solution, for he had to carry not only Fairfax but also Cromwell along with him, and Cromwell was likely to regard any advocacy of a *programme* as 'fleshly reasoning', a sinful assertion of human will and a slighting of God's providences. His way was to 'wait upon the Lord' for a dispensation, a posture which the unsympathetic understandably saw as mere opportunism. While the judgments of the Second Civil War convinced Cromwell of the inappropriateness of his strictures of 1647 against the use of force, those judgments did not show a clear way forward. Accordingly, while he made no move to alter Ireton's course, he only arrived in London – and it must have been intentional – *after* his son-in-law had initiated the revolution.

Ireton did not, however, have a completely free hand. On 5 December the Commons voted by 129:83 that Charles's answers at Newport were grounds to continue negotiating, a vote that the army concluded – probably rightly – heralded the return of Charles to London, upon which all attempts to impose conditions on the king would collapse. Next day Colonel Pride's musketeers blocked the stairs into parliament, to enforce the army's will. Ireton had wanted to dissolve an assembly which he saw as hardened in corruption and – in not the last instance of misplaced military faith in the electorate – to hold new elections on a reformed franchise; but he was dissuaded by radical MPs like Edmund Ludlow and Thomas Scot, who had a more realistic sense of public opinion. Furthermore, although republicans, they recoiled both from the breach with the past that a dissolution would bring, and from the prospect of the soldiers in power. Ireton's own readiness to appeal to history against the Levellers at Putney may have made him easier to persuade. But in succumbing to the promptings of those desperate for a semblance of continuity he took the incipient revolution the first of its many steps towards conservatism; Cromwell, far more conservative by temperament, was to accelerate the process. Pride's Purge was therefore a purge and not a dissolution, excluding about 110 MPs; around 160 more, including some radicals like the younger Vane (who had eventually denounced the Newport treaty), withdrew in protest. By the middle of January 1649 the remaining 'rump' had difficulty in reaching a quorum of forty.

But Cromwell, who took the initiative after his arrival on 7 December, intended neither that the revolution should become uncontrolled nor that it should degenerate into farce. He immediately set about persuading seceders to return, however much this diluted godly fire with constitutionalist scruples. And in late December he made a last effort to persuade Charles to surrender all his powers. Although it is often assumed that Pride's Purge led inevitably to the republic, to Cromwell and certainly to a number of others in the Commons a drastic purge to avert a sell-out did not mean regicide. Nevertheless, fearful lest his more radical subordinates should seek a real revolution, Cromwell dared go no further, and responded to Charles's rebuff by characteristically bending with opinion in the army in order to contain it. No republican himself, he now concluded that 'providence and necessity' gave a united verdict – the king's head must be the price of the preservation of order. Relieving his tensions in bouts of horseplay, he was urged onwards by the vengeful cries of Hugh Peter from the Whitehall pulpit.

The high court of justice which the leaders of the Commons and the army appointed had the unprecedented task of bringing a king to his death in the open: not for these godly men a hugger-mugger murder. In the attempt to substantiate the *Remonstrance*'s claims that sovereignty lay in the people – and to substitute for the refusal of the judges and the Lords to co-operate – the managers nominated to the high court a cross-section of the godly cause in parliament, army, London and the country. With few exceptions the handful of peers and greater gentry refused to accept their nominations; but even had Fairfax, the younger Vane, or Haselrig, agreed to serve on the court, it would have made little difference to the attitude of king or country. Charles refused to recognize the court's authority, and instead maintained as he had always done that his trust came from God rather than the people. His bearing at the trial, and then in the cold on the scaffold on 30 January 1649, was undoubtedly the most dignified of his career, and for once his stammer left him. He did far more for the cause of kingship than he had ever achieved during his life, and the cult of Charles the Martyr was not wholly generated by the pious meditations of *Eikon Basilike*, ghost-written by the royalist cleric John Gauden. The huge groan that rose from the crowd when the axe fell challenged the radicals' claims that power originated in the people. To the appalled watchers, and to the eager purchasers of the thirty-six editions of *Eikon Basilike* which appeared in the next year, the headsman had seemed to strike at a divine order.

The widespread fears that regicide betokened a total overturning were, however, unfounded. To some of the zealots, Charles's execution indeed heralded the millennium, foretold in *Revelations*. But for Cromwell, although a saint, even for Ireton, and certainly for many of their allies in the Commons, Charles had not died for any ideological reasons. He had died because, as the Scots had found earlier, it was impossible to come to an agreement with him; and in a monarchical state it was impossible to come to a settlement without him.

10 The Commonwealth 1649-1653

In a society so custom-bound, the killing of the king could not but seem to have special meaning. For probably the overwhelming majority of the political nation it reinforced the fears of social disintegration which had long been evident. Many even of the godly followed the course taken by the voluble William Prynne – who had been Laud's victim as well as one of Colonel Pride's – from hopes of a new dawn at the start of the decade to grim outrage at the end. The steady drift into disillusionment is one of the most obvious features of the 1640s and 1650s. Yet equally important is the counterpoint, as some radical protestants grew more than ever convinced that the age of the spirit, in which Antichrist would fall, was at hand. Even Cromwell, who had not been driven onwards by prophetic hopes, soon looked back to a remarkable manifestation of God's purpose. Colonel Harrison went further, greeting 'the day, God's own day, wherein he is coming forth in glory in the world'.

In the revolutionary years, therefore, a daunting array of groups and individuals claimed to bear witness to a new divine dispensation. The 1640s had seen the appearance of 'seekers', lonely consciences who passed through one after another of the gathered churches in search of some sign from God which would redeem the corruption of all current forms of worship. The collapse of political institutions made it easy to conclude that the age of the law, and not merely the age of churches, had ended – to the gleeful proto-communist Gerrard Winstanley, 'the old world' seemed to be 'running up like parchment in the fire'. What more natural than that the spirit should fill the void?

It is important not to attribute too great a coherence to radical thought. Many were the unlettered men and women who grew convinced in these turbulent and iconoclastic times that God had granted them some personal illumination, or even union with the godhead, empowering them to denounce existing authorities. The John Robins who claimed to be God the Father and his wife the expectant mother of the new Christ may not have been typical, but the strain of crude popular enthusiasm, blasphemy, and often sheer cynical irreligion, cannot be ignored. Nevertheless, one very common theme can be identified. The early Christian church had defused the apocalypse by asserting an undying church on earth and an immortal soul: Christ's kingdom upon earth was thus both now and – in practice – never. That device shattered as belief in an imminent end to time heightened. Perhaps encouraged by fashionable neo-Platonism and by the materialism of the early scientists, as well as by the millennialist climate, Milton, Overton, Walwyn, Winstanley and many less famous names held that the soul perished with the body, to be revived at the approaching Armageddon. Mortalism, 'soul-sleeping', challenged the claims of all established churches to be *the* visible church, since if the saints died, the church could only be the congregations of which they were members for their time on earth. Mortalism also seemed to guarantee the end of all order, as its conservative opponents readily misidentified it with materialist atheism, and assumed that mortalists denied the existence of an after-life. Such a denial was appalling enough as a religious heresy. But as Hobbes recognized in *The Leviathan,* belief in divine rewards and punishments hereafter was the ultimate prop of states with inadequate coercive powers. Worse still, a soul that perished might be of one substance with the body, which would imply that the flesh was good in the same way as was the soul. Freedom of the spirit might, and did, then become freedom for the flesh. Gentry as well as clergy felt they had much to lose.

Freud rather than the more fashionable Marx might better interpret these radicals, for the prevalence of libertarian antinomianism in the revolution suggests a reaction against the insistent authoritarianism of a patriarchal Calvinist society. The Ranters above all, few in number though prominent in the nightmares of their many enemies, are the most revealing. Laurence Clarkson, 'captain of the Rant', held a characteristic antinomian position when he asserted that to the pure in spirit all things are pure, and that sin 'hath its conception only in the imagination'; yet Abiezer Coppe's remarkable advocacy of swearing probably served not only as an affirmation of spiritual freedom but also as therapy for consciences overburdened by the puritan stress on sin. Equally novel was the way Ranters and other enthusiasts revelled in those seventeenth-century narcotics, alcohol and tobacco, in hopes of releasing the spirit within the flesh. But the impact of the Ranters cannot be appreciated merely by imagining the eruption of 1960s flower children into high Victorian society. The orthodox held that property and government had been instituted to restrain the consequences of sin. If there were no more sin, if God had his 'light and dark sides', in the words of Joseph Bauthumley, then what would follow, especially in such a time of hunger and resentment? Coppe provided an answer in his 1649 pamphlet, *A Fiery Flying Roll,* in which he coupled an extravagant hymn to the unity of spirit and flesh, to 'my majesty within me', with a violent denunciation of the great ones of the earth.

Another manifestation of the widespread reaction against the Calvinist disjuncture between the corrupt material world – the flesh – and the spirit proved just as unnerving. On 1 April 1649 a small group of poor men and women followed in the footsteps of countless squatters on waste land by digging up the common at St George's Hill in what is now suburban Surrey. But the leadership of Gerrard Winstanley, a bankrupt cloth merchant, transformed these 'Diggers'. Like the Ranters, the idealistic Winstanley believed that the spirit was within all men; but more than that, like some neo-Platonists before him he saw God in the material world too. The way to save mankind was therefore through harmony with the world, and he even advocated scientific lectures instead of church services on Sundays. Believing that private property had corrupted man, he saw salvation only in the holding of all things in common. St George's Hill was to be but a beginning. But as the Digger colony failed in face of local harassment and harsh weather, Winstanley retreated from his millennial hopes. In his communistic utopia, *The Law of Freedom,* of 1652 he showed an almost Calvinist sense of man's propensity to sin and of the importance of government.

Winstanley was not the only radical to grow pessimistic. The world was not turned upside down. A political revolution occurring in a context of enormous suffering in fact bred surprisingly little popular excitement, for the poor did little more than try to keep alive. At one level their response was of momentous significance. Although the economy was by now sufficiently varied for the population as a whole to avoid the starvation that devastated parts of Europe and Scotland, the appalling harvests and epidemics of the later 1640s confirmed a conclusion that with hindsight we can see had long been evident. Rising prices, the mounting pressure of squatters on wastes and woodland, the migration to the towns and to the New World, had all pointed to the exhaustion of resources. A higher proportion of the population, particularly of the unmarried males, emigrated in the later 1640s and the 1650s than at any other time until the late nineteenth century. Intimate responses to the years of adversity were similarly unambiguous. Couples with only gloomy prospects before them delayed their marriages for some two or three years, and seem too to have practised other primitive forms of contraception, thus limiting the size of their families – an effect achieved equally by endemic disease, which had by this time measurably reduced life expectancy. The easing in the 1650s of population pressure ushered in the long and economically decisive period of more stable food prices.

The social record too underlines how unfounded were the fears of the gentry. As we have seen, class consciousness was extremely limited, and there was only one major strike – by Newcastle keelmen – in the 1650s. Moreover, arguments that the 'industrious sort' were the power-house of radicalism clash with the hostility of London craftsmen and artisans to competition in these years from projects to employ the poor, or of urban craftsmen everywhere to attempts to help disbanded soldiers by relaxing corporate restrictions. Still more revealing, in view of widespread troubles in the sixteenth century and in 1607, was the agrarian quiet. After some scattered enclosure riots in the turmoil of the early 1640s, agrarian protest during the revolution was confined to the old flash-points of the fens and the south-western forests. The absence of any wider outbreak says much of the impact of the economic and cultural polarization of the villages – realizing how much they had to lose, yeomen who might have given a political lead acquiesced as parish officers across the country raised the poor rate to feed the hungry. The tranquillizing effect of such social fissures may also have been reinforced by a change in popular attitudes. The deaths of monarchs in 1603 and, to a lesser extent, in 1625 seem to have occasioned minor crime waves, as the criminous alleged that the law had died with the prince; the silence in 1649, when monarchy itself died, suggests the steady spread of the sense that law and the state were impersonal. It also points to the basic orderliness of society.

If the poor were not revolutionaries, no more were their masters. The pragmatic origins of the republic were reflected in its subsequent uneasy history, as those in power were driven to take a step back for each one they took forward.

The ambiguities of the Rump are clear. 1648–9 brought the only revolution in English history, not only in the forms of politics, in the abolition of monarchy and the house of Lords, but also in the personnel. With the possible exception of Barebone's parliament in 1653 the Rump was accompanied by the greatest ever displacement of the traditional governors from office. Precious few noblemen were active at the centre or in the localities during the commonwealth – the disgusted Lord Saye even retired to his island fastness of Lundy. But this was not 1789, for the men who ruled were still gentlemen, albeit somewhat poorer than those they replaced; and they conspicuously lacked a revolutionary ideology. Many aspired towards the millennium, and the commonwealth's admiral, Robert Blake, was in 1651 to proclaim in the city square at Cadiz the imminent end of all earthly monarchies. But most remained content with the conventional – and imprecise – ideal of the godly commonwealth. Some even made a virtue of their imprecision. The characteristic Independent position, advanced repreatedly by Cromwell, and by the great Independent divine John Owen in the 1650s, was merely that God had left mankind free – and obliged – to erect the state which best conduced to godliness. The Rump contained only a handful of convinced republicans, classically educated, often rationalist figures like Algernon Sidney and Henry Nevile.

The essential pragmatism of the Rumpers is apparent in the way they acted first and only later justified themselves. Thus, Charles died on 30 January, while monarchy was only abolished on 17 March; only in May was England declared 'a commonwealth and free state'. The disparaging reference of the royalist John Evelyn to 'unkingship' was not inappropriate. The demise of the house of Lords was similarly undoctrinaire. It was voted down on 6 February, to be abolished, 'useless and dangerous', on 19 March – its 'uselessness' was apparent in the shrinking attendances during the 1640s, to a mere half-dozen after the Purge.

The Rump's ideological lameness is apparent in its supporters' accounts. John Goodwin, a religious Independent, argued in 1649 in *Right and Might Well Met* that consent was essential to government and that the people might change their rulers; but faced with the obvious *lack* of consent, he lamely retorted that necessity justified the army's actions. John Milton had already made a similar prudent retreat from the cause of godly nation and people into his characteristic élitism. Denouncing the 'besotted' people for being taken in by *Eikon Basilike,* he now proclaimed an aristocracy of the virtuous, 'fit though few' as he was to call them later in his greatest poem. Such men had a God-given right, which he propounded in 1649 in *The Tenure of Kings and Magistrates,* to change their rulers when they saw fit to preserve *their* – and not the people's – liberty. Little wonder that most justifications of the Rump by local magistrates merely counselled acceptance of St Paul's injunction to obey 'the powers that be'.

Such lack of fervour gives the measure of the Rump, and paradoxically explains how it gained the acquiescence of much of the political nation. Dangers loomed on every hand: vengeful Scots to the north, the festering sore of Ireland, Leveller stirrings in the army, across the Channel an outraged continent which applauded as royalist exiles assassinated English ambassadors to the Netherlands and to Spain, an empty treasury groaning under the burden of dishonoured wartime debts. Furthermore, the old problem of low attendances at Westminster had grown to embarrassing proportions. Now was not the time for a reforming crusade which might further estrange conservatives from the old parliamentarian coalition. Accordingly, in the spring of 1649 Cromwell laboured to persuade MPs who had withdrawn in protest to return to Westminster. In this he appears, remarkably, to have gained the co-operation of harder men such as Ludlow, Scot and Colonel Harrison. The revolutionaries themselves ensured the frustration of reformers' hopes by willingly admitting mere conformists. They were, after all, gentlemen, and when so much seemed at risk they deliberately turned to fellow-gentlemen rather than the assorted radicals who urged them in other directions.

Those early reinforcing the consequences of Ireton's decision to purge rather than to dissolve, exposed what was to prove the Rump's fatal dilemma. Although the sword was its only preservative, the soldiers to whom the Rump was beholden signified both a distasteful social and political radicalism and also military interference. If there was one thing parliament-men had acquired during the long decade of parliamentary rule in the 1640s it was a sense of the importance of parliament, and Pride's Purge offended that sense. Throughout its life the Rump tried to distance itself from its creator, seeking instead the support of the conservative gentlemen against whom the Purge had been directed. In the spring of 1649 the Rump conspicuously failed to elect Ireton to its new executive, the council of state. Thereafter, army pressure for reform bred an equal and opposite reaction.

The history of the Rump must be written around the problem of survival. And for all the threatening noises from Europe about the blasphemous English, and for all the Scots' anger at the death of *their* king, the immediate threat was a domestic one.

The grievances of the soldiery still rankled, and the Levellers were still eager to profit. The Leveller leaders had been confirmed in their suspicions of the grandees when the officers failed to press on parliament in the New Year the compromise Agreement of the People thrashed out in the discussions of late 1648. However impressive his advocacy of electoral reform, separation of powers and freedom for godly consciences, it was clear that Ireton had sought to buy time. Lilburne, Walwyn and Overton greeted this new hypocrisy with a devastating series of pamphlets in the spring of 1649. *England's New Chains Discovered* lambasted the alliance of army and Rump for its unprecedented consolidation of powers, and *The Hunting of the Foxes* vividly indicted Cromwell's now notorious ability to share the aspirations of both radicals and conservatives:

> You shall scarce speak to Cromwell about any thing, but he will lay his hands on his breast, elevate his eyes, and call God to record, he will weep, howl and repent, even while he doth smite you under the first rib.

The Rump seemed frightened enough, and arrested the authors; Cromwell for his part warned the council of state, 'If you do not break them, they will break you.'

But the Levellers' constituency was disintegrating. The saints gathered in the London churches and amongst the junior officers grew wary of the two heretics, Walwyn and Overton, and embarrassed too at disruptive Leveller tactics. More importantly, Ireton had in the immediate aftermath of the revolution persuaded the Rump to increase the soldiers' pay and to secure their arrears through the sale of crown lands – only time was to reveal the damage such moves did to the regime's precarious finances. Disturbances in the spring of 1649 amongst the soldiers were in consequence easily quelled. A swift onslaught by Fairfax and Cromwell at Burford in Oxfordshire on 14 May, and a handful of executions, effectively ended the Leveller threat, though 'freeborn John' Lilburne's voice continued to resound in the wilderness into the 1650s. Occasional murmurings in the army greeted officers' speculation in lands sold to redeem the soldiers' debentures for their back-pay; but once arrears began to be paid off the army never again seemed likely to rise. Furthermore, the execution of Charles and of leading royalists like Hamilton and Holland seems to have satisfied some of the resentful passions of the troops. Political revolution thus helped avert social upheaval.

The pacification of the army cleared the way for the Rump to turn its attention to Ireland, where its efforts were to prove as notorious to posterity as the killing of the king did to contemporaries.

The Rump's motives for looking to Ireland were various. Despite the hysteria it had generated, Ireland remained a secondary concern during the Civil War. Parliament diverted resources to campaigns closer to home, and Charles in the 1643 Cessation sought to co-opt the few English troops left in the country. It had been left to a small Scottish expeditionary force in Ulster to conduct a holding operation as the Catholic Confederacy tightened its grip. But the malign neglect could not continue, since the end of the Thirty Years War put a flood of mercenaries on the market while Ireland offered a potential base for Charles I's young heir, the future Charles II. Furthermore, a campaign against the Catholic Irish might unite English protestants and more important, preoccupy a potentially dangerous army. The army's council of officers in 1649 and Walwyn the Leveller were virtually alone in calling for humane treatment for the Irish. But while the latter may have been doomed by the thirst for vengeance for the massacre of 1641, their sufferings were intensified by the Rump's financial problems. Both king and parliament had in 1642 invited private capital to finance the reconquest, and both had seen Irish lands as the only feasible repayment for the 'adventurers' for Ireland. The need to reward unpaid soldiers from the same source only intensified the destruction.

The Irish campaign is the great blot on Cromwell's record, although his success preserved the regime. In the care with which he prepared the impressive expedition which set out in July 1649 he had an eye to a hostile audience on both sides of the Irish Sea. Knowing that the gathering Scottish threat required his speedy return, immediately after landing Cromwell stormed Drogheda, to the north of Dublin, and put its garrison to the sword for refusing to surrender. Many civilians perished in the slaughter, and Drogheda forms the basis for a legend of Cromwellian atrocity which gained strength from a second massacre at Wexford. His actions certainly accorded with the laws of war – Prince Rupert's sack of Bolton in 1644 had been brutal enough – and Hiroshima has made his calculation familiar: harshness now will save time and avert future bloodshed. But the exultation of his letter to parliament on the 'marvellous great mercy', the 'righteous judgment of God', shows that the blood guilt of 1641 was being avenged; and the disturbing fact that Drogheda had only fallen to the Confederacy in 1649, rather than 1641, shows that Cromwell was willing to damn the whole nation. In this he was not unusual. Protestant settlers in Ireland were eager to magnify Irish guilt in order to maximize the amount of land to be seized. But Cromwell, like so many English protestants, had been swept up in the apocalyptic fervour of 1641, and saw in the Irish in arms not only a troublesome enemy but Antichrist.

Although in the spring of 1650 Cromwell returned to England, leaving only a mopping-up for his successors, attitudes changed little. Indeed, they probably hardened when the war became less a matter of sieges and more of anti-guerilla operations. As the commander of the new Wexford garrison reported,

> In searching the woods and bogs, we found great store of corn, which we burnt, also all the houses and cabins we could find: in all which we found great plenty of corn. We continued burning and destroying for four days: in which time we wanted no provision for horse or man, finding housing enough to lie in; though we burnt our quarters every morning, and continued burning all day.

The autumn of 1649 saw the beginning of what was to become a characteristic cycle. Victories in Ireland, like other victories later, relieved the worst pressures on the regime and allowed most Rumpers to hope for a return to normality. Yet victory also encouraged the army to speak up for reform. In 1649 in particular the council of officers could not help but raise its voice, for continuing rains had ruined another harvest, and all around could be heard the tramping feet of the hungry. Although few officers contemplated major social change, they were soon discussing law and tithe reform. But the Rumpers recoiled in horror from reform at a time of radical upsurge.

September brought the last Leveller mutiny in the army; in October, to the Rump's dismay, a London grand jury tumultuously acquitted Lilburne of treason. The strength of discontent in the capital was made even clearer in December when Lilburne and Colonel Pride were elected to the common council by groups pressing for a democratic restructuring of London's politics.

Although the Rump responded to army promptings by taking up good causes, it as always found the sheer doing of business more urgent than the luxury of reform. It had other reasons too for inaction. Fear of the king rather than commitment to reform had brought together this heterogeneous body of puritans, and there was still much to be afraid of. The radicals were dangerous enough, and the Rump promptly blocked Lilburne's election; but more alarming was the sullenness of the country as the rain and rents continued to fall and prices soared. In December 1649 the Rump propitiated its enemies by reducing the assessment from £90,000 a month – inadequate enough to support an army of 47,000 – to £60,000 after three months, thus plunging the commonwealth deeper into financial crisis. Its financial desperation also drove it to remove the main prop of the county committees, long the object of universal hostility. By taking into its own hands control over sequestered royalist estates and over the 'composition' fines for their release it deprived the committees of their main revenue, and the support for their local troops.

Even more striking than this display of political presbyterianism was the Rump's donning of the presbyterians' religious clothes. It moved swiftly to counter sectarian excesses by reimposing the censorship which had collapsed in 1641, and its success can be seen as the flood of pamphlets from the presses abated after 1650. Although in August 1649 the Rumpers failed by the narrow margin of the Speaker's casting vote to reinforce the national presbyterian church, in the following spring an act for the observance of the sabbath was followed by others against adultery, fornication, swearing and blasphemy, all hastened by dismay at the Ranters. The act against adultery is the most notorious of these measures, though contemporaries appear not to have been shocked by the double standard which reserved the death penalty for women. Local courts anyway were reluctant to use the fierce penalties, even against Ranters; there are only four known death sentences for adultery, and perhaps twenty prosecutions under the blasphemy act. But the drive for discipline may have had some effect – the corporation of Newcastle in 1652 bought 500 copies of an abridgement of the moral statutes, and many puritans in the Restoration wilderness paid tribute to the good effects of the 1650 code. To the frustration of many in the army, the Rump was by no means the tolerant creature of the Independents.

The defensive posture does not however, seem to have impressed its intended audience, and discontent continued. Accordingly, in January 1650 the frightened Rumpers extended a new loyalty test, the Engagement, to all adult males, barring non-subscribers from office, and from legal proceedings. Although the undertaking required was minimal, a mere declaration of obedience to the current government, the Engagement was a major political mistake. In demanding more than mere passive acquiescence as the warrant for full citizenship it concentrated attention on the propriety of allegiance to usurpers and on the degree to which other oaths were being breached. Fairfax was driven 'melancholy mad' over it, and the diaries of presbyterian clergy tell an anguished story of attempts to square providences with past obligations.

The Engagement had the great benefit, for posterity at least, of driving men to think of the grounds of government. While obligations to duly constituted authority had been the central theme of political thought since the Reformation, theorizing about *power* had been strikingly absent in England. But the execution of the king underlined a conclusion which had become steadily more apparent throughout the decade, that duly constituted authorities were disappearing fast. The controversy over the Engagement thus forced Englishmen to confront what government was and what its claims were, questions the avowed conservatism of both sides in the civil war had enabled them to avoid.

The appeal to conservatives was the most eye-catching part of the debate. Several works, such as the turncoat Marchamont Nedham's *Case of the Commonwealth Truly Stated,* urged the novel thesis of the irrelevance of moral considerations to government. Taking to an extreme the Calvinist view of human depravity they bleakly saw in protection the over-riding purpose, and therefore in the sword the inescapable reality, of government. But in his essays in the government's newspaper *Mercurius Politicus,* whose editorship he earned for his labours, Nedham introduced a more positive element. His contention, that in a republic shaped after republican Rome the citizen could best find liberty as well as a dynamic national purpose, suggests that the Rump's supporters may not have been limited to the radical godly. A similar ambiguity is visible in Andrew Marvell's brilliant appreciation of Cromwell in his 'Horatian Ode'. While the poem closes with Cromwell holding the sword erect in a way which puts Marvell close to the other Engagement theorists, it also raises the possibility that Cromwell might introduce an apparently classical liberty to Europe. But neither Nedham nor even Marvell quite represents the high-point of the Engagement controversy. Thomas Hobbes's masterpiece, *The Leviathan,* appeared in 1651. Hobbes had for some time been endeavouring to build a *science* of politics, based on fashionable Euclidean geometry and divorced from the private judgments which had brought ruin to England. In *The Leviathan,* which is so much part of the contemporary debate, he argued forcefully and coherently that the only criterion of the legitimacy of government is, not some subjective religious standard or the false aura of antiquity, but the ruler's capacity to offer protection. For, given the essential egotism of mankind, it is protection that all need. This – Hobbes left unspoken – the Rump as the sitting tenant could provide.

The nature of the Rump's campaign for support, and of local reactions to it, is revealing. Where local administrators had been closely identified with political presbyterianism the Rump deemed action necessary. In Herefordshire, dominated by the presbyterian Harley family, about 40 per cent of the membership of the county's various committees changed in 1649. Equally sweeping were the changes in south Wales, where the rebellions of 1648 had revealed the moderation, or blatant royalism, of many of the gentry; the outcome was the hegemony for the next decade of a tiny Baptist clique around Philip Jones. Still more obviously, London had to be purged, and in the carefully controlled City elections of 21 December 1648 two-thirds of the common councillors departed. The new purge completed the transfer of power, begun in 1641, from the merchant princes of the older European and eastern trades towards lesser, and more adventurous, traders to the colonies. But where it could the Rump avoided sweeping purges in fear of driving further wedges into the political nation. In Chester at least the Engagement seems never to have been tendered, and it was not until July 1651 that the corporation of Coventry was purged.

Many local officials were equally willing to live and let live: thus, almost 40 per cent of the members of Barnstaple corporation in 1642 were still serving in 1650. But it is unwise to assume with some recent historians that the overriding philosophy of all local governors was that government must go on. The mayor of Exeter threw into the gutter the proclamation of the commonwealth, and there and in Southampton a quorum for corporation meetings proved hard to find. While few JPs had been active in Devon even before Pride's Purge, thereafter order collapsed in some places, especially in the moorlands, and reports of a rise in crime elsewhere probably owed something to the reluctance of many JPs to act as well as to the stricken economy. The overburdening of the few active 'pack horses', as the Cornish Rumper John Moyle called them, as much as the desire to remove enemies exposed by the Engagement led the Rump to a more widespread purge later in 1650. In the extreme cases of Bedfordshire and Cheshire over one-third of the JPs were removed. The Rump thereby

confessed the failure of its moderate courses of 1649–50, and by calling yet more new men, and army officers, into local government
further increased gentry resentment.

Matters scarcely improved. 1651 saw demoralizingly sparse attendances of the Somerset gentry at the local assizes, and all over the
country assize courts rang with a remarkable series of defensive
sermons by reliable clergy on the necessity of magistracy.

The winter of 1649–50 was a bleak time for those in power. The
council of officers wondered if God had turned away his face, and the
younger Vane was convinced that 'the whole kingdom would rise and
cut their throats upon the first good occasion.'

The Rump's vulnerability grew patent when in the early months of
1650 the young Charles Stuart, his hopes in Ireland dashed, swallowed his pride and moved towards the Scottish Covenanters his
father had thought so hostile to monarchy. To meet the threat of a
royalist-presbyterian alliance the Rump determined on a pre-emptive
strike across the border, though this only increased the regime's
domestic problems as Fairfax resigned his command in protest.

Fortunately for the Rump, the Scots were equally disunited.
Hamilton's defeat in 1648 had brought the proscription from political
life of the Engagers, those who had 'engaged with' Charles I, creating
an enduring fissure between the nobility and the clericalists. The
government of the kirk party with which the young Charles II reluctantly came to terms was therefore politically isolated, its support
largely confined to the fervently presbyterian south-west, and with
Argyll its only major noble ally. It was a marriage of desperation for
both sides, since the kirk had few illusions about the roystering
Charles Stuart. Nevertheless, in June 1650 the Covenanters set about
raising a godly host, dismaying their generals by purging any supporters of the Engagers.

Cromwell, Fairfax's successor as lord general and by now in the
eyes of some Rumpers their sole prop, must have seen little to hope
for. He had characteristically preserved his rear by conciliating the
radicals, Lilburne, Ludlow and ex-Cornet Joyce; but June was late in
the campaigning season to be heading north, and he lacked men,
money and supplies. The army's fervently millenarian declaration
from Musselburgh on its way into Scotland, that it had taken Jesus to
be its king, can be taken as a gesture of desperation rather than
of confidence. David Leslie, Cromwell's old ally and rival for the
credit of Marston Moor, had built an immensely strong defensive
line between Berwick and Edinburgh, and Cromwell spent weeks in
appalling weather trying to draw the Scots out to fight. By the end
of August disease and privation had destroyed about a third of the

English force, and supplies were dwindling. Sensing victory, and pressed on too by the dissensions in his own camp, Leslie left his fortifications and pinned the English down around the small port of Dunbar. There Cromwell, grimly conscious of the consequences of defeat, determined to risk everything by charging the much larger enemy force. In the dark morning of 3 September he sent in the dashing young Colonel Lambert. Caught by surprise, the Covenanters were routed. It was Cromwell's most remarkable victory, and since it was won over an army which itself militantly claimed to be God's chosen instrument it only heightened the sense of election the general shared with his officers.

Dunbar did not end the threat from Scotland, but it changed its complexion, for Charles Stuart now turned to the moderate wing of the kirk and to the remnants of the old Engagers. But if the pure army of the Covenant had fallen before the New Model, that of the king fared little better. Although Cromwell's long illness in the spring of 1651 gave Leslie time to consolidate, the summer saw the New Model cut the Scottish lines of communication. Overruling Leslie, who wanted to fight on friendly ground and exploit Cromwell's supply problems, Charles determined to march south. The Rump steeled itself for disaster, since the Engagement had loosed a flood of presbyterian anger.

Charles had, however, been misled by tales of the universal unpopularity of the Rump. Unpopular it might be, but few were willing to risk ruin by reopening the old scars, least of all for a king at the head of the hated Scots. In fact, the Scottish invasion generated considerable support for the regime, and the godly flocked to the county militias the Rump raised in the summer of 1651 in its bid to conciliate county feeling – even Fairfax gave his support. With presbyterians deterred by the judicious execution of a clerical plotter, Christopher Love, and royalists cowed by defeat and sequestration, only about 2,000 Englishmen joined Charles. Cromwell therefore had a heavy numerical superiority when he caught up with the Scots at Worcester on 3 September 1651, the anniversary of Dunbar. However unsurprising the victory, to Cromwell it was God's 'crowning mercy'.

The commonwealth was safe. Irish, Scots, presbyterians, royalists, all were defeated, and Charles Stuart barely escaped into an ignominious exile. The Rump could at last seek a final solution to the British problem which had plagued successive English regimes, and in the following months it planned the total unification of Ireland and Scotland with England.

Physical security made it easier for the Rump to appeal to the nation for acceptance. The time-serving lawyer Sir Thomas Widdrington, who had refused to co-operate with the regime in 1649, was by 1651 a member of the council of state; likewise, the Independent lord Wharton, who had broken with Cromwell at Pride's Purge, in 1651 declared himself 'now satisfied'. Amongst the royalists too there were changes of heart. That year John Evelyn followed the self-exiled Thomas Hobbes home to England, 'there being now so little appearance of any change for the better'. Though this did not mean willing support – a Dutch visitor in the winter of 1651–2 noted many tokens of royalist sympathies, as in the inn signs which read 'Here *was* the King's Head – it might suffice.

In the longer term, however, Dunbar and Worcester were disastrous for the Rump. For victory as usual persuaded the army to speak out. After Dunbar the elated Cromwell urged parliament to stand out for God's people,

> for they are the chariots and horsemen of Israel . . . relieve the oppressed, hear the groans of poor prisoners . . . be pleased to reform the abuses of all professions; and if there be any one that makes many poor to make a few rich, that suits not a commonwealth.

But though after Worcester there were no more enemies to interrupt such calls, they achieved little.

What reforming energy the Rump possessed was always diverted by those MPs who craved stability most of all. But inertia also claimed some of the more zealous amongst the Rumpers and their supporters. Such godly men as Haselrig, a temperamental oligarch, or the provincial lawyer John Bradshaw, who presided at the king's trial and over the commonwealth's first council of state, came to rank the preservation of the republic as an end in itself; these 'commonwealthsmen' were loath to consider the Rump as merely the path to better things. The prospects for reform dimmed further with the moderating of another group of republicans, more secular this time, who derived their inspiration from Tacitus and Machiavelli rather than the Old Testament. Henry Marten in particular, and Tom Chalenor and Algernon Sidney too, had shown a genuine concern for the poor. But, as the military victories flowed in, they became as entranced as Nedham by the republican virtue of antiquity, and hoped to build, as Milton put it, 'another Rome in the west'. Increasingly after 1651 they sank their considerable energies into extending the benefits of citizenship to the conquered Scots; the all-consuming war against the Dutch, on which the Rump embarked in 1652, was also to be their memorial as they pursued republican glory. And perhaps most important of all, the Rump was an executive as well as a legislature, and all its members were seduced by the pleasures of administration.

Reform met other obstacles. It cost money, and the debts left by the civil wars – even without the later burden of the Dutch war – were a millstone, forcing one parliamentarian government after another into a breathless and crippling sale of assets. First came the episcopal lands after 1646, and then under the Rump the crown lands, the lands of the deans and chapters (the senior cathedral clergy), and finally in 1651–2 the estates of 780 assorted unrepentant royalists. Some have seen these sales as further proof of radicalism, assuming that they must have facilitated the rise of a new class of progressive landowners. But as so often, detailed studies of this unrevolutionary revolution tell a story of continuity: thus, the vast majority of royalists had regained their estates through loans or mortgages even by the end of the 1650s. More interesting is what the sales show of the Rump's plight.

The financial gains were smaller – since the political risks involved ensured that the estates sold at a discount – than the political losses. So desperate was parliament from 1646–52 that it used the land sales to entice unrepaid creditors to 'double', or lend as much again, with repayment to come from the confiscated estates. Those unable to lend more had little hope save to sell their notes at an alarming discount of 50–70 per cent, to widespread public and army resentments, especially as the Rump failed to reform the laws against poor debtors. The bigger lenders, who could double, equally resented the crude treatment they received when in 1649 the Rump threatened to repudiate its debts unless creditors lent again for the Irish campaign. The scandalous mistreatment of the state's creditors meant that soon there was nobody left to lend to it, particularly as the worsening relations with the army after 1651 made a bad risk worse. However much more efficient its administration than that of the early Stuarts, its solutions to the enduring problem of how to provide long-term funding were no better. Its political options were thus as severely constricted.

Financial stringency narrowed the Rump's range of options most obviously over church reform. The Rumpers had two major practical objectives – like Laud, they wished to improve the financial position of the ministry, and they also sought to make preaching more available. But though they devoted every Friday to their undoubted good intentions, they found the Word harder to deploy than the sword.

The Rump was beset by both internal and external problems. There was little agreement on solutions, for on the one hand Baptists urged an end to the national church, and the replacement of tithes with voluntary contributions to ministers, while on the other, presbyterians sought to retain, and even strengthen the tithe system; meanwhile, Independents inclined towards the abolition of tithes but favoured some form of compulsory support – understandably enough, since there were at least 130 Independent parish ministers, while other Independents occupied virtually separatist positions. But any national measure would have been prohibitively costly, all the more so in view of the devastation caused by war, and the Rump's solutions were therefore piecemeal. In June 1649, in a revealing gesture of commitment to an established church, the Rump voted £20,000 p.a. from confiscated church and crown revenues to provide 'augmentations' to bring inadequate livings up to £100 p.a. More was intended, but parliament's chronic indebtedness meant that redemption of the 'public faith' claimed most of the church lands sold off between 1646 and 1650, lands which might have been put to the constructive uses dreamed of in 1641. Something was achieved: by 1650 seventy-three augmentations had been awarded to Essex clergy and 129 to Lancashire. But around half of these had been lost by the time of the Rump's fall, as the financial crisis deepened. The 'root and branchers' of 1641 would certainly have approved of the use of Lichfield cathedral to employ the poor; but they would have been impressed neither with the whole achievement nor with the transformation of St Paul's cathedral into a barracks and St Asaph's into a wine shop.

The refurbishment of the national church was to be by way of improving its efficiency as well as by material strengthening. Prompted by local petitions, parliament in 1649 instituted a survey of the unwieldy parochial structure, and was soon receiving careful reports and proposals for putting everyone within three miles of a parish church. The detail of the commonwealth survey even today looks impressive. But the alteration of parish boundaries raised huge problems of property rights, in pews, to tithes, to appointments, to charitable endowments. Colchester and a few other towns on their own initiative amalgamated ill-supplied parishes; but late in the 1650s Cromwell's council was still wrestling with the petty disputes which blocked the survey's recommendations. Similar frustrations arose from the schemes for dealing with even graver deficiencies in local provision, by propagating the gospel into the 'dark corners of the land'. The widespread puritan concern about the backward, Catholic and politically suspect north and Wales was at last given focus by local pressure groups allied to powerful parliamentarians, as when the energetic Colonel Harrison and Philip Jones, the south Wales boss, supported the calls of the charismatic Welsh millenarian preachers Vavasour Powell and Morgan Llwd. In early 1650 the Rump established the twin commissions for propagation in the north and in Wales; it also set up similar bodies for Ireland and New England, although these inevitably were more ephemeral. Both the northern and the Welsh commissioners ejected assorted 'scandalous' clergy – nearly 300 in Wales – but replacements proved hard to find, especially in Wales, with its language barrier. There the commissioners had to rely on some ninety itinerant preachers, who scandalized conservative opinion in England because their learning often matched their zeal as little as did their respect for parish boundaries. The drive for propagation led to the publication of several evangelical works in Welsh, as well as some for American Indians. But as always, good intentions were thwarted by financial stringency, and only a third of perhaps sixty new schools founded in Wales between 1650 and 1653 survived to 1660.

The conservatism which led Rumpers to concentrate on reforming rather than replacing the national church was still more evident in the social and political fields. There were certainly ideas aplenty, for the widespread expectation of change led many to look for the creation of a new heaven on earth. The most prolific generator of proposals was perhaps Samuel Hartlib, one of the pious reformers of 1641. Throwing himself after Francis Bacon's dream of the advancement of mankind through technology, Hartlib circulated to anybody he thought might be interested, or helpful, plans for reform in all walks of life: agriculture, medicine, education, commerce, all could be improved in order to reduce human misery and reform men and women. But the Rump remained unmoved by the technological millennium. One of Hartlib's followers, Henry Robinson, did in 1650 come close to converting the post office into an 'office of addresses', to serve as a glorified patent office and scientific labour exchange; but the intellectual ferment was carried closest to the centre of power by the whirlwind figure of Hugh Peter. A favourite of Cromwell since their New Model days, Peter – an irrepressible busybody – preached often at Whitehall; like Hartlib he saw glimmerings of the millennium in social improvement, and his social conscience was as broad as that of many of his radical contemporaries. He had as early as 1646 urged the army to 'teach [Irish] peasants to understand liberty', and in his call for guaranteed agricultural prices he was unusual in thinking hard about farmers. His fertile mind ranged from the usual radical schemes for abolishing imprisonment for debt and for establishing state hospitals and cheap local courts to the advocacy of a national bank.

But the cries of the saints from the depths of the worst economic depression in a generation hardly encouraged gentlemen to give calm consideration to the myriad schemes aired in print. The Rump's social reforms were as limited as had been the Stuarts', and – as in the municipal workhouse it helped establish in London in 1649 – as disciplinarian. Nor was there much encouragement in the localities.

In Yorkshire the JPs countered the dearth in time-honoured fashion, harrying both traders in grain and the hapless squatters on wasteland; in Norwich, despite political changes in the corporation, there were no new initiatives. Most revealingly of all, measures for fen drainage, which would worsen the lot of many commoners, and bills against deer poaching fared better in this parliament of property-owners than did reform of the poor laws. Colonel Robert Bennet, a Cornish Baptist supporter of the Rump, thought it 'a sad omen . . . in these days of pretended reformation' that property should be set higher than compassion.

Much the same story can be told of law and electoral reform. The widespread prejudices against the lawyers had sharpened in the 1640s. Litigants had suffered as the war dislocated the courts, and the poor had probably suffered most as parliament overthrew the accessible provincial royal councils at York and Ludlow, the equity courts in the palatinates of Lancaster and Durham, and the hugely popular court of requests, the central equity court for the poor. The Levellers accordingly advocated a radical decentralization of the courts and the removal of the 'Norman yoke' whose legal complexities and French law enriched lawyers while condemning poor men to death for minor property offences; millenarians meanwhile pleaded for the godly simplicity of the Mosaic code. Such enthusiasm, when about a fifth of the two hundred or so Rumpers were lawyers and most of the rest gentry, doomed even moderate schemes. The furthest the Rump would go was to concede the replacement of the archaic law French with English as the language of the courts. It also moved to fill one of the worst vacuums left by the collapse of the ecclesiastical courts by at last establishing a procedure for probate of wills. It would be wrong to think that parliament was simply hidebound. The Rump established an impressive law reform commission under the chairmanship of the eminent Restoration judge Mathew Hale in the aftermath of Worcester; while this was partly a response to radical pressure, even conservative Rumpers could recognize the need for some reform of the antiquated structure and the scandalously expensive and unpredictable procedures of the courts. With the goodwill at first of lawyer MPs such as Bulstrode Whitelocke, the Hale commission proposed thoughtful limits on the worst anomalies, as in the matter of imprisonment for debt. But unfortunately Rumpers could never view law reform in isolation. Reluctant as ever to offend conservatives outside the house, and more reluctant than ever to gratify the army, in February 1653 they failed to proceed with the Hale commission's report.

Creeping paralysis similarly beset the Rump's progress towards electoral reform. Members could scarcely ignore their peculiar status, evident in the Purge itself, the paucity of their numbers, and the complaints of unrepresented constituencies. But they not unnaturally treasured their own seats, and had few illusions about their support in the country; nor did they relish cutting the state adrift from the last of its constitutional moorings. It therefore required the seasonal nudges of the army to drive them into action. Although Ireton's sweeping proposals remained anathema, in the aftermath of Dunbar Vane drew up a clever compromise which would have left the Rumpers undisturbed in their seats and 'recruited' new members for the vacant, but reapportioned, constituencies. The army, however, fully reciprocated the Rump's resentments, and saw Vane's scheme as a disguise for self-interest. After Worcester tensions grew, and although the Rump at last agreed to a dissolution, albeit at the distant date of November 1654, it moved offensively slowly to give substance to its electoral proposals.

The army thus found itself powerless to effect reform: its commanding position merely enabled it to block hostile measures. Its solitary gain after Dunbar was the toleration act of September 1650, which redeemed the Rump's earlier promises to tender consciences by repealing the statutory requirement that all attend parish churches every Sunday. But the grudging Rump gave far more publicity to its blasphemy act than to toleration, and it is unclear how much effect the new measure had. Clergy in these years certainly had trouble in filling their churches, but this probably owed more to materialist irreligion, and to the general confusion, than to radical dissent.

The prospects for reform dwindled further after Worcester as Marten, Chalenor and their republican friends turned their attention not just to the problem of Scotland but also to the economic regulation which has constituted the Rump's claim to fame.

The crisis which seemed to call for action was undeniable, as the European peace of 1648 exposed English shipping to superior Dutch competition. By 1651 there were fifty Dutch ships to every one English in the Baltic trade, and the Dutch were edging English carriers out of the colonial ports too, taking with them European rather than English manufactures, and returning the colonial products, with their re-export profits, to Dutch rather than English ports. The threat was broad: to manufacturing, to shipping and ship-building, which was after agriculture the largest employer of men, and to national security, since ships and men were conscripted for wartime service as needed. The Rump responded by erecting protectionist barriers.

Considerable controversy has built up around the two navigation acts of 1650–1. They have been seen as the foundation of the 'mercantilist system', and, in their treatment of the colonies' trade as subservient to that of England, the first decisive step in England's progress towards colonial imperialism. Some have accordingly sought to identify the 'bourgeois' pressure groups which must have been behind the acts. Such efforts seem misguided, for virtually all commercial sectors, as well as the state itself, stood to gain from curbs on Dutch competition. The navigation acts were conceived in good Tudor fashion, to benefit the 'commonweal'. That fact points to another qualification to the legend, for 'mercantilism', as a code, did not orginate in 1651. Shipping and manufactures had been the subject of occasional legislation for generations, since their importance was so obvious. The scale of the crisis, rather than innovative protectionist theorizing, drove the Rumpers to lay down a broader, national, framework; and pragmatism rarely shapes coherent policies.

Ironically, the Rump and its London merchant advisers first reacted by seeking not to exclude but to copy the Dutch and their low-cost ways. Admiration for the Dutch economy reinforced a very different strain within the Rump. The old dream of a union of protestants against the popish Antichrist, strengthened by memories of the Elizabethan quasi-protectorate over the Dutch, was given firmer shape by Sidney's and Chaloner's increasingly jingoistic vision of republican expansion. In the winter of 1650–1 the Rumpers sought to persuade the Dutch to submerge themselves, and their economy, in union with England. The Dutch were unimpressed.

Affection for the Dutch was anyway luke-warm. Merchants urged retaliation against competition, while others dreamed of revenge for all the injuries incurred in the east and in the fishing grounds. The jealous outcome was the navigation acts. These did not, as the Restoration's measures did, seek to monopolize colonial trade for England; rather, they were concerned with the threat to English shipping, and decreed that all imports must come either in English ships or in ships of the country of origin. But as long as English freight charges remained high, Dutch ships would carry the cargoes.

It was therefore the bellicose aftermath rather than the navigation acts themselves which changed England's fortunes. England plunged into war in mid-1652 amid growing commercial and political resentments after the failure of union. But there was also an ominous pointer to the later disintegration of the godly cause in the support Sidney's expansionism found amongst some of the saints. Vane saw the war as a means to break 'the great silence in heaven' after Worcester, and in this he echoed a widespread unease; for, like Cromwell after them, the godly who looked for reassurance in God's providence had found scant encouragement on a political stage which proved far more opaque than the battlefield. The saints were not to be disappointed. After an unnerving beginning, the fast-growing English navy gradually gained the advantage; here the brilliance of Admiral Blake was perhaps of less importance than the prevailing westerly winds which favoured England. That advantage was consolidated the following winter when the energetic Vane took over the running of the navy. By the war's end in 1654 the ratio of Dutch to English losses was over four to one, and the prizes at last allowed English shipowners to compete more effectively.

The war was not all gain, however. The scale of the military establishment meant that the Rump ran constantly at a deficit, and it dared not raise the assessment, its major tax, much further; sporadic riots showed that the excise was still more resented. The war was therefore fought in an even more hand-to-mouth fashion than most early-modern wars as the republic drifted closer towards bankruptcy – even in 1652 the excise was mortgaged, 'anticipated', for four years into the future. Equally damaging were the political consequences, for just as the army could be fired by its victories, so too could the Rump. Naval and commercial successes, and organizational efficiency, fostered an unrepentant pride in what 'commonwealthsmen' from the godly Haselrig and Scot to Sidney saw as a virtuous oligarchy. Increasingly convinced of their own legitimacy, they set on a collision course with the soldiers.

A growing religious reaction fuelled the confrontation. It was in the early 1650s rather than in the 1640s that the sectarian challenge extended beyond the towns into the countryside as a whole. Thomas Hall, minister of King's Norton in Warwickshire, had prided himself on the unity of his parish, but early in 1651 he lamented the first signs of heresy in his flock, and denounced Baptist missionaries from nearby towns. Similarly, in the spring of 1652 the clerical participants in a combination lecture at Wiveliscombe in Somerset agreed to concentrate on fundamental doctrinal and ecclesiological points in order to fortify themselves against a growing sectarian onslaught.* Perhaps even more alarming was the learned biblical exegesis of the Socinian John Biddle which questioned the divinity of Christ, and in so doing challenged all those who had been taught that their salvation lay in the merits of Christ alone. The last year or so of the Rump therefore brought a new spate of county petitions in favour of the established ministry, order and protestant truth.

The Rump responded by setting itself more firmly against the radicals. The old faithful of mainstream puritanism, Stephen Marshall, once more became a favourite preacher to parliament;

*Brit. Lib., E628(4); E671(2).

meanwhile, the leading Independent divines, John Owen and Philip Nye, attracted considerable support in their campaign to establish certain 'fundamentals' in doctrine against Biddle and the sects. The crowning blow for the saints came early in 1653 when the Rump discontinued the Welsh commission for propagation. Nowhere that winter did the Rump appear an agent of reform. The dashing of the Hale commission for law reform underlined the message of the Rump's legislative record, which showed only one-third as many public bills passed in 1652 as in 1649. The pressure of business on a weary legislature which was also a wartime executive explains much; furthermore, leading reformers were gone, Ireton dead in Ireland in 1651, Vane immersed in his navy work. But radicals took more notice of the members' concern for their own interests.

The worst of the charges of corruption levelled against the Rump were unwarranted. A different concept of office was emerging, centring on service to the state, fostered as much by the puritan self-denial celebrated in Lucy Hutchinson's portrayal of Ireton as by the classical republicanism of so many commonwealthsmen. There were moves towards a salaried administration, the sale of offices declined, and the taking of fees incurred disapproval. The few signs of corruption under the commonwealth, when the administration had mushroomed and when the proliferation of treasuries and of committees provided abundant opportunities for concealment, speaks well of the puritan consciences of the Independents and Baptists who provided so many of the servants of the new state. Nevertheless, there had been no dramatic change in the pattern of office-holding, and offices still tended to be seen as private property; furthermore, the increase in the number of minor gentry and attornies who came to hold them resulted more from the alienation of their betters than from the advance of 'meritocracy'. The widespread accumulation of offices by MPs encouraged charges of self-seeking; and where the Rump undeniably erred was in its concentration of executive, legislative and judicial power. The Rump's harassment of Lilburne in 1652 for a feud with Haselrig left a sour taste of tyranny, and when the interests of God's people were jeopardized by the tired Rumpers' long week-ends, Cromwell could but scent gross worldliness. His angry tirade when he eventually expelled the Rump did have some substance.

Others were less restrained in their denunciations. Most Baptists and radical Independents had sought Christian rather than political liberty, and had accordingly parted company with the Levellers. But the growing conviction, especially in the months of frustration after Worcester, that the men and the institutions the saints had trusted were irredeemably corrupt drove some of them to ask the fundamental questions about the nature of authority they had earlier avoided.

Members of various gathered churches, already millenarians in general terms, now put a firmer interpretation upon prophecy. Charles's execution in 1649 seemed the end of the fourth, and last, earthly monarchy foretold in scripture; the fifth monarchy, of Christ and his saints, was beginning. The inchoate and unprogrammatic Fifth Monarchist groups, which probably numbered less than 10,000, doubtless found such radical conclusions the more plausible in the dislocation of the time – indeed, the readiness of artisans and craftsmen in London and elsewhere to seize on apocalyptic solutions perhaps indicates a suppressed strand of class hostility in the revolution. They listened eagerly as the Londoners Christopher Feake and John Simpson, the Welshman Vavasour Powell, and their great patron Colonel Harrison, preached that the time for the politicians was past and that the hour of the saints had come. The threat was the greater in that Harrison had supporters in the army too.

The conflict between a radical army and parliament was not perhaps as inherently explosive as it had been in 1647. The submissiveness of the country in 1652–3 allowed greater latitude to the Rump; conversely, the army was not the monolith it had been, for the soldiers' quarters were now more scattered across the country and their sense of injured pride had diminished. Yet opinion in the army had hardened in other respects. While probably no more of the soldiers were saints than in 1647, their Musselburgh declaration of 1650 for King Jesus, which cast the whole struggle of the 1640s in apocalyptic terms, boded ill for a parliament whose reformism had died. Furthermore, Nedham's editorials in *Mercurius Politicus* in 1651–2 had developed Machiavelli's argument that a vigorous people in arms was the mainstay of a free republic, and as several radical outbursts during the protectorate were to show, the contention had considerable appeal to an army whose central political tenet remained its 1647 denial that it was a 'mere mercenary army'. The officers' commitment to a 'freedom' they found difficult to define – Edmund Ludlow, an officer and Rumper, later claimed vaguely that the soldiers had fought 'that the nation might be governed by its own consent' – meant that they were as trapped by their principles as was the Rump. They demanded free elections, yet no matter how careful the electoral provisions no new representative would be any less hostile to the army and its goals than was the Rump. Nevertheless, so intense was the army's frustration that by the winter of 1652–3 getting rid of the Rump had become an end in itself. There was recurrent talk of a coup.

They key to the conflict lay in Cromwell. He personified the tension which had always characterized the parliamentarian cause, between the moderate constitutionalism of the gentry and radical

puritanism. Tithes were to him both a grievous anomaly *and* a matter
of property rights. Though he was far more merciful towards royalists
than, for example, Haselrig, unlike most MPs he had not lost his
millenarian enthusiasm in the disillusionment of politics; and he
shared his officers' impatience with the Rump's evident desire to
hang on to power when its energy and its moral credit were exhausted.
His priorities were as they had been in 1647, a settlement along
traditional lines *and* reform. He was still the man of the old middle
group, the friend of St John; and in the aftermath of Worcester he had
talked of a settlement with 'somewhat of monarchical power in it'. In
all probability it was his growing sense of the need for an executive
with the power to reform as well as his weariness of the incessant
hostility between Rump and army that led in November 1652 to his
outburst, 'What if a man should take upon him to be king?'

The exact cause of Cromwell's expulsion of the Rump will never be
known, since he seems to have destroyed the evidence. In the winter
of 1652–3 he strove to avoid the use of force as he had in 1647. Acting
as moderator between the officers and MPs he even persuaded the
Rump to bring forward the date for its dissolution to November 1653.
But though he came to recognize reality, and concluded that fresh
elections would be a disaster, he remained adamant that the Rump
must go, if only to preserve the all-important unity of the army. He
seems to have hoped that the Rumpers would entrust power to a small
body of godly and reformist men until the world became safe for
elections.

In April 1653 Cromwell discovered how violently the Rumpers
opposed the army. His plan would necessarily have allowed the officers an indefinitely extended role in politics, and this the Rumpers
could not tolerate. The Rump does not seem to have revived Vane's
old plan for recruiter elections in order to perpetuate itself, as the
army later claimed and historians long believed: rather, it rushed
ahead with a bill for a November dissolution and fresh elections which
would leave a committee of former Rumpers the sole judge of those
elected. The officers rightly saw it as a recipe for a still more conservative parliament. After weeks of withdrawal from politics – his customary 'waiting on the Lord' – Cromwell angrily called in the
troops on 20 April.

As so often, Cromwell acted first and then tried to work out the implications later. He later testified that the move into the constitutional
unknown made his hair stand on end, but the nation seems to have
been less unnerved by the demise of such a long parliament. Uncertainty about the future was clearly outweighed by relief at the fall of
the Rump, and as Cromwell himself noted, 'there was not so much as

the barking of a dog' in protest. One Independent minister observed accurately enough that all was quiet, 'and could we but be eased of taxes, we should not much mind who ruled over us'* – for the general response, as so often in these years, was conformist. Quarter sessions continued to meet, and the country to function, although all legitimate authority had gone. A major worry for the officers had been the expiry in June of the current act for the monthly assessment; but the readiness of taxpayers to defer to what became thereafter merely an arbitrary demand illuminates the power of the sword.

Nevertheless, the army needed a long-term solution, for Cromwell as lord general was left the only power in the land. The council of officers, dominated by Independents and Baptists, had given little thought to the future, and was, like Cromwell, more interested in godliness than in constitutions. But some amongst them felt capable of filling the void. The secular-minded Lambert advocated a small executive council, to govern until the time was ripe for a new parliament, while Harrison urged that an assembly of saints, modelled on the Old Testament sanhedrin, should fit the land to the imminent coming of Christ. Although few officers were Fifth Monarchists, Harrison could appeal to the broad millenarian hopes of many. Not least of these was Cromwell, who repeatedly declared his belief that the kingdom of Christ would be realized spiritually, in the hearts of men, and not physically on earth: the way to it was through liberty of conscience and the elimination of evils. Characteristically, he achieved an unlikely compromise in the council. A nominated assembly – nominated by the officers and not by the sectarian churches as some had hoped – was to win the people over to godliness by its reforms, thus preparing the way for a new, and godly, parliament. In the meantime the officers appointed a new and army-dominated council of state.

Through May and June the interim government struggled with the problems of security. The demands of the Dutch war were compounded by the beginnings of an almost nationalist revolt in Scotland, which caused trouble as far south as the Borders; there were reports too of armed bands in Yorkshire as the economic crisis proved slow to ease. In this tense atmosphere the council of officers prepared nominations to the new assembly. Cromwell must have breathed a sigh of relief as he handed over power.

The nominated assembly was soon to be satirized as 'the Barebone's Parliament', so called after one of its members, the London leather-seller and radical Independent, Praise-God Barebone. The first 'British' assembly in history, containing both (hand-picked)

---

* *Thurloe State Papers*, I, 290.

Scottish and Irish members, the Barebone's has been more renowned for its social composition. Recent research has, however, modified the old caricature of an assembly of humble and ignorant saints from the gathered churches. The officers drew on their knowledge of local conditions, rather than on any sectarian 'slate', to nominate members, and the assembly was by no means disreputable. Since Cromwell was eager to take the army out of politics there were few regular officers; furthermore, over one-third of the members might have warranted election to any ordinary parliament, and nearly two-thirds had been JPs for more than three years. Some hardly fit the zealous profile: thus Sir Anthony Ashley Cooper, future earl of Shaftesbury and patron of John Locke, and inscrutable in his religion, had probably attracted Cromwell's notice as a reformer on the Hale commission. But the assembly did contain many more minor gentry than had other parliaments, and it contained too perhaps a dozen Fifth Monarchists, mostly allies of Harrison and Powell from north Wales, in a total of 144 members. Their impact was the greater both for their energy and for the way that just as in the army command they acted as a leaven in a larger lump: probably a majority of members held millenarian beliefs of some kind.

Cromwell is typical of that broader millenarianism. In his opening speech to the assembly on 4 July he enthusiastically declared that 'this may be the door to usher in things that God hath promised and prophesied of.' But while Harrison was certain that the time had come to break down earthly powers Cromwell warned, 'These things are dark.' Though he looked towards a time when all the nation were God's people, he made clear that the new sovereign authority, to which the army surrendered its power, was only to sit for a limited time, and was to prepare for a return to parliaments. This was not to be the constituent assembly, reshaping England, to which it has sometimes been likened. Any reshaping was to be moral, not constitutional.

The early proceedings must have gratified Cromwell's hopes that zeal might combine with continuity. There was at first little sign of polarization, and the act of self-aggrandizement by which the assembly promptly declared itself a parliament was opposed both by Fifth Monarchists and by moderates who saw this as no true parliament. The new council of state the parliament elected in July was also reassuringly bipartisan, balancing a handful of Fifth Monarchists with moderates and officers. Most impressive, however, was the conscientiousness of members; in its five months' existence the Barebone's passed over thirty acts and had other major ones in preparation.

Much of its business was eminently worthy. There were bills

continuing Rumper efforts to unite the commonwealths of England, Scotland and Ireland, to settle Ireland, to revise the excise and to limit both confusion and corruption by uniting the many separate treasuries into one. Predictably, the members turned too to law reform. Although lack of time was to handicap their efforts, they had been given a good start by the Hale commission, on whose work they drew heavily. One of their few successful measures, the civil marriage act, was another belated attempt to repair damage done by the destruction of the church courts. Few doubted the need for some matrimonial jurisdiction, though the requirement that marriages must be performed by a JP rather than the parish minister may have been more honoured in the breach than the observance – one MP reported in 1657 that 'not one marriage in one hundred . . . is made pursuant to this act'. Further pragmatic reforms gave some relief both to suffering debtors and to creditors. Even the notoriously peremptory August vote to abolish the court of Chancery forthwith can be seen in this moderate light; it came in the context of other moves to reduce lawyers' fees and foibles, and there seems to have been surprisingly little opposition to it. Chancery had long been widely disliked as the most arbitrary, clogged and expensive of all courts; there were said to be 23,000 cases pending in 1653. In the country even Anthony Nicoll, one of the conservative 'eleven members' of 1647, could view its abolition with equanimity, provided it was replaced with another equity court.* But chancery was also vulnerable *as* an equity court, a court of conscience, when some radicals felt the consciences of lawyers should give way to the consciences of saints.

In the overlap between moderate and radical purposes lay both the strength and weakness of Barebone's. Progress was assured by the reduction in the conservative presence, and even some of the handful of lawyers in the house, such as Andrew Broughton of Kent, were among the zealous. But conversely the reformism of the moderates meant that they were not always well prepared to counter the fire of Vavasour Powell's friends, particularly as wealthier members withdrew to the country to escape the City's heat and bustle. The Hale commission's report was not the only model for reform. The prospect of change had brought a new flurry of Leveller activity, and demands were heard in the streets and in the press for the laws to be reduced to 'the bigness of a pocket book' in the interests of cheapness and justice. Likewise, the Fifth-Monarchists' pulpits resounded with calls for the Mosaic code, the only positive laws given by God. Vavasour Powell caught the spirit of both groups when he declared, 'Laws should stream down like a river freely, . . . impartially as the saints please

* Folger Library, Washington, Ms. X. d. 483(112).

[*sic*], and . . . should run as rivers do, close to the doors.' Rather than the rationalization which many sought, a wholesale onslaught on the body of law seemed at hand. Others beside the parliamentary moderates grew alarmed. A Cheshire gentleman concluded gloomily that a sale of land would be difficult because his father's 'uncertainty of what alterations may now be in the law, and his doubt how to draw any present assurances [i.e. deeds of sale], doth so much amaze him.'*

The course of religious reform ran parallel. On one extreme stood the conservative gentry who owned tithes and advowsons and saw them as legal property to be touched only at great peril; on the other stood the increasingly clamorous sects, who rejected all compulsion, whether in worship or in payment. In the middle, as during the Rump, were the many who recognized the abuses of the tithe system but feared the disintegrative effects of complete voluntarism. It was the strength of the last group which brought a vote in November for the introduction of a bill outlawing patronage in church livings, and the crucial vote of 10 December rejecting an aggressively conservative defence of tithes. Moderates could vote with radicals for perfectly respectable reasons. But the times were fast becoming less than respectable, as the sects and the Fifth Monarchists petitioned the house against a national church and the universities too as a relic of the old popish Antichristian captivity. The threat to the ministry in 1653 was to shape clerical and conservative attitudes in the following years.

Polarization was not as total as the close vote on tithes – 56:52 – suggests, and considerable bipartisan reform work went on until the end. Nor was there a radical take-over: the house's November poll for the council of state produced a more moderate body than had the July vote. Perhaps the most dangerous development was the resurfacing of the old parliamentary hostility to the army, as the well-organized radical caucus in the house blocked the renewal of the excise and attacked the monthly assessment, the army's chief support. When sailors were rioting for lack of pay this led Cromwell, who had studiously left the new sovereign power undisturbed, to complain that he was now 'more troubled with the fool than before [during the Rump] with the knave'. Indeed, the house's executive capacity was sadly deficient, and its council of state too large and inexperienced to deal with the Dutch war. Furthermore, while some Fifth Monarchists embraced that war as the best place to begin breaking down earthly powers – since the Dutch were notoriously more interested in commerce than in God – Cromwell still hoped for a protestant union. Other moderates thought that recent naval successes should allow a

*Bodleian Library, Ms. Top. Cheshire E.3, f.18v.

speedy and favourable peace. Cromwell's manifest impatience with the council, and with what he saw as the divisive haste of parliament's reforms, encouraged the moderates to act.

The December vote on tithes drove some in the house to accept the conviction of conservatives in the country that the entire social order was at risk. Huge popular demonstrations in London in the autumn had celebrated Lilburne's acquittal on yet another capital charge, and while these were more a comment on Lilburne himself and on hostility to the government, rather than on Levelling as a movement, they were bad enough. Equally ominous were the changes in local government. At some point between mid-1652 and late 1653, and probably in the Barebone's period, massive changes occurred in many county commissions of the peace. Over two-thirds of the Surrey names were deleted, over a half in five more counties, and while some of the newcomers were probably mere anti-Rumpers rather than fiery radicals, it was certainly in late 1653 that yeomen and shopkeepers first appeared on the Cumberland commission. In order to stop the rot, forty or more moderates in the house – who included the aged Speaker, Francis Rous, Sir Charles Wolseley and other future Cromwellians – exploited the absence of radicals at a prayer meeting, and trooped off to Whitehall on 12 December to return their power to the lord general.

This time the army leaders were more prepared. Lambert had in late November urged Cromwell to take the crown, in hope of the reform mixed with stability they both craved. But Cromwell flinched once again from the prospect of using force, and from the crown too – as he assured future audiences frequently enough for plausibility, he did not seek self-exaltation. Furthermore, he had never taken a political initiative unless necessity enforced it. It was only when providence, or rather the members who had doubtless been schooled by Lambert, thrust power into his hands that he took it. He did so the more willingly for being able to console himself later with the thought that Barebone's would have brought 'the confusion of all things'. Those sentiments were a far cry from his zeal in July for the cause of 'the people of God'; but unlike Harrison, Cromwell always coupled the interests of 'men as men and Christians as Christians', and protested that 'He sings sweetly that sings a song of reconciliation between these two interests.' Like countless other parliamentarian gentlemen before him, he was to come to recognize the difficulty of harmonizing them.

11   The Protectorate
1653–1658

The inauguration of the protectorate has strong claims to be a turning-point, as England retraced its steps towards the safely monarchical order of the Restoration. Dominant figures of the Rump, such as Vane and Haselrig, were excluded from power in 1653, as was Harrison, so influential in Barebone's. They were replaced at the centre by a small group of less millenarian officers and by civilians like Wolseley and Ashley Cooper, many of whom had no connection at all with the revolution of 1648–9. More striking was the constitutional framework. The collective leadership of the single-chamber parliament and elective council of state of 1649–53 gave way to something akin to Pym's objective in 1641, with a single-person executive, the lord protector, restrained by a council as well as by a parliament. Cromwell's talk of 'healing and settling' underpins the common assumption that the protectorate represented an attempt to sheathe the sword which the army had turned to naked political use.

Such an analysis needs to be qualified. Cromwell had always been reluctant to take the army into politics, and at no point in his 'revolutionary' career would he have disagreed with his remark to his first parliament in 1654, 'A nobleman, a gentlemen, a yeoman, that is a good interest of the nation and a great one.' On the other hand, sheathing the sword was not the same as laying it down. Although he increasingly donned the trappings of monarchy, and although there were more civilians than serving officers on his council, the dominant figure, after Cromwell himself, was the brilliant, witty, but still soldierly, John Lambert. More revealing was the situation in the localities, where Cromwell left intact the remaining garrisons which so troubled the gentry and clergy; nor did he purge the many army officers from the ranks of the JPs. He had too much to lose. Not only did the soldiers keep the royalists down; they were also his only hope of combining godly rule with godly liberty.

These tensions were reflected in an order which sought to present itself as a golden mean between monarchy and republic as much as between licence and tyranny. Cromwell took upon himself a quasi-

regal style, signing documents 'Oliver P.' in a slight departure from
the regal form 'Charles R.' He also reclaimed some of the dispersed
treasures and palaces of the late king, and established a distinct protectoral court. Yet he had rejected Lambert's suggestion that he take
the crown. In his celebratory poem, 'The First Anniversary', Andrew
Marvell deftly caught the undefinable when he concluded, 'Abroad a
king he seems, and something more,/At home a subject on the equal
floor.' In stark contrast to the flattering grandeur of the portraits of
Charles I, Cromwell's famous instructions were that he be painted
'warts and all'. Similarly, he habitually appeared simply clad on state
occasions, and austerity was a hallmark of his court. The installation
of the protectorate, with Lambert bearing the sword of state and
Oliver himself clothed in plain black, carefully sought to combine the
military and godly with regal forms.

The polity of the protectorate was no less ambivalent. In December
1653 Lambert dusted off the scheme he had urged in the spring and
presented it as the Instrument of Government, England's first written
constitution. The Instrument resounds with earlier attempts at constitutional reform. There was to be no legislation nor taxation without
the consent of parliament, and control over the militia was to be
shared between protector and parliament. More striking, in stipulated areas the protector was bound to act only with the consent of his
council; that these restrictions proved effective is indicated by
Cromwell's complaint to his second parliament in 1657 that he had
been hemmed in as 'a child in swaddling clouts'. John Pym would
have approved, as he would of the presence of his old ally Oliver St
John at Cromwell's elbow throughout the protectorate. There were
other debts, for Lambert drew heavily on his work with Ireton in
1647, and on the labours of the winter of 1648–9, for the Instrument's electoral reforms and for its weakening of the ruler's legislative veto. But perhaps most important were the lessons learned under
the commonwealth, both of parliament's tyranny and of its obstructionism. The novel theme of the separation of powers is implicit in
the Instrument, and indeed explicit in some of the early defences of
the protectorate; and while the Nineteen Propositions and the *Heads
of Proposals* had sought to limit the executive, the Instrument provided government with considerable freedom of action. Until the first
parliament met – on 3 September 1654 – the protector could issue
ordinances with the force of law; he could raise funds indefinitely
for the support of the army and navy independently of parliament;
and parliament was to have only limited control over the council.
Appropriately, the main defence of the Instrument, Nedham's *True
State of the Case of the Commonwealth,* showed a certain weariness with
parliaments.

The Instrument's weaknesses are obvious in retrospect. There was no provision for amendment, nor for the adjudication of disputes. Its provisions for liberty of conscience and for the independence of the government ignored the very different concerns of most parliament-men since 1642. Nevertheless, the Instrument did wrestle with the central problems of an over-mighty prince and an over-mighty parliament, and given mutual tolerance and adequate funding it might have worked.

None could be sure of the willingness of the nation to obey. But though the council lost no time in preparing a new treason ordinance and in reincarcerating Lilburne, and though the first of many half-baked royalist and Leveller assassination plots soon troubled the protector's peace, Oliver had a large asset in the reaction against Barebone's. The Fifth-Monarchist groups might denounce him as 'the dissemblingest perjured villain in the world', but the silence in the army which greeted Harrison's dismissal showed that discipline was far stronger than millenarian fervour where it really mattered. Elsewhere, the initial response to the change was at worst resignation in face of the sword, at best mild relief. Mathew Hale probably spoke for many when he accepted judicial office, thinking it 'absolutely necessary to have justice and property kept up at all times'. Most important of all, taxes kept coming in, for as always, men deferred to authority when chaos was the alternative. But Cromwell hoped for more than this, and true to his old 'middle group' credentials he sought to reconcile the moderate, unpartisan country gentry. The council purged some of Harrison's radical allies from the Welsh commissions of the peace, and smiled as a few 'presbyterians', such as Sir George Booth in Cheshire, crept back into local office. Although fewer moderates responded than Oliver must have hoped, there were some gains; by 1655 the progress of reconciliation was apparent in the increase in the average income of the Worcestershire JPs, to almost twice what it had been in 1652. Gentry life slowly regained a semblance of normality, and Buckinghamshire hunting parties sometimes included the formerly royalist Verneys as well as Oliver's son Richard and his son-in-law John Claypole.

But Cromwell's aim was never simply to conciliate the gentry. It does not seem to have been merely inertia and the overwhelming pressure of business which delayed any general remodelling of the commissions of the peace until 1657, and left the administration of Devon, of Cumberland, of Buckinghamshire, virtually untouched. To return power to the gentry might foster political stability, but scarcely reform.

Accordingly, the Instrument delayed the summoning of a parliament not only to ensure stability but also to secure a modicum of reform. The council's activities in the interim, as it went about government and reform by *fiat*, certainly smack more of pragmatism than of original thought, but both the parliamentary reformers of 1641 and the army in 1647 had – with Cromwell's support – focused primarily on making the existing constitution work. The army's declarations of 1647 had denounced private interest, and the two main defences of the protectorate in 1654, *The True State of the Case of the Commonwealth* and Milton's *Second Defence of the English People,* had echoed them in their insistence on Cromwell's stern probity and breadth of vision. The protectorate is often criticized for its lack of an inspiring ideology, and while it betrayed no great millennial fervour or classical republican idealism it was surprisingly faithful to the ideals of the army in the days of its awakening. Those ideals are reflected in the protectorate's relatively uncorrupt administration and in the high calibre of its judicial appointments. Although the protector must have calculated that better judges would win wider approval, in Hale he appointed one of the finest lawyers of the century.

Some problems were, however, more intractable than administrative reform. The Rump had baulked at the Hale commission's proposal for local courts and registers of title to land, and the hostility of the legal profession to the decentralization which had been such a strong radical demand blocked Cromwell equally. The protector showed his good intentions by bringing in as his legal adviser William Sheppard, a provincial lawyer and – as author of *England's Balme* in 1656 – the most far-sighted legal reformer of his day. Yet revealingly Oliver's one successful move to improve legal provision in distant areas was the restoration of the ancient palatine, or semi-independent, jurisdiction of Lancaster in 1654. Not for nothing had John Thurloe, soon to be secretary of state, confided in January that henceforth the people would be 'governed by the good old laws': ignoring army pressure, the council duly entrusted reform of chancery and the common law courts to senior lawyers. The resulting chancery ordinance of August 1654 therefore introduced thoroughly moderate measures – moderate enough to have some effect – for simplifying procedure and reducing frauds and fees. Still less far-reaching were the internal orders the common law judges introduced that December to regulate their courts. The protector was finding the level of reform consonant with 'healing and settling'.

The small extent of social and economic reform indicates still more clearly how little gratification the Levellers and other radicals had gained from the revolution of 1649. In general, the protectorate's economic policy departed little from that of its royal predecessors, and while Oliver did not grant private monopoly patents he was not averse to the forms of monopoly permitted by the 1624 statute. Thus, the only new urban corporation established, at Swansea in 1655, featured both an oligarchic magistracy and a monopolistic merchant guild. Equally revealingly, the council bowed before local interests in 1657 and brought framework-knitting, a new craft omitted from the Elizabethan regulatory statutes, under corporate control. Furthermore, while under the Rump the trade of the East India Company had been open to interlopers, the protectorate saw government and company return to the old mutual dependency, of loans in return for privileges, as in 1657 the company gained a new charter. Whatever the limited consequences for international trade of the navigation act, the revolution had patently not brought with it an expansive new economic framework.

The social consequences were equally limited. In a suggestive sign of his priorities, Oliver began to grant titles of knighthood, and the new élite often aped the old; Lambert for one resided in palatial splendour at Wimbledon house. The poor obtained little consolation, as in March 1654 the hard-pressed government extended the excise to virtually all saleable goods. The social issues on which the army – let alone the Levellers – had campaigned, such as pensions for soldiers' widows and orphans, remained as dependent as ever on local initiatives at quarter sessions.

The protectorate was closest to the army's ideals of 1647 in its religious policy. The soldiers had declared that their intentions were to maintain unity and to secure freedom for tender consciences, rather than to establish Independency. Cromwell's lamentations for the disunity he saw all around, and his avowed detestation of those who sought to 'press their finger upon their brethren's conscience', were thus entirely in keeping. But while Cromwell's record has been celebrated as one of protestant ecumenicism at its finest, the protector aimed as little at toleration as had the soldier-saints in 1647. The Instrument guaranteed freedom to all save papists, prelatists (or episcopalians), deniers of Christ and disturbers of the peace. In practice toleration was certainly wider than that, and despite the abolition of the prayer book and occasional bursts of repression in political crises, Anglicans on the whole worshipped unmolested. Visitors to London seem to have had little difficulty in obtaining Anglican sacraments which were probably readily available in many parts of the countryside. Similarly, whatever the government's political anti-Catholicism, individual English Catholics fared better than they had under kings greedy for money from recusancy fines. But the liberty for which Oliver strove was emphatically a liberty for godly protestants: he contemplated with equanimity the punishment of such a denier of the divinity of Christ as the Socinian John Biddle, or of Quakers and the Ranters whom he regarded as 'diabolical'.

Despite allegations both then and since that there was no church at all in the 1650s, continuity with an older order was remarkably strong. The parochial system more or less functioned as before, especially in the countryside, and indeed, the national presbyterian church was never formally disestablished. Perhaps most important, many of the old ministers survived. Despite Laud, most parish clergy in the 1630s had probably remained loosely 'puritan' in the broad Elizabethan–Jacobean tradition, and they conformed readily enough to subsequent changes – just as the majority were to do at the Restoration. Probably only between a quarter and a third of the clergy were purged under the various parliamentarian regimes: in Herefordshire, only thirty-three parishes were affected, out of more than 200. Nationally, probably half the parish pulpits were occupied in the 1650s by those who had filled them in 1642.

Not content with such continuities, Oliver strove to build a broad national church. As an Independent he was little troubled at godly differences or at congregational initiatives in the appointment of ministers. But it was not simply the conservative gentleman in him that sympathized with the outcries against antinomian and antitrinitarian excesses. Like most others, he saw these as heresies, not simply errors, and as invitations to God to punish the land. His solution – a March 1654 ordinance establishing a commission of 'triers' in London to examine those seeking appointment as 'public ministers' in parish livings – was by no means original, for it owed much to the 'fundamentals' proposed in 1652 by the alarmed clerical Independents, Owen and Nye. Nor was it without defects. But while the triers sometimes sought evidence of the spiritual arousal dear to the saints rather than of pastoral sufficiency, the episcopal examinations of old had often been haphazard enough. And Cromwell was careful to balance Independent and Baptist triers with presbyterians in a bid to build a broad, and doctrinally orthodox, church. He hoped yet to reunite the godly.

Cromwell's establishment was completed by an August ordinance setting up county commissions of 'ejectors'. Composed like the triers of both laity and clergy, the ejectors offset the centralization of the triers with an element of local control. Their task was to purge ministers and schoolmasters guilty of moral, political or gross pastoral failings, and also to enforce the payment of tithes. In some counties the ejectors were active on the latter score,* but except in the aftermath of the royalist risings of 1655 they initiated few purges. A

---

*See, for example, Brit. Lib. E910(6), and Somerset Record Office, D.P. dum 4/1/1.

Berkshire minister with Ranter and Digger associations was swiftly removed, but otherwise, as Major-General Desborough complained in 1656, ejectors would not proceed against the livings of ministers without statutory warrant. It was the old story of the obstruction of reform by property rights.

Cromwell proudly boasted of his triers and ejectors, 'There hath not been such a service to England since the Christian religion was perfect in England', and Richard Baxter looking back after the Restoration could agree. Furthermore, it seemed not unlikely that his church would prove successful, for the ageing of the surviving bishops meant that, unless renewed, the episcopal church must die out in the next decade. But still, despite the Rump's efforts, little had been done to rectify the material deficiencies of the parochial system: in 1656 only one out of the five parish churches in Leicester had a settled minister. Perhaps more seriously, the protector's church was largely shorn of coercive powers. It could neither enforce attendance nor discipline those within or without, save the licentious and disturbers of the peace. And the consequences of the failure to erect a discipline were just what many had warned they would be in the ecclesiastical debates of the 1640s. The spread to the countryside of the sectarian challenge was as alarming as was the fissiparous history of the gathered churches themselves. Godly ministers waxed gloomy as they saw their congregations fall away to the sects, and the sects in turn fall asunder. Reams of paper are the visible fruit of their anxieties, for probably the major single theme of 1650s pamphleteering was the sectarian threat.

The scale of the threat can be appreciated from the drift of Baxter, the most important moderate clergyman of the decade, away from the Calvinist doctrine of election which seemed to fuel so much of antinomianism. He carried many other clergy with him into an Arminianism, an emphasis on godly works as well as faith, which would probably have disturbed them two decades earlier. And he joined other ordained clergy in stressing the dangers to the church as heatedly as their High Church successors were to do after 1688. The London presbyterian Zachary Crofton in 1657 confessed his astonishment that in these days of hatred 'a gospel minister should die in his bed'.* The common cry that this was 'the dregs of time' showed how far the world had fallen from the hopes of 1641. The support of many presbyterians, the largest single group after the covert 'episcopal men', for royalist plans and plotting in the 1650s did not owe everything to a merely political distaste for Cromwell the usurper.

*Brit. Lib., E909(1), pp. 8–9.

If millions of words were poured out through the presses to confront sectarianism, then millions more lamented the continuing problem of the communion service. Cromwell's triers and ejectors provided no means of coercing sinners, and the 1650s therefore brought no solution to the dilemma which godly ministers had already begun to face a decade earlier. Left with no legal basis for excluding the ungodly from communion, their unpalatable alternatives were either total cessation or the admission of all 'promiscuously'. Either meant the abandonment not only of the godly ideal of 'frequent' communion to seal the faith of the believer, but also of discipline; for exclusion was a minister's chief sanction. Some stalwarts, especially Independents who looked for 'visible saints', did strive to maintain their standards, but the social cost was high – the minister of Gateshead, Durham, was accused of having excluded all but eight of a congregation of 1,000. In response, angry parishioners often joined sectaries in refusing tithes, on the grounds that they had been denied their due. But surviving churchwardens' accounts suggest that the overwhelming majority of ministers either ceased the communion entirely or returned to the traditional practice of parochial celebration at the great festivals of Christmas, Easter and Whitsun. The confusion, and the withdrawal from any attempt at discipline, contributed enormously to a ministerial crisis of confidence.

The 1650s therefore brought a broad clerical response. On the one hand, denominational lines hardened. Baptist ministers formed regional associations, amongst the presbyterians the leadership of the London provincial assembly gained acceptance, while 120 Independent ministers conferred at the Savoy palace in London in 1658. And on the other hand, clergy of all denominations could see the need to repair the fragmentation of the 1640s as parliament failed to institute a state church. In at least seventeen counties ministers formed 'associations', which were often non-denominational, to meet a variety of needs. One pressing concern was the provision of some local means to ordain new clergy, but the major preoccupation of the model association – that of Worcestershire, whose guiding spirit was Baxter – was with the two great problems of antinomianism and the sacrament. The association hoped to nerve its members to deal with challengers to the doctrine and the position of the clergy; and on the sacrament it sought to formulate a common position and eliminate the scandalous diversity of practice.

The ministerial response involved more than organization. Several associations, and surviving presbyterian *classes* too, saw the vital solution to their problems in parochial catechizing, which seemed the way to bring congregations up to the minimum standard of godliness sufficient to allow their admission to the communion service. More generally, catechizing might have the further advantage of being pitched in simple enough terms for the uneducated populace. The implications were startling. The Worcestershire association in 1656 made a striking confession of the failure of preaching, for so long seen as 'the effectual means to salvation':

> We find by sad experience, that the people understand not our public teaching, though we study to speak as plain as we can, and that after many years preaching, even of these same fundamentals, too many can scarce tell anything that we have said.

Baxter, in his *Reformed Pastor* of 1656, confessed, 'We never took the rightest course to demolish the kingdom of darkness till now.'* While catechizing had certainly been a feature of the pre-civil war church, most had probably been performed in the household; but the catechisms of the 1640s and 50s – such as the Westminster Assembly's *Shorter Catechism,* which attracted strong support in Cromwell's parliaments – were primarily ministerial and parochial. They proliferated because many clergy had come to recognize the ineffectiveness of the pulpit, to which they had pinned their trust. With that discovery we can perhaps speak of the pastoral failure of puritanism. Instead, a new era opened with the beginnings of the parochial catechizing movement which was to be so fundamental a feature of later English protestantism.

But catechizing did not provide the answer fast enough. Even Baxter, who had in 1656 rejoiced at the prospects for godliness in the land, in 1657 complained that though he had 'waited a year or two . . . none but a few' were willing to appear as Christians on his terms; the rest 'continue silently to hear'. And if this was true of Kidderminster under Baxter, a pastoral genius, how much more so elsewhere? England, to the bafflement of the godly, remained unreformed, though it might seem no surprise to us. Fierce Calvinism, or the varied enthusiasms of recent years, was not necessarily well-suited to the work of evangelism. John Evelyn in 1656 noted that preaching on the southern outskirts of London was only on 'high and speculative points and strains . . . there was nothing practical preached, or that pressed reformation of life'. Even Crofton, a more sympathetic witness, warned his readers, 'You have been too long pleased and puffed up with high flown doctrines . . . heady disorderly knowledge, uttered in free but very confused discourses.'* The publications of the 1650s bear out such complaints, and testify to the failure of the godly cause. It was no wonder that Oliver's calls for

*Brit. Lib., E1653(2), p. 11; E1574(1), preface.
*Brit. Lib., E906(1), preface; *Diary of John Evelyn,* III, p. 184; Brit. Lib., E1165(1), preface.

national fasts lamented the prevailing ingratitude to the Lord, manifested in the often bitter disunity of the godly and the unrepentance of the rest.

If ideals were tarnished in England, so they were elsewhere. Marvell, assessing Cromwell in the 'Horatian Ode', had thought the general might be a 'climacteric' to 'all states not free'; and some amongst the regime's supporters hoped that conquered Ireland might be made a blueprint for reform in England. But abroad as well as at home pragmatism and financial constraints tempered the protector's achievements.

The effect of financial pressures was clearest in Ireland. The novelty of the so-called 'Cromwellian settlement' did not lie in its outline: the protector merely implemented the plans of the Rump, which in turn – in its reliance on private interest – had followed in the steps of other governments before it. Rather, the novelty of the measures of the 1650s lay in their sweeping scale. Debts dictated policy. The Rump, and the protectorate after it, needed to recoup an expenditure of £2.5M. on the reconquest, over £300,000 was due to those who had 'adventured' loans for Ireland in 1642, while the pay of 35,000 soldiers was in arrears. Massive expropriation of Irish landowners, Antichristian by definition, seemed to offer the only chance of financial stability.

As the remarkable land survey carried out by William Petty proceeded, it grew apparent that the land could never satisfy the demands on it. Successive governments in 1653 therefore determined to transplant all Catholic landowners 'to hell or Connaught', as the later saying went, in the rocky west; they would thus clear the way for the creation of a loyal protestant yeomanry in the hinterland. But protestant settlers proved as hard to attract as James had found them for his Ulster plantation of 1607. The easing of economic conditions in England, and delays in the settlement of claims, ensured that only about 12,000 of the 35,000 soldiers entitled finally settled in the country. The rest, weary and disillusioned, sold out to officers and speculators who then in their need for labour connived at the presence of Catholic tenant farmers; similarly, town corporations winked at Catholic townsmen who illegally stayed on. For the Irish landless poor, about three-quarters of the total population, the Cromwellian settlement probably made little practical difference to the hardships they already suffered.

Nevertheless, the effects of the settlement should not be minimized. The enforced winter migration of some 40,000 Catholic landowners and their families is a story of horror. There was not enough land in Connaught, and many of the dispossessed therefore took to

brigandage, becoming 'tories' in the language of the time and prolonging the brutalities inflicted by one side or other on the survivors.
Others emigrated, whether forcibly or voluntarily. More far-reaching
were the social consequences of the settlement, which laid the grounds
for the later 'protestant ascendancy'. Catholics held some 60 per cent
of the land in Ireland in 1641, but only about 20 per cent in 1660. The
exclusion of Catholics from urban trades and offices left little chance
of a Catholic middle class forming, while religion became more than
ever an index of nationalism.

Despite the government's hopes there were few positive achievements to balance the equation. The protectorate's near-bankruptcy
thwarted plans for educational and ecclesiastical expansion. Furthermore, too much energy was dissipated in internecine friction amongst
the diverse protestants, military and settler, especially during the
1653–5 rule of Cromwell's tolerant son-in-law, Charles Fleetwood.
As Fleetwood was succeeded by Cromwell's determined but conservative son Henry, English policy focused increasingly on Strafford's
old goals of raising revenue and fostering trade.

Scotland too disappointed reformers. Although no such sweeping
overhaul was intended in protestant Scotland as in Ireland, there were
some similarities in treatment: for ironically, the republic pursued
uniformity even more aggressively than had the luckless Charles I.
Not only did the protectorate, following the Rump's plans, abolish
the Scottish and Irish parliament and allot each subordinate 'commonwealth' thirty seats in the British parliament at Westminster; it
also sought to extend English law into partly feudal Scotland. No less
chauvinist than those who in 1607 urged the abrogation of Scottish
law, the Rumpers had combined an idealistic desire to free the common people with a realistic attempt to bring down the magnates who
had led the Scottish invasions of 1648 and 1651. The republic thus
went far beyond the old royal policy of attacking the hereditary jurisdictions of the nobility. English officials and officers in conquered
Scotland favoured tenants and creditors in actions against nobles,
while at the same time they strove to comfort the godly by limiting the
overmighty kirk and fostering Independency. The results were explosive. As English policy became clear, recruits flocked to the remaining embattled royalists under Glencairn and Middleton, in revolt in
1653–5 in the Highlands. The resentful kirk stood aside as debt-
ridden Scottish magnates, threatened with ruin by the government's
stand, took arms.

The rebellion occasioned further retreats from reform. The commander in Scotland, Robert Lilburne, brother to the Leveller,
recognized the economic grievances and imparted a needed flexibility
to English policy; but he lacked the harshness to subdue a guerilla

war. George Monck, who succeeded him in 1654, was not only pragmatic in his politics but also well-versed in scorched-earth tactics after serving in the royal army in Ireland in the early 1640s. Reformist goals were finally sacrificed to political stability with the arrival in 1655 of another former royalist, lord Broghill. Sent to head the civil administration, Broghill, a brilliant younger son of the the earl of Cork, sought to propitiate the kirk and to build better relations with the nobility. He did not implement a total reaction, though, for the suppression of heritable jurisdictions, and Monck's troops eliminated some of the worst aristocratic excesses. Better justice and order, and the benefits from freer trade in peacetime, gained the Cromwellian government considerable local co-operation. But imperialism proved a wasting asset. Expenditures exceeded revenues in Ireland by around £100,000 p.a., and in Scotland by at least £130,000 p.a., thus further dashing the hopes of those who had looked for reforms in England, let alone elsewhere.

The growing financial restraints on the government might seem to have dictated a policy of retrenchment, and indeed, the protector moved swiftly to come to terms with the Dutch. But Marvell had spoken prophetically when he declared that 'restless Cromwell' could not rest content in 'the inglorious arts of peace'. Conscious of a prophetic mission, and haunted too by England's decline from its legendary Elizabethan glories, Cromwell told his council in the summer of 1654, 'God has not brought us hither where we are but to consider the work that we may do in the world as well as at home.' Doing that work was to make England the most respected state in Europe in the 1650s; but the resentments at the taxes Cromwell's foreign policy required contributed to the reaction which brought the Restoration.

That ambiguous outcome is an appropriate comment on Oliver's ambivalent policies. The eventual shape of his relations with the Dutch – peace, the end to Dutch aid to the exiled Charles Stuart, and commercial concessions from Portugal in the East Indies and Sweden in the Baltic to balance Dutch strength in those areas – suggest considerable realism. Yet in the treaty of Westminster which in April 1654 put an end to the Dutch war Oliver steadfastly refused to exploit fully England's naval advantage. Not only did he seek security, conciliating the Dutch in fear lest they turn again to the royalists; he also hoped for a protestant alliance against 'the old enemy', Rome and its – alleged – lackey, the king of Spain. He even contemplated abandoning England's interests in the East Indies in return for a Dutch alliance against the Spanish western empire. Similarly mixed motives underlay the protector's policy towards Sweden which took shape in the middle of the decade. The Baltic was vital as the prime source for naval supplies, and Oliver's friendship with Sweden which balanced the Dutch alliance with Denmark can be seen as a major act of statesmanship. Yet he had sought more than that. Myopically seeing in the energetic and expansionist Charles X of Sweden a protestant hero, the protector dreamed of a pan-protestant alliance which might yet permit a march on Habsburg Vienna. Oliver was too much the realist to allow Charles X to achieve the Baltic hegemony which the latter coveted; but he failed to recognize that a selfish hegemony was the goal of protestant Sweden, though he came to suspect it of protestant Denmark and the Dutch. Zeal tempered with realism might be the verdict on his stance towards the protestant states.

Assessment of the protector's relations with the Catholic powers is more complex. Had stability and reform at home been the over-riding concerns they seemed, he would have been best served by seeking peace; for neither France nor Spain, exhausted as both were, constituted a threat. French support for Charles Stuart was an embarrassment, but one that might have been ended with fewer costs than those Oliver brought on himself. But he dreamed still of dislodging the pope, or of aiding the suffering French Huguenots around Bordeaux, and of bringing godly liberty to Europe. And as always there were more painful considerations. Just as the Long Parliament had been unable to pay off the army in 1647, so Oliver in 1654 was trapped, unable to pay off the fleet used against the Dutch and left only with the hope that it might be cheaper in the short run to keep ships and men in active service. Accordingly, despite his instinctual dislike of Spain, despite his detestation of the persecution of protestants in the French dependency of Savoy, and despite too his dreams of a protestant union, Oliver allowed himself to be courted throughout 1654 by the two great Catholic powers. At the end of the year he finally opted for an assault on Spain's West Indian colonies and drifted slowly towards friendship with France.

The protector's reasons for turning against Spain were revealing. Madrid had allowed no freedom of worship to English merchants, nor security to English colonies; furthermore, it had an empire from which a rich trade in slaves, sugar and tobacco was hoped, and in which protestantism might be advanced. The chance of seizing a Spanish treasure fleet was as always a further strong incentive, reinforced now by the possibility of helping captive Portugal secure independence from Spain. And as in the case of the Dutch peace there was a strong political argument. Royalists sheltered by a Spanish enemy would be less dangerous, both for geographical and ideological reasons, than royalists in French ports. That mixture of motives – the concerns of the 'Elizabethan' gentlemen, the aggressive imperialist,

the protestant zealot and the pragmatist – could be readily reconciled
by one who believed his country God's chosen nation.

Oliver's foreign policy is remarkable for its readiness to use force in
the nation's interests, not only against Spain in the Caribbean but
also against Dutch and French colonists on the North American
mainland. Yet as on the British mainland, imperialism had its costs,
and reservations expressed by the hard-headed Lambert in the summer of 1654 were to be borne out. Cromwell's 'western design' in the
Caribbean took England in 1655 into a conflict with Spain which was
to prove both economically and politically disastrous.

Despite the achievements, then, the reforms fell far short of the
hopes. Everywhere financial and political realities drove the protector
to temper the desirable with the possible. In 1654 the accumulated
debt stood at the level of one year's total revenue, or about £1.5M.
– manageable enough, had long-term credit been available. But the
scandal of the 'public faith' left Oliver's borrowings even more hand-
to-mouth than the Stuarts' had been. The likelihood that diplomacy
would occasion new burdens must have made a welcome prospect of
the parliament which the Instrument of Government required Oliver
to meet on 3 September 1654.

How that parliament would behave was unclear, for it was to be
elected on a new franchise. True to Ireton's proposals of 1647–9, the
Instrument redistributed the 400 English seats for the new single-
chamber assembly in accordance with the tax burden – not, as the
Levellers would have had it, with population. While it eliminated
many rotten boroughs and enfranchised the new industrial towns
of Leeds, Manchester and Halifax, it awarded most seats to the
counties. There were anomalies – London, long the butt of provincial jealousy and also perhaps of the army's political suspicions, was
markedly under-represented – but on the whole representation was
fairer than it was to be again until the later nineteenth century. More
disputed is the significance of the Instrument's replacement of the
trifling forty-shilling freehold franchise in the counties with a requirement of £200 in either real of personal property. Although this
marked an important shift away from the concept of land as the only
title to political action, it seems clear that it also narrowed the electorate, despite the arguments about democracy in 1647. Nevertheless, consistency underlay the change, for the army had in 1647
denounced corruption and the pursuit of private interest, and the
Instrument now aimed at an *independent* electorate; impoverished
cottagers and rotten boroughs were alike vulnerable to corruption.
But sadly for the protector, idealism proved politically counter-
productive. Although the military in Scotland and Ireland controlled

the elections there, the rotten boroughs included the few English constituencies where government interest could have been deployed – had Oliver been willing to deploy it. In the counties too, independent property-owning voters were likely to oppose the army and the social ramifications of religious reform. Lambert's Instrument had strengthened the backwoods.

The 1654 elections revealed much of political attitudes. Turn-out seems to have been low, suggesting a large measure of apathy, though the threat to the clerical profession mounted in Barebone's generated a fierce clerical backlash. 20 per cent of the Essex voters were reported to have been clergy, a clerical party canvassed in Wiltshire, and clergy deluged the new parliament with calls for support. Ranged against them in vain in counties like Oxfordshire* and Wiltshire were local alliances of radical saints and of commonwealthsmen striving to recover from the blows of 1653. With royalists excluded from the polls, most MPs were moderate puritan gentlemen, of the sort who had eagerly supported the 'presbyterian' drive for settlement in 1647–8. While they might applaud Cromwell's opening appeal for 'healing and settling', their attitude to the sects and the soldiers was another matter.

Oliver's unease was clear. He desperately needed this parliament, and not just for the permanent settlement which would allow him to shake off military rule as the country gentleman in him so craved to do. His short-term purposes also demanded a settlement, since the Instrument sanctioned the rule of protector and council no longer than this parliament. Accordingly, before the opening the council cut the monthly assessment from £120,000 to £90,000, a major sacrifice for a régime near bankruptcy; lest this move fail to buy 'country' support, the council also rushed through a flurry of ordinances, some reforming, some administrative, while it still could.

The government's apprehensions were well-founded. Its hopes of speedy parliamentary ratification of the Instrument were blocked both by a handful of obdurate commonwealthsmen and by many more country gentlemen eager to avenge all the affronts they had suffered since 1647. Cromwell's problems were compounded by his characteristic reluctance to impose his will until necessity dictated, which meant that the regime's defence in parliament was totally inadequate. The troops which once more surrounded parliament on 12 September were thus a confession of political failure. In an impassioned speech, Oliver justified himself as he so often did by appealing to history and to the record of God's providences, and pointed too to the support of 'the good people – although most of his audience

*Longleat, Whitelocke Mss., vol. 16, f. 69.

would have questioned his definition. He then insisted that MPs take a 'recognition' to accept 'the government, as it is settled in one single person, and a parliament'. About a hundred intransigents withdrew in protest – country gentlemen outraged by one more display of military power joining commonwealthsmen like Haselrig and Thomas Scot in a dramatic if futile gesture.

The remaining members were not to be diverted from their campaign to erode what Oliver had declared to be 'fundamentals': liberty of conscience and the status of the army. Oliver had intimated his willingness to limit the expression of 'prodigious blasphemies' such as those of Biddle, but the fierce clerical campaign against the sects indicated that any such limits were likely to trench on the freedom of Baptists too, whom Oliver held dear. It was one thing for MPs to encourage Owen to revive his doctrinal 'fundamentals' of 1652, but quite another for them to emulate the Long Parliament in attacking 'damnable heresies'. MPs showed themselves the heirs of the Long Parliament in other ways. Fired by the failure of rents to regain their pre-war levels, they voted down the monthly assessment's tax on land, and with it the number of troops, from the present 54,000 to the 30,000 the Instrument envisaged as a permanent force. The legalism of the latter demand suggests that these MPs would have been at home too in the 1620s, as does their refusal of Cromwell's offer to involve them in the detail of foreign policy. Indeed, several close divisions suggest some support for the government, and parliament willingly voted funds for the upkeep of its civil, if not its military, side. It accepted too the compromise proposal of that formidable home-spun orator, the presbyterian ex-Colonel John Birch, that for the present the assessment be merely reduced to £60,000 a month. But Oliver knew well what the army could expect from MPs cast in the 1620s mould.

This was anyway not the time to alarm the solidery, for there were stirrings afoot. The new ecclesiastical order of triers and ejectors infuriated the Fifth Monarchists, and that autumn Feake and Simpson cried out to the soldiers against the protector as 'the father of lies', and as the father too of a new papalism. Equally, Oliver's protectoral dignity offended commonwealthsmen, and in October a group of officers prepared to denounce the retreat from the Engagement of 1647: only 'constant successive parliaments, freely chosen by the people', would save England from corruption. 'The three colonels', following was as small as their trust in the voters was misplaced, and Oliver dismissed them without incident. But that winter discontent spread, amongst the officers in Scotland and in the major garrison at Hull; there were signs too of links between Leveller and royalist terrorists. Over Christmas Oliver reinforced the strong points in

London, and waited impatiently for the expiry of the five lunar months which would give him at least a semblance of legality under the Instrument for dissolving this obstructionist parliament.

But Oliver was not simply speaking for the soldiers when he angrily dissolved parliament on 22 January 1655. He then characterized the army as in effect a separate estate in the nation, its position warranted by the protection it gave the godly, and in so doing pointed to the dilemma of his rule. He craved a parliamentary settlement which would secure the liberty of 'men as men'; yet he had also fought for liberty for the Christian conscience, and only the army could guarantee the latter. One of his supporters in parliament urged against parliamentary control over the army in terms Oliver himself might have used: 'for such parliaments might hereafter be chosen as would betray the glorious cause of the people of God'. In 1642 the godly cause and the constitutionalist cause had appeared to many to go hand-in-hand. Although Cromwell fought hard to reconcile them, they had long ago parted company in the eyes of the traditional political nation.

The spring of 1655 brought the crisis of Oliver's protectorate. Among the least of his worries was the conspiracy which had troubled him over Christmas. Most royalists were cowed into submission, and the hot-heads too divided to co-ordinate effectively – their ill-planned rising fizzled limply on 8 March, when a handful of cavaliers in the north and midlands slunk away from each other, 'strangely frightened with their own shadows'. Only in the south-west did serious trouble occur, when perhaps 200 royalists, led by the former colonel John Penruddock, seized the assize judges in Salisbury; but finding little support they fled westwards, into the arms of watchful troops.

The constitutional predicament was more alarming. The Instrument had provided for rule by the executive until the first parliament. Parliament had of course refused the necessary endorsement, and thus cast doubt on the protector's powers to legislate by ordinance, even to raise taxes. Oliver evaded the issue by simply ordering that taxes be collected, but he was on weak ground. The Norfolk assessment commissioners debated uncomfortably in March whether to act, since the protector had not dared 'meddle with the legislative power himself, but put it upon us, and we must by action establish it a law, and so may be sued, and may prove a ship-money cause';* but in the end they conformed. The parallels with the 1630s were indeed close, not least in that few relished confrontation – the only opposition seems to have come from radicals, from Barebone and a few

*Thurloe State Papers, III, 328.

purged commonwealthsmen. Nevertheless, constitutional scruples
were more widespread, and the crisis grew during May and June
when Oliver was driven to replace five of the central court judges.
Like the nation at large these had adapted themselves remarkably
swiftly to the various changes of 1653 – doubtless encouraged to do so
by Oliver's alleged observation that if the men of the red robe would
not enforce the law his men in red coats would. The judges' professional bias in favour of political stability inclined them to support
Oliver just as earlier judges had supported Charles, and they had not
flinched when the protector, like his various predecessors in government, ignored the niceties of *habeas corpus*. But parliament's failure to
ratify the Instrument now forced them to confront issues they would
clearly rather have overlooked.

In court after court the protectorate came under challenge. The
trials of the royalist rebels that spring occasioned considerable heart-
searching amongst the judges about the 1654 treason ordinance. Still
more disturbing was the concurrent case of George Cony, a merchant
and religious radical who had refused to pay customs duties. In May
his counsel – all prominent conservatives, revealing the kind of alliances the protectorate had created – challenged the entire Instrument, and although they were promptly imprisoned their arguments
swayed the bench. Oliver's replacement of Chief Justice Rolle and
two others, and his exasperation at the use of 'magna farta' by
pettifogging constitutionalists, shows how far government was
becoming business as usual rather than a matter of high ideals.
Further embarrassments in chancery increased the protector's impatience. Bulstrode Whitelocke and Sir Thomas Widdrington, two of
the three commissioners of the great seal, rejected the 1654 chancery
reforms, alleging their inconvenience; but the usually pliant
Whitelocke's real objections were clearly constitutional. The council
quickly found replacements, including the old middle-grouper
Nathaniel Fiennes, willing to do the work; nevertheless, confusion in
the north midlands suggests that the constitutional crisis may have
caused a temporary breakdown of legal process.* It also encouraged
London presbyterians to exploit the apparent lapse of the Instrument
by mounting a new attack in the courts on Baptists and on Biddle,
alleging that the swingeing 1648 blasphemy ordinance was still in
force. Oliver had to forestall further moves against the Baptists by
reluctantly sending Biddle, whom he abhorred, into exile beyond the
reach of the common law. Coming after the frustrations in parliament
the debacles emphasized his failure to obtain much more than the
barest acquiescence from the political nation.

*H.M.C. 12th Report, Appendix part II, pp. 343, 344.

Characteristically, Cromwell responded to the turmoil in quite contradictory ways. Showing the flexibility that was his political strength he moved to appease the gentry. Cutting the assessment to the £60,000-per-month level that Birch had urged in parliament, he then made a virtue of necessity by reducing the soldiers' pay, and their numbers to 40,000. The desperately needed savings totalled about £300,000 p.a., though they did not make good the loss on the assessment.

But despite the fiscal concessions, Oliver's solution to the constitutional dilemma was a military one. A few of his civilian advisers seem to have sought a Cromwellian monarchy as the only way to wean the protector from the soldiers, but Oliver was no readier to take the crown than he had been in 1653; one of the earliest 'kinglings', Ashley Cooper, had already withdrawn in defeat from the council during the 1654 parliament. Convinced by the failure of his attempt at 'healing and settling' that the nation was as unregenerate as he had thought it in the summer of 1653, the protector now swung sharply against civilian counsels. Yet Cromwell was no tennis-ball of the factions. The growing divisions at court in the spring of 1655 were real enough as the military interest vied with the new 'courtiers' – some of them (such as Wolseley and Charles Howard, like the unlamented Ashley Cooper) the more objectionable to those who had won the war in that they were pragmatic ex-royalists still in their twenties or early thirties. Nevertheless, the sudden unsheathing of the sword stemmed from the incessant clash between Oliver's conflicting visions of rule.

If Oliver was reluctantly coming to the conclusion that the hand of providence was no longer clearly visible in a history which was turning out to be one damn thing after another, he hoped yet to salvage something for the godly cause. The ensuing rule of the major-generals combined police work and tax-gathering with moral reform in a way that shaped the legend of the Cromwellian years as the triumph of blue-nosed puritanism.

Security remained a prime concern. The enforced troop cuts left the council uneasy in face of the latent discontent uncovered by Secretary Thurloe's efficient intelligence work, but the response of some of the godly to Penruddock's rising suggested a solution. 3,000 were reported to have turned out in Somerset, 400 in the old parliamentarian fortress of Gloucester; the council therefore sought a new militia from this godly remnant. Like the militia of old, the new militia would be cheap, and might even placate those who disliked a standing army. But, to ensure its political reliability, the local militia commissioners were to include a powerful leaven of regular army officers serving in the counties, under the direction of the major-general heading each of the eleven districts into which the country was eventually divided.

The militia only revealed the narrow base of the regime's support. Although the influential Sir Thomas Barnardiston in Suffolk and a few other members of the pre-war ruling élites were ready to serve, the commissioners everywhere included lesser gentry who had proved their zeal, or their worth, in minor and often disreputable posts. A clearer indication of the government's sense of isolation is found in the funding for the new forces. The major-generals were to 'decimate' royalists who had not demonstrated their change of heart, imposing fines of 10 per cent on those with a landed income of over £100 p.a., or with over £1,500 in goods. In justification the council cited the wave of conspiracies – since the royalists' intransigence made protection necessary, better that they rather than the innocent should pay. For, Oliver maintained, the cavaliers were separating themselves from the nation, intermarrying as a caste; 'that generation of men', argued Thurloe, must be dealt with 'as the Irish are'. But the evidence of non-partisan social gatherings of gentry in counties from Sussex to Cheshire belies these wild allegations.

Despite the fears of a massacre aroused amongst alarmed western royalists,* decimation was not entirely the instrument of tyranny it seemed. It was indeed a fundamentally arbitrary executive procedure, based, since the lapse of the protector's power to issue ordinances, only in the council's instructions to those concerned. It breached the Rump's act of oblivion, and its flavour is best caught in the plea of Major-General Berry, responsible for Wales and the Marches, that the protector 'let us alone awhile with my lord Coventry'. But this Oliver was reluctant to do. Still the man of the old middle group, he could see the dangers in alienating those otherwise quiet. His congenital ambivalence is nowhere clearer than in the way he held back subordinates he had empowered as extraordinary agents. His often sympathetic response to aggrieved royalists dismayed major-generals who saw their revenues from decimation, and thus the readiness of their militias, decline in consequence. The yield of decimation was also limited by the need to rely on evidence of income provided by royalists themselves, and by the relatively high level of the income threshhold, which left too few royalists in some counties to yield sufficient fines. The major-generals spent most of their first six months in office on decimation work, yet the militia had been reduced by one-fifth by the following summer and the pay of the soldiers fell up to a year in arrears. The demoralization of the royalists

---

*G. Davies, ed., *Memoirs of the Family of Guise of Elmore* (Camden Soc., 1917), pp. 129–30.

certainly gave the agents of Charles Stuart diminishing hope of winning back the kingdom. Nevertheless, the inability of many major-generals to muster the militias in the summer of 1656 for fear of meeting demands for pay suggests that the government could hardly regard this military interlude as an unqualified success.

But as Oliver in council in the autumn of 1655 shaped the instrument providence, and the careful Lambert, had put into his hands, decimation became overlaid with other activities. In successive calls for days of humiliation in 1654–5 the protector had preached jeremiads upon the sinfulness of the nation; his prophetic zeal was heightened by the approach of what was widely thought to be the climacteric year, 1656. Throughout Europe, Christians and Jews alike expected great things of a year so close to apocalyptic '666', and such expectations led the council into intensive discussion late in 1655 on the readmission of the Jews to England. The way to the millennium had to be prepared.

Accordingly, the instructions to the major-generals turned increasingly to godly rule, to varied effect. Local studies have indicated the remarkable conscientiousness of local administrators in the 1650s. Poor rate expenditures rose as far afield as Yorkshire and Essex, even though food prices were falling fast; quarter sessions from Warwickshire to Kent dealt with the poor more urgently than in the 1630s by means of almshouses for the infirm as well as by out-relief and the fierce punishment of both parents of bastards. Yet social regulation was far from godly evangelism, and there was even widespread evasiveness when the council called for lists of Catholics in 1655. Oliver, who in his second parliament was to denounce the JPs as 'owls', loath to be scorned by their neighbours for exerting themselves, intended the major-generals to compensate by spreading zeal throughout the land. Accordingly, in county after county quarter sessions' orders against alehouses coincided with a major-general's presence; Charles Worsley, the most energetic of them all, saw to the suppression of 215 alehouses in a single hundred, or subdivision of Lancashire, and almost 200 in the city of Chester. But Worsley found aid locally for, isolated amongst religious conservatives, the godly of the north-west were more self-conscious than most and Worsley was able to rely on them for information. Where local puritans were less aggressive, the impact of the major-generals depended on their own efforts. While Worsley literally worked himself to death, the godly William Goffe, Cromwell's least successful appointment, wrung his hands ineffectually in Hampshire and Sussex.

In few respects were the major-generals' activities entirely novel. Throughout the republic, army officers had acted as a godly leaven in local commissions. Furthermore, others before the Cromwellians had sought to purify the land: sixteenth-century humanists had urged the death penalty for adulterers, and Archbishop Laud had, in his moral concerns at least, been thoroughly puritanical. Major-General Boteler's determined harrying of vagabonds in the south midlands would have been applauded by generations of JPs. Still less revolutionary was the major-generals' attempt to inculcate that honesty of purpose which the early defences of the protectorate had proclaimed. Edward Whalley in particular, in the midlands, checked weights and measures and saw to the enforcement of market regulations and the antiquated enclosure laws; significantly, he applauded the unradical judge Hale as a 'godly man' for his even-handed justice.

Even the assumption that the major-generals represent the high-point of early-modern centralization is open to question. In the patchy central register of information on royalists – which shows that in the security field at least Hartlib's passion for useful statistics had taken effect – some grounds can be found for the legend. But historians have been misled by the intensity of the major-generals' labours, epitomized in the astonishing total of over 5,000 bonds for good behaviour taken from suspects from all walks of life by Cromwell's brother-in-law Desborough in the south-western counties. Cromwell had characteristically turned not to institutional reform and centralized procedures for enforcement, but to godly men; his anger at the brief vacation from Wales taken by the hugely burdened Berry is symptomatic, both of his hopes and of his failure. No more than Charles I, therefore, could he create an obedient local administration – any 'system' in the major-generals' rule extended no further than the paper of their instructions. Indeed, these 'satraps and bashaws', or local despots, were subject to the same complex tensions as all local officers before them. They were soon acting as mediators, speaking for their localities to the central government as well as *vice versa*. Robert Lilburne in the north-east backed local demands for local courts and for what was to be the short-lived third university at Durham, while Whalley echoed some lord lieutenant of old when he told Thurloe he had 'in the face of all my counties' declared 'that they cannot be so forward to desire and propound any thing for the good of the country, but his highness . . . will be as forward to promote it.' It was ironic, though not inappropriate, that the major-generals should be denounced in the ensuing parliament as 'cantonizers' for dividing up the country, rather than as centralizers.

The problems of the towns, far more than of the counties, drove the major-generals into arbitrary acts. There had been occasional outbursts of urban zeal to gratify them – thus, influenced by the radical garrison, Bristol's magistrates stopped the water conduits on the sabbath. But the major-generals complained incessantly that on the whole urban magistrates were 'all asleep'. The jurisdictional autonomy of towns gave central government far less control than it possessed over the appointive JPs in the counties, and after the sporadic purges stemming from the Engagement conservatives had crept back in municipal elections. Determined monarchs both before and after might have sympathized with the protector in his dilemma. A characteristically blunt proclamation in September 1655, of no legal validity, extended the Rump's expiring statute against royalist participation in municipal politics, and added a new demand that magistrates be godly. On that flimsy basis the major-generals systematically purged town corporations, pressing their victims to resign 'by an usurped, illegal, pretended power', as the outraged town clerk of Lincoln noted. The impact of such tactics, which extended to surrounding the town hall of Hythe in Kent with troops, was remarkable. Desborough drove nine to resign from Tewkesbury corporation, five from Tiverton, two from Bristol, four from Gloucester, and probably more.

Purges were no guarantee of permanency, and in the spring of 1656 the council duly set up a committee to regulate town charters. This has sometimes been seen as a bid to reshape the country by creating packed parliamentary electorates, a gambit which Charles II and James II were later to follow profitably. The new charter for Colchester, steered through by Major-General Haynes, certainly vested power in a rigid, and unrepresentatively radical, oligarchy. But Cromwell was always more concerned with individuals than with structures; and even at the height of his arbitrary rule he still hoped to return to ways of settlement. Accordingly, despite Haynes's prompting and despite the eagerness of many towns for some *quid pro quo* in new charters, the council did little to pack the boroughs. As ever, other business intervened, and few charters were issued. Furthermore, the fact that the leading light on the council's committee was the reformist lawyer, William Sheppard, suggests that the protector's aim may not have been simply partisan.

Oliver's decision in the summer of 1656 to swing from repressing the nation to seeking its aid in a new parliament was not therefore wholly quixotic, for he had never lost hope of a settlement. As always, however, events rushed him on. Lambert's misgivings of 1654 about the costs and consequences of a 'western design', an assault on Spain's empire, had been borne out.

Few Englishmen understood the problems of amphibious warfare, least of all in the tropics, and Oliver trusted too much to God's aid to give his usual care to the preparations. Instead, he optimistically advised the expedition's commanders, 'The Lord himself hath a controversy with your enemies; even with that Romish Babylon.' He sought a substitute for the lost Providence Island colony of his old middle group friends, a base for attacks on Spain's treasure fleets as well as its empire. But when in the spring of 1655, ill-led and supplied and ravaged by disease, the raw recruits reached their destination of Hispaniola in the West Indies even the weak Spanish presence proved too much for them. Oliver drew little consolation from the capture of Jamaica, which was eventually to prove far more valuable, and concluded that God was chastising a sinful nation and its magistrate.

The protector was therefore ready for a European war when Spain retaliated against English shipping. Amidst the humiliations of the 1660s and 70s Oliver's efforts dazzled in retrospect; all Europe had courted his alliance, and Admiral Blake swept the seas of pirate and foe alike. At the time it seemed different. A Spanish war could arouse patriotic fervour, but Spain unlike the Dutch had little shipping to attack, while English merchants were as vulnerable as ever to Dunkirk privateers. By mid-1656 the council was deluged with protests about losses; still more politically damaging was the discontent in the new draperies regions which depended on trade with Spain. Funding was in shorter supply than ever, with scant prospect of loans from a City whose long suspicion of government credit was heightened in 1656 by the levy of a virtual forced loan of £50,000 on the East India Company. In desperation, the protector in July resorted to the intensely provocative step of ordering the payment in advance of the monthly assessment for the following December–June, in effect doubling the rate for late 1656. The political nation's remarkable submissiveness is again evident in its compliance with this arbitrary demand. Still, there seemed neither to the council nor to the major-generals, anxious for money to pay their militias, any alternative to a parliament.

Most of the major-generals contemplated elections with equanimity, and indeed some actually urged them on Oliver. They had troops and they had, as Whalley had exulted, struck 'an awe . . . into the spirits of wicked men'. Their optimism was not wholly unfounded, for the perennial eagerness of constituencies to secure friends at court ensured the election of an unprecedented total of over forty officers, who helped constitute an official and 'courtier' group which comprised a respectable third of the attenuated house. That achievement is the more notable in that the government did little to influence the polls. The emergency of 1655 had brought tighter censorship and the suppression of all but the two government newspapers, but no propaganda was deployed. And since most militia troops were unpaid, the major-generals dared not muster them. Furthermore, the government's local agents were as unco-ordinated as ever.

The unusually blatant electoral manipulation in Herefordshire was offset by the conservative sheriffs who countered the officers' efforts in Cheshire and Suffolk. The disorganization common to all governments was undoubtedly partly responsible for these anomalies, but so were the divisions at the centre, which had been inflamed by the recent military interlude. A coherent approach to the elections was anyway rendered less likely by Oliver's own confusion: country gentleman as he was, he seems to have determined that elections ought to be free.

'Free' elections, even under the Instrument, could mean only one thing. The rule of the 'swordmen and decimators' had united the gentry, whether presbyterian, neuter or crypto-royalist, against military high-handedness. As Henry Verney complained in Buckinghamshire, 'All sports put down, and the gentry not permitted to meet,' for the major-generals' quest for order had brought the suppression of horse-racing and cock-fighting. Accordingly, the electoral apathy of 1654 had evaporated: contests were more frequent and the turn-out higher. The consequences were clear everywhere in 'presbyterian' triumphs, in Major-General Kelsey's failure to gain one of the eleven Kent seats, or in the bottom place secured by the collaborationist Sir Thomas Barnardiston in Suffolk. The radicals paid the penalty too, although many had been equally distrustful of Oliver's arbitrary and imperial tendencies. Baptist candidates in Middlesex were nearly lynched, and violence disturbed the Westminster poll. Sir Henry Vane's attempt to unite godly and republican dissidents with his *A Healing Question* was a damp squib, although his appeal to the usefully vague 'good old cause' proved potent in the later protectorate.

The outcry at the hustings against 'soldiers and courtiers' aroused fears of a new rising, and hopes of counter-measures: as Kelsey protested, 'The interest of God's people is to be preferred before a thousand parliaments.' But the new parliament-men took care not to provoke such a response, and for three months avoided any attack on the major-generals. They had learned the lesson of 1654, that confrontation would only bring more military rule. Anyway, the sitting MPs were consciously conformist, for the council disingenuously exploited the Instrument's insistence on godly MPs to exclude a hundred or so political opponents at the start. Commonwealthsmen such as the inseparable duo of Haselrig and Scot, presbyterians like Birch, as well as known royalists and all the City's MPs had gone, taking with them another fifty who withdrew in protest.

Those remaining quickly got down to business. Quietly passing over the massive breach of privileges, they declared their goodwill by repudiating Stuart claims to the throne: Thurloe's complacency at the end of October at the absence of any 'contradictory spirit to any thing' had some foundation. Most MPs evidently hoped to persuade the protector to 'civilianize' himself; in the meantime they worked at all the mundane bills, for law courts at York, for draining lands in Hampshire, against 'undecent' dress, that had been so long neglected. The impression of a house pursuing 'business as usual' in the manner of some of its 1620s predecessors is strengthened by its attitude to the Spanish war. While it rallied willingly enough to the protestant banner – all the more so after the exhilarating seizure in September of part of the Spanish treasure fleet – it preferred to fight an anti-Catholic war not by voting taxes but by passing anti-Catholic measures, to the embarrassment of the more tolerant Oliver. Members preferred 'jogging on' after their own affairs, as an increasingly anxious Thurloe noted.

In fact, the confusion of the parliament in late 1656 says much of the protector's failings. Historians often see him as a congenital back-bencher, temperamentally averse to government, and as such responsible for his parliamentary failures, and there is some truth to the verdict – though we should remember that kings born to rule had equally had problems with parliaments. Oliver can be faulted for allowing the large court and military contingent to join in the stampede after private bills in late 1656, and for making little effort to divert it towards revenue matters. His opening address too had spoken largely but vaguely of a host of reforms for which he yearned but had not planned, and he chose a fatally weak Speaker in the time-serving lawyer Sir Thomas Widdrington. His providentialist posture of 'waiting on the Lord' was as ill-suited to giving a lead through the minutiae of politics, as opposed to the crises, as it had always been.

Consideration of the revenue was further disrupted in December by the case of James Nayler. This brought into relief still more brutally than had the successive attempts to punish John Biddle the Socinian the limits to the puritan concern for freedom for godly consciences. It underline too the constitutional problems of the protectorate.

A former soldier, James Nayler was as charismatic a leader of the early Quakers as his more famous ally, George Fox. But he lacked Fox's sense of balance, and erred catastrophically when he allowed enthusiastic followers to re-enact Christ's entry into Jerusalem as he rode into Bristol on an ass in October 1656. His gesture symbolized the Quaker teaching that Christ was within all men and women, and that in the spiritual sense Christ had come again. But uncomprehending gentlemen and magistrates saw in Nayler and all Quakers only grotesque blasphemy, the most disturbing manifestation yet of the sectarian spirit.

The Quakers flourished in the millenarian context of spiritual arousal which had given rise to so many groups in the previous decade. Independents, and still more the presbyterians, stressed the primacy of the scriptures in order to hedge in the antinomian implications in a fallen world of any appeal to a spiritual freedom in which in principle they too believed; but more than most sects, the emphatically unpredestinarian Quakers had moved outside the Calvinist consensus. Believing as fully as did the Ranters in an 'inner light' which supplemented, or even in some cases superseded, scripture, the Quakers – so-called from their ecstatic habit of 'quaking' before a God of whom they claimed immediate knowledge – felt commanded to transcend conventional ways. While they emphatically did not reject the moral teachings of the Old Testament, their emphasis on 'Christ within' all men led Nayler and many others towards a nearly Ranter belief in freedom from sin. Those early Quakers who went 'naked for a sign', re-enacting the provocative behaviour of the Old Testament prophets to whom God had also spoken, seemed dangerously flamboyant. Like Ranters too they often testified to their belief in the immediate presence of God by disrupting the mediated rituals of the 'priests' in the 'steeple-houses', as they called the parish churches. Mainstream protestantism had never been more directly challenged.

Even more than did the Ranters, the Quakers also challenged the underpinnings of a society based ultimately upon deference. Eager to bring down pride in men who were all equal before God, they refused 'hat-honour', the doffing of hats before those in authority; refusing to take God's name in vain, they shunned oaths, on which all legal proceedings hinged. And most alarming of all, thanks to the organizing genius of Fox as well as to the heroism of other missionaries, their numbers soared, from nothing to perhaps 50,000 in the 1650s. Their successes, particularly in the north, point to the neglect of large parts of the country by the established church; they also indicate a reaction against the Calvinist stress on predestination. Although the evidence for their social composition is patchy, there were Quakers in all walks of life, and – doubly distressing to a male-dominated society – disproportionate numbers of women responded to the Quaker teaching of Christ within men and women alike. Moreover, the Quakers were not the pious, respectable pacifists of later years. 'Friends' were instructed to go 'as one man' to the 1656 Yorkshire election;* many soldiers turned Quaker, as did radicals of various hues, John Lilburne certainly, Gerrard Winstanley probably. The vituperative Quaker denunciations of unjust magistrates

---

* *Journal of the Friends' Historical Society* xxi (1924), p. 22.

and their millennial rhetoric of God's impending judgment on 'the great ones of the earth' could not be ignored.

More than any other group, the Quakers made a reality of the sectarian challenge. Although Baptist missionaries had already caused some alarm to rural clergy, the gathered churches had until the early 1650s been largely confined to the towns. The dynamism of Fox, Nayler and their associates took Quakerism into all the counties, to the army in Scotland and Ireland, and even overseas. Clergy everywhere might now encounter challenges to their beliefs, to their authority and to their position; and with lay impropriators they might face refusals of tithe, which could, many feared, be a prelude to the refusal of rents. The response was immediate and almost pathological. JPs eagerly whipped Quaker missionaries as vagrants, while clergymen turned from anxious debates with Quaker challengers long enough to howl in anguish as their world seemed to turn upside down. London pulpits rang during the ensuing parliament with clarions to the defence of the established ministry.

Nayler inflamed nerves already rubbed raw by too many affronts to the old order. Stoning to death was one popular suggestion for retribution, as MPs waxed hysterical about the dangers of toleration. 'If this be liberty, God defend me from such liberty', cried that simple old puritan, Major-General Philip Skippon. But the issue was both legally and theologically awkward. The Instrument guaranteed freedom to all protestants except the immoral and breakers of the peace, and several of Skippon's colleagues on the council recognized that Nayler was neither of these; furthermore, his teachings on the inner light were uncomfortably close to the 'glorious truth', as one councillor put it, which any protestant could accept. But in a house thinned by purge and growing weariness, the 'merciful men' were outnumbered. While the urbane Lambert, with an author's interest in the Instrument, defended liberty of conscience and pointed to the constitutional implications of any parliamentary action, a narrow majority sought an escape by appropriating to the new single chamber the judicial power of the old house of Lords. They proceeded to vote Nayler guilty of 'horrid blasphemy', an offence they found as hard to define as they did the authority by which they decreed that he be branded, bored through the tongue and twice flogged.

Cromwell's response was muted, for he had no wish to offend a parliament which had yet to vote supply, and probably more important he too believed that Nayler had blasphemed appallingly. Evidently seeking only to limit any future encroachments on freedom of conscience, he waited until the first part of Nayler's punishment had been inflicted and then on 25 December wrote temperately to ask for parliament's 'grounds and reasons'. Once more the house agonized until, as averse as the protector to a confrontation, it let the matter slip by. But Nayler's case had done more than underline the continuing lack of support for toleration. It had also exposed the difficulties of interpreting the Instrument. When the protector faced a parliament trying to regain powers the Instrument had sought to curtail there was, as one member pointed out, 'No judge upon earth' between them.

Arbitrariness now seemed all around, both at Westminster and in the localities. The arguments for some revision of the *status quo* therefore appealed increasingly to the officers as well as to civilian 'courtiers' and to country gentry. Ironically, the major-generals themselves began the work when, encouraged by the low attendance, Desborough called on 25 December for statutory confirmation of the decimation tax. His aim was not simply to protect the commissioners against any retribution from vindictive gentlemen; some of the major-generals subsequently referred to the need to reassure the 'honest party' in the country who, like the 'seeker' William Sedgwick, saw in decimation the only evidence that Oliver was not leading the godly back to Egypt. The long deferential silence of the early months of the parliament was at last broken when – suggestively echoing the occasions in the 1620s when courtiers headed an 'opposition' – Cromwell's unsaintly son-in-law John Claypole and his former-royalist confidant Lord Broghill opened the attack on the soldiers whom they had long opposed at court.

Military rule, so terrible a prospect in 1628, was now familiar. That fact, and the exclusion of leading orators like Haselrig and Birch at the start of the session, ensured that the debates were a pale shadow of those a generation earlier. Nevertheless, they sufficed, when reinforced by the hope of supply, to persuade Oliver that either providence or necessity was speaking and he should withhold his hand from the balance. His tact was rewarded, and a vote of £400,000 for the Spanish war followed immediately on the defeat on 28 January 1657 of the decimation bill – like so many of their contemporaries, these parliament-men had evidently hidden their political objections behind quibbles when asked for money. The votes signalled Oliver's abandonment of the major-generals and the slow withering away of their rule.

However blundering his response, Desborough's suspicions that a change was in the offing had been correct. The uncertainties of an elective succession were underlined that January by the discovery of Sindercombe's plot, an unholy alliance of ex-army Levellers and royalists, all hoping to profit from the protector's assassination. The constitutional crises and abhorrent expedients made the issue doubly urgent, and a move to reconstitute the government in hereditary rule and 'ancient constitution' quickly gathered momentum. On 23 February Sir Christopher Packe, a former lord mayor of London, proposed a broad platform which included a revived upper house of parliament and the crown for Oliver. The conservative gentry and merchants in the house responded eagerly, led by the Surrey member Sir Richard Onslow; but probably the most important figure was Broghill, who was convinced that only the crown would enable Oliver to break with the sword. He was supported by lawyers such as Whitelocke, who longed to see the common law reign supreme again, despite the recent inability of monarchy to ensure harmony. All were spurred on by the realization that otherwise Oliver's successor would be the strongest man in the army – and personable though he was, the young and ambitious Lambert was a frightening prospect.

The hostility of sections of the army to these developments was predictable. The triumph of the gentry must endanger freedom of conscience, and also the hard-won position of the officers themselves. Furthermore, in the eyes of Fleetwood, Desborough and many other officers, God had condemned kingship in 1648–9. While Lambert had contemplated monarchy in 1653, there was a world of difference between an Oliver crowned by the officers and an Oliver enthroned by parliamentary gentry desperate to distance him from Lambert and his comrades. The generals therefore seconded their passionately republican speeches to parliament with nudges to gatherings of alarmed officers in London.

The proposals which emerged in the house as the Humble Petition and Advice after long debates in March 1657 seemed almost to encapsulate the parliamentary war aims of 1642. A limited monarchy, with the great officers of state and councillors approved by a bi-cameral parliament, taxation by parliamentary consent, a reduction in the army necessitated by the ending of monthly assessments, and new limitations on the exuberant conscience: there were many who would have supported such a programme between 1642 and 1648. The wagers ran strongly for Oliver's acceptance.

Much has been made of the officers' role in blocking kingship, but as general Monck later correctly pointed out, an officer had only to be dismissed to be deprived of his capacity to do mischief. Furthermore, Cromwell always justly trusted in his comrades' regard for himself and for the unity of the army. Despite Secretary Thurloe's alarm lest the 'grandees', Lambert, Fleetwood, Desborough, try to split the army, the height of their threats now was to offer to resign. The junior officers for their part listened thoughtfully as Oliver reminded them of the inadequacies of an Instrument which had failed to protect Nayler – 'The case of James Nayler might happen to be your own case.' Why then did he reject the crown?

There were aspects of the package to which he could object. He had doubts about the sufficiency of the £1.3M. p.a. offered to him as revenue. He also had, as the curious ceremonial of his court suggests, genuine reservations about the exaltation of his own position, and had accordingly hesitated long before appointing his forceful younger son Henry to a carefully restricted office in Ireland. Nevertheless, such reservations could be overcome by his country gentleman's anxiety to clothe the sword in decent constitutional garb. The ceremonial of his court was to become more lavish, and he soon allowed his elder son Richard to emerge from obscurity. On the financial side, negotiations during April persuaded parliament to increase the revenue by £600,000 p.a. for three years by means of the assessment. Furthermore, he was more than a little attracted by the religious clauses of the Petition, which promised to do more than the Instrument had done to restrain the likes of Biddle and Nayler. Perhaps surprisingly, in view of his tolerationist reputation and his council's occasional efforts to protect individual Quakers from persecution, Oliver greeted the new constitution as 'the greatest provision that was ever made' for liberty for 'the people of God'.

Perhaps most important of all, Cromwell had joined the countless other gentlemen who had grown uncertain about God's purposes. He confessed to parliament in April that the Barebone's episode had been 'a story of my own weakness and folly'; indeed, he concluded, he had often been unable to tell 'what my business was, . . . save comparing it with a good constable to keep the peace of the parish'. Kingship was hardly incompatible with that minimal vision. Worn out as he was by the cares of office, it was no wonder that Oliver wavered that spring as the crown seemed to offer an easier path. His weeks of illness testify to his indecision, as does the tortured syntax of speeches in which, as so often, he raked over the past in order to discern God's will.

In this instance providence did not clearly tell in favour of kingship. Although the parliamentary majority pressed the crown on him, there were none of the addresses from the country for which he might he might have hoped if, as he persisted in doing, he saw the voice of the godly people as the voice of God. The continuing divisions of the godly throughout the 1650s had shown that England was not yet walking in God's ways. Now the army, the only gathered church Cromwell had known, as well as Independent and Baptist congregations in the country, and John Owen closer to hand, indicated their disquiet. They served as a sounding-board for a conscience already shaken by the failure at Hispaniola. Furthermore, to the end of his life he continued to set religious freedom higher than civil liberty, and whatever his distaste for Nayler the parliamentary outcry warned him that, without the army, liberty of conscience would suffer further erosion.

Cromwell's rejection of the crown drove many MPs to join Broghill in withdrawing in disgust: yet others still saw value in a document which insisted that government run 'according to the laws of these nations'. And for his part, once the crown was put aside Oliver seized on the chance to regularize his position. The revised Humble Petition and Advice allowed him to nominate a new upper house of parliament, whose value even the officers could see after Nayler's case, and made his protectorship effectively hereditary by allowing him to name his successor. Parliament then underlined the return to parliamentary ways by passing a spate of mundane legislation and at last ratifying the protector's contentious ordinances. On 26 June 1657 the Speaker of parliament filled the place of the defunct archbishop of Canterbury as Oliver was installed as protector a second time, with all the trappings of kingship but the crown. The government's new reliance on parliamentary sanction could not have been more clearly indicated. As MPs adjourned until the following January many expected the drift towards a parliamentary monarchy to continue.

Both the structure and the tone of political life in the later protectorate point to a reaction which was to culminate in the Restoration. The Quaker menace occasioned a 1657 statute which brought a return to compulsory attendance at some religious worship on Sundays. And at the centre, to match the two-chamber parliament, the protector's council was now called the 'privy council'. Equally revealingly, while courtly ceremonial became more ornate Oliver's daughters married, amidst unsabbatarian dancing, into noble families, one to his confidant Lord Fauconberg and another to the heir of the earl of Warwick. Yet the Humble Petition and Advice in fact inaugurated few significant political shifts. It can even be argued that by accepting the Petition Oliver did not so much wearily turn back towards the old world as bind himself to preserve a balance more assiduously; he was merely to eschew ventures like Barebone's and the major-generals.

Cromwell's careful balancing of interests to the end can be seen in his appointments. The council changed little. Secretary Thurloe, a moderate, a great intelligence gatherer, but hardly a major politician, came in alone; not until the end of the year did Oliver conquer his reservations about the hereditary principle by admitting his elder son Richard. The only departure was Lambert, cashiered in July for his opposition and probably also for his ambition. The military contingent survived, still checking if not quite balancing Oliver's civilian entourage, his old friends St John and Nathaniel Fiennes, both now judges, and new supporters like Wolseley, Broghill and Fauconberg. The split between soldiers and the military 'party' on the one hand

and civilians and the 'civilian' on the other was by no means total. Charles Howard and Edward Montague, members of noble families and beneficiaries of the Restoration, were both colonels and yet both acted with the 'courtiers', as did General Monck from Scotland; conversely, the civilians Walter Strickland and Sir Gilbert Pickering aligned with the soldiers on the council. Nevertheless, the division existed, and that Oliver did not resolve it owed more to his sense that the soldiers' seats around his chair were their due, as custodians of the godly 'interest', than from unease about the army. The silence which greeted the dismissal of the popular Lambert would have dispelled any such doubts.

Still more revealing are the appointments to the new second chamber of parliament, over which the protector brooded throughout late 1657. The sixty-three nominees included seven conformist peers, five sons of peers, four baronets, one Scottish and one Irish peer, and about a dozen substantial country gentlemen. But these were balanced by a cluster of officials and by seventeen serving regimental officers, including the egregiously plebeian colonels Hewson, Pride and Barkstead. Not only was the second chamber to interpose between protector and parliament and avert another Nayler case. Oliver also seemed to be trying to square the circle by institutionalizing the interest of the army within the conventional political system.

The localities tell a similar story. While each county is obviously distinct, the slight impact of the ostensibly civilian constitution on the localities stands out. In March 1657 the Hertfordshire JPs took over the remaining decimation funds for use on such worthy causes as bridge repair, and the following year a Berkshire JP sent a militia officer for trial for disarming an alleged dissident; in Surrey Onslow's influence grew, while in Somerset the remnant of John Pyne's unpopular regime of the 1640s was further dismembered. But such developments were balanced by the withdrawal of gentry whose hopes had been dashed by Cromwell's rejection of the crown – in Essex fewer titled gentlemen acted at quarter sessions in 1657–8 than in 1655. More remarkable were the commissions of the peace issued in 1657, the first of the protectorate. These removed several anomalous Quakers, but otherwise made only minor changes, and left undisturbed many of the religious radicals of Barebone's parliament. The partisan machine in Kent survived, while the Cumberland commission consisted of one knight, two esquires, three merchants, a handful of yeomen and an army officer. There were too many of 'Cromwell's hangmen', as the Cheshire magnate Sir George Booth fulminated. Indeed, most commissions of the peace included more officers than had those of 1652 – fourteen, of whom six were mere captains, in the West Riding of Yorkshire. Furthermore, more officers served on the local assessment commissions in 1657 than at any other time. Early-modern regimes were never capable of implementing a coherent programme, and the protectorate's inertia, and its failure to attract new support, may have enabled conscientious officers to survive. Yet the appointments of 1657 may, like Cromwell's limp electioneering in 1656, indicate that he did not aim to commit himself wholeheartedly but rather to reconcile the twin objectives of moderation and reform. The history of the protectorate cannot be told entirely in terms of sudden swings – real enough those these were – between reform and reaction.

Political conditions in 1657 were not, however, such as to favour Cromwell's synthesis. His hopes of confining the war with Spain, on which he had embarked so needlessly in 1655, to the New World had long ago proved vain. Even within Europe it was expanding, since British assertions of the right to search neutral shipping risked driving the Dutch into alliance with Spain. Aware of the risks of isolation, Cromwell at last heeded the long-standing French offer of an alliance, and in March 1657 he bound himself to send 6,000 troops to aid against the Spanish in Flanders. His excessive admiration for Sweden, his hostility to Spain and his friendship with France have led many to tax the protector with, in the words of a contemporary, being 'not guilty of too much knowledge' in foreign affairs. Although the anachronistically religious dimension of his policy does lend the charge some justification even his new continental commitment to France addressed some vital interests. The return on the alliance was to be the cession to Britain of the Spanish Netherlands towns of Dunkirk and Mardyke, whose privateers had long threatened English shipping. Furthermore, Cromwell had more immediate objectives. While Dunkirk might not be the step on the road to Vienna and Rome for which he yearned, its capture would deter Spain from backing any future royalist attempt on England. The argument that the balance of power required support for declining Spain rather than rising France is one that appeals only to those with hindsight.

Not unrealistic it may have been, but expensive it certainly was. Although France would pay for the troops on campaign, England had to equip and transport them, and the treasury was empty. Naval activity had added £500,000 p.a. to the government's expenditure since 1655. The reduction of the monthly assessment required by the Humble Petition and Advice, from £60,000 to £35,000, left the tax able to bear less than half the military and naval burden. In its effort to spare the landed taxpayer parliament had granted an additional tax, the old royal standby of a levy on new building in London, which it had fondly hoped would raise £300,000 p.a.: but by the end of 1658 it had yielded only £41,000. In desperation, the government was increasingly driven in 1657–8 to resort to free quarter for its troops, a move hardly calculated to please the public. Relations were further strained by deteriorating harvests in the later 1650s, which as usual increased the unpopularity of the excise, and by the war's accompaniments of losses of shipping and trade. Significantly, arrears on payments of the assessment began to rise in 1657, after keeping at a remarkably low level throughout the republic.

The demands of war preoccupied the protector and his council, and dulled their reforming energies. Perhaps more damaging, the business of war – compounded by his habitual slowness in matters of political strategy – diverted Oliver from other matters. Not until December, little over a month before the new parliamentary session, were the nominations of members of the second chamber complete, leaving little time for anyone concerned to think about their functions.

The council's unpreparedness was also manifest in its inability to explain its financial needs to parliament. Both Oliver and his spokesman, Fiennes, lord commissioner of the seal, stressed the crying need for money, but could only promise that details would soon be ready. Unforeseen consequences of the Humble Petition and Advice created more serious problems. Oliver's opening speech on 20 January 1658 was remarkably optimistic, lauding his achievements in securing peace and religious and civil liberty, and praising the last session for harmonizing 'all interests'; Fiennes then wove the theme into a long hymn to the ancient constitution. Many in the audience were unmoved. Not only had the protector fewer friends in the Commons since he had elevated eloquent civilian supporters like Broghill and Onslow as well as officers to his new second chamber. Worse, the revised constitution also allowed the members excluded by the council in 1656 to return.

The 1658 session ended in disaster, though not because the Cromwellians were numerically overwhelmed. Rather, the breakdown reflected the weakness of the parliamentary process in face of genuine ideological division. In Haselrig and Scot the commonwealthsmen had parliamentary tacticians of genius who, recognizing the suspicions of the Commons for an institutional rival, seized on the 'other house' in order to embarrass the protector they hated. They sought to wreck the new parliamentary order while exciting radical disaffection in the army and City, with the ultimate goal of reviving the Rump – though the anarchy of 1659 was to show that goodwill between Rump and army was no more likely than it had been in 1652–3. Haselrig proclaimed, accurately enough, that he 'could speak till four o'clock' on the virtues of the Rump; neither did his allies lack for arguments.

In late 1656, when constitutional change had been so widely expected, James Harrington in his *Oceana* had provided the coherent secular defence of republicanism which Marchamont Nedham had begun to shape in the early 1650s. Harrington argued that the basis of political power lay in property, and that the king had been defeated because his post-feudal nobility no longer held the balance of property. The only path not just to freedom but also to political stability was, concluded Harrington, to vest political power in the people, who now held the preponderance of property. The argument was to shape both English and American republicanism. But more compelling to snobbish country gentlemen than echoes of Harrington, or the commonwealthsmen's vague evocations of the glories of the Rump, was the presence amongst the thirty or so who attended the 'other house' of 'cobbler' Colonel Hewson and 'drayman' Colonel Pride. Some royalists had thought it only natural that Oliver should create peers. Yet even to a fairly sympathetic observer like the protector's steward John Maidstone it hardly seemed a house of Lords.

Oliver watched in frustration as paralysis set in. On 25 January he spoke forcefully of the domestic and foreign dangers, in face of which an uncaring parliament left the hungry soldiers to freeze in the streets. As at the end of his first parliament he declared his commitment to the army; but equally striking is his conviction that the achievements of his rule warranted a settlement, if only 'the nation would be content with rule'. He sounded here uncomfortably like his royal predecessor. But the wranglers proved unstoppable, and on 4 February the protector angrily dissolved the parliament, over the anxious protests of his son-in-law General Fleetwood, whom he not unjustly brushed aside as a 'milksop'.

It was not frustration that spurred Oliver on, but the grim consciousness that the reconciliation for which he had pleaded was doomed as City radicals prepared to petition both parliament and army under the umbrella of the 'good old cause'. As so often when the unity of the army seemed at risk he acted swiftly, calling a meeting of officers to whom he made his usual long speech on the history of their common cause. Though he extracted from them their usual resolve to 'live and die' with him, he sought out doubters, and dismissed the major of his own regiment, Packer, and his five captains, all Baptists. That he should have broken with comrades from the early days of the Eastern Association suggests his desperation at the polarization of his twin props, parliament and army. Observers agreed that the protector was near emotional and physical breakdown.

Oliver's last months showed that his protectorate had put down no deeper roots into popular affections. The continuing tensions, both domestic and external, combined to hurry Oliver into his grave.

Circumstances now seemed to favour the royalists. The major-generals and the Quakers had between them intensified country resentments, and Charles Stuart therefore looked not only to the crown's old supporters and to Spain but also to former 'presbyterians' like Waller and even Fairfax. He looked too to the City of London, where the restive apprentices had grown frustrated with the moralist discipline which had brought the suppression of bear-baiting and theatres, and had eagerly purchased scurrilous royalist broadsheets before the tighter censorship of 1655. Economic dislocation brought by the Spanish war had increased the citizens' impatience, and the hated excise fuelled the flames. The success of men who had been purged in the 1640s in gaining election for the City in 1654 and 1656 hinted at the sympathies of the more respectable. But though Thurloe's intelligence reports predicted dire things, the royalists were no better placed to rise than in 1655. Indeed, the passage of time saw many, who echoed parliamentary puritans in reading history as the fruit of God's purposes, drift into acquiescence: as one royalist facing decimation concluded, 'Afflictions are God's messengers to bring us nearer him; 'twas for the sins of the Israelites that God led them into captivity.'* Not coincidentally, the classic royalist-Anglican literary product of these years is Isaac Walton's *Compleat Angler*. Going fishing offered as in most times an escape from care; but it also offered a clear conscience. As former enemies intermingled – the marriage in 1657 between the disreputable young duke of Buckingham and Fairfax's daughter is only the most notorious of such contacts – the most astute of Charles Stuart's advisers placed their hopes in an assassin's bullet or in the internal collapse of the regime. Thurloe's intelligence work increased the demoralization by exploiting divisions amongst the royalists themselves. A wave of arrests in March 1658, followed by ostentatious troop movements through the City, reinforced the implications of the English capture of the Spanish Netherlands port of Ostend. The protectorate was unlikely to be upset by force.

But however physically secure, Cromwell's problems remained. He had told parliament in 1657 that the deficit then ran at about £500,000 p.a., and thereafter it was to increase sharply as a result of the shortfall of the taxes granted in 1657; by the end of that year the use of free quarter had increased dangerously. The ghosts of the councillors of the 1620s must have smiled when within weeks of the dissolution of the parliament in 1658 there were rumours that the desperate council was about to call a new one. Yet the financial crisis

*W.C. and C.E. Trevelyan, ed., *The Trevelyan Papers* (Camden Soc., 1872), p. 280.

was not as bad as it might seem. The debt at Oliver's death stood at the equivalent of about one year's revenue, in relative terms perhaps a third of that of the French crown. But Oliver, like Charles and the Rump before him, could not persuade people to lend. In the summer the council was 'forced to go a-begging' to individual London aldermen for loans for the upkeep of newly captured Dunkirk, to little effect. Although the City fathers as always favoured stability and did not relish the prospect of collapse and anarchy, they had little cause to commit themselves to as bad a debtor as the protectorate, least of all in the current war-generated depression. The wheel had come almost full circle. Charles I had depended on a narrow coterie of lenders, and Cromwell now could only rely on Martin Noel, whose web of credit was unfortunately no stronger than his predecessors'; furthermore, the reluctance of financiers to pay the high price demanded in negotiations in 1657 for a return to customs farming meant that there were no customs farmers to call on. Indeed, the paralysis of successive regimes facing small wars and minor debts underlines how limited was the freedom of action of any government before the financial revolution of the end of the century.

In its desperation, the military party on the council, led by Desborough, urged a return to the strong measures of 1655–6, doubtless citing as justification the new royalist conspiracy. The outrage of the 'civilians', and probably Cromwell's own distaste, blocked this and other 'as well non-legal as contra-legal ways of raising money', as Henry Cromwell in Ireland called them. But there were no other solutions, and the divided council was now literally living on borrowed time. In April it again ordered that the next six months' assessment be paid in advance to prevent the extension of free quarter, 'which otherwise will inevitably follow'. Equally inevitable, therefore, was another parliament, although Desborough and his allies were no more ready than they had been in 1657 to concede the constitutionalist measures which must be the price of any grant.

Oliver seems to have tried to the end to continue his balancing act. The appointment of a new commander of the protector's own regiment was seen as a test case, and to the dismay of the civilians Oliver that summer turned to Boteler, perhaps the most unpopular of all the major-generals. Equally revealingly, a majority of the 'junto' he established in June to plan for a new parliament was military. But their prolonged inability to act persuaded Thurloe at least that Oliver was preparing to abandon his characteristic 'waiting posture'. It was widely assumed that the parliament intended for later in the year would renew the offer of the crown; wearied of his government's paralysis and desperate for money, Oliver might not refuse this time. Grand juries in several counties gave voice to their hopes that summer in a volley of loyal addresses, a tribute to the protector that was both unusual and significant.

The hopes were fruitless. Although the majority in the Commons in the next parliament proved extremely favourable to the house of Cromwell, Oliver was dead. His health had never been strong, and he was now worn out by the political crisis he found so much more burdensome than the reflex choices of the battlefield. He died on 3 September 1658, the anniversary of Dunbar and Worcester, though few joined the poets in celebrating the symbolism of that fact. His awkward funeral procession elicited little mourning, and in the Essex countryside Ralph Josselin noted, 'Cromwell died, people not much minding it.' Even the sympathetic Andrew Marvell, who had sounded high millenarian notes in his 'First Anniversary' of 1654, did not know quite what to make of it all in the rambling eulogy he wrote for the dead protector.

Not all contemporaries scorned Oliver's achievements. As hostile an observer as Clarendon could acknowledge that 'brave bad man', for Cromwell's soldiers and sailors had made England the most respected military power in Europe. The contrast with that record was to embarrass Charles II. More generally, Cromwell had astonished the world and gratified republican political theorists by showing that a strong state could be built, as it seemed, from scratch. Fortified by his belief in God's providence, he had coped with that doctrine of necessity which had caused his predecessors, Charles I and the Long Parliament, such unease. He would have impressed those earlier students of fortune and necessity, the Roman Tacitus and the Italian Machiavelli.

Oliver of course prided himself on his efforts not only as an Englishman but as a Christian. He had ensured freedom of worship for the godly and brought good men into public life. Others too could praise him, and not merely in retrospect – even in 1656 Richard Baxter could 'bless God for the change that I see in this country'. The rooting of dissent in the previously unevangelized uplands of Wales and the north is one of the most lasting achievements of the Interregnum. Fittingly, the gathered church at Broadmead, Bristol, looked back after the Restoration to 'those halcyon days of prosperity, liberty and peace'. The majority view was, however, less favourable.

The protectorate did not die with its founder. The royalists were cast down by the frustrations of the spring, and the loyalists buoyed up by the capture of Dunkirk. With some reason Clarendon concluded that Cromwell's 'power and greatness [seemed] to be better established than ever' at his death. The greatest testimony to the royalists' weakness came in the uneventful succession of Oliver's chosen heir,

Richard. But Richard did not seem to the gentry who greeted him in the ensuing parliament merely the *only* way; he also seemed the better way. The civilians on the council backed him eagerly, despite the greater capacities of his younger brother Henry, because he represented the principle of primogeniture and thus promised stability. He was also appreciated for his unmilitary background and for his many friendships amongst the gentry. The flood of congratulatory addresses far outnumbered those to his father that summer, and their contrast to the country's silence over Oliver's elevation in 1657 testified to the widespread hopes of a reduction in the army's role.

But while it must remain forever in doubt whether Oliver was on the point of breaking with the officers before his death, he was far better placed to do so than Richard. His comradeship with them allowed him to draw on their loyalties, while Richard's relations were bound to be more tense, particularly since reform had run out of steam. The protectorate's survival had depended overwhelmingly on Oliver's personality and his ability to reconcile conflicting interests, and he left a vulnerable inheritance. The army's presence, in the council and around London, could hardly be ignored, and the officers had a strong sense of their own claims and interests. While they had always been slow to move against the civilian authorities, too much would hang on Richard's ability to impose his will on a divided council.

12   Conclusion: a Turning-point?

The long-term consequences of the mid-seventeenth-century upheaval have proved as elusive as its long-term causes. English society at 1700 was not as it had been at Elizabeth's death, but the role of political and religious turmoil in the transformation is not readily apparent. Since it is currently fashionable for historians to argue that the real climacteric occurred in 1688–9, and that therefore text-books should terminate there, it behoves us to examine the claims that the late 1650s mark a significant break in historical continuity.

The most obvious objections to any long-term emphasis on the mid-century troubles lie in the field of politics. That weaknesses persisted in the structure of government is apparent in Charles II's temporary repudiation of royal debts in 1672 in the celebrated 'Stop of the Exchequer' and in his periodic recourse to a French dole. Rulers still lived from hand to mouth; it was to take the increase in customs revenues of the 1680s, and still more the financial revolution of the 1690s, before governments could undertake major operations without bringing catastrophe upon themselves. Furthermore, the political tensions of the later 1660s and the 1670s, and the very occurrence of a revolution in 1688, show how few of the constitutional dilemmas had been solved by the Restoration. In 1660–1 the parliamentary gentry in the Convention, and their more royalist successors in the Cavalier Parliament, aimed above all to take the sword from their backs and to still the cries of the radicals. They therefore surrendered to the restored Charles II control over the enlarged machinery of state, both military and bureaucratic, which was an undoubted product of the revolutionary years. The conviction that Ranters, Quakers and military rule had been too high a price to pay for resistance meant that the restoration of the monarchy in 1660 was unconditional. It also meant that England only escaped absolutism under both later Stuart kings by a narrow margin. Property-owners and parliament-men had by no means forgotten the concerns for property and liberty which had moved them in 1628 and 1640–1; such concerns had after all distanced them from the protector. But they had concluded that the greatest threat to those valuable commodities came not from the crown but from another direction.

The resulting conservative reaction tipped the balance towards the crown. Most of the legislation of 1641 survived the Restoration – the crown's power to intervene in the localities was lessened after the fall of the prerogative courts and its fiscal prerogative diminished with the demise of fiscal feudalism. Moreover, parliamentary sophistication had grown with experience. These developments were, however, politically outweighed by the fears of renewed disorder. 1649's brutal reminder that kings had joints in their necks cut more than one way. It may have emboldened the small remnant of commonwealthsmen and discontented magnates who sought in the Rye House plot of 1683 to kill the king in the name of free and regular parliaments; and his desire never to go 'on his travels' again may have inclined Charles towards conciliation. Yet others besides the king looked back on 1649 and its aftermath with horror and their reaction gave Charles assets his father might have envied. The world of the 1660s was in many respects no less monarchical than that of the 1620s. Such considerations have led some historians to argue plausibly that the years 1641–60 represent a false start.

Some of the apparent novelty of the Restoration era stemmed, furthermore, not from the revolution but from long-term changes. The scientific revolution was clearly the product of broad cultural shifts rather than of any commercial or puritan vanguard. Equally, while government in the later period was certainly less given to direct intervention in the economy, the triumph of private enterprise and initiative had been a gradual process. Even in the dearth of the later 1630s Charles I's council appears to have been significantly less activist than it had been a half-dozen years earlier when it issued the books of orders. That gradual change in government's response to crises suggests too that the later shift of the grain laws in favour of the producer rather than the consumer was as much the result of demographic and economic developments as of any social reaction. And as we have seen, the ensuing 'mercantilism' was not a sudden and revolutionary awakening but a generally applauded response, which had long been emerging, to enduring trading problems.

Yet the 'broken times', as euphemists called them, did have consequences. Not least, they occasioned a social reaction. The game laws became ever more draconian, and 'fleering' – crudely contemptuous behaviour towards the meaner sort – grew popular amongst some of the gentry. Other social changes can also be traced to the impact of civil war. If the confiscation of royal, royalist and church property during the Interregnum failed signally to transform the composition of the landowning classes, the polarization of the rural populace into the landed few and the landless many proceeded apace. Wartime seizures of stock and plough animals ruined many smallholders. Moreover, the enormous burden of taxes and the rapid if often temporary transfer of lands encouraged landowners to maximize their returns, and so further undermined the competitiveness of smallholders.

If such shifts seem like the small change of history, firmer evidence exists to suggest that the last years of the protectorate mark a crucial watershed. Fittingly, when much of the impulse towards civil war had been religious, the prime consequences of that war were religious. Although the constitutional battles remained to be fought again, the struggle for godly rule was over.

The strength of both urban and rural dissent in face of persecution after the Restoration shows that generations of godly edification in the parishes had done their work. But the many frustrations of the Interregnum killed puritanism as a national cause. National reformation failed, and the godly party fragmented; equally important, since anti-Catholicism had been so central to that cause, the Catholic threat failed to materialize, though all was chaos and Catholics at the gates were so widely expected. Preaching to the house of Commons on 5 November 1678, on the anniversary of the Gunpowder Plot of 1605 and at the height of the great scare of the 'Popish Plot', John Tillotson, a relative by marriage of Oliver Cromwell, could express no opinion on whether the pope was Antichrist, and saw in Catholicism primarily a political threat. Amongst his audience, virtually the only MP who during the heated debates of the ensuing Exclusion Crisis spoke in the once-familiar tones of strenuous protestantism was the aged Colonel Birch; to Birch's colleagues, popery seems to have meant absolutism, secular evils and something un-English, but not the apocalypse. Even Birch later cast himself for his funeral monument as a Roman patriot rather than as one of God's Englishmen. He was far from alone in this, for memorials to Roman virtue abound in the epitaphs and monuments of the later seventeenth century.

That supremely important retreat from the vision of England as Jerusalem which had for decades shaped the nation's politics did not simply result from the catastrophe of 1659–60. Central to Roman virtue were moderation, stoicism, the tempering of the passions – values directly at odds, or so those who subscribed to them believed, with religious 'enthusiasm'. The sterility of the doctrinal battles, the confusion brought to the church by the attempts to establish godly rule, and the dangerously heady excitement of the sects, enormously reinforced a strain of distaste for controversy which had already been evident before the civil war. In despair at the arid disputes between

Calvinists and Arminians, a group of scholars and theologians had gathered in the 1630s at Great Tew, the Oxfordshire estate of Lord Falkland, the unhappy royalist of the 1640s; there they had aired distinctly humanist views. Their insistence that what mattered were not formal theological systems – which could never be verified until God made all things clear at the millennium – but the way Christians lived was to sound increasingly plausible as the next two decades unfolded.

Support for the anti-rigorists came simultaneously from the philosophers, who grew increasingly preoccupied with the problem of how ideas formed in the mind. The importance of physical data in the steadily more impressive work of the scientists encouraged examination of the nature of experience and of sense-impressions, sources of knowledge very different from those which concerned the theologians. The probings of the philosophers, which gathered momentum around-mid-century, could not help but breed a certain scepticism, exemplified by René Descartes' famous reduction to fundamentals, '*cogito ergo sum*' ['I think therefore I am']. In the hands of Thomas Hobbes, himself a member of the Tew circle, materialist scepticism about the grounds of knowledge could prove devastating to claims to religious certainty. Yet it should not be thought that the impact of the new science on religious claims was wholly coincidental. No less than the cult of Roman virtue, science in the seventeenth century was an ideology for use against the zealots. Both Robert Boyle and Thomas Sprat, in his propagandist *History of the Royal Society* of 1667, urged the scientific approach as an antidote to enthusiasm. In particular, the scientists' dissociation of the material from the spiritual world offered the welcome prospect of an end to the radical sectarians' claims that the spirit was in the flesh. Not surprisingly, many Restoration bishops smiled on science.

One of the most vivid manifestations of this cultural realignment which presaged 'the age of reason' lay in the transformation of language. Scientists from Francis Bacon onwards had cause to regret the Renaissance delight in words and affection for ornate metaphors and double-meanings. The Royal Society's adoption in the 1660s of Bacon's motto 'nullius in verba' ['nothing in words'] is symptomatic of a wider conviction that rhetoric did not always aid communication, and that belief ought to rest upon evidence rather than persuasion. In like vein, the Oxford mathematician John Wallis published in 1653 his *Grammatica Lingua Anglicanae*, which sought to discern intrinsic meanings in words by analysis of sounds, and thereby to provide an incontrovertible basis for usage; meanwhile Hobbes had in his *Leviathan* unequivocally insisted that words were simply names for objects. It was a short way to the blunt contention in 1668 of John Wilkins, Oliver Cromwell's brother-in-law, that 'things are better than words', as he endeavoured to lay the foundations for a universal, and purified, language. There could have been no starker contrast with the faith of the godly that in 'the Word' – of scripture – lay the key to all things.

The reaction against extravagance was a European as much as an English phenomenon. But it seems no accident that it began in England as the flood of books from the printing presses crested in the middle years of the century. In denouncing those who indulged in 'insignificant speech' Hobbes had two enemies in view, traditional Aristotelian philosophers on the one hand and on the other the sectarians who claimed religious inspiration for their utterances. Sprat in his *History* saw the same two groups as abusers of 'rhetoric'. The conviction gained ground that language had been perverted, by the zealots whose printed pages sometimes resemble modern 'stream-of-consciousness' prose, and by politicians and clerics fighting the partisan wars of the pen which Milton lamented in his *History of Britain*. Not for nothing did Milton in both *Paradise Lost* and *Samson Agonistes* see in words the agents of corruption. Equally revealing of an intense distrust for the effects of words is the silence which prevailed while Quakers waited for the spirit to move one of the 'friends' to speak in their meetings. The contrast between the florid style of Lancelot Andrewes, James I's favourite preacher, and the spare argument of John Tillotson, a future archbishop of Canterbury, after the Restoration did not owe everything to the scientists' rules for controversy.

The corollary of this revaluation of language was a significant change in religious expression. However time-serving his politics, Bulstrode Whitelocke was undeniably one of the godly; yet in the later stages of the Rump he had in his dismay at the divisions amongst the saints already turned towards private rather than public worship. Even the Quakers, chastened by the Nayler episode, withdrew into the quietism and restraint which has become characteristic of them. Others made no bones of their distaste for religious feeling. The intensity with which poets such as Donne and Herbert, or even the dourly Calvinist Fulke Greville, Lord Brooke, had explored their faith in the first half of the century is absent, rather than merely out of place, in the second. True, in adversity one persecuted dissenter, John Bunyan, wrote a best-seller when in *Pilgrim's Progress* he recorded the spiritual pilgrimage of the soul, while another, John Milton, provided in *Samson Agonistes* what is amongst other things the finest account of the relation of the individual to a providentialist God. Yet in more respectable circles John Dryden was almost alone in making public a personal statement of faith; and that testament, his poem *Religio Laici* of 1682, is chiefly remarkable for its lack of religious sentiment. Piety and morality had become the order of the day, and 'zeal' an insult.

The ground had already been laid even before the political disasters of 1659 for Samuel Butler's definitive identification of puritanism with hypocrisy in his Restoration best-seller, *Hudibras*. Before Oliver's death one of Richard Baxter's female correspondents apologized for troubling him rather than going to her own minister, and observed that to her neighbours, and to 'most of the gentry of England', a woman's private conferences with a minister were worse than 'gaming or mixed dancing or bare breasts'. A Scottish MP in 1657 was appalled when the house burst out laughing at a speaker who too readily referred to scriptural texts. Most revealing of all of the sense that conviction had been lost and a cause perverted was the warning given to the army by a radical dissident in 1654:

> Consider how the people of God are scorned and reproached, and the name of God blasphemed daily for your sakes. It's now the common word, when any one speaks of a false dissembler and treacherous faith-breaker, 'There's a saint', say they.*

Puritanism in power contained within itself the seeds of its own destruction. Puritans who declared that they were fighting the Lord's battles and setting themselves against 'self-ends', in Cromwell's phrase, found themselves in positions of power and profit. Whatever the general probity of its administrators, this revolution like every other attracted fellow-travellers. Even as conscientious a public servant as Major-General Berry could worry that if any of the assassination plots against Oliver 'should take . . . what will come of our preferments?' Contemporaries thought it quite proper that those who ruled should be rewarded for so doing; but puritans had made a virtue of self-denial for too long to be given the benefit of the doubt when they prospered while stopping others from going about their enjoyments. Few would have had much sympathy for the low-born regicide Colonel Barkstead, lieutenant of the Tower of London, who early in 1654 wanted more money since he must live 'suitable to his place'. Nor did they appreciate Colonel Pride's possession of Nonesuch Palace and its Great Park. In 1659 there were moves to impeach for corruption Philip Jones, who had turned his suzerainty over much of Wales into a profitable concern. The drive for reform had petered out, and 'the glorious cause of the people of God' had come to look too much like self-seeking under a shell of piety. There were certainly grounds for the caricature so often drawn of hypocrites: thus, an officer pleading for Desborough's favour in 1655 used the revealing arguments that he did not wear costly clothes, did not powder his hair

---

*Brit. Lib., E813(20), p. 7.

and had never been in a barber's shop. The maypoles and the frolicking at the Restoration command sympathy. Nevertheless, we can still be moved by the failed hopes as Milton in *The Ready and Easy Way*, his last-minute battle-cry for the republic, contemplated 'the perpetual bowings and cringings of an abject people' under monarchy.

Bibliography

Those seeking further enlightenment than this volume could provide will have to negotiate a vast sea of articles and monographs. They will, however, receive invaluable guidance from two recent bibliographies. M.F. Keeler, *Bibliography of British History: Stuart Period, 1603–1714* (Oxford, 1970), points to older works and the more accessible primary sources, while the strength of J.S. Morrill, *Seventeenth Century Britain* (Folkestone, 1980), lies in its wide coverage of recent scholarship. In addition, two other recent aids to research have appeared – A. Macfarlane, *Guide to English Historical Records* (Cambridge, 1983), and G.E. Aylmer and J.S. Morrill, *Civil War and Interregnum: Sources for Local Historians* (London, 1979).

Since Morrill's bibliography is so helpful, this section will largely content itself with highlighting the leading works in a field and with bringing the record up to date.

General

Of brief modern surveys, by far the best is B. Coward, *The Stuart Age* (London, 1980); other works have on the whole been rendered less useful by the flood of modern scholarship, but still worth consulting, especially for the European context, is J.P. Cooper, ed., *The New Cambridge Modern History. IV. The decline of Spain and the Thirty Years War* (Cambridge, 1970).

Economic and Social

The literature of these fields has blossomed in recent decades. The best surveys are D.C. Coleman, *The Economy of England 1450–1750* (London, 1977), and C.G.A. Clay, *Economic Expansion and Social Change: England 1500–1700* (2 vols. Cambridge, 1984). D.M. Palliser, *The Age of Elizabeth* (London, 1983), although sometimes over-optimistic, provides more than merely a chronological starting-point for the study of our period.

Since the papers of government tend to be better preserved and more accessible than other sources, economic policy has been particularly well studied. The seminal work is B.E. Supple, *Commercial Crisis and Change 1600–1642* (Cambridge, 1970); for the domestic economy, see J. Thirsk, *Economic Policy and Projects* (Oxford, 1978). D.C. Coleman, 'Mercantilism Revisited', *Historical Journal* 1980, and B. Outhwaite, 'Dearth and Government Intervention in English Grain Markets, 1590–1700', *Economic History Review* 1981, are also essential. Further afield, D.B. Quinn and A.N. Ryan, *England's Sea Empire 1550–1642* (London, 1983) provides a valuable introduction to colonization, both in policy and practice.

On agriculture the essays in J. Thirsk, ed., *Agrarian History of England and Wales. IV. 1500–1640* (Cambridge, 1967), have yet to be supplanted, though they should be read in conjunction with Clay, cited above, which is an essential introduction to urban history and to economic policy too. A greater historiographical transformation has, however, occurred in the study of demography and social relations. E.A. Wrigley and R. Schofield, *Population History of England 1541–1871* (London, 1981), must be the definitive demographic analysis; K. Wrightson, *English Society 1580–1680* (London, 1982) is vital, though his work needs to be read with M. Slater, *Family Life in the Seventeenth Century* (London, 1984), and R. Houlbrooke, *The English Family 1450–1700* (London, 1984). The position of women is excellently surveyed in M. Prior, ed., *Women in English Society 1500–1800* (London, 1984).

The history of other social groups has longer been the subject of scholars' attention. L. Stone's blockbuster, *The Crisis of the Aristocracy* (Oxford, 1965, abridged 1967) is brilliant on the social characteristics of the peerage, but its assertion of widespread financial debility has been widely challenged: see especially R. Ashton, 'The Aristocracy in Transition', *Econ. Hist. Rev.*, 1969. The 'gentry controversy' is devastatingly addressed by J. Hexter in 'Storm over the Gentry', in his *Reappraisals in History* (London, 1961), while J.S. Morrill, 'The Northern Gentry and the Great Rebellion', *Northern History* 1979, provides a helpful perspective. H.J. Habakkuk synthesizes much recent work on landowners in three essays in *Transactions of the Royal Historical Society* 1979–81, while J.P. Cooper, 'The Social Distribution of Lands and Men', *Econ. Hist. Rev.* 1967, suggests that the magnates maintained their economic position. Groups lower down the social scale have been best addressed in a number of recent village studies, one of the most productive of all recent scholarly approaches. Two of the most thoughtful are K. Wrightson and D. Levine, *Poverty and Piety in an English Village* (London, 1979), and C. Howell, *Land, Family and Inheritance in Transition* (Cambridge, 1983).

Suggestive observations on social mobility and social change are to be found in A. Everitt, *Change in the Provinces; the Seventeenth Century* (Leicester, 1969), which takes issue with L. Stone, 'Social Mobility in England, 1500–1700', *Past and Present* 1966. The demand for education has been most thoroughly considered by L. Stone in 'The Size and Composition of the Oxford Student Body', in his *University and Society* (Princeton, 1974), vol. 1, and in D. Cressy, *Literacy and Schooling in Early-Modern England* (Cambridge, 1980). The literature on crime is growing fast, and a useful introduction to it can be found in C. Herrup, 'Law and Morality in Seventeenth-Century England', *Past and Present* 1985.

Religion and Intellectual Life

The literature on religious currents, and particularly on puritanism, is now immense. A helpful introduction to the problems, if not to the recent literature, can be found in H.G. Alexander, *Religion in England 1558–1662* (London, 1968). Perhaps the major theme of recent research has been the rehabilitation of the pre-Laudian church, and here the outstanding exercise is P. Collinson, *The Religion of Protestants* (Oxford, 1982). But Collinson's terminal date is 1625, before the Laudian storm, and to understand how protestantism might have a radical potential we need to turn -with care -to the far too schematic M. Walzer, *Revolution of the Saints* (Cambridge, Mass., 1965). A local case-study that straddles uneasily a Collinsonian appreciation of protestantism as an ideology of order and a sense that puritanism could become an ideology of opposition is W. Hunt, *The Puritan Moment* (Cambridge, Mass., 1983).

The theological content if any, of puritanism has been variously argued. The seminal study of the broad orthodoxy of predestinarian Calvinism is N. Tyacke, 'Puritanism, Arminianism and Counter-Revolution', in C. Russell, ed., *Origins of the English Civil War* (London, 1973). An excellent study of the Calvinist theology of grace is P. Coolidge, *The Pauline Renaissance in England* (Oxford, 1970); but see also D. Wallace, *Puritans and Predestination* (Chapel, Hill, 1982). Still the best account of millenarianism is W.M. Lamont, *Godly Rule 1603–1660* (London, 1969). The political dimensions of anti-Catholicism are illuminated by P. Lake, 'The Significance of the Elizabethan Identification of the Pope as Antichrist', *Journal of Ecclesiastical History* 1980, and R. Cust and P. Lake, 'Sir Richard Grosvenor and the Rhetoric of Godly Magistracy', *Bulletin of the Institute of Historical Research* 1981.

It used to be that to move from the historiography of puritanism to that of Catholicism was to move from an almost scholastic logic-chopping to pious hagiography. That that is no longer the case owes much to J. Bossy, whose *English Catholic Community* (London, 1976) opened new frontiers. But his views have been challenged by, especially, C. Haigh, 'From Monopoly to Minority', *Trans. Roy. Hist. Soc.* 1981. C. Hibbard, 'Early Stuart Catholicism', *Journal of Modern History* 1980, is excellent on the relations between the reality and the contemporary perceptions.

That K. Thomas, *Religion and the Decline of Magic* (London, 1971) appears at the end of the section does little justice to its stature as the most outstanding work on English folk-religion and superstition to appear in the last generation. Its analysis of the role of religion in a predominantly agrarian society is breath-taking in its scope. Its argument about witchcraft is broadened conceptually by S. Clark, 'Inversion, Misrule and the Meaning of Witchcraft', *Past and Present* 1980.

Political thought has been a strangely neglected subject. There are no general surveys of the whole period, though P. Zagorin's brief *History of Political Thought in the English Revolution* (London, 1954) is good for the later part, while A. Sharp, *Political Ideas of the English Civil War* (London, 1983) prints some valuable documents. Perhaps the most central thematic surveys are J.G.A. Pocock, *The Ancient Constitution and the Feudal Law* (Cambridge, 1957) and R. Tuck, *Natural Rights Theories* (Cambridge, 1979). Pocock's *Machiavellian Moment* (Princeton, 1975) and his 'Authority and Property: the Question of Liberal Origins' in B. Malament, ed., *After the Reformation* (Manchester, 1980) are dazzling on republicanism, while M.J. Mendle, *Dangerous Positions* (Alabama, 1985) threads his way dexterously through the controversies of the outbreak of the Civil War. A provocative interpretation of what is seen as the main, 'bourgeois' current of seventeenth-century thought is C.B. Macpherson, *The Political Theory of Possessive Individualism* (Oxford, 1962).

The history of science has lately been as lively a field as political and religious history. Two recent surveys, R.S. Westfall, *The Construction of Modern Science* (Cambridge, 1977) and A.R. Hall, *The Revolution in Science* (London, 1983), stress the ultimate winner, the mechanical approach, and challenge C. Webster's massive *The Great Instauration* (London, 1975). H. Kearney's brief *Science and Change* (New York, 1971) attempts a synthesis of the various traditions. Although concerned with later years, M. Hunter, *Science and Society in Restoration England* (Cambridge, 1981) is helpful, while B. Shapiro, *Probability and Certainty in Seventeenth-Century England* (Princeton, 1982) points out the unwisdom of segregating science from other intellectual fields. M. Macdonald, *Mystical Bedlam* (Cambridge, 1981), sensitively treats of insanity, while M. Feingold, *The Mathematician's Apprenticeship* (Cambridge, 1984) is now the best study of a particular branch of science, and does much to rescue the universities from the intellectual garbage-heap to which they have often been consigned (that rescue operation has also been joined by K. Sharpe's 'The First History Lectureships', *History of the Universities* 1982). The religious affiliations of science are variously argued in C. Webster, ed. *The Intellectual Revolution of the Seventeenth Century* (London, 1974), which should be supplemented with the valuable N. Tyacke, 'Science and Religion at Oxford' in D. Pennington and K. Thomas, *Puritans and Revolutionaries* (Oxford, 1978).

The expansion of mental horizons can be traced in F.J. Levy, 'How Information Spread among the Gentry', *Journal of British Studies* 1982, while K. Thomas, *Man and the Natural World: Changing Attitudes in England 1500-1800* (London, 1982), is a fascinating study of changing horizons of another sort. C.A. Patrides and R.B. Waddington, ed., *The Age of Milton* (Manchester, 1980), is the most helpful general introduction to the cultural world of the mid-seventeenth century.

Politics

Only when we turn to politics does the full weight of scholarship become evident, and here above all Morrill's bibliography cited above is an essential aid. Essential too is S.R. Gardiner's massive *History of England* (London 1864-1903), covering the period 1603-56, and continued down to 1658 by C.H. Firth, *The Last Years of the Protectorate* (London, 1909). Collectively, the nineteen volumes are a monument of historical scholarship, and although recent years have seen some reaction against their judgments they must still be read by all serious students. Almost as long, and better reading, is Clarendon, *History of the Rebellion* (Oxford, 1888, and still in print); those who lack the time should read G. Huehns, *Selections from Clarendon* (Oxford, 1978), with an introduction by H.R. Trevor-Roper.

Documents and sources

There is as yet nothing to match the acuteness of J.P. Kenyon's commentary and selection of documents in his *Stuart Constitution* (Cambridge, 1966), though both are growing a little dated. While the source-books are well-surveyed in the bibliographies, some major additions should be noted. Students can now turn to superb modern editions of *Stuart Royal Proclamations,* edited, successively, by J.F. Larkin and P.L. Hughes (Oxford, 1973) and J.F. Larkin (Oxford, 1982), vital sources for governmental attitudes on a surprising range of topics. Amongst the many parliamentary collections, M.F. Keeler *et al* ed., *Proceedings in Parliament 1628* (six vols., New Haven, 1977-83) is a remarkable exercise in completeness, while the printed diaries from the Long Parliament have been joined by collections edited by W.H. Coates, A.S. Young and V.F. Snow (New Haven, 1982), and M. Jansson (New York, 1984).

Other works

The magisterial works of G.E. Aylmer, *The King's Servants* (London, 1961) and *The State's Servants* (London, 1973) are indispensable to an understanding of both royal and republican government. P. Williams, 'The Activity of the Council in the Marches under the Early Stuarts', *Welsh History Review* 1961, provides a useful introduction to one of the provincial councils, while L. Peck, 'Court Patronage and Government Policy', in G.F. Lytle and S. Orgel, ed., *Patronage in the Renaissance* (Princeton, 1981), suggestively examines the assumptions of office-holders. M. Hawkins, 'Government: Its Role and Aims', in Russell, *Origins of the Civil War,* is the best brief introduction to royal government.

Local government and the localities are best approached through the invaluable summary by G.C.F. Forster in A.G.R. Smith, ed., *The Reign of James VI and I* (London, 1973). A slew of local studies have given rise to one of the most vehement assertions of recent scholarship, the claim that the localities were essentially insular and introverted – for a forthright assertion of this case, see J.S. Morrill, *The Revolt of the Provinces* (London, 1976), a stimulating and forceful study of c.1637-48. The argument has been challenged by C.A. Holmes, '"County Community" in History and Historiography', *Jnl. Brit. Studs.* 1980 and by A. Hughes, 'Warwickshire on the

Eve of the Civil War', *Midland History* 1982. Undoubtedly the best study of the relation of centre and locality is B. Quintrell, 'Government in Perspective: Lancashire and the Privy Council 1570–1640', *Transactions of the Historic Society of Lancashire and Cheshire* 1982.

The essential account of the political role of the judiciary is W.J. Jones, *Politics and the Bench* (London, 1971), while J.S. Cockburn, *History of English Assizes 1558–1714* (Cambridge, 1972) gives a useful account of the local work of the judges. W.R. Prest, ed., *Lawyers in Early Modern Europe and America* (New York, 1981) contains two helpful essays on English lawyers. S. Black, '*Coram Protectore*: The Judges of Westminster Hall under the Protectorate', *American Journal of Legal History* 1976, covers a neglected field, and B. Shapiro, 'Law Reform in Seventeenth Century England', *ibid.* 1975, gives a useful survey of a contentious subject. The best study of the thought of Sir Edward Coke is C. Gray, 'Reason, Authority and Imagination', in P. Zagorin, ed. *Culture and Revolution* (Berkeley, 1980).

The liveliest area of recent scholarship has, however, undoubtedly been the study of parliament. The Victorian confidence of the great S.R. Gardiner, reinforced by W. Notestein, 'The Winning of the Initiative by the House of Commons', *Proceedings of the British Academy* 1925, was frontally challenged by C. Russell, 'Parliamentary History in Perspective', *History* 1976, and more fully in his fundamentally important *Parliaments and English Politics 1621–1629* (Oxford, 1979). Russell has extended his attack geographically and chronologically in 'Monarchies, Wars and Estates', *Legislative Studies Quarterly* 1982. The excesses of post-Russell revisionism have brought some riposte from T. Rabb and D. Hirst in *Past and Present* 1981 and – more entertaining if more partisan – by J.H. Hexter, in *Parliamentary History* 1982. Recent less embattled studies have included E.R. Foster's measured *The House of Lords 1603–1649* (Chapel Hill, 1983), J. Hart, 'The House of Lords and Appellate Jurisdiction', *Parl. Hist.* 1983, and S. Lambert's important 'Procedure in the House of Commons', *English Historical Review* 1980.

There are unfortunately few good biographies for this period. James I in particular is badly in need of rescue from prejudices and misunderstandings. J. Wormald, 'Two Kings or one?' *History* 1983, has made a start, as, for Scotland, has M. Lee, *Government by Pen* (Urbana, 1980). The recent biographies of Charles I, by P. Gregg (London, 1981) and C. Carlton (London, 1983) both fail – despite the psychologizing of the latter – to get their subject in perspective; as useful as either is M. Havran, 'The Character and Principles of an English King: the Case of Charles I', *Catholic Historical Review* 1983. But R. Strong, *Charles I on Horseback* (London, 1970) yields greater insights. Although the recent biography of Buckingham, by R. Lockyer (London, 1981), is a valuable work of scholarship, it takes the duke as a statesman at his own estimate. C. V. Wedgwood, *Thomas Wentworth, Earl of Strafford. A Revaluation* (London, 1961) also tends to identify with her subject, and needs to be qualified by the essays in J.P. Cooper, *Land, Men and Beliefs* (Hambledon, 1983), and by P. Salt in *Northern History* 1980. Strikingly immune to the vice of hero-worship is H.R. Trevor-Roper, *Archbishop Laud* (London, 1940), although its author's unabashed anticlericalism vitiates what might have been a brilliant 'life'. We badly need a modern full-length portrait, as we do of Salisbury and Pym. The best biography of Cromwell remains that by C.H. Firth (London, 1900), although R.S. Paul, *The Lord Protector* (London, 1955) is good on Cromwell's religion, and C. Hill, *God's Englishman* (London, 1970) is always stimulating and provocative. Among the most illuminating of all studies are B.H.G. Wormald, *Clarendon* (Cambridge, 1951), and W.M. Lamont's difficult but rewarding *Richard Baxter and the Millennium* (London, 1979).

To examine the proliferating literature on specific topics is to understand how hard it is to write a balanced biography. Recent years have brought several admirable collections of essays. For the pre-war period Russell's *Origins of the Civil War* has been joined by K.M. Sharpe, ed., *Faction and Parliament* (Oxford, 1978), with essays on themes ranging from parliamentary history and taxation to the relations of court and country; by P. Clark, A.G.R. Smith and N. Tyacke, ed., *The English Commonwealth 1547-1640* (London, 1979), with valuable analysis by Russell of John Pym's parliamentary career and by A.H. Smith of militia rates; and by H. Tomlinson, ed., *Before the English Civil War* (London, 1983), with an important essay by Russell on parliaments and valuable suggestions by Thomas on royal financers and by Collinson on the Hampton Court conference of 1604. Also of value on the last theme is B. Quintrell in *Jnl. Eccles. Hist.* 1980. James's relations with Catholics and with the church receive stimulating attention from J. Wormald, K. Fincham and P. Lake in *Jnl. Brit. Studs.* 1985, while F.C. Youngs helpfully discusses royal proclamations in D. Guth and J. McKenna, ed., *Tudor Rule and Revolution* (Cambridge, 1982); another Jacobean theme, the proposed Anglo-Scottish union, is discussed by B.P. Levack in Malament, *After the Reformation.* L. Peck, *Northampton* (London, 1982), provides a provocative revaluation of the unpopular earl.

The major work on the 1620s parliaments is of course that by Russell cited aboved. The beginnings of a reaction may be apparent in T. Cogswell, 'Foreign Policy and Parliament', *Eng. Hist. Rev.* 1984, and R. Cust, 'Charles I, the Privy Council and the Forced Loan', *Jnl. Brit. Studs.* 1985. Charles's duplicity emerges clearly from J. Guy, 'The Origins of the Petition of Right Reconsidered', *Historical Journal* 1982, and from E. R. Foster, 'Printing the Petition of Right', *Huntington Library Quarterly* 1974.

The 1630s have been little studied. K. Sharpe's revaluation in Tomlinson's *Before the Civil War* goes too far towards the king's stand-point, but several full-length studies are in preparation. The best survey of Laud's efforts is J.S. McGee, 'William Laud and the Outward Face of Religion', in R.L. DeMolen, ed., *Leaders of the Reformation* (Cranbury, N.J., 1984) for some responses see J.T. Cliffe, *The Puritan Gentry* (London, 1984). Excellent on the books of orders are P. Slack and B. Quintrell in *Trans. Roy. Hist. Soc.* 1980 and *Eng. Hist. Rev.* 1980 respectively; the need for, and the coherence of, governmental response is touched on in B. Sharp, *In Contempt of All Authority* (Berkeley, 1980), on the woodland riots of the 1630s. G.E. Aylmer, 'Attempts at Administrative Reform 1625-1640', *Eng. Hist. Rev.* 1957, discusses one side of the government's coin, while K. Sharpe on the reform of the foreign posts in *Bull. Inst. Hist. Research* 1984 gives a more favourable verdict; but the basic study of government remains Aylmer's *King's Servants.* Important studies of local responses to ship money are K. Fincham, 'The Judges' Decision on Ship Money: the Reaction of Kent', *Bull. Inst. Hist. Research* 1984, and P. Lake, 'The Collection of Ship Money in Cheshire', *Northern Hist.* 1981. But for studies of ship money in general, and of star chamber, we have to turn to M.D. Gordon in *Trans. Roy. Hist. Soc.* 1910 and H.E.I. Phillips, *ibid.,* 1939. There has however, been good work on the court by S. Orgel, *The Illusion of Power* (Berkeley, 1975), R Strong, *Britannia Triumphans* (London, 1980), and P. Thomas in Russell's *Origins of the Civil War* – although the last overstates the case for a cultural clash. R. Smuts, 'The Puritan Followers of Henrietta Maria', *Eng. Hist. Rev.* 1978, provides some corrective.

Of fundamental importance for the crisis which destroyed Charles I's rule is C. Hibbard, *Charles I and the Popish Plot* (Chapel Hill, 1983). Charles's own expectations are laid bare in C. Russell, 'Why did Charles I call the Long Parliament?' *History* 1984; to be used with care is S. Lambert, 'The Calling of the Long Parliament', *Hist. Jnl.* 1984. Avoiding those questions, but tackling much else, is A. Fletcher, *The Outbreak of the English Civil War* (London, 1981), which gives a minutely detailed analysis of 1640–42 and at last supplants the narrative of S.R. Gardiner. Fletcher's strength lies in his relation of the localities to the centre. Equally vital insights are afforded by J.S. Morrill, 'The Religious Context of the English Civil War', *Trans. Roy. Hist. Soc.* 1984, and (on parliamentary administration) D. Pennington, 'The Making of War', in Pennington and Thomas, *Puritans and Revolutionaries,* An important non-parliamentary context is sketched in J.H. Elliott, 'The Year of the Three Ambassadors', in H. Lloyd-Jones, V. Pearl and B. Worden, ed., *History and Imagination* (London, 1981).

Pym's organization of the fledging parliamentarian cause is described with great insight in J.H. Hexter, *The Reign of King Pym* (Cambridge, Mass., 1941), in an argument which has on the whole stood the test of time. P. Crawford's biography of Denzil Holles (London, 1979) is valuable on another of the parliamentarian heavy-weights. P. Young and R. Holmes, *The English Civil War* (London, 1974) provides the best military account, while R. Ashton, *The English Civil War* (London, 1978), offers a helpful political narrative. R. Hutton's 'The Structure of the Royalist Party', *Hist. Jnl.* 1981 and *The Royalist War Effort* (London, 1981) have transformed our understanding of the royalist cause, though they have been challenged by J. Daley in *Hist. Jnl.* 1984; and see also P.R. Newman, 'The Royalist Officer Corps', *ibid.,* 1983. On the parliamentarian side, C. Holmes, *The Eastern Association* (Cambridge, 1975), is a masterly exercise in relating parliamentary to local and military developments. Equally important in arguing against the segregation of local from national politics is A. Hughes, 'The King, the Parliament and the Localities during the English Civil War', *Jnl. Brit. Studs.* 1985, which, with her 'Warwickshire Politics and Westminster Politics 1643–1647', *Trans. Roy. Hist. Soc.* 1981, needs to be set against Morrill's stress on localism in *Revolt of the Provinces.* M. Kishlansky, *The Rise of the New Model Army* (Cambridge, 1979) argues the non-partisan genesis of the army, challenging some though not all of the arguments of C.H. Firth's classic *Cromwell's Army* (London, 1902).

J.S. Morrill, ed., *Reactions to the English Civil War* (London, 1982) covers many developments outside parliament: Morrill's own essay on the church and Pennington's on the impact of war are particularly valuable. The case for class alignments in the war is strongly argued in C. Hill, 'Parliament and the People', *Past and Present* 1981. D. Underdown, 'Community and Class', in Malament, *After the Reformation,* provides a judicious synthesis of various interpretations of popular allegiance and of neutralism, while the ecological case he elaborates in *Trans. Roy. Hist. Soc.* 1981 is undoubtedly the most original approach to the problem to date; see also his discussion of the Clubmen in *Past and Present* 1979. Underdown's 'Honest Radicals in the Counties' in Pennington and Thomas, *Puritans and Revolutionaries,* valuably demonstrates the existence of popular commitment outside London.

D. Underdown, *Pride's Purge* (Oxford, 1971), is the indispensable analysis of post-war politics. It should be read with V. Pearl, 'London's Counter-Revolution', in G.E. Aylmer's excellent collection, *The Interregnum* (London, 1972). The best introduction to the Levellers is G.E. Aylmer, *The Levellers in the English Revolution* (London, 1975); the conventional account does, however, need to be modified in light of essays by M. Kishlansky in *Hist. Jnl.* 1979, *ibid.* 1982, and in Morrill's *Reactions to the Civil War,* and also by R.B. Seaberg in *Hist. Jnl.* 1981. There are several anthologies of Leveller material: perhaps the best is A.S.P. Woodhouse, *Puritanism and Liberty* (London, 1938).

The history of the Rump is definitively told in B. Worden, *The Rump Parliament* (Cambridge, 1974), and of the Barebone's Parliament in A. Woolrych, *Commonwealth and Protectorate* (Oxford, 1982). Worden's 'Classical Republicanism and the English Revolution', in Lloyd-Jones, Pearl and Worden, *History and Imagination,* is invaluable on the politics, while Lodewijk Huygens, *The English Journal, 1651–1652,* ed. A.G.H. Bachrach and R.G. Collmer (Leiden, 1982), provides an all-too-rare glimpse of life under the Rump. Material aspects of the Interregnum are discussed excellently in M. Ashley, *Financial and Commercial Policy of the Commonwealth and Protectorate* (2nd edn., Oxford, 1962) and by J.P. Cooper and V. Pearl in the collections edited by Aylmer and by Pennington and Thomas respectively.

The best introduction to the ecclesiastical fragmentation of the period is by way of Morrill's essay on the church in his collection, and through the essays in J.F. McGregor and B. Reay, ed., *Radical Religion in the English Revolution* (Oxford, 1984): the essays by the editors and by Aylmer in the latter are especially helpful. Also of value on the Baptists is B.R. White, *The English Baptists of the Seventeenth Century* (London, 1983), while M. Tolmie, *Triumph of the Saints* (Cambridge, 1977) skilfully untangles the Independents. I. Green surveys the fate of the losers, the 'scandalous' clergy, in *Eng. Hist. Rev.* 1979, while W.B. Patterson looks sympathetically at one conformist in D. Baker, ed., *Studies in Church History* xvi (1979). The essential entry to the less mainstream sects is C. Hill, *The World Turned Upside Down* (London, 1972), the best of his many books. N. Smith, ed., *A Collection of Ranter Writings* (London, 1982), also includes a perceptive introduction. C. Hill, B. Reay and W. Lamont, *The World of the Muggletonians* (London, 1983), is a fascinating study of an insistently non-proselytizing sect, while R. Bauman, *Let Your Words Be Few* (Cambridge, 1983), provides a novel study of the Quakers' outlook.

On the Protectorate surprisingly little work had been done. Woolrych's *Commonwealth and Protectorate* is the best account of its genesis, while C.H. Firth, 'Cromwell and the Crown', *Eng. Hist. Rev.* 1902, 1903, and B. Worden, 'Toleration and the Protectorate', in W.J. Sheils, ed., *Studies in Church History* xxi (1984) survey its central dilemmas. I. Roots, 'Cromwell's Ordinances', in Aylmer, *Interregnum,* examines the Protector's legislative activities, while H.R. Trevor-Roper, 'Cromwell and his Parliaments', in his *Religion, the Reformation and Social Change* (London, 1967), gives an incisive if one-sided account of the Cromwellian parliaments. The workings of government during the whole of the republic are of course surveyed in Aylmer's *State's Servants;* D. Hirst, '"That Sober Liberty"', in J.M. Wallace, ed., *The Golden and the Brazen World* (Berkeley, 1985), studies the public image. The best introduction to the many studies of the personnel of local government during the Interregnum is G.E. Aylmer, 'Crisis and Regrouping in the Political Elites: England from the 1630s to the 1660s', in J.G.A. Pocock, ed., *Three British Revolutions* (Princeton, 1980), which needs to be read with D. Underdown, 'Settlement in the Counties', in Aylmer, *Interregnum.* An excellent brief survey of local government in action is G.C.F. Forster's account of Yorkshire in *Northern History,* 1976; J.S. Morrill, *Cheshire 1630–1660* (Oxford, 1974) is also of value.

The successor to this volume, J.R. Jones's *Country and Court* (London, 1978), carries the story to its disjointed close, while the aftermath is also discussed in J. Miller, 'The Potential for "Absolutism" in Later Stuart England', *History* 1984, and, from a very different perspective, C. Hill, *The Experience of Defeat* (London, 1984).

Foreign Policy

The best survey is J.R. Jones, *Britain and Europe in the Seventeenth Century* (London, 1966). S.L. Adams, 'Spain or the Netherlands?' in Tomlinson, *Before the Civil War,* and R. Crabtree, 'The Idea of a Protestant Foreign Policy', in I. Roots, ed., *Cromwell* (New York, 1973), provide invaluable perspectives on the earlier and later parts of the period.

Wales

As so often happens in histories of England, Wales has received short shrift in this volume. A.H. Dodd, *Studies in Stuart Wales* (Cardiff, 1952, reprint 1971) may help to redress the balance; and G. Williams, ed., *Glamorgan County History 1536–c.1770* (Cardiff, 1974) is one of the better county histories. P. Jenkins, *The Making of a Ruling Class* (Cambridge, 1983), further illuminates the affairs of the Glamorganshire gentry.

Scotland

Lately Scottish historiography has undergone a renaissance, and B. Lenman, 'Reinterpreting Scotland's Last Two Centuries of Independence', *Hist. Jnl.* 1982, provides a thoughtful review. Essential reading for the years when Scottish and English affairs were intertwined are D. Stevenson, *The Scottish Revolution 1637–1644* (Newton Abbot, 1973) and *Revolution and Counter-Revolution in Scotland 1644–1651* (London, 1977); W. Makey, *The Church of the Covenant 1637–1651* (Edinburgh, 1979), advances a suggestive hypothesis about the relations of church and society. F.D. Dow, *Cromwellian Scotland* (Edinburgh, 1979) is the basic work for the 1650s.

Ireland

The starting-point for a study of Ireland's calamitous relations with England in this period is T.W. Moody, F.X. Martin and F.J. Byrne, ed., *A New History of Ireland. III. Early Modern Ireland* (Oxford, 1976). English colonization in its various forms has been excellently studied, by A. Clarke in T.W. Moody, ed., *Nationality and the Pursuit of National Independence* (Belfast, 1978); by T.W. Moody, *The Londonderry Plantation* (Belfast, 1939), and by K. Bottigheimer, *English Money and Irish Land* (Oxford, 1971). The best study of the 1641 revolt is A. Clarke, 'The Genesis of the Ulster Rising', in P. Roebuck, ed., *Plantation to Partition* (Belfast, 1981). On the role of Irish troops during the Civil War, see J.L. Malcolm, 'All the King's Men', *Irish Historical Studies,* 1979, T. Barnard, *Cromwellian Ireland* (Oxford, 1975) fully analyses the English administration after 1649. And, finally, a work which cannot be categorized, revealing as it does the destructive ties between the three kingdoms, D. Stevenson, *Scottish Covenanters and Irish Confederates* (Belfast, 1981).

Index

373